Computational Intelligence and Human–Computer Interaction: Modern Methods and Applications, 2nd Edition

Computational Intelligence and Human–Computer Interaction: Modern Methods and Applications, 2nd Edition

Guest Editors

Grigoreta-Sofia Cojocar
Adriana-Mihaela Guran
Laura-Silvia Dioşan

Basel • Beijing • Wuhan • Barcelona • Belgrade • Novi Sad • Cluj • Manchester

Guest Editors

Grigoreta-Sofia Cojocar
Department of Computer
Science
Faculty of Mathematics and
Computer Science
Babeș-Bolyai University
Cluj-Napoca
Romania

Adriana-Mihaela Guran
Department of Computer
Science
Faculty of Mathematics and
Computer Science
Babeș-Bolyai University
Cluj-Napoca
Romania

Laura-Silvia Dioşan
Department of Computer
Science
Faculty of Mathematics and
Computer Science
Babeș-Bolyai University
Cluj-Napoca
Romania

Editorial Office
MDPI AG
Grosspeteranlage 5
4052 Basel, Switzerland

This is a reprint of the Special Issue, published open access by the journal *Mathematics* (ISSN 2227-7390), freely accessible at: https://www.mdpi.com/si/mathematics/CI_HCI.

For citation purposes, cite each article independently as indicated on the article page online and as indicated below:

Lastname, A.A.; Lastname, B.B. Article Title. *Journal Name* **Year**, *Volume Number*, Page Range.

ISBN 978-3-7258-3655-0 (Hbk)
ISBN 978-3-7258-3656-7 (PDF)
https://doi.org/10.3390/books978-3-7258-3656-7

© 2025 by the authors. Articles in this book are Open Access and distributed under the Creative Commons Attribution (CC BY) license. The book as a whole is distributed by MDPI under the terms and conditions of the Creative Commons Attribution-NonCommercial-NoDerivs (CC BY-NC-ND) license (https://creativecommons.org/licenses/by-nc-nd/4.0/).

Contents

About the Editors vii

Hancheng Zhu, Yong Zhou, Zhiwen Shao, Wen-Liang, Guangcheng Wang and Qiaoyue Li
Personalized Image Aesthetics Assessment via Multi-Attribute Interactive Reasoning
Reprinted from: *Mathematics* 2022, 10, 4181, https://doi.org/10.3390/math10224181 1

Damjan Vlaj and Andrej Zgank
Acoustic Gender and Age Classification as an Aid to Human–Computer Interaction in a Smart Home Environment
Reprinted from: *Mathematics* 2022, 11, 169, https://doi.org/10.3390/math11010169 16

Xizhong Shen and Ran Li
BroadBand-Adaptive VMD with Flattest Response
Reprinted from: *Mathematics* 2023, 11, 1858, https://doi.org/10.3390/math11081858 38

Md. Humaun Kabir, Shabbir Mahmood, Abdullah Al Shiam, Abu Saleh Musa Miah, Jungpil Shin and Md. Khademul Islam Molla
Investigating Feature Selection Techniques to Enhance the Performance of EEG-Based Motor Imagery Tasks Classification
Reprinted from: *Mathematics* 2023, 11, 1921, https://doi.org/10.3390/math11081921 53

Sandi Ljubic and Alen Salkanovic
Generating Representative Phrase Sets for Text Entry Experiments by GA-Based Text Corpora Sampling
Reprinted from: *Mathematics* 2023, 11, 2550, https://doi.org/10.3390/math11112550 72

Jamshaid Ul Rahman, Sana Danish and Dianchen Lu
Deep Neural Network-Based Simulation of Sel'kov Model in Glycolysis: A Comprehensive Analysis
Reprinted from: *Mathematics* 2023, 11, 3216, https://doi.org/10.3390/math11143216 98

June-Woo Kim, Hoon Chung and Ho-Young Jung
Spectral Salt-and-Pepper Patch Masking for Self-Supervised Speech Representation Learning
Reprinted from: *Mathematics* 2023, 11, 3418, https://doi.org/10.3390/math11153418 107

Anamaria Briciu, Alina-Delia Călin, Diana-Lucia Miholca, Cristiana Moroz-Dubenco, Vladiela Petrașcu and George Dascălu
Machine-Learning-Based Approaches for Multi-Level Sentiment Analysis of Romanian Reviews
Reprinted from: *Mathematics* 2024, 12, 456, https://doi.org/10.3390/math12030456 129

Jin-Long Lin and Meng-Cong Zheng
An Empirical Investigation on the Visual Imagery of Augmented Reality User Interfaces for Smart Electric Vehicles Based on Kansei Engineering and FAHP-GRA
Reprinted from: *Mathematics* 2024, 12, 2712, https://doi.org/10.3390/math12172712 165

Laila Alshehri and Muhammad Hussain
A Lightweight GCT-EEGNet for EEG-Based Individual Recognition Under Diverse Brain Conditions
Reprinted from: *Mathematics* 2024, 12, 3286, https://doi.org/10.3390/math12203286 186

About the Editors

Grigoreta-Sofia Cojocar

Grigoreta-Sofia Cojocar, Ph.D., is an Associate Professor at the Department of Computer Science at Babeș-Bolyai University, Cluj-Napoca, Romania. She received a Ph.D. in Computer Science in 2008. Her research interests are in software engineering, focusing on aspect mining, programming paradigms, formal methods, and computational intelligence. Recently, she has been interested in how advances in artificial intelligence can be used to improve the human–computer experience of young and very young users.

Adriana-Mihaela Guran

Adriana-Mihaela Guran, Ph.D., is an Associate Professor at the Department of Computer Science at Babeș-Bolyai University, Cluj-Napoca, Romania. She received a Ph.D. in Computer Science in 2008. Her research interests mainly focus on designing interactive software systems using a user-centered approach. She wants to apply participatory design with special user groups such as preschoolers. Combining HCI approaches with AI is one subject of interest in her recent research, and her main research focus is on using AI techniques to recognize emotions while interacting with edutainment and on adapting interaction based on the identified emotions.

Laura-Silvia Dioșan

Laura-Silvia Dioșan, Ph.D., is a Professor at the Department of Computer Science at Babeș-Bolyai University, Cluj-Napoca, Romania. She received a Ph.D. in Computer Science in 2008. She has been a director and member of several projects. Her research interests mainly focus on evolutionary computation, genetic programming, np-complete problems, financial modeling, machine learning, and robotics.

Article

Personalized Image Aesthetics Assessment via Multi-Attribute Interactive Reasoning

Hancheng Zhu [1], Yong Zhou [1,*], Zhiwen Shao [1], Wenliang Du [1], Guangcheng Wang [2] and Qiaoyue Li [3]

1. School of Computer Science and Technology, China University of Mining and Technology, Xuzhou 221116, China
2. School of Transportation and Civil Engineering, Nantong University, Nantong 226019, China
3. Department of Optoelectronics and Energy Engineering, Suzhou City University, Suzhou 215104, China
* Correspondence: yzhou@cumt.edu.cn

Abstract: Due to the subjective nature of people's aesthetic experiences with respect to images, personalized image aesthetics assessment (PIAA), which can simulate the aesthetic experiences of individual users to estimate images, has received extensive attention from researchers in the computational intelligence and computer vision communities. Existing PIAA models are usually built on prior knowledge that directly learns the generic aesthetic results of images from most people or the personalized aesthetic results of images from a large number of individuals. However, the learned prior knowledge ignores the mutual influence of the multiple attributes of images and users in their personalized aesthetic experiences. To this end, this paper proposes a personalized image aesthetics assessment method via multi-attribute interactive reasoning. Different from existing PIAA models, the multi-attribute interaction constructed from both images and users is used as more effective prior knowledge. First, we designed a generic aesthetics extraction module from the perspective of images to obtain the aesthetic score distribution and multiple objective attributes of images rated by most users. Then, we propose a multi-attribute interactive reasoning network from the perspective of users. By interacting multiple subjective attributes of users with multiple objective attributes of images, we fused the obtained multi-attribute interactive features and aesthetic score distribution to predict personalized aesthetic scores. Experimental results on multiple PIAA datasets demonstrated our method outperformed state-of-the-art PIAA methods.

Keywords: image aesthetics assessment; personalized aesthetic experiences; multiple attributes; interactive reasoning

MSC: 68U10; 68T05

Citation: Zhu, H.; Zhou, Y.; Shao, Z.; Du, W.; Wang, G.; Li, Q. Personalized Image Aesthetics Assessment via Multi-Attribute Interactive Reasoning. *Mathematics* 2022, 10, 4181. https://doi.org/10.3390/math10224181

Academic Editors: Grigoreta-Sofia Cojocar, Adriana-Mihaela Guran and Laura-Silvia Dioşan

Received: 8 October 2022
Accepted: 7 November 2022
Published: 9 November 2022

Publisher's Note: MDPI stays neutral with regard to jurisdictional claims in published maps and institutional affiliations.

Copyright: © 2022 by the authors. Licensee MDPI, Basel, Switzerland. This article is an open access article distributed under the terms and conditions of the Creative Commons Attribution (CC BY) license (https://creativecommons.org/licenses/by/4.0/).

1. Introduction

In the past few years, with the prevalence of social networks (such as Facebook and Wechat), people usually use multimedia data such as images to obtain information and for other visual needs. Therefore, the visual experience of providing images in these social networks plays a key role in attracting users. In this context, it is desirable to develop image aesthetics assessment (IAA), which can simulate users' visual experiences and automatically assesses the aesthetics of images, e.g., digital cameras provide users with aesthetic evaluation suggestions when taking photos. Consequently, massive IAA methods [1,2] have been proposed by researchers in the pattern recognition and computer vision communities, which has applicable value for various tasks, e.g., photo retrieval [3], image management [4], image enhancement [5], image synthesis [6], and image recommendation [7].

Typically, IAA approaches can be classified into two broad categories: generic image aesthetics assessment (GIAA) and personalized image aesthetics assessment (PIAA) [8]. As the name indicates, GIAA aims to infer the aesthetic experiences perceived by most people [9], whereas PIAA is designed for the aesthetic ratings of a certain individual user for images [10]. Early IAA methods mainly leveraged general attributes in photography and artistic painting (e.g., composition, color, light) to measure the aesthetics of images for most people (GIAA) [2]. Specifically, the average rating of an image annotated by different people is used as the "ground truth" to classify the image into high and low aesthetic categories [11,12] or to map the image to a certain aesthetic score [13,14]. However, these average results ignore an important fact that people's aesthetic experience of images is subjective. In view of this, existing GIAA methods mainly focus on directly predicting the aesthetic distribution of most people's ratings on images [15–18]. Although the image aesthetic distribution can reflect the aesthetic subjectivity of people to a certain extent, this task only measures people's aesthetic ratings from the perspective of images. All in all, GIAA methods are unable to infer individual users' aesthetic preferences for images, which is very valuable in many user-centric applications (e.g., personalized image recommendation [19], personalized image captioning [20] and personalized image enhancement [21]). To deal with this issue, PIAA is proposed to obtain individual users' personalized aesthetic experience of images [22].

PIAA is a user-oriented approach that can only utilize the annotated data provided by each individual user to build a PIAA model [10]. Usually, the number of annotated data provided by a user is limited, which is unable to directly train an efficient PIAA model based on a deep learning framework. Consequently, existing PIAA models mainly rely on a large amount of labeled data rated by most users to train a prior model and further use the labeled data of individual users for model fine-tuning [22–29]. These prior models can be summarized into two types, including learning from the generic aesthetic results of most users [22–26] or learning from the personalized aesthetic results of a large number of individual users [27–29]. The former prior model can capture generic aesthetic experience from the perspective of images, while the latter prior model directly obtains personalized aesthetic experience from the perspective of users. However, the prior knowledge obtained from images eliminates the aesthetic differences among individual users, while the prior knowledge achieved directly from individual users cannot efficiently capture the general aesthetics of images.

To alleviate the above issues, the prior model for PIAA should not only learn the general aesthetics of images, but also model the aesthetic differences of individual users. Specifically, the general aesthetics of an image is usually determined by its objective attributes [30]. For example, Figure 1a shows an image and the corresponding objective attributes. We can observe that the generic (average) aesthetics is closely related to multiple attributes, and these attributes jointly influence most users' aesthetic experience of images. Besides, the aesthetic differences among individual users are usually affected by their own subjective attributes [10]. As shown in Figure 1b, the subjective attributes of the two users are quite different. For instance, User #1 has better education and photography skills than User #2, which makes User #1 more stringent about the attributes such as composition and light of the image. User #2 may prefer scenes such as buildings. All in all, User #1 gives the image a lower aesthetic score (0.3), while User #2 has a higher aesthetic score for the image (0.9). Therefore, exploring the close relationship between the multiple objective attributes of images and the multiple subjective attributes of users is the premise of inferring the personalized aesthetics of a specific user. However, this interactive relationship has not been exploited in the prior model of existing PIAA methods [22–29]. To this end, we can leverage the interactive relationship between subjective and objective attributes to capture aesthetic prior knowledge (multi-attribute interactions). Even when a user provides limited annotated data, the aesthetic prior knowledge can also stably utilize the relationship between the subjective attributes of similar users and the objective attributes of images for reasoning about the user's aesthetic preferences.

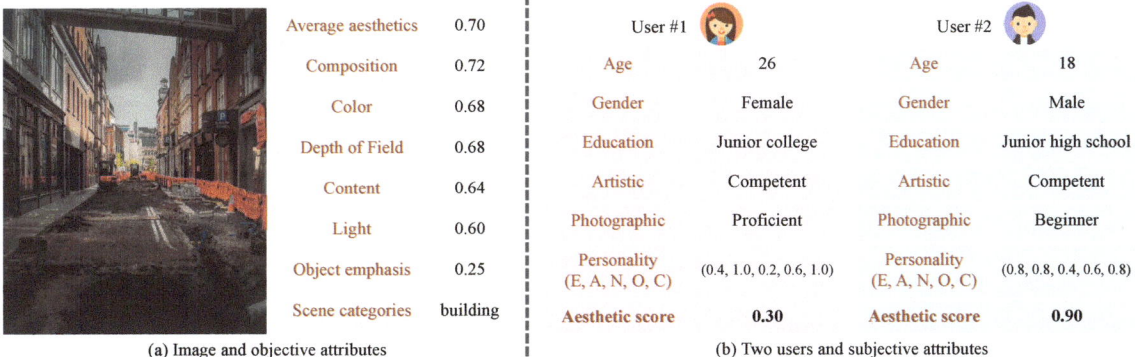

Figure 1. An image and two different users who rated it from the Personalized image Aesthetics database with Rich Attributes (PAPA) [10]. To their right, some objective attributes of the image and several subjective attributes of the users are shown. These numerical attributes and aesthetic scores are normalized between 0 and 1, and higher values indicate stronger attributes and aesthetics. The personality of users here is measured by the Big-Five traits (extroversion (E), agreeableness (A), neuroticism (N), openness (O), and conscientiousness (C)) [31].

In this paper, we propose a personalized image aesthetics assessment method via multi-attribute interactive reasoning (PIAA-MIR). In order to reveal the personalized aesthetic preference of users for images, we expect to capture the aesthetic prior model that reflects the potential interaction between the subjective attributes of users and the objective attributes of images. Compared with the existing prior models that only learn the generic aesthetics of most users [22–26] or the personalized aesthetics of a large number of individual users [27–29], the proposed multi-attribute interaction can effectively characterize the aesthetic mutual influence of users and images to accurately evaluate personalized aesthetic preferences. Specifically, we first propose a generic aesthetics extraction module from the perspective of images to simultaneously predict multiple objective attributes and aesthetic distributions of images. From the perspective of users, a multi-attribute interaction reasoning network is then introduced to capture the interaction between multiple attributes of users and images. To obtain the multi-attribute interaction, we utilized the outer-product [32] to calculate the pairwise correlations between multiple attributes of users and images. Based on the multi-attribute interactive features and aesthetic score distribution, we used a regressor to fuse them for obtaining personalized aesthetic scores. To sum up, the main contributions of the proposed method are as follows:

- We excavated the fundamental factors of users' personalized aesthetic preferences for images by constructing a multi-attribute interaction, which alleviates the insufficient problem of directly obtaining prior knowledge only from the generic aesthetics of images or the personalized aesthetics of a large number of individual users.
- We propose a generic aesthetics extraction module that can simultaneously predict multiple attributes and aesthetic distributions of images. In the multi-attribute interactive reasoning network, we can not only leverage multiple attributes of images and users to construct an effective interaction, but also further use the multi-attribute interactive features and aesthetic score distribution to jointly model personalized aesthetic scores.
- We propose a personalized image aesthetics assessment method via multi-attribute interactive reasoning (PIAA-MIR), whose experimental results on several PIAA databases demonstrated that the proposed PIAA-MIR outperformed state-of-the-art PIAA methods. Besides, ablation studies also showed the effectiveness of our method in learning a personalized aesthetic prior model.

2. Related Works

Since existing PIAA methods are mainly built on the GIAA model, we first review some works related to the GIAA methods and then introduce the PIAA methods.

2.1. Generic Image Aesthetics Assessment

Early researchers believed that people had a consensus on the aesthetic experience of images [33] and generic image aesthetics perceived by most people could be measured by aesthetic rules in photography (e.g., light, colorfulness, and composition) [34]. Generally, GIAA methods can be divided into three categories: aesthetic binary classification [11,12], aesthetic score regression [13,14], and aesthetic distribution prediction [15–18]. The goal of the aesthetic binary classification task is to classify images into "high" and "low" categories according to the aesthetic ratings of most people. Specifically, Murray et al. [11] introduced a large general-purpose IAA database, AVA, and utilized hand-crafted features to train an SVM for image aesthetic classification. Compared with the aesthetic binary classification task, aesthetic score regression needs to more accurately predict image aesthetic scores. For instance, Kong et al. [13] employed a deep Siamese network based on image pair ranking learning, which can simultaneously predict the aesthetic attributes and content of images and further learn to rank the aesthetic scores of images on the basis of aesthetic attributes and content information.

Regardless of aesthetic binary classification or aesthetic score regression, it is necessary to process the aesthetic ratings of different people into a unified result ("high" or "low" and aesthetic score), which will introduce label uncertainty to a certain extent. The main reason is that people's aesthetic experiences are highly subjective, which makes the unified result unable to effectively describe the image aesthetics perceived by different people. Therefore, the task of aesthetic distribution prediction that directly models the image score distribution rated by most people has received great attention from researchers. For example, Talebi et al. [2] used the earth mover's distance (EMD) loss function to train an IAA model for predicting the image aesthetic distribution. The above methods mainly focus on the image aesthetic distribution, ignoring the intrinsic relationship among the three tasks of image aesthetics binary classification, aesthetic score regression, and aesthetic distribution prediction. Therefore, some recent studies have proposed a unified deep learning framework for the three GIAA tasks [15–17]. For example, Zeng et al. [16] proposed a deep model with a unified probabilistic formula and introduced a loss function that is effective for all three GIAA tasks to optimize the deep model. Based on the above analysis, we can find that the current GIAA research mainly focuses on aesthetic distribution prediction. Therefore, our generic aesthetics extraction module exploits the score distribution to represent generic image aesthetics.

2.2. Personalized Image Aesthetics Assessment

The purpose of PIAA is to evaluate images by simulating the visual aesthetics of individual users [22]. Since users' aesthetic preferences are affected by multiple factors such as age, education, and behavioral habits [35,36], the PIAA for a specific user is more complicated and difficult than the GIAA for generic users. Due to the limited labeled samples provided by individuals, PIAA is a small sample learning task [28]. Existing PIAA models are usually built on a prior model with generic aesthetic knowledge, which utilizes aesthetic data annotated by massive users for model training [22–29].

Among them, one approach is to take generic aesthetic results rated by most users as the target for prior model learning from the perspective of images. For instance, Ren et al. [22] found that users' aesthetic preferences were closely related to image content and aesthetic attributes and leveraged the average aesthetic scores of images, image content, and aesthetic attributes to jointly infer personalized aesthetic scores. Li et al. [8] built a prior model for the PIAA task by using the aesthetic distribution of images and the Big-Five personality traits of users who prefer these images. However, these prior models learned from images eliminate the aesthetic differences among individual users.

Another approach is to learn the prior model directly from the personalized aesthetic results of a large number of individual users from the perspective of users. In [28], Zhu et al. proposed a PIAA model based on bi-level gradient optimization meta-learning, which directly captured an aesthetic prior knowledge by training the PIAA tasks of extensive users. Hou et al. [29] trained a prior aesthetic pattern for all individual users by leveraging the interaction between user preferences and image content. In [27], the authors inferred the Big-Five traits of users from their rated images and used the personalized aesthetics of massive individual users to train a prior model. However, the above aesthetic prior models learned directly from individual users are inefficient in capturing the general aesthetics of images. To this end, we expect that the prior model of PIAA can both learn the general aesthetics of images and model the aesthetic differences of various users. Therefore, we utilized multiple attributes of images and users to characterize general aesthetics and aesthetic differences, respectively, and capture the stable interactive relationship between objective attributes and subjective attributes for easily inferring users' personalized aesthetics of images.

3. Proposed Method

This section introduces the personalized image aesthetics assessment method via multi-attribute interactive reasoning, which is called PIAA-MIR. In the proposed PIAA-MIR, we obtain the prior model for the PIAA task of an individual user by implementing a multi-attribute interaction between users and images. Figure 2 shows the overview architecture of our PIAA-MIR, whose training process can be divided into three steps. In the first step, a generic aesthetics extraction module is the software command line to proceed with the extraction, which is trained with images and the annotated multiple aesthetic attributes and score distribution. In the second step, we built a prior model from a multi-attribute interaction between users, as well as their rated images, which further reasons personalized scores by fusing interactive features and the score distribution. In the third step, we leveraged an individual user's personalized aesthetic data to fine-tune the prior model for obtaining the PIAA model of the user.

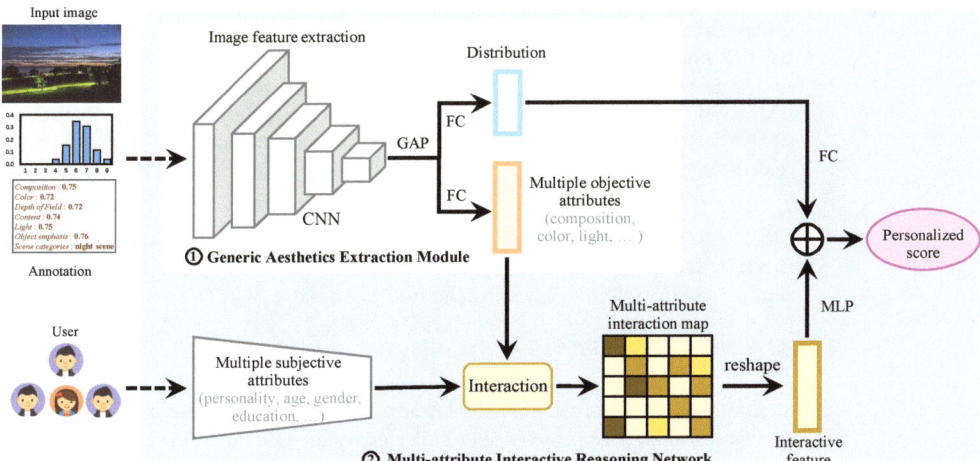

Figure 2. The overview architecture of our PIAA model, whose training process can be divided into three steps. In the first step, a generic aesthetics extraction module is used to simultaneously predict multiple attributes and aesthetic distributions from the perspective of images. In the second step, a multi-attribute interaction reasoning network is then introduced from the perspective of users to capture a multi-attribute interaction between users, as well as their rated images. Based on interactive features and the score distribution, a prior model is built to fuse them for obtaining personalized aesthetic scores. In the third step, the PIAA model of an individual user can be obtained by fine-tuning the user's personalized data.

3.1. Generic Aesthetics Extraction

To obtain the generic aesthetics of images, we designed a generic aesthetic extraction module to jointly infer multiple objective attributes and the aesthetic score distribution. Consequently, we introduced a convolutional-neural-network (CNN)-based multi-task learning [8,37] to extract the shared image features of generic aesthetic attributes and the distribution. The proposed CNN was inherited from the typical ResNet [38], which removes the full connection layer. As shown in the upper part of Figure 2, we adopted the CNN parameters pre-trained on ImageNet [39] as initial weights, which further use a global average pooling (GAP) and two fully connected layers (FC) for mapping images to multiple aesthetic attributes and score distributions.

In particular, for an input image x, the generic aesthetic extraction module can be formulated as

$$\hat{a} = FC_{\theta_a}(GAP(f_\theta(x))), \hat{d} = FC_{\theta_d}(GAP(f_\theta(x))), \quad (1)$$

where θ represents the CNN parameters f_θ and FC_{θ_a} and FC_{θ_d} denote the parameters of an FC layer corresponding to the predicted multiple aesthetic attributes $\hat{a}$ and score distribution $\hat{d}$, respectively. Since this module aims to extract the aesthetic attributes and score distributions of images rated by most people, we assumed $\mathcal{D}_{img} = \{x_i, a_i, d_i\}_{i=1}^{N_a}$ as the set for training the generic aesthetic extraction module, where a_i and d_i indicate some annotated aesthetic attributes and score distribution of the i-th image x_i ($i = 1, 2, 3, \ldots, N_a$), respectively. Besides, N_a denotes the number of images in this training set.

To enable the proposed generic aesthetic extraction module to effectively predict aesthetic attributes and the score distribution, we employed the earth mover's distance (EMD) [40] and l_2 loss functions to jointly optimize the parameters of this module (θ, θ_a, and θ_d), which is defined as

$$\mathcal{L}_a = \frac{1}{N_a} \sum_{i=1}^{N_a} \left((a_i - \hat{a}_i)^2 + \left(\frac{1}{P} \sum_{k=1}^{P} |CDF_{d_i}(k) - CDF_{\hat{d}_i}(k)|^2 \right)^{\frac{1}{2}} \right), \quad (2)$$

where $\hat{a}_i$ and $\hat{d}_i$ are the predicted aesthetic attributes and score distribution by feeding the i-th image into the generic aesthetic extraction module. Similar to [2], classes in the image aesthetic score distribution are inherently ordered as $d_i^{p_1} < \ldots < d_i^{p_P}$. Therefore, the EMD, which contains the cumulative distribution function (CDF), is sensitive to the order of aesthetic score buckets, which is suitable for calculating the loss of the image aesthetic distribution. Specifically, P indicates the number of aesthetic score buckets, and $CDF_{d_i}(k) = \sum_{j=1}^{k} d_i^{p_j}$ represents the cumulative distribution function, where $d_i^{p_j}$ denotes the probability of the j-th score bucket and $\sum_{j=1}^{P} d_i^{p_j} = 1$. In this way, the generic aesthetics extraction module that can simultaneously predict multiple attributes and aesthetic distributions of images can be obtained by using the training data of $\mathcal{D}_{img}$ from the perspective of images.

3.2. Multi-Attribute Interaction Reasoning

Before building the multi-attribute interaction, we need to utilize multiple subjective attributes to characterize individual users. Assume that s represents the subjective attributes of an individual user, which can be collected by users answering several questionnaires [10]. To enable the prior model also to robustly capture personalized aesthetic differences from the perspective of users, we leveraged a large number of users' personalized aesthetic data on images to train the multi-attribute interactive inference network.

Suppose that $\mathcal{D}_{users} = \{s_j, \{x_{i,j}, y_{i,j}\}_{i=1}^{N_s}\}_{j=1}^{N_b}$ denotes the set for training the multi-attribute interactive inference network, where s_j represents some subjective attributes of the j-th user ($j = 1, 2, 3, \ldots, N_b$) and $y_{i,j}$ indicates the user's personalized score for the image $x_{i,j}$ ($i = 1, 2, 3, \ldots, N_s$). For the image $x_{i,j}$, the multiple objective attributes and score distribution can be extracted from the trained generic aesthetics extraction module, which is formulated as

$$\hat{a}_{i,j} = FC_{\theta_a}(GAP(f_\theta(x_{i,j}))), \hat{d}_{i,j} = FC_{\theta_d}(GAP(f_\theta(x_{i,j}))), \quad (3)$$

where $\hat{a}_{i,j}$ and $\hat{d}_{i,j}$ are the predicted aesthetic attributes and score distribution of the i-th image in the subset of the j-th user. As shown in Figure 1, since the user's personalized aesthetic preference for images is affected by multiple attributes from both sides, we need to obtain all pairwise interactive relationships between subjective attributes and objective attributes. To achieve this, we employed the outer-product [32] to obtain the pairwise interactions between multiple attributes of users and images, which takes the form

$$\mathcal{A}_{i,j} = s_j \otimes \hat{a}_{i,j}, \quad (4)$$

where $\mathcal{A}_{i,j} \in \mathbb{R}^{d_s \times d_a}$ denotes the multi-attribute interaction map, $s_j \in \mathbb{R}^{d_s \times 1}$ represents the attributes of the j-th user, $\hat{a}_{i,j} \in \mathbb{R}^{d_a \times 1}$ represents the attributes of the i-th rated image, and $\otimes$ is the operation of the outer-product. In addition, d_s and d_a indicate the number of users' subjective attributes and image objective attributes, respectively. The elements in the interaction map $\mathcal{A}_{i,j}$ reflect the aesthetic preferences of users' subjective attributes to image objective attributes at different dimensions. For example, if a testing user has similar subjective attributes to some trained users, his/her aesthetic preference for images can be inferred from the stable relationships learned from the multi-attribute interaction map.

To make the prior model learn the aesthetic differences among individual users, we further used the interaction map for reasoning users' personalized aesthetic scores for images. For this purpose, the interaction map $\mathcal{A}_{i,j}$ was reshaped to an interactive feature $I_{i,j}$, and we leveraged a two-layer multilayer perceptron (MLP) to map the interactive feature into aesthetic difference scores between different users, which is given by

$$\hat{r}_{i,j} = MLP_{\theta_r}(I_{i,j}), \quad (5)$$

where $\hat{r}_{i,j}$ denotes the aesthetic difference score of the j-th user for the i-th image relative to most users and θ_r indicates the parameters of MLP_{θ_r}, which contains two FC layers. As mentioned above, the generic aesthetics of images can also affect users' personalized aesthetic preferences. Instead of taking the average ratings as the generic scores [8,27], we utilized an FC layer to fuse the score distribution and aesthetic difference score for obtaining a personalized score, which can be formulated as

$$\hat{y}_{i,j} = FC_{\theta_s}(\hat{d}_{i,j}) + \hat{r}_{i,j}, \quad (6)$$

where $\hat{y}_{i,j}$ indicates the predicted aesthetic score and θ_s denotes the parameters of FC_{θ_s}. Then, we employed the l_2 loss function to optimize the parameters of the MLP and FC layers (θ_r and θ_s), which is defined as

$$\mathcal{L}_s = \frac{1}{N_b} \sum_{j=1}^{N_b} \left(\frac{1}{N_s} \sum_{i=1}^{N_s} (y_{i,j} - \hat{y}_{i,j})^2 \right), \quad (7)$$

where N_b and N_s represent the number of training users and the corresponding rated images, respectively. In this way, the proposed prior model can capture a robust multi-attribute interaction map by learning extensive users' personalized aesthetic ratings of images from the perspective of users. Based on the learned multi-attribute interaction, the proposed prior model can be efficiently transferred to the personalized aesthetics of a target user through fine-tuning a small number of user-specific aesthetic data.

3.3. PIAA Fine-Tuning for a Specific User

Since PIAA is aimed at the aesthetic preferences of a specific individual user, we leveraged a user's personalized aesthetic data to fine-tune the prior model for obtaining the PIAA model. Assume that $\mathcal{D}_u = \{s_u, \{x_i^u, y_i^u\}_{i=1}^{N_s}\}$ represents the training set of a specific user, where N_s denotes the number of small samples annotated by the user and s_u denotes subjective attributes. Besides, x_i^u and y_i^u represent the i-th image, as well as the corresponding aesthetic score. Firstly, we leveraged the generic aesthetics extraction module to obtain the objective attributes and score distribution of the image, which can be defined as

$$\hat{a}_i^u = FC_{\theta_a}(GAP(f_\theta(x_i^u))), \hat{d}_i^u = FC_{\theta_d}(GAP(f_\theta(x_i^u))), \quad (8)$$

where $\hat{a}_i^u$ and $\hat{d}_i^u$ are the predicted aesthetic attributes and score distribution of the i-th image. Then, we leveraged the user's subjective attributes s_u and predicted objective attributes $\hat{a}_i^u$ for interaction and fused the interactive feature I_i^u and score distribution $\hat{d}_i^u$ to obtain a personalized aesthetic score, which can be computed by

$$\hat{y}_i^u = FC_{\theta_s}(\hat{d}_i^u) + MLP_{\theta_r}(I_i^u), \quad (9)$$

where $\hat{y}_i^u$ indicates the predicted aesthetic score. In general, a specific user can only provide a small number of annotated samples for model fine-tuning. Therefore, we only optimized the parameters of the MLP and FC layers (θ_r and θ_s) by using the l_2 loss function, which is formulated as

$$\mathcal{L}_u = \frac{1}{N_u}\sum_{i=1}^{N_u}(y_i^u - \hat{y}_i^u)^2. \quad (10)$$

In this manner, fine-tuning a small number of parameters (θ_r and θ_s) with annotated samples can enable the prior model to be easily transferred to the PIAA model of the specific user. For a testing image, we fed it into the PIAA model and obtained the user's personalized aesthetic score for the image.

4. Experimental Results

In this section, we employ extensive experiments to verify the effectiveness of our PIAA-MIR, which were mainly performed on three public PIAA databases: PAPA (https://web.xidian.edu.cn/ldli/en/dataset.html, accessed on 7 October 2022) [10], FLICKR-AES, and REAL-CUR (https://github.com/alanspike/personalizedImageAesthetics, accessed on 7 October 2022) [22].

4.1. Databases

The **PAPA** [10] database contains 31,220 images with rich annotation rated by 438 users. Besides the aesthetic score, each image was annotated by several users with seven objective attributes: *composition, light, color, depth of field, object emphasis, content*, and *scene category*. For each user, the database also provided some subjective attributes: *age, gender, education experience, artistic experience, photographic experience*, and *Big-Five personality traits* [41]. The education experience was divided into six steps: junior high school, senior high school, technical secondary school, junior college, and university. The artistic experience and photographic experience included beginner, competent, proficient, and expert. The Big-Five traits (extroversion (E), agreeableness (A), neuroticism (N), openness (O), and conscientiousness (C)) of each user were collected by asking them to fill in the BFI-10 questionnaire [42]. In this database, 40 users and their corresponding rated images were randomly selected as the testing set, and the remaining users and their corresponding rated images were used as the training set. Therefore, we can use the interaction between the multiple attributes of images and users to train the proposed PIAA-MIR model.

The **FLICKR-AES** [22] database contains 40,000 images rated by 210 users. Among them, 173 users and their rated 35,263 images were chosen as the training set, and the remaining 37 users and their rated 4,737 images were used as the testing set. Since the database only provided each user's personalized aesthetic score for the images, we could use the general aesthetic extraction module trained by the PAPA database to obtain multiple attributes of images. Similar to [27], we also could leverage users' aesthetic ratings on images to obtain their Big-Five personality traits. In this way, the Big-Five personality traits were used as subjective attributes to interact with the objective attributes of images to train our PIAA-MIR model.

The **REAL-CUR** [22] is a relatively small database that contains 14 users and their personalized aesthetic ratings on images in their own photo albums. Each photo album only consists of images ranging from 197 to 222. Due to the small number of users in this database, we directly fine-tuned the prior model trained on the PAPA database with the PIAA tasks of these 14 users, which can verify the generalization performance of the proposed prior model for inferring users' personalized aesthetics in a real scenario.

In the following experiments on these three databases, all aesthetic scores and numerical attributes were normalized to the range of 0 to 1, and higher values indicate stronger aesthetics and attributes.

4.2. Experimental Settings

Implementation details: The initialized parameters of our CNN model (f_θ) came from ResNet50 [38], which is pre-trained on ImageNet [39]. In the multi-attribute interaction reasoning network, MLP_{θ_r} consists of two FC layers with 1024 nodes and 1 node. All parameters of FC layers were randomly initialized. In the training process of the generic aesthetics extraction module and multi-attribute interaction reasoning network, we set the initial learning rate to 5×10^{-5}, and the learning rate was multiplied by 0.1 every 5 epochs. Besides, the batch size and the number of epochs were set to 100 and 20, respectively. In the PIAA model's fine-tuning, the number of epochs was set to 5, and the learning rate was set to 1×10^{-5}. The proposed PIAA-MIR was performed on PyTorch, and Adam was used as the optimizer of our model.

Evaluation criterion: As with the previous approaches [27,28], the Spearman rank-order correlation coefficient (SROCC) was adopted to evaluate the effectiveness of the PIAA models in predicting users' personalized aesthetic scores on images. The values of the SROCC range from −1 to 1, and higher values of the SROCC indicate better performance of the PIAA methods.

4.3. Comparing with the State-of-the-Art PIAA Methods

Since PAPA is a recently released PIAA database, only a few results of the PIAA models have been reported in this database [10]. To further examine the performance of the proposed method, we also compared our PIAA-MIR with a generic aesthetic prior-based method (PA_IAA [8]) and two personalized aesthetic prior-based methods (BLG-PIAA [28] and PIAA-SOA [27]). Similar to [10], we randomly selected 40 users for testing and report the average results of 10 repeated experiments. For each user, 10 or 100 images rated by the user were selected to fine-tune the prior model for obtaining the PIAA model. To avoid random bias, the fine-tuning process for each user was repeated 10 times, and the average results and the corresponding standard deviation are reported.

Table 1 lists the comparison results of our PIAA-MIR with several PIAA methods on the PAPA database [10], where the mean SROCC results of 40 testing users were used as the final results, and the best results are highlighted in bold font. Overall, our PIAA-MIR method achieved the best performance when fine-tuning with 10 or 100 images, which indicates the effectiveness of the proposed multi-attribute interaction-based prior model. Compared with the PIAA models only using a generic aesthetic prior (PAPA (unconditional) and PA_IAA) or a personalized aesthetic prior (BLG-PIAA and PIAA-SOA), PIAA-MIR achieved superior performance, demonstrating that it is efficient in jointly learning the prior model from the perspectives of both users and images. In addition, the proposed PIAA-MIR outperformed the three types of conditional PIAA models (PAPA (artistic), PAPA (photographic), and PAPA (photographic)), which shows that it is more effective at learning users' aesthetic preferences through multiple attributes' interaction than directly embedding subjective attributes.

Table 1. SROCC results of our PIAA-MIR with several PIAA methods on the PAPA database [10]. PAPA (unconditional) indicates the unconditional PIAA model proposed by the authors of PAPA. Similarly, PAPA (artistic), PAPA (photographic), and PAPA (photographic) denote the PIAA model by embedding three types of conditional information (artistic experience, photographic experience, and personality traits).

Methods	10 Images	100 Images
PAPA (unconditional) [10]	0.681 ± 0.0015	0.695 ± 0.0014
PAPA (artistic) [10]	0.686 ± 0.0016	0.698 ± 0.0012
PAPA (photographic) [10]	0.683 ± 0.0014	0.698 ± 0.0010
PAPA (personality) [10]	0.691 ± 0.0009	0.705 ± 0.0015
PA_IAA [8]	0.683 ± 0.0013	0.690 ± 0.0016
BLG-PIAA [28]	0.688 ± 0.0015	0.697 ± 0.0013
PIAA-SOA [27]	0.692 ± 0.0014	0.703 ± 0.0012
PIAA-MIR	**0.702 ± 0.00010**	**0.716 ± 0.0008**

As with the experimental setup in [27], we verified the performance of the proposed method on the FLICKR-AES and REAL-CUR databases. In Table 2, we summarize the average SROCC results of the proposed PIAA-MIR and several state-of-the-art methods on the 37 testing users of the FLICKR-AES database, where the best results are highlighted in bold font. From the table, we can see that the proposed method significantly outperformed all the PIAA methods, except PIAA-SOA. This illustrates that the objective attributes of images learned on the PAPA database are also beneficial to building the prior model on the FLICKR-AES database. Compared with PIAA-SOA, which directly integrates objective attributes and subjective attributes, the proposed method utilizes multi-attribute interaction to learn better personalized aesthetic prior knowledge for individual users. To verify the effectiveness of the proposed prior model in adapting to users' personalized aesthetic preferences in real scenarios, we list the average SROCC results of our PIAA-MIR and three PIAA methods reported in [27] on the 14 album users of the REAL-CUR database in Table 3. As shown in the table, the proposed PIAA-MIR yielded the best performance in learning the aesthetic preferences of individual users in real applications. This further proves that our prior model learned on the PAPA database also has satisfactory generalization performance for users of other databases.

Table 2. SROCC results of our PIAA-MIR with several PIAA methods on the FLICKR-AES database [22].

Methods	10 Images	100 Images
PAM (attribute) [22]	0.518 ± 0.003	0.539 ± 0.013
PAM (content) [22]	0.515 ± 0.004	0.535 ± 0.017
PAM (content and attribute) [22]	0.520 ± 0.003	0.553 ± 0.012
USAR_PPR [23]	0.521 ± 0.002	0.544 ± 0.007
USAR_PAD [23]	0.520 ± 0.003	0.537 ± 0.003
USAR_PPR&PAD [23]	0.525 ± 0.004	0.552 ± 0.015
ML-PIAA [25]	0.522 ± 0.005	0.562 ± 0.015
PA_IAA [8]	0.543 ± 0.003	0.639 ± 0.011
BLG-PIAA [28]	0.561 ± 0.005	0.669 ± 0.013
UG-PIAA [26]	0.559 ± 0.002	0.660 ± 0.013
PIAA-SOA [27]	0.618 ± 0.006	0.691 ± 0.015
PIAA-MIR	**0.621 ± 0.005**	**0.713 ± 0.00016**

Table 3. SROCC results of our PIAA-MIR with three PIAA methods on the REAL-CUR database [22].

Methods	10 Images	100 Images
PA_IAA [8]	0.443 ± 0.004	0.562 ± 0.013
BLG-PIAA [28]	0.448 ± 0.007	0.578 ± 0.015
PIAA-SOA [27]	0.487 ± 0.006	0.589 ± 0.014
PIAA-MIR	**0.498 ± 0.008**	**0.606 ± 0.013**

To further verify the efficiency of our method in learning each user's personalized aesthetic experience from the proposed prior model, we examined the performance of the prior model and the PIAA model fine-tuned on 100 images of each testing user from the PAPA database [10]. To highlight the comparative results, we compared our PIAA-MIR with the state-of-the-art PIAA-SOA and show the average SROCC results of 10 experiments on 40 testing users in Figure 3. For both PIAA-SOA and the proposed PIAA-MIR, the PIAA model yielded better performance than the prior model. For most users (27 out of 40), PIAA-MIR outperformed PIAA-SOA in terms of the prior model (0.695 versus 0.686), which shows the effectiveness of the proposed prior model in capturing the personalized aesthetic experiences of individual users by using the interaction between multiple objective and subjective attributes. In addition, when the prior model was fine-tuned on 100 images rated by individual users, our method was also superior to PIAA-SOA in transferring users' personalized aesthetics from the prior model (0.021 (from 0.695 to 0.716) versus 0.018 (from 0.686 to 0.703)). In summary, the proposed PIAA-MIR builds a robust prior model through multi-attribute interaction, which can easily adapt to personalized aesthetic preferences with a small number of annotated samples.

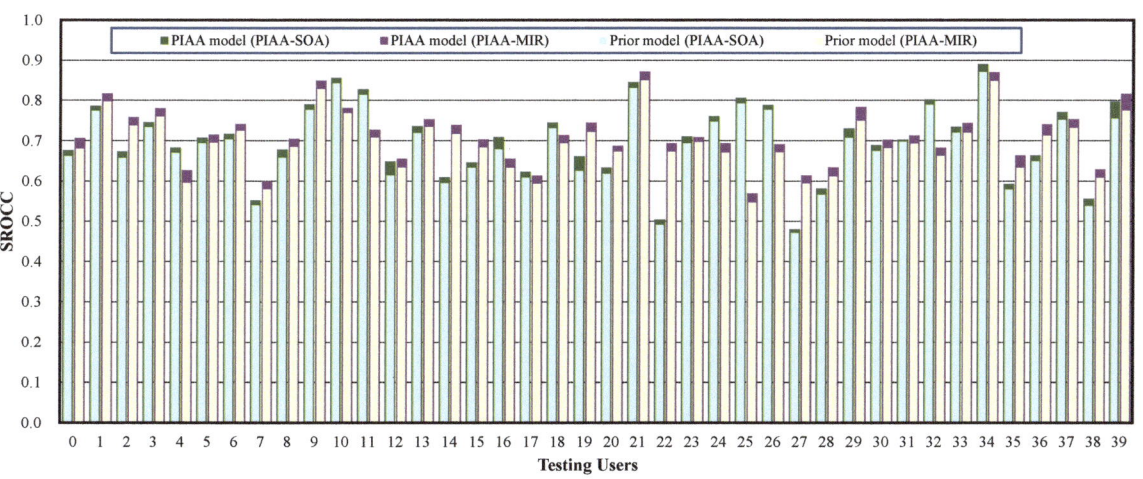

Figure 3. SROCC results of PIAA-SOA [27] and our PIAA-MIR on the 40 testing users of the PAPA database [10]. The testing results of the prior model and PIAA model on each user are shown. Specifically, the testing results of PIAA-SOA are displayed with blue and green bars, and the testing results of PIAA-MIR are displayed with yellow and purple bars.

4.4. Ablation Study

To further examine the contribution of each module in the proposed multi-attribute interactive reasoning network for learning users' personalized aesthetic preferences for images, an ablation study was conducted on the PAPA database [10]. In the generic aesthetics extraction module, we removed the prediction branch of multiple objective attributes and only leveraged multiple subjective attributes and score distributions to predict personalized aesthetic scores, which is termed "PIAA-MIR w/o objective". In the multi-attribute interactive reasoning network, we replaced multiple subjective attributes with a one-hot encoding vector to characterize users (PIAA-MIR w/o subjective). We replaced the multi-attribute interaction with simple attributes combined to predict personalized aesthetic scores, which is called "PIAA-MIR w/o interaction". In addition, to compare the prior model learned only from generic aesthetics or personalized aesthetics, we introduced the baseline model by only training the generic aesthetics extraction module from the perspective of images (Baseline (generic)) or the multi-attribute interaction reasoning network from the perspective of users (Baseline (personalized)).

Table 4 lists the test results of the ablation experiments. As shown in the table, the full version of PIAA-MIR obtained the best results on the testing users of the PAPA database. Compared with the baseline model learned only from generic aesthetics (Baseline (generic)) or personalized aesthetics (Baseline (personalized)), the proposed PIAA-MIR yielded significant performance improvements, which shows that it is efficient at learning a prior model from the perspectives of both images and users. When eliminating multiple objective attributes (PIAA-MIR w/o objective) or multiple subjective attributes (PIAA-MIR w/o subjective) in our model, PIAA-MIR showed worse prediction performance in learning personalized aesthetics, which demonstrates the importance of embedding subjective and objective attributes in the proposed PIAA-MIR. Besides, PIAA-MIR was also superior to "PIAA-MIR w/o interaction", which indicates that the proposed multi-attribute interaction is crucial for exploring the underlying factors for users' personalized aesthetic experiences. All in all, the above modules contributed to promoting the evaluation performance of the proposed method.

Table 4. SROCC results of our PIAA-MIR on the PAPA database [10] by eliminating different ablation modules, where the best results of fine-tuning on 10 and 100 images are shown in boldface.

Methods	10 Images	100 Images
Baseline (generic)	0.679 ± 0.0014	0.692 ± 0.0015
Baseline (personalized)	0.682 ± 0.0015	0.698 ± 0.0016
PIAA-MIR w/o objective	0.689 ± 0.0011	0.700 ± 0.0011
PIAA-MIR w/o subjective	0.684 ± 0.0013	0.693 ± 0.0014
PIAA-MIR w/o interaction	0.696 ± 0.0012	0.707 ± 0.0010
PIAA-MIR	**0.702 ± 0.00010**	**0.716 ± 0.0008**

4.5. Visual Analysis

To intuitively show how PIAA-MIR leverages the interaction between multiple subjective and objective attributes for personalized aesthetic preferences reasoning, we randomly selected two testing users, as well as two testing images rated by them from the PAPA database [10]. The predicted results of our method are shown in Figure 4. We can see from the figure that the predicted attributes and aesthetic scores of the proposed PIAA-MIR for the four images were close to the ground truth (GT) results, which indicates that the proposed generic aesthetics extraction module is efficient in predicting aesthetic attributes and the score distribution. Since User #1 is a man with expert photography experience, he tends to give higher aesthetic ratings to images with better composition and content. In addition, User #1 is also a person with strong agreeableness and conscientiousness, so he prefers the left image containing animals. By contrast, User #2 is a person with strong neuroticism and has preliminary art and photography experience. Although the two images rated by User #2 have the same average aesthetics, the user's personalized aesthetic scores for these two images differ greatly. This is because neurotic people prefer images with dim light and monotonous color [41], which led User #2 to give a higher aesthetic score to the left image than the right image. From the above analysis, we can draw a conclusion that the multiple objective attributes of images and the multiple subjective attributes of users jointly affect users' personalized aesthetic experiences for images, and the proposed multi-attribute interaction can effectively reveal the potential impact relationship between them.

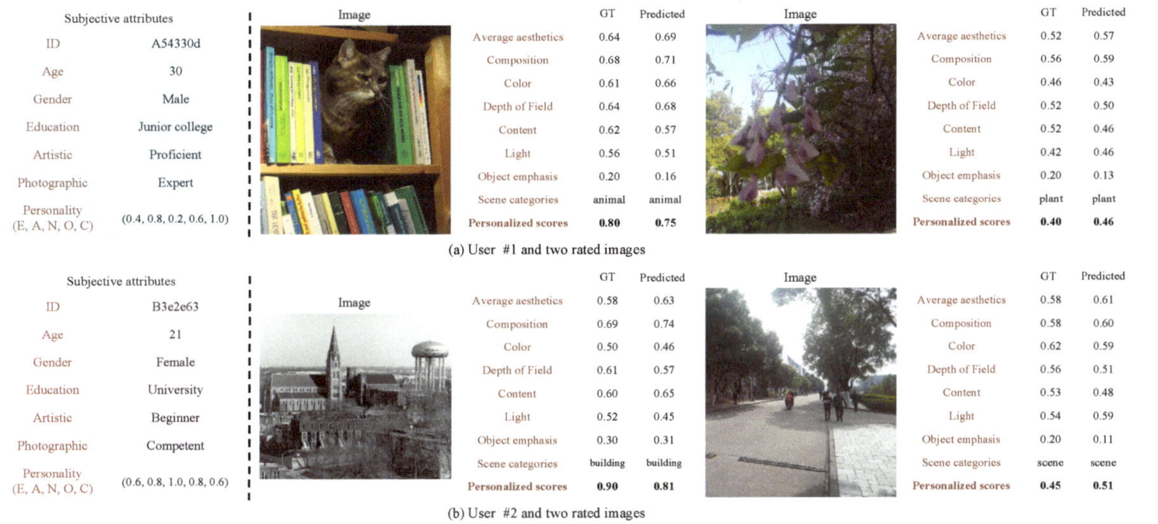

Figure 4. Qualitative results of the proposed model on two testing users from the PAPA database [10]. The identification (ID) information and some subjective attributes of these two users are shown on the left side. The average aesthetics of score distribution, objective attributes, and personalized scores of images are shown on the right side. For comparison, we show both the ground truth (GT) and predicted results, where aesthetic scores and numerical attributes are normalized to the range of 0 to 1 and higher values indicate stronger aesthetics and attributes.

5. Conclusions

In this paper, we introduced a personalized image aesthetics assessment method via multi-attribute interactive reasoning (PIAA-MIR). Compared with existing PIAA methods, the proposed method can effectively reason users' personalized image aesthetic experiences, which benefits from learning the prior model for PIAA from the perspectives of both images and users. Specifically, the proposed generic aesthetics extraction module showed its efficiency in predicting multiple aesthetic attributes and score distributions of images. In addition, the multi-attribute interaction-based prior model learned from extensive users' PIAA tasks can capture the robust impact of multiple subjective and objective attributes on users' personalized aesthetic preferences for images. Therefore, when an individual user only provides a small number of annotation samples, the proposed multi-attribute interaction can use this robust interactive relationship to effectively transfer the prior model to the PIAA model for the individual user. The experimental results and visual analysis of three PIAA databases demonstrated that the proposed PIAA model is effective in reasoning individual users' personalized visual aesthetics. In the future, our method will highlight a novel strategy to analyze the implicit reasons for personalized aesthetic preferences from the perspectives of both users and images.

Author Contributions: Conceptualization, H.Z. and Y.Z.; methodology, H.Z. and Z.S.; software, H.Z.; validation, W.D., G.W. and Q.L.; formal analysis, W.D.; investigation, H.Z.; resources, H.Z.; data collection, H.Z.; writing—original draft preparation, H.Z.; writing—review and editing, Y.Z. and Z.S.; visualization, H.Z.; supervision, Y.Z.; project administration, Y.Z.; funding acquisition, H.Z. All authors have read and agreed to the published version of the manuscript.

Funding: This work was supported by the National Natural Science Foundation of China (No. 62101555), the Natural Science Foundation of Jiangsu Province (No. BK20210488), the Project funded by China Postdoctoral Science Foundation (No. 2022M713379), and the Fundamental Research Funds for the Central Universities (No. 2021QN1071). It was also partially supported by the National Natural Science Foundation of China (Nos. 62272461, 62106268, and 62002360), the Natural Science Foundation of Jiangsu Province (No. BK20201346), the High-Level Talent Program for Innovation and Entrepreneurship (ShuangChuang Doctor) of Jiangsu Province (No. JSSCBS20211220), and the Six Talent Peaks High-level Talents in Jiangsu Province (No. 2015-DZXX-010).

Institutional Review Board Statement: Not applicable.

Informed Consent Statement: Not applicable.

Data Availability Statement: The experiment used three public PIAA databases, which are available in the PAPA [10], FLICKR-AES [22], and REAL-CUR [22] databases.

Conflicts of Interest: The authors declare no conflict of interest.

References

1. Deng, Y.; Chen, C.L.; Tang, X. Image Aesthetic Assessment: An Experimental Survey. *IEEE Signal Process. Mag.* **2017**, *34*, 80–106. [CrossRef]
2. Talebi, H.; Milanfar, P. NIMA: Neural Image Assessment. *IEEE Trans. Image Process.* **2018**, *27*, 3998–4011. [CrossRef]
3. Ma, W.; Qin, J.; Xiang, X.; Tan, Y.; He, Z. Searchable Encrypted Image Retrieval Based on Multi-Feature Adaptive Late-Fusion. *Mathematics* **2020**, *8*, 1019. [CrossRef]
4. Karlsson, K.; Jiang, W.; Zhang, D.Q. Mobile photo album management with multiscale timeline. In Proceedings of the 22nd ACM International Conference on Multimedia, Orlando, FL, USA, 3–7 November 2014; pp. 1061–1064. [CrossRef]
5. Lozano-Vázquez, L.V.; Miura, J.; Rosales-Silva, A.J.; Luviano-Juárez, A.; Mújica-Vargas, D. Analysis of Different Image Enhancement and Feature Extraction Methods. *Mathematics* **2022**, *10*, 2407. [CrossRef]
6. Esser, P.; Rombach, R.; Ommer, B. Taming Transformers for High-Resolution Image Synthesis. In Proceedings of the IEEE/CVF Conference on Computer Vision and Pattern Recognition, Nashville, TN, USA, 20–25 June 2021; pp. 12873–12883. [CrossRef]
7. Zhang, Y.; Yamasaki, T. Style-Aware Image Recommendation for Social Media Marketing. In Proceedings of the 29th ACM International Conference on Multimedia, Virtual, China, 20–24 October 2021; pp. 3106–3114. [CrossRef]
8. Li, L.; Zhu, H.; Zhao, S.; Ding, G.; Lin, W. Personality-Assisted Multi-Task Learning for Generic and Personalized Image Aesthetics Assessment. *IEEE Trans. Image Process.* **2020**, *29*, 3898–3910. [CrossRef]
9. Zhang, X.; Zhang, X.; Xiao, Y.; Liu, G. Theme-Aware Semi-Supervised Image Aesthetic Quality Assessment. *Mathematics* **2022**, *10*, 2609. [CrossRef]
10. Yang, Y.; Xu, L.; Li, L.; Qie, N.; Li, Y.; Zhang, P.; Guo, Y. Personalized Image Aesthetics Assessment With Rich Attributes. In Proceedings of the IEEE/CVF Conference on Computer Vision and Pattern Recognition, New Orleans, LA, USA, 19–20 June 2022; pp. 19861–19869. [CrossRef]
11. Murray, N.; Marchesotti, L.; Perronnin, F. AVA: A large-scale database for aesthetic visual analysis. In Proceedings of the IEEE Conference on Computer Vision and Pattern Recognition, Providence, RI, USA, 16–21 June 2012; pp. 2408–2415. [CrossRef]
12. Kao, Y.; He, R.; Huang, K. Deep Aesthetic Quality Assessment With Semantic Information. *IEEE Trans. Image Process.* **2017**, *26*, 1482–1495. [CrossRef]
13. Kong, S.; Shen, X.; Lin, Z.; Mech, R.; Fowlkes, C. Photo Aesthetics Ranking Network with Attributes and Content Adaptation. In Proceedings of the European Conference on Computer Vision, Amsterdam, The Netherlands, 11–14 October 2016; pp. 662–679. [CrossRef]
14. Pan, B.; Wang, S.; Jiang, Q. Image Aesthetic Assessment Assisted by Attributes through Adversarial Learning. In Proceedings of the AAAI Conference on Artificial Intelligence, Honolulu, HI, USA, 27 January 27–1 February 2019; pp. 679–686. [CrossRef]
15. Zhang, X.; Gao, X.; Lu, W.; He, L. A Gated Peripheral-Foveal Convolutional Neural Network for Unified Image Aesthetic Prediction. *IEEE Trans. Multimedia* **2019**, *21*, 2815–2826. [CrossRef]
16. Zeng, H.; Cao, Z.; Zhang, L.; Bovik, A.C. A Unified Probabilistic Formulation of Image Aesthetic Assessment. *IEEE Trans. Image Process.* **2020**, *29*, 1548–1561. [CrossRef]
17. She, D.; Lai, Y.K.; Yi, G.; Xu, K. Hierarchical Layout-Aware Graph Convolutional Network for Unified Aesthetics Assessment. In Proceedings of the IEEE/CVF Conference on Computer Vision and Pattern Recognition, Nashville, TN, USA, 19–25 June 2021; pp. 8475–8484. [CrossRef]
18. Zhang, X.; Song, Q.; Liu, G. Multimodal Image Aesthetic Prediction with Missing Modality. *Mathematics* **2022**, *10*, 2312. [CrossRef]
19. Zhang, J.; Yang, Y.; Zhuo, L.; Tian, Q.; Liang, X. Personalized Recommendation of Social Images by Constructing a User Interest Tree with Deep Features and Tag Trees. *IEEE Trans. Multimedia* **2019**, *21*, 2762–2775. [CrossRef]
20. Park, C.C.; Kim, B.; KIM, G. Towards Personalized Image Captioning via Multimodal Memory Networks. *IEEE Trans. Pattern Anal. Mach. Intell.* **2019**, *41*, 999–1012. [CrossRef] [PubMed]
21. Bianco, S.; Cusano, C.; Piccoli, F.; Schettini, R. Personalized Image Enhancement Using Neural Spline Color Transforms. *IEEE Trans. Image Process.* **2020**, *29*, 6223–6236. [CrossRef] [PubMed]
22. Ren, J.; Shen, X.; Lin, Z.; Mech, R.; Foran, D.J. Personalized Image Aesthetics. In Proceedings of the IEEE International Conference on Computer Vision, Venice, Italy, 22–29 October 2017; pp. 638–647. [CrossRef]
23. Lv, P.; Wang, M.; Xu, Y.; Peng, Z.; Sun, J.; Su, S.; Zhou, B.; Xu, M. USAR: An Interactive User-Specific Aesthetic Ranking Framework for Images. In Proceedings of the 26th ACM International Conference on Multimedia, Seoul, Korea, 22–26 October 2018; pp. 1328–1336. [CrossRef]

24. Wang, G.; Yan, J.; Qin, Z. Collaborative and Attentive Learning for Personalized Image Aesthetic Assessment. In Proceedings of the International Joint Conference on Artificial Intelligence, Stockholm, Sweden, 13–19 July 2018; pp. 957–963. [CrossRef]
25. Wang, W.; Su, J.; Li, L.; Xu, X.; Luo, J. Meta-Learning Perspective for Personalized Image Aesthetics Assessment. In Proceedings of the IEEE International Conference on Image Processing, Taipei, Taiwan, 22–25 September 2019; pp. 1875–1879. [CrossRef]
26. Lv, P.; Fan, J.; Nie, X.; Dong, W.; Jiang, X.; Zhou, B.; Xu, M.; Xu, C. User-Guided Personalized Image Aesthetic Assessment based on Deep Reinforcement Learning. *IEEE Trans. Multimedia* **2021**, 1–14. [CrossRef]
27. Zhu, H.; Zhou, Y.; Li, L.; Li, Y.; Guo, Y. Learning Personalized Image Aesthetics from Subjective and Objective Attributes. *IEEE Trans. Multimedia* **2021**, 1–12. [CrossRef]
28. Zhu, H.; Li, L.; Wu, J.; Zhao, S.; Ding, G.; Shi, G. Personalized Image Aesthetics Assessment via Meta-Learning with Bilevel Gradient Optimization. *IEEE Trans. Cybern.* **2022**, *52*, 1798–1811. [CrossRef]
29. Hou, J.; Lin, W.; Yue, G.; Liu, W.; Zhao, B. Interaction-Matrix Based Personalized Image Aesthetics Assessment. *IEEE Trans. Multimedia* **2022**, 1–16. [CrossRef]
30. Kucer, M.; Loui, A.C.; Messinger, D.W. Leveraging Expert Feature Knowledge for Predicting Image Aesthetics. *IEEE Trans. Image Process.* **2018**, *27*, 5100–5112. [CrossRef]
31. Vinciarelli, A.; Mohammadi, G. A Survey of Personality Computing. *IEEE Trans. Affect. Comput.* **2014**, *5*, 273–291. [CrossRef]
32. He, X.; Du, X.; Wang, X.; Tian, F.; Tang, J.; Chua, T. Outer Product-based Neural Collaborative Filtering. In Proceedings of the International Joint Conference on Artificial Intelligence, Stockholm, Sweden, 13–19 July 2018; pp. 2227–2233. [CrossRef]
33. Zeki, S. Clive Bell's "Significant Form" and the neurobiology of aesthetics. *Front. Hum. Neurosci.* **2013**, *7*, 730. [CrossRef]
34. Perona, P.R.; Gallego, M.J.F.; Callejón, J.M.P. An Application for Aesthetic Quality Assessment in Photography with Interpretability Features. *Entropy* **2021**, *23*, 1389. [CrossRef] [PubMed]
35. Gelli, F.; Uricchio, T.; He, X.; Del Bimbo, A.; Chua, T.S. Learning Subjective Attributes of Images from Auxiliary Sources. In Proceedings of the ACM International Conference on Multimedia, Nice, France, 21–25 October 2019; pp. 2263–2271. [CrossRef]
36. Kim, W.H.; Choi, J.H.; Lee, J.S. Objectivity and Subjectivity in Aesthetic Quality Assessment of Digital Photographs. *IEEE Trans. Affect. Comput.* **2020**, *11*, 493–506. [CrossRef]
37. Zhao, W.; Wang, B.; Ye, J.; Yang, M.; Zhao, Z.; Luo, R.; Qiao, Y. A Multi-task Learning Approach for Image Captioning. In Proceedings of the International Joint Conference on Artificial Intelligence, Stockholm, Sweden, 13–19 July 2018; pp. 1205–1211. [CrossRef]
38. He, K.; Zhang, X.; Ren, S.; Sun, J. Deep Residual Learning for Image Recognition. In Proceedings of the IEEE Conference on Computer Vision and Pattern Recognition, Las Vegas, NV, USA, 27–30 June 2016; pp. 770–778. [CrossRef]
39. Krizhevsky, A.; Sutskever, I.; Hinton, G.E. ImageNet Classification with Deep Convolutional Neural Networks. *Commun. ACM* **2017**, *60*, 84–90. [CrossRef]
40. Levina, E.; Bickel, P. The Earth Mover's distance is the Mallows distance: Some insights from statistics. In Proceedings of the IEEE International Conference on Computer Vision, Vancouver, BC, Canada, 7–14 July 2001; Volume 2, pp. 251–256. [CrossRef]
41. Zhu, H.; Li, L.; Zhao, S.; Jiang, H. Evaluating attributed personality traits from scene perception probability. *Pattern Recognit. Lett.* **2018**, *116*, 121–126. [CrossRef]
42. Rammstedt, B.; John, O.P. Measuring personality in one minute or less: A 10-item short version of the Big Five Inventory in English and German. *J. Res. Pers.* **2007**, *41*, 203–212. [CrossRef]

Article

Acoustic Gender and Age Classification as an Aid to Human–Computer Interaction in a Smart Home Environment

Damjan Vlaj and Andrej Zgank *

Faculty of Electrical Engineering and Computer Science, University of Maribor, 2000 Maribor, Slovenia
* Correspondence: andrej.zgank@um.si; Tel.: +386-2-220-7206

Abstract: The advanced smart home environment presents an important trend for the future of human wellbeing. One of the prerequisites for applying its rich functionality is the ability to differentiate between various user categories, such as gender, age, speakers, etc. We propose a model for an efficient acoustic gender and age classification system for human–computer interaction in a smart home. The objective was to improve acoustic classification without using high-complexity feature extraction. This was realized with pitch as an additional feature, combined with additional acoustic modeling approaches. In the first step, the classification is based on Gaussian mixture models. In the second step, two new procedures are introduced for gender and age classification. The first is based on the count of the frames with the speaker's pitch values, and the second is based on the sum of the frames with pitch values belonging to a certain speaker. Since both procedures are based on pitch values, we have proposed a new, effective algorithm for pitch value calculation. In order to improve gender and age classification, we also incorporated speech segmentation with the proposed voice activity detection algorithm. We also propose a procedure that enables the quick adaptation of the classification algorithm to frequent smart home users. The proposed classification model with pitch values has improved the results in comparison with the baseline system.

Keywords: acoustic classification; acoustic signal processing; Gaussian mixture model; pitch analysis; smart home

MSC: 68T10

Citation: Vlaj, D.; Zgank, A. Acoustic Gender and Age Classification as an Aid to Human–Computer Interaction in a Smart Home Environment. *Mathematics* **2023**, *11*, 169. https://doi.org/10.3390/math11010169

Academic Editor: Daniel-Ioan Curiac

Received: 24 November 2022
Revised: 21 December 2022
Accepted: 26 December 2022
Published: 29 December 2022

Copyright: © 2022 by the authors. Licensee MDPI, Basel, Switzerland. This article is an open access article distributed under the terms and conditions of the Creative Commons Attribution (CC BY) license (https://creativecommons.org/licenses/by/4.0/).

1. Introduction

The intensive development of information communications technology (ICT) has spread into all sections of everyday life, including the human living environment. Real-life smart home systems already include successful automation and control support for the variety of scenarios that human users are confronted with. Currently, the majority of smart home users belong to the category of early adopters, but it is expected that the future development of the technology will increase its broad acceptance in the general population [1,2].

An important functionality in a smart home environment is the detection of the user's presence in a room. This can be fulfilled in different ways, focusing on non-invasive methods, wherein users do not need to wear any dedicated device. One of the traditional methods is passive infrared (PIR) motion detection, which yields relatively simple and robust sensors. The disadvantage of this technology is its inability to distinguish between different user categories, such as gender, age, speakers' identity [3], etc. Another method that cannot cope with user categories is speech activity detection (SAD) [4], which provides the smart home system with information about a user's presence solely from the captured speech signal.

Human–computer interaction (HCI) can, in advanced smart home environments, provide rich functionality if it can differentiate between various user categories. To distinguish between them, machine learning classification can be used. The classification accuracy and, in particular, system complexity largely depends on the category characteristics and intra-category variance. The decision regarding which type of user classification (e.g., gender) to apply is based on HCI scenarios and requested functionalities that need to be applied in the smart home environment. The resulting HCI system in a smart home environment can act accordingly, applying user scenarios, adapting functionality, or deploying entity personalization. The area of personalization [5] covers a large number of possible scenarios. Some smart home entities that are frequently included in the personalization process include the user interface, media and users' content, a recommendation system, AAL functions, etc. The main personalization objective is to achieve better usage acceptability and higher quality of experience. To be able to carry out such category-based presence detection, a more sophisticated approach must be used than IR motion detection or SAD. One possibility is to use image processing [6], and another is to use more complex audio processing. The advantage of presence detection using audio as a modality is its lower computational complexity, lower cost, and better acceptability among users. The user's acceptability is tightly connected with the data privacy question. In the case of audio, a well-considered design can lead to local processing, without the need to use cloud-based speech processing services.

Based on the above characteristics of the advanced HCI interface, we propose an acoustic classification model that determines the age and gender of the speaker from the captured speech signal. Such a classification approach can be used in a smart home environment for precise presence detection. Broadly accepted smart home usage scenarios were analyzed and a decision was made to classify users into three categories: male, female, and child. This represents an effective combination of all speakers' characteristics. A special characteristic of the proposed model is the inclusion of the category of children in the classification, which is not typically represented in speech technologies. This aspect is important due to the smart home user interface design and content-processing process. In the case of children, the personalization steps must be more intensive and age-oriented, emphasizing domain control and the adequacy of the information available to them. The first objective of the proposed acoustic classification model is to provide accurate performance for all three defined categories using pitch processing. Pitch is one of the signal processing values that can contribute most extensively to classification accuracy, as it depends significantly on the speakers' characteristics. We propose an algorithm for efficient pitch calculation. We also propose two-step solutions for including pitch in the classification to enable adaptation in the second step. The second objective of the proposed model is to simplify the development of acoustic age and gender classification for presence detection in a smart home environment. The motivation was to reuse available speech recognition modules from a smart home environment. This results in less complex speech technology methods that can even be used by resource-constrained devices.

Using speech as an input modality has both advantages and disadvantages. The speech signal propagates through the room, which means that the capture devices need not focus directly on the user. This can significantly improve the system's usability. There are two shortcomings present for speech modality. The first one is the sensitivity of the speech signal in relation to other audio sources co-existing in the room. The disturbing audio sources' types vary according to the scenario: background music/TV, home appliances, other speakers, domestic animals, street noise, etc. The second one is the issue of the privacy of uttered information, which can be successfully handled by local processing in the scope of the embedded systems. The speech-based presence detection system can be combined with other presence detection entities, such as PIR motion detection sensors. This can result in improved performance, as the modalities of signals and noises differ. The end result is the limiting of shortcomings connected with the pure speech-oriented system.

The paper is organized as follows. Section 2 presents a literature review from two perspectives: gender classification and smart home systems. Section 3 first presents the proposed model and then describes the theory of acoustic gender classification, with an emphasis on approaches used in the experiments. Then, the system design applied in the experiments is presented. The speech processing results are presented in Section 4. The discussion is provided in Section 5, and the conclusion is provided in Section 6.

2. Literature Review

The objective of this work was to establish a back-end smart home service, which could be used for detecting the presence of users solely via speech modality and classify them accordingly. Thus, the addressed related work also covers two fields. The first one is the field of digital signal processing and gender classification from speech. The second one is the field of smart home systems and services.

The topic of acoustic gender classification is an area in spoken language technology with a long history. The first systems emerged decades ago [7–9], mainly as sub-components of automatic speech recognition systems. The basic idea—of how to detect gender from acoustic signals—is usually pursued via the spectral and temporal characteristics of the captured speech signal [10]. To be able to carry out gender classification, two approaches need to be combined: first, the representative features are extracted from the captured audio signal [11], and second, the appropriate machine learning approach is used to classify them [12].

The acoustic feature extraction procedure is a key factor in successful gender classification. Various approaches, such as mel-frequency cepstral coefficients (MFCC) [13,14], pitch [15], and RASTA [15], have been used for the gender classification task. In general, MFCC feature extraction usually provides good classification results. The speech rate, pauses, loudness, intonation, and voice quality can be categorized as paralinguistic features. Similar to acoustic features, paralinguistic features can also be used for gender classification [16], with the objective of broadening the data available for classification. This can improve the overall classification accuracy.

An important issue in the case of gender classification from speech is its robustness against the acoustic background and other degradation events. The background signal and noise can reach high energy levels and, consequently, significantly disturb system operation in smart home scenarios. Islam [17] showed that GFCC features also significantly improve the robustness and effectiveness of gender classification in a harsh environment.

One of the baseline approaches to addressing gender classification is Gaussian mixture models (GMMs) [18]. The GMM gender classification approach can show high precision with relatively low complexity, which is important for smart home scenarios, where limited embedded resources are frequently available. Ranjan et al. [19] also showed that GMM gender classification achieves good results in different languages, or even in a multilingual environment.

Hidden Markov models (HMMs) have been used for gender and age classification [20], and also for the classification of various human activities in natural environments [21]. The use of HMMs introduces another model's architecture to the classification task, which can improve the robustness, accuracy, and reusability of real-life systems. The combination of several statistical approaches is presented in [22], where universal modeling (UM) based on GMM clustering was used.

Another machine learning approach used for gender classification is support vector machines (SVMs). Bocklet et al. [23] showed that SVM can achieve high-accuracy gender recognition results. The i-vector approach proposed by Dehak [24] was also applied successfully for gender classification in complex spoken scenarios [19].

Deep neural networks (DNNs) were used for gender classification by various authors [25,26]. The main objective was to improve accuracy and combine the gender classification system with the main automatic speech recognition system using the same architecture. Prior to DNNs, other neural network methods, such as multi-layer perceptrons (MLPs) [27], were also successfully implemented for gender classification.

The majority of gender classification systems found in the literature only deal with adult speech, thus classifying between males and females (and unknown). In the case of a smart home, distinguishing between adult and child can also be important. The Paralinguistic Special Session of Interspeech 2010 [28] addressed this topic. The aGender speech database [29], which is applied for the classification task, originated from long conversational telephone sessions, and the speakers were classified into three gender categories and seven combined categories. Meinedo and Trancoso [30] presented a system that used a combination of four different corpora with the fusion of acoustic and prosodic features, and this was able to classify gender with an 84.3% average recall. Yücesoy and Nabiyev [29] carried out gender classification on the aGender speech database with a combination of three subsystems at the score level. The experimental system provided a 90.39% classification success rate for the gender category. This result shows that there are still challenges in the area of gender classification when children's speech is incorporated into experiments.

With the development of algorithms, systems, and terminal equipment, the number of possible use cases increased, and nowadays, gender classification systems can be used successfully in the smart home environment [31]. Speech activity detection, which can be seen as a simplified gender classification approach for the smart home, was addressed by SASLODOM, part of the EVALITA 2014 challenge [32], wherein three different SAD systems were presented. The best system achieved a 2.0% SAD error rate at the frame level, which is already usable in real-life scenarios applicable to SAD. Gender classification can also be helpful for social robots as part of the smart home environment [33]. The availability of extended speech databases also enables a combined approach, whereby age and gender were processed in parallel [34,35].

The literature review presents a general overview of approaches to carrying out the gender classification task. In our work, the emphasis will be placed on particular solutions for acoustic presence detection, as well as gender and age classification, in the smart home environment, where the combination of accuracy and required system resources plays an important role.

3. Materials and Methods

This section presents the proposed procedure used for gender and age classification from input speech signals. First, we present the entire process of preprocessing and extracting the necessary information from the input speech signal so that, in the end, we can determine the presence of a male, female, or child in the environment through classification procedures. Then, we present, in more detail, the voice activity detection (VAD) algorithm and the procedure for determining the pitch value from the input speech signal. The pitch value of an individual speaker gives essential information about whether the speaker is a male, female, or child. Therefore, we chose the pitch value as one of the more essential features in our proposed procedure. We presented the VAD algorithm and the pitch value determination in one of our previous works [36]. We enhance the procedures in this paper to improve the algorithm's performance, which we also describe in more detail in this section's second and third subsections. Next, we present the feature extraction algorithm included in our setup. The training of Gaussian mixture models (GMMs) is presented thereafter.

3.1. Proposed Gender and Age Classification

Here, we present the proposed gender and age classification procedure in detail. Figure 1 will form the basis for describing the details of the proposed procedure. We want to extract information about a person's gender (male or female) and age (adult or child) from the speech signal spoken by a person present in an intelligent environment. The input speech signal is divided into overlapping frames. All further information extraction is from the frames. In the speech signal, most information about gender and age is present in the voiced frames of the speech signal. The voice activity detection (VAD) algorithm detects the voiced frames in the speech signal. The voiced frames of the speech signal are the basis for determining the speaker's pitch value. The next step in the procedure is calculating the 12 mel-frequency cepstral coefficient (C1–C12) features and energy, as specified in the standard [37]. After that, we carried out the composition of the feature vectors that were finally used. Because we did not want to change the size of the feature vector, we decided to replace coefficient C12 with the pitch value. To improve the effectiveness of gender and age classification, we have also calculated the first and second derivatives of the feature vector coefficients. Once we derived the final feature vector and the pitch value for each frame, we began classifying the person's gender and age.

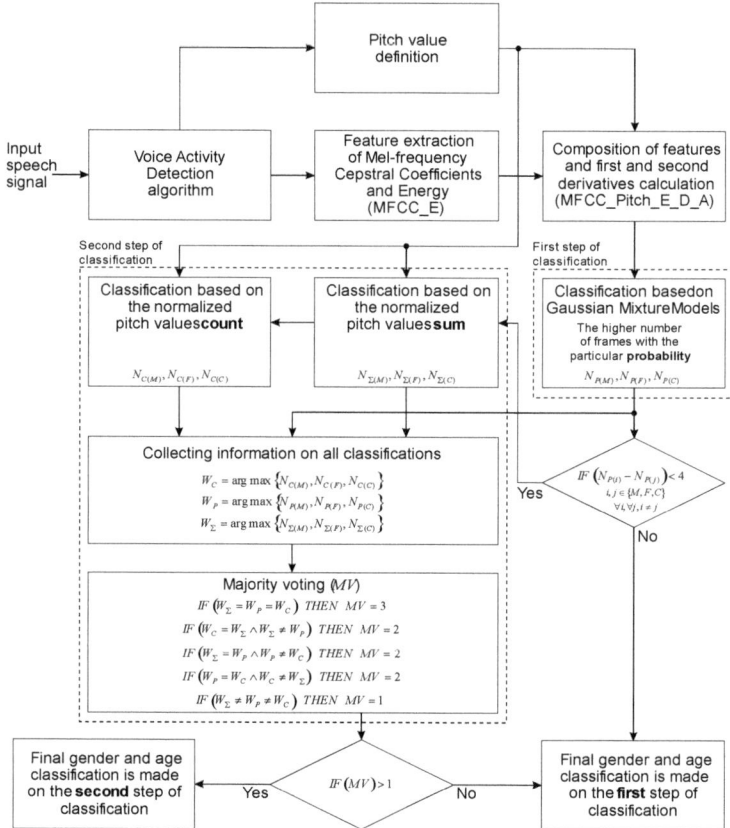

Figure 1. The proposed gender and age classification procedure.

We propose a gender and age classification procedure comprising two steps [38]. We decided on a two-step classification process because, in the second step, based on the analysis of the pitch value of the speakers present in an intelligent environment, we can improve the classification. In the first step, gender and age classifications are based on Gaussian mixture models (GMMs). For each frame, three probabilities, $P(M)$, $P(F)$, and $P(C)$, are determined, representing the probabilities of a male, a female, or a child. The higher probability determines to which gender or age the frame belongs. Next, the frame counters ($N_{P(M)}$, $N_{P(F)}$, and $N_{P(C)}$) are determined for all three classification categories. For each frame, only one frame counter is incremented; that is, the one whose frame has a higher probability. The frame counter with the higher value indicates which gender or age the entire input speech signal belongs to, and it is presented as the winner, W_P, of the classification based on GMMs. We completed the classification process if any frame counter value stood out and was at least four counts greater than the other two. In this case, we considered the GMM-based classification as a final conclusion of gender and age classification. However, if the difference between the two frame counters was less than four, we continued with the second classification step. The right decision block in Figure 1 presents this decision.

In the second step, we propose two procedures of gender and age classification. These are (a) classification based on the normalized pitch value counts and (b) classification based on the normalized pitch value sums. The normalized pitch values are obtained in both procedures by analyzing the speech recordings used to train the GMMs. All frames in which we can determine the pitch value were used for analysis. First, we established three groups of male, female, and child speakers. After that, we divided the pitch values into intervals of 10 Hz. In the 80 Hz interval, there are pitch values between 80 and 90 Hz; the 90 Hz interval covers all pitch values between 90 and 100 Hz, etc. The male speakers' recordings exhibited the most pitch values between 110 and 120 Hz. All the counted pitch values from the male, female, and child speakers were normalized according to the highest value observed by the male speaker.

For the classification based on the normalized pitch value counts, we analyzed the occurrence of the normalized pitch values for the male, female, and child speakers. For each frame, three count areas, $C(M)$, $C(F)$, and $C(C)$, were determined, representing the areas for a male, a female, or a child speaker. If the normalized pitch value for a current frame was below 160 Hz, it belonged to the count area $C(M)$; if it was between 160 and 230 Hz, it belonged to the count area $C(F)$, and if it was above 230 Hz, it belonged to count area $C(C)$. Here, we also determined the frame counters ($N_{C(M)}$, $N_{C(F)}$, and $N_{C(C)}$) for all three classification categories. For each frame, only one frame counter was incremented—the one whose frame belongs to a particular count area. The frame counter with the higher value was used to determine to which gender or age group the entire input speech signal belonged and was presented as the winner, W_C, of the classification based on the normalized pitch value counts.

The classification based on the normalized pitch value sums also uses the analysis results. We have defined three sums: for male $N_{\Sigma(M)}$, female $N_{\Sigma(F)}$, and child $N_{\Sigma(C)}$ speakers. For each frame in which we could detect the pitch value in the speech signal, we added the normalized values obtained from the analysis to the sums of each speaker. For example, a pitch value of 173 Hz was determined within a particular frame. This pitch value was between 170 and 180 Hz, so a 170 Hz interval was selected for all classification groups. Consequently, the normalized value of 0.14 was added to the $N_{\Sigma(M)}$, the normalized value of 0.37 was added to the $N_{\Sigma(F)}$, and the normalized value of 0.08 was added to the $N_{\Sigma(C)}$. Here, can be seen that a normalized value of 0.37, which was added to the $N_{\Sigma(F)}$, was the largest compared to the other two values. This is understandable since this normalized value is located between 160 Hz and 230 Hz, which belongs to the female speakers' count area $C(F)$. The most significant sum value of three sums ($N_{\Sigma(M)}$, $N_{\Sigma(F)}$, and $N_{\Sigma(C)}$) was used to classify to which gender or age the entire input speech signal belonged, and was presented as the winner, W_Σ, of the classification based on the normalized pitch value sums.

The second classification step ends with collecting information about the winners (W_C, W_P, and W_Σ) of all three described classification procedures and majority voting, MV. We performed all three classification procedures on the same speech signal. The results of all three might be the same, but sometimes they give different results. When the results are the same, the majority vote equals three. Then, all classification procedures can be used to determine whether the speaker in the recording is a male, a female, or a child. In such a case, the final decision of the second classification step is simple. If the majority vote is equal to two, this means that at least two processes give an identical classification. In this case, the final classification is the same as the majority vote winner. However, if all three classification procedures give different results, the majority vote is equal to one. In such a case, the final classification of gender and age is based on the first classification step or GMM-based classification.

We will use the proposed gender and age classification system in a smart home environment. There is always the question of how to update and improve such a system.

In this paper, we propose another procedure that would allow for the fast adaptation of the system to users who appear frequently in a smart home environment. The idea of the procedure is based on the fact that the classification based on GMM remains the same. It means that the test set does not influence the trained GMMs. The change is that the system monitors the correctness of the classification and records pitch values on the basis of the frame of the user in the smart home environment. When we have a sufficiently large number of captured pitch values for users, we use these values to adapt the gender and age classification system to them. This sufficiently large number of pitch values can be taken from the analysis. An experiment has been performed to confirm the adaptation procedure, and the results are provided in Section 4.

3.2. Voice Activity Detection Algorithm

An essential contribution of the voice activity detection (VAD) algorithm is real-time noise energy estimation. Such an algorithm can be used in smart home environments where the noise level can vary significantly. Frame energy and zero-crossing measures are used for the VAD on each acoustic frame. A speech signal is cut into 50 percentage overlapped frames with durations of 25 milliseconds. Owing to the fact that the speech signal is sampled with a frequency of 16 kHz, the duration of each frame can be presented as a 400-sample window. To explain the process of VAD decision determination, we will use Figure 2. The frequency spectrum (Figure 2a) and signal representation in the time domain (Figure 2b–f) of the specific values are provided for a captured spoken sample in which the digit sequence "seven six one three" is uttered.

The frame energy, E_f, values are presented as a blue line in Figure 2b. The frame energy, E_f, value is calculated as in (1) from the N samples of the input signal, s.

$$E_f = \frac{\sum_{i=1}^{N}(s[i])^2}{N} \quad (1)$$

We did not use the logarithmic function in calculating the frame energy, because it would be more difficult to define the threshold that determines the presence of speech. The noise area energy values, E_n, are presented in Figure 2c. The value E_n is calculated for each frame as in (2) from the 10 values of the cyclic noise buffer, N_{buff}.

$$E_n = \frac{\sum_{i=0}^{9} N_{buff}[i]}{10} \quad (2)$$

The value E_n is calculated as an average value within a cyclic noise buffer, N_{buff}, that contains the frame energy, E_f, of the last 10 noisy frames.

The energy values, E_f, of the first 10 frames in the captured audio signal are mapped into the cyclic noise buffer, N_{buff}. After the first 10 frames, only the noisy frames with the weighted energy values, E_f, are added in the last place of the cyclic noise buffer, N_{buff}. The decision regarding which energy value, E_f, contains noise is presented in

$$N_{buff}[9] = \begin{cases} E_f; & E_f \leq 2 \cdot E_n \\ E_f/2; & 2 \cdot E_n < E_f \leq 4 \cdot E_n \\ E_f/4; & 4 \cdot E_n < E_f \leq 8 \cdot E_n \end{cases} \quad (3)$$

As can be seen in (3), the cyclic noise buffer, N_{buff}, is not updated when the current frame energy value, E_f, is 8 times larger than the noise area energy value, E_n, in the same frame. This limit has been determined empirically. If the cyclic noise buffer, N_{buff}, is not updated, then the noise area energy value, E_n, is also not updated according to (2). This is also presented in Figure 2c. This coincides with the beginning of the speech occurrence (digit "seven") in the captured audio signal and can be seen in Figure 2a.

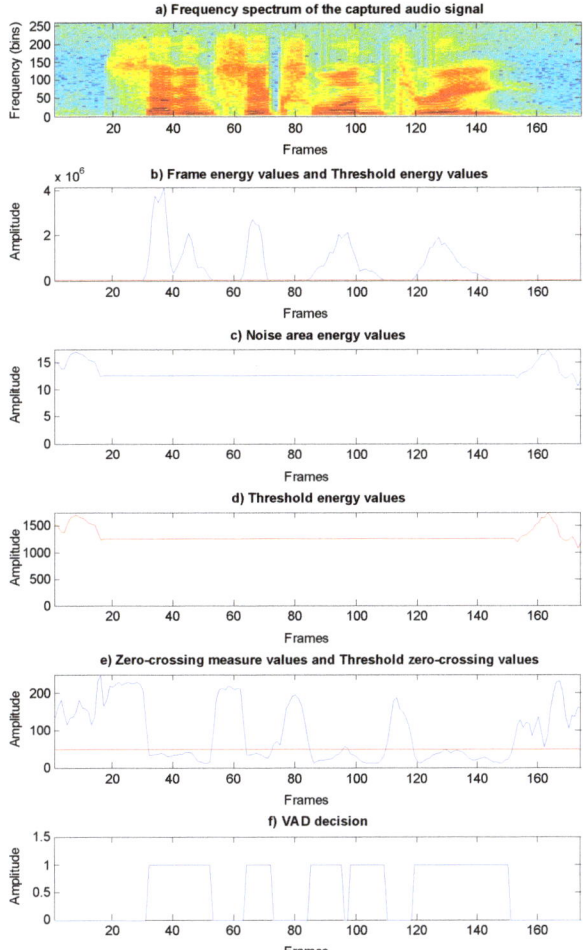

Figure 2. VAD decision determination: (**a**) Captured audio signal frequency spectrum. (**b**) Frame energy values and threshold energy values. (**c**) Noise area energy values. (**d**) Threshold energy values. (**e**) Zero-crossing measure values and threshold zero-crossing values. (**f**) VAD decision.

The next step in determining the VAD decision is to determine the threshold energy value, E_{Th}. The threshold energy value, E_{Th} is calculated as in (4) with the help of factor, f, and the noise area energy value, E_n.

$$f = \begin{cases} 100; & E_n \leq 100 \\ 100 - 0.1 \cdot E_n; & (E_n > 100) \wedge (E_n < 900) \\ 10; & E_n \geq 900 \end{cases} \quad (4)$$

$$E_{Th} = f \cdot E_n$$

The achieved result can be seen in Figure 2d. It is evident from the decision procedure that we used a different factor value, f, to determine the threshold energy value, E_{Th}. If the noise area energy value, E_n, is small (smaller than or equal to 100), it is necessary to raise the threshold energy value, E_{Th}. If the value of factor f is 10, then a slight increase in frame energy value E_f would lead to the wrong VAD decision, since the zero-crossing values

(Figure 2e) in the non-speech areas are also large. Therefore, we need to use a larger factor value, f, (in our case it is 100) so that wrong VAD decisions are less probable. On the other hand, if the noise area energy value, E_n, is large (larger than or equal to 900), it is necessary to reduce the threshold energy value, E_{Th}. Such high energy values of E_n occur if there is no silence at the beginning of the captured audio signal and speech occurs immediately. If the value of factor f is 100, then the threshold energy value, E_{Th}, would be too high, which would mean that the VAD algorithm would not detect the voiced speech segments in the captured audio signal. Therefore, in this case, we set a smaller factor value, f, (in our case, 10) so that the VAD algorithm can detect the speech segments in the captured audio signal. The high noise area energy value, E_n, decreases as soon as the conditions in (3) are met. However, if the noise area energy value, E_n, is between 100 and 900, then the value of factor f, as well as the threshold energy value, E_{Th}, changes linearly according to (4). Typically, for the captured audio signal, the time domain representations of the noise area energy values, E_n, (Figure 2c) and the threshold energy values, E_{Th}, (Figure 2d) are identical but multiplied by the constant factor, f, used. The time domain representations of the threshold energy values, E_{Th}, in Figure 2d are presented with a red line. The same value is also presented with a red line in Figure 2b.

We can derive additional information for better VAD decisions from the zero-crossing measure value, ZC_m. The enormous zero-crossing measure value in the frame represents the frame containing noise, or unvoiced speech, in the audio signal. For example, consonants in the speech signal belong to unvoiced speech. Figure 2a shows the frequency spectrum of the digit sequence "seven six one three", and the words seven and six contain the consonant "s". In word seven, the consonant "s" is present from frame 18 to frame 30, while in word six it is present from frame 53 to frame 63, and from frame 75 to frame 84. The value of the zero-crossing measure is presented as a blue line in Figure 2e. The ZC_m values in the unvoiced speech and noise signal regions are large and much more significant than those in a voiced speech signal region. The zero-crossing threshold value, ZC_{Th}, determines the segments of unvoiced speech and segments of the voiced speech signal. We set this value to 50, which is presented in Figure 2e as a red line. As mentioned before, one frame contains 400 samples. Having the value ZC_{Th} set at 50 means that the signal crosses the zero value at every 8 samples. This also means that the signal reaches its positive peak at every 16 samples. In this case, for a sampling frequency of 16 kHz, the pitch value would be 1000 Hz, which is almost impossible.

The proposed VAD decision is calculated from frame energy value E_f, zero-crossing measure value ZC_m, threshold energy value E_{Th}, and zero-crossing threshold value ZC_{Th}, as presented in (5). For each frame, the VAD decides if it contains voiced speech or not. Figure 2f shows the VAD decision on the captured audio signal. Voiced frames are then used for pitch value determination.

$$VAD = \begin{cases} 1; & (E_f > E_{Th}) \wedge (ZC_m < ZC_{Th}) \\ 0; & (E_f > E_{Th}) \wedge (ZC_m \geq ZC_{Th}) \\ 0; & E_f \leq E_{Th} \end{cases} \quad (5)$$

3.3. Pitch Definition

A pitch value, or speaker's fundamental frequency, can be determined from the speech signal's time domain representation or the frequency spectrum. Our pitch determination process is based on a periodic pattern, which can be found in the time domain representation of the speech signal. A repeating periodic pattern can be found in all vowels, sonorant consonants (/n/, /m/, /l/, etc.), and also in voiced obstruents (such as /b/, /d/, /g/) [39]. To facilitate the interpretation of the pitch determination process, we will use time domain representation of the vowel /i/ in word six of the captured audio signal with the digit sequence "seven six one three". The frequency spectrum of this digit sequence is presented in Figure 2a. The time domain representation of the 65th frame of this sequence is presented in Figure 3a. The blue line represents speech signal samples, and we can see a repeating periodic pattern. In the next paragraph, we will present the procedure by which the peaks are detected in each frame. The pitch can then be calculated from the difference between correct peaks.

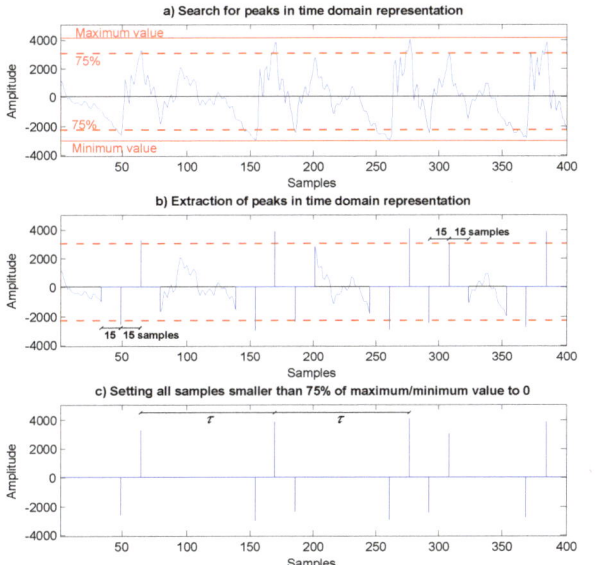

Figure 3. The time domain representation of the 65th frame in the digit sequence "seven six one three": (**a**) Search for peaks in one speech signal frame. (**b**) Extraction of peaks, where 15 samples left and right of the peak are set to 0. (**c**) All samples smaller than 75% of maximum/minimum value are set to 0.

When we define pitch value, we must first define the highest maximum value between positive samples' values and the lowest minimum value between negative samples' values. The samples' highest maximum and lowest minimum values in the frame are presented as red lines in Figure 3a. After that, we must define positive and negative peaks. The current peak maximums or minimums are detected in samples where greater than 75% of the maximum or minimum value is detected in the frame. The maximums are searched from the highest maximum to 75% of their value. The 15 samples left and right of the positive or negative peaks are set to 0. Figure 3b shows the result of this procedure. In the end, all other samples below 75% of the highest maximum or lowest minimum are set to 0. Figure 3c shows this result. If we look at the positive peaks that we have found, we can see that the first, second, third, and fifth are detected correctly. The fourth positive peak is incorrect. For negative peaks, two peaks (third and fifth) are defined incorrectly.

Finding the difference or the number of samples between the peaks is the next step in the procedure. As can be seen in Figure 3c, the difference is represented by the variable τ. Differences are calculated between all adjacent peaks. Positive and negative peaks' positions and the calculated differences between adjacent peaks can be seen in Table 1. Only the differences between the first and the second peak and between the second and the third peak of the positive peaks, and the difference between the first and the second peak of the negative peaks, gave correct results that could be used to determine the correct pitch value. After the calculation, the differences are sorted from the highest to the lowest value. To determine the pitch, the maximum calculated difference is used, along with those that deviate from this value by 10% or less. In the presented frame, only the first two differences from the positive peaks are used (see Table 1, values 106 and 107), as well as the first difference from the negative peaks (see Table 1, value 106). The average difference is determined from the differences that are used. The fundamental frequency, F_0, or pitch value can be calculated as in (6), where f_{samp} is the sampling frequency and $\bar{\tau}$ is the average difference between the peaks.

$$F_0 = \frac{f_{samp}}{\bar{\tau}} \qquad (6)$$

Table 1. Positive and negative peaks' positions in the 65th frame in the digit sequence "seven six one three" and differences calculated between adjacent peaks.

Positive peak position	Difference between adjacent peaks
64	106
170	107
277	31
308	76
384	
Negative peak position	**Difference between adjacent peaks**
49	106
155	31
186	75
261	31
292	77
369	

This method of determining a pitch is only applicable when a repeating periodic pattern is detected in the speech signal. In any case, such a signal is not present when the VAD algorithm does not detect the presence of a voiced segment in the speech signal. When we know the pitch of the speech signal's voiced segments, then this information can be used to detect the speaker's gender in two ways. One is that we use different levels of thresholds for determining a speaker's gender, while the other is to use the pitch as a feature for training different models. In this paper, Gaussian mixture models (GMMs) are used for the model training process. When training GMMs, specific cases may arise wherein it is not possible to train them if all the training values are not defined. In the noisy or silent segments in the audio signal, and in the unvoiced speech segment, we do not have information about the pitch, because it cannot be determined in these segments. Now the question concerns which value to set in these audio signal segments. Our approach here is that these values should be smaller than the value of the pitch that may occur in the voiced part of the speech signal. We decided that this value should be less than 40 Hz. For the modeling process, it is not appropriate that this value be constant for the whole unvoiced speech signal segment. Therefore, we determined the apparent value of the fundamental frequency, F_0, or pitch value as in (7), where F_{max} is the maximum apparent value of the pitch, *frameLength* is the length of the frame, and *averagePeak* is the average value of the peaks' positions in the frame.

$$F_0 = \frac{F_{max} \cdot averagePeak}{frameLength} \qquad (7)$$

From Figure 4, we can determine these values. If the value *frameLength* is 400, the value F_{max} is set to 40, while the value of *averagePeak* is calculated by summing the positions of the three positive peaks (218, 329, and 348) and the positions of the two negative peaks (201 and 313). This gives the calculated average value of 281.8. The apparent pitch value is then taken as 28.18 Hz.

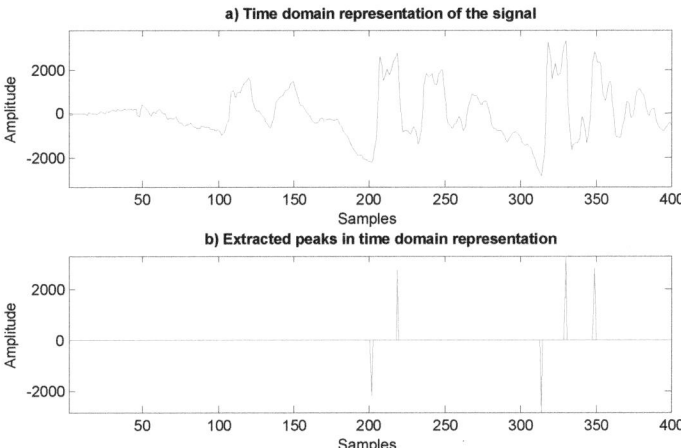

Figure 4. The time domain representation of the frame at the boundaries of the transition from the unvoiced to the voiced segment of the audio signal: (**a**) The time domain representation of the signal. (**b**) Extracted peaks in the time domain representation.

The proposed Equation (7) makes it possible to determine the apparent pitch in the unvoiced speech signal segments. We also used (7) when we could not define the pitch in the voiced speech signal segment. This occurs at the boundaries of the transition from the voiced to the unvoiced segment of the speech signal, and vice versa. Figure 4 shows an example in which we could not determine the pitch from the detected peaks correctly. We decided to use (7) when the procedure did not detect any positive or negative peaks between 0 and 200, or between 200 and 400 samples. This equation and procedure (7) are also used in cases when we detect the following:

(a) Less than two positive or negative peaks;
(b) Twice as many positive or negative peaks between 0 and 200 as between 200 and 400 samples;
(c) Twice as many positive or negative peaks between 200 and 400 as between 0 and 200 samples;
(d) Two peaks where the difference between them is greater than 200 or less than 25 samples.

3.4. GMM Training

The Gaussian mixture models (GMMs) belong to the group of statistical speech recognition methods that apply the weighted sum of the Gaussian probability density functions as components. Each component is defined by the mean vector, mixture weights, and covariance matrix, which is, in the case of speech processing, frequently diagonal. The GMMs are trained in an iterative way with the Baum–Welch algorithm [40], which applies the expectation-maximization (EM) algorithm to determine the maximum likelihood estimation of the unknown models' parameters on a set of training feature vectors.

To train GMMs, we used 12 mel-frequency cepstral coefficient (C1–C12) features. We replaced the coefficient C12 with the pitch value and added the energy coefficient. We thus derived 13 coefficients in the feature vector. The most significant coefficients' values in the feature vector are the values of the energy coefficient, and these are in the range of 20. However, since pitch values can also be up to 500 and over, we decided to divide the pitch values by 10 so that these coefficient values would not be too high. To improve the effectiveness of gender and age classifications, we have also calculated the first and second derivatives of the feature vector coefficients.

The next step is to determine the number of models we have trained. The VAD algorithm gives us the information wherein the audio recordings are speech signals and there is also silence. Based on this information, we trained four GMMs. On the speech signal parts, we trained the models for a male, a female, and a child (a boy or a girl), and for the rest of the signal, we trained silence. We used the hidden Markov model toolkit [40] for the GMMs' training. The GMMs' training procedure is provided in Figure 5.

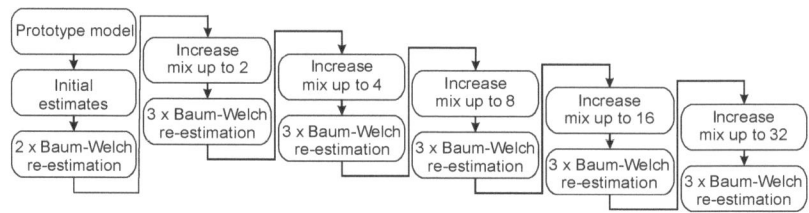

Figure 5. The GMM training procedure with up to 32 Gaussian mixtures per state.

When training GMMs, we started with a prototype model, which defines the required model topology. The topology of a single GMM is presented as a single-state model, and has the form of the required model, except that means are set to 0, variances are set to 1, and mixture weights are set to 1. The next step is to provide initial estimates for the feature vector single model parameters using a set of observation sequences for each model (male, female, child, and silence, if used). The next step is to perform two basic Baum–Welch re-estimations of the single model parameters using a set of observation sequences. Then, we used the procedure to increase the number of Gaussian mixtures. In the following, we again perform Baum–Welch re-estimation of the parameters, but it is now completed three times. The last two steps are repeated all the way to training GMMs with up to 32 Gaussian mixtures.

3.5. Experimental Design

For the experimental design, we used the speaker-independent connected digits American English speech database TIDIGITS [41]. This speech database is widely used for speech technology research, and it is one of the few that also includes utterances spoken by children in an equally balanced way. The original audio recordings were collected in a quiet environment and digitized at a 20 kHz sampling rate. For the needs of this research and the needs of the developed application, which will be used in the smart home environment, we downsampled the original audio recordings to the 16 kHz sampling frequency. The complete speech database contains 326 speakers, of which 111 are male, 114 are female, and 101 are child speakers (50 boys and 51 girls). In our research, we did not separate child speakers by gender. The age of male speakers is between 21 and 70 years, females are between 17 and 59, and children are between 6 and 15 years. The recordings of the speech database are divided into a training and a test set, which is proposed by the authors of the speech database. The training material contains 163 speakers, of which 55 are male, 57 are female, and 51 are child speakers—together representing 12,549 audio recordings. For the test material, 163 speakers remained, of which 56 were men, 57 were female, and 50 were children, which together represented 12,547 audio recordings. The speakers pronounced the following English digits in the recorded database: zero, one, two, ..., nine, and oh. Almost all of the speakers pronounced 77 isolated or connected digits, of which 22 were isolated, and digit sequences two, three, four, five, and seven digits long were uttered 11 times.

4. Results

In this section, we will first present a pitch value analysis of each recording in a speech database using the procedure for determining the pitch value presented in this paper. This analysis helps us in the later interpretation of the results. For those frames in the audio recording for which we were able to determine the pitch value, we compared their values. The pitch value most often detected is determined as the pitch value of the speaker's voice in the audio recording. The analyses are presented in Figure 6. As can be seen from the analysis, the male speaker's pitch value was the least distributed. Most of the recordings with the male speakers had a pitch value of 110 Hz for both the training and test set materials. The pitch values in recordings with female and child speakers were more dispersed. When we look at the analysis results of the children's recordings in Figure 6c, we can see that most of the speakers in the training set of the audio recordings had slightly higher pitch values than most speakers in the test set of the recordings, where their pitch values were somewhat lower. Thus, the pitch values of the child speakers in the test set recordings were closer to the pitch values of the female speakers that were used in the recordings for the training set. If we look only at the pitch values, we can see frequent confusion between child and female speakers in the gender and age classifications.

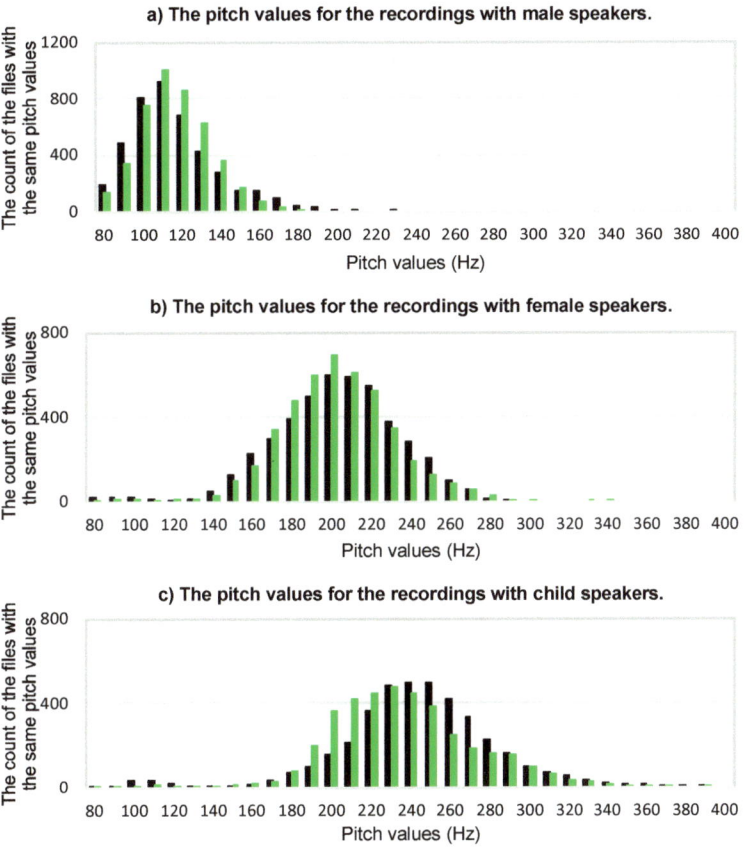

Figure 6. The count of the files with the same pitch values for the recordings with (**a**) male, (**b**) female, and (**c**) child speakers.

We will continue with presenting the results of the speaker's gender and age classification derived from experiments. The accuracy results of gender and age classification, and the statistical analyses of the results with confidence intervals, are presented in Table 2. The associated confusion matrices with recall results are provided in Table 3. The experiments and associated notations used in Tables 2 and 3 are explained in the following list, where (c)–(e) were experiments that were compared with the algorithms presented in the paper:

(a) The classification was based on the count of the pitch values in all frames with calculated pitch values. We performed a classification regarding whether it belongs to a male, female, or child speaker. This decision is presented as a classification based on the normalized pitch value counts. For this classification, we used the notation *Pitch value counts*;

(b) The classification was based on the normalized pitch value counts in all frames in which we could determine the pitch value. We have defined three sums of the normalized pitch value counts for male, female, and child speakers. This decision is presented as a classification based on the normalized pitch value sums. For this classification, we used the notation *Pitch value sums*;

(c) The classification was completed on the basis of the trained three states of the left-to-right monophone HMMs, the topology of which is described elsewhere [40]. In this case, we used three HMMs for male, female, and child speakers and one additional state, a silence HMM. HMMs were trained on the recordings with 11 mel-frequency cepstral coefficients (C1–C11), the pitch value divided by 10, logarithmic energy, and the first and second derivatives of those coefficients. For this classification, we used the notation *Three-state monophone HMMs—MFCC_Pitch_E_D_A*;

(d) The classification was completed on the basis of the trained sixteen states of the word HMMs, the topology of which is presented elsewhere [42]. In this case, we used three sixteen-state HMMs for male, female, and child speakers and one additional 3-state silence HMM. HMMs were trained on the recordings with 11 mel-frequency cepstral coefficients (C1–C11), the pitch value divided by 10, logarithmic energy, and the first and second derivatives of those coefficients. For this classification, we used the notation *Sixteen-state word HMMs—MFCC_Pitch_E_D_A*;

(e) The classification was based on an idea presented in previous work [22], where universal modeling (UM) based on GMM clustering was used. In this case, we used three types of features. The first type of feature was 13 mel-frequency cepstral coefficients (C0–C12); the second type of feature was MPEG-7 low-level descriptors (LLDs), as presented in [21]; and the third type of feature was perceptual wavelet packets (PWP), as presented in [43]. For this classification, we used the notation *Universal modeling based on GMM clustering*;

(f) GMMs were trained on segmented recordings with 12 basic mel-frequency cepstral coefficients (C1–C12), logarithmic energy, and the first and second derivatives of those coefficients. For this classification, we used the notation *GMMs with segmentation—MFCC_E_D_A*;

(g) GMMs were trained on segmented recordings with 11 mel-frequency cepstral coefficients (C1–C11), the pitch value divided by 10, logarithmic energy, and the first and second derivatives of those coefficients. For this classification, we used the notation *GMMs with segmentation—MFCC_Pitch_E_D_A*;

(h) The proposed final gender and age classification was based on a combination of the classifications used in all three experiments (a), (b), and (g). This proposed classification is presented in Section 3.1. For this classification, we used the notation *Proposed algorithm with segmentation*;

(i) The experiment applies in the same way as in experiment (h), with the exception that, in this case, an adaptation of the proposed gender and age classification algorithm is made. With a sufficiently large number of pitch values of the users, we can adapt the normalized pitch value counts and sum. In the last paragraph of Section 3.1, we propose a procedure that would allow for the fast adaptation of the system to the users who occur most frequently in the smart home environment and would use such a gender and age classification system. For this classification, we used the notation *Proposed algorithm with segmentation and pitch adaptation*.

Table 2. Accuracy results obtained by gender and age classification of the speaker and statistical analysis of the results with a 95% confidence interval.

Gender and Age Classification of the Speaker	Acc [%]	Mean [%]	95% CI [min max]
(a) Pitch value counts	78.02	78.00	[77.33 78.66]
(b) Pitch value sums	80.98	80.99	[80.32 81.65]
(c) Three-state monophone HMMs—MFCC_Pitch_E_D_A	90.44	90.44	[89.94 90.95]
(d) Sixteen-state word HMMs—MFCC_Pitch_E_D_A	87.18	87.19	[86.63 87.70]
(e) Universal modeling based on GMM clustering [22]	93.32	93.31	[92.88 93.74]
(f) GMMs with segmentation—MFCC_E_D_A	89.32	89.31	[88.77 89.86]
(g) GMMs with segmentation—MFCC_Pitch_E_D_A	91.38	91.39	[90.88 91.85]
(h) Proposed algorithm with segmentation	91.46	91.47	[91.00 91.89]
(i) Proposed algorithm with seg. and pitch adaptation	92.25	92.25	[91.79 92.69]

Table 3. Confusion matrix results obtained by gender and age classification with recall results.

	Male	Female	Child	Recall [%]
(a) Pitch value counts				
Male	4217	94	0	97.8
Female	514	3034	841	69.1
Child	185	1124	2538	66.0
(b) Pitch value sums				
Male	4262	49	0	98.9
Female	142	3571	676	81.4
Child	41	1479	2327	60.5
(c) Three-state monophone HMMs—MFCC_Pitch_E_D_A				
Male	4270	31	10	99.0
Female	52	4010	327	91.4
Child	0	780	3067	79.7
(d) Sixteen-state word HMMs—MFCC_Pitch_E_D_A				
Male	4282	19	10	99.3
Female	58	3136	1195	71.5
Child	3	323	3521	91.5
(e) Universal modeling based on GMM clustering [22]				
Male	4279	23	9	99.3
Female	76	4080	233	93.0
Child	12	485	3350	87.1
(f) GMMs with segmentation—MFCC_E_D_A				
Male	4108	159	44	95.3
Female	190	3811	388	86.8
Child	24	535	3288	85.5
(g) GMMs with segmentation—MFCC_Pitch_E_D_A				
Male	4264	43	4	98.9
Female	88	4014	287	91.5
Child	2	657	3188	82.9
(h) Proposed algorithm with segmentation				
Male	4271	36	4	99.1
Female	91	4026	272	91.7
Child	3	665	3179	82.6
(i) Proposed algorithm with segmentation and pitch adaptation				
Male	4276	29	6	99.2
Female	62	4085	242	93.1
Child	5	628	3214	83.5

The accuracy, *Acc*, presented in Table 2 is defined in (8), where H is the sum of all correct classifications for male, female, and child speakers, divided by the number of all classifications, N.

$$Acc = \frac{H}{N} \cdot 100[\%] \quad (8)$$

The correct classifications for male, female, and child speakers are marked in bold as integer values in Table 3. In Table 3, the results are provided with a different evaluation metric called *Recall*, which is defined in (9), where H_R is the number of correct classifications for male, female, or child speakers in the row divided by the number of all classifications, N_R, in the row for the corresponding class.

$$Recall = \frac{H_R}{N_R} \cdot 100[\%] \quad (9)$$

The number of all classifications, N_R, in the row for the male speakers is 4,311, for the female speakers is 4,389, and for the child speakers is 3,847. From the confusion matrices in Table 3, the calculated *Recall* value can be seen easily. For each classification, the integer value in the row marked in bold is divided by the number of all possible classifications, N_R, in the row for a particular class.

5. Discussion

In this section, we will comment on the results of the experiments in the previous section. First, we will describe the results in Table 2. In addition to the accuracy results, the statistical analysis results with the given confidence interval are also provided. Bootstrapping with 1000 replications was performed for each experiment. As we can see, there were no significant differences between the mean values and the accuracy of the defined test set. If we compare the proposed algorithm with segmentation (experiment h) and the proposed algorithm with segmentation and pitch adaptation (experiment i), it can be seen that the first's accuracy was outside of the second's confidence interval. Thus, we can conclude that the obtained results were statistically significant and not due to chance in the selected test set of the TIDIGITS database [41]. The experiments presented in Table 3 under (a) and (b) mainly obtained their information from the pitch value when determining the speaker's gender and age classification from the recordings. The confusion matrices' results show that, in both cases, the male speaker in the recording was never incorrectly classified as a child speaker. However, the maximum number of confusions in both experiments was present when a female speaker was classified in the recordings even though there was actually a child speaker in the recording. These gender and age classification errors were derived from the pitch values in the training and test sets of the speech database itself, the values of which are presented in Figure 6. The pitch values were determined on the basis of the entire audio recording and the pitch value, which was in the majority of frames in the audio recording, as presented in Figure 6. The pitch values in the children's test set material (Figure 6c) overlapped more severely with the pitch values in the training set material of the female speakers (Figure 6b). Figure 6c shows that the pitch values in the test set were more diffused than in the training set. Experiments (c) and (d) were both based on HMMs. The first used three-state monophone HMMs, and the second used sixteen-state word HMMs. The sixteen-state word HMMs provided worse accuracy (Table 2), most likely due to the use of pitch value as a coefficient in the feature vector. This conclusion is based on the fact that pitch values could only be defined in the voiced speech segment of the word and not through the duration of the whole word, where there were also consonants. Experiment (e) was carried out according to instructions provided elsewhere [22]. Here, the best accuracy was achieved (Table 2), and the recall classification was very good (Table 3)—especially for the child speakers, although the classification of a child speaker was still the most problematic. Such good results were based on more advanced modeling techniques and the use of a larger number of features, such as MPEG-7 low-level descriptors (LLDs), as presented elsewhere [21], and perceptual wavelet packets (PWPs), as presented elsewhere [43]. Our motivation in this paper was to get closer to these results using less complex procedures that would be more suitable for embedded systems in smart home environments. In the following four experiments—(f)–(i)—we used segmentation based on the proposed VAD algorithm. Experiment (f) was taken as a baseline since it used only MFCC_E_D_A features without pitch values. Comparing experiments (f) and (g), Table 2 shows a more than 2% accuracy improvement in classification performance when the pitch value was used as an additional feature. In the subsequent two experiments—(h) and (i)—an additional contribution can be seen, as we used the classification split into two steps, as proposed in Section 3.1. A more significant contribution was made by the last experiment, (i), when we adapted pitch values. With this experiment, we wanted to present the procedure by which the classification system can be quickly adapted to the normalized pitch values of the users in a smart home environment. As can be seen from experiment (i) in Table 2, the accuracy was better when we performed the adaptation of the proposed classification algorithm with a new set of normalized pitch values. The results in Table 3 show that the recall values of the female speakers for this experiment were the highest of all experiments. After reviewing all the experiments provided in Tables 2 and 3, we can conclude that the biggest problems lie in the classification of female and child speakers. In the classification of male speakers, it is possible to achieve very good results, the values of which were above 99%.

The presented gender and age classification solution can be derived via an embedded system or as a microphone array that captures the signal, and processing is completed on a server. From the user's perspective, how accurately users can be detected by such systems is important. It is required that the system classify the gender and age of the user correctly as often as possible. The speech database used in the tests included 163 speakers, most of whom pronounced 77 isolated or connected digits. Table 4 presents an analysis of the results wherein four parts were identified. First, we checked the number of speakers in which the gender and age classification of the speaker was correct for all audio recordings. In the second and third parts of the analysis, we checked the number of speakers for whom the gender and age were classified incorrectly in 1 to 10 recordings or classified incorrectly in 11 to 20 recordings. If incorrect gender and age classification occurred, the requirement was that the number of these errors be as small as possible. In the fourth and final part of the analysis, we checked the number of speakers in which the gender and age of the speaker were classified incorrectly in 21 to 77 recordings. In this case, in most tests, there were 13 to 17 speakers for which the gender and age were classified incorrectly. When we analyzed these 17 speakers, we found that 11 of them appeared in all tests. There were no male speakers among them, which is also understandable since the male speaker classification was, in most cases, correct. There were eight child speakers and three female speakers for whom gender and age classifications were incorrect in all tests. For these 11 speakers, most confusions in gender and age classification were between the female speaker and child speaker, and vice versa. Of these 11 speakers, 5 speakers were almost entirely incorrectly classified by gender and age in all experiments, which represents 3% of the test material. For these speakers, we can say that they present a challenging task, due to their characteristics, and they will almost always be classified as errors. As can be seen from Table 4, the gender and age classification is presented for all three classes separately (M for male, F for female, and C for child). The column labeled with S represents the sum of values in individual classes. To understand the table better, let us remember that the number of male, female, and child speakers in the test set were 56, 57, and 50, respectively. In experiment (d), for 75 speakers, classification was correct for all audio recordings of these speakers. This represents the best result, but this experiment has as many as 31 speakers for which the gender and age of the speaker were classified incorrectly in 21 to 77 audio recordings. Good results were achieved in experiment (e) due to the very complex methodology, while the results of the proposed algorithm with segmentation and pitch adaptation (experiment (i)) were very similar. However, if we compare experiments (h) and (i), we can see that the adaptation of the system helped to improve the classification of the female speaker. The number of female speakers for which the female gender was classified correctly in all recordings increased from 10 to 14.

Table 4. Gender and age classification analysis (M—male, F—female, C—child, S—sum of all gender and age classifications) for all 163 speakers.

The Number of Speakers for Which the Gender and Age of the Speaker Were Classified:	Correctly in All Recordings				Incorrectly in 1 to 10 Recordings				Incorrectly in 11 to 20 Recordings				Incorrectly in 21 to 77 Recordings			
Experiments: Gender and age:	M	F	C	S	M	F	C	S	M	F	C	S	M	F	C	S
(a) Pitch value counts	49	0	4	53	4	16	19	39	1	17	6	24	2	24	21	47
(b) Pitch value sums	50	11	1	62	4	26	16	46	0	6	10	16	2	14	23	39
(c) Three-state monophone HMMs—MFCC_Pitch_E_D_A	46	9	9	64	9	37	21	67	1	7	9	17	0	4	11	15
(d) Sixteen-state word HMMs—MFCC_Pitch_E_D_A	49	2	24	75	6	11	18	35	1	20	1	22	0	24	7	31
(e) Universal modeling based on GMM clustering [22]	46	12	14	72	10	33	24	67	0	6	4	10	0	6	8	14
(f) GMMs with segmentation—MFCC_E_D_A	30	6	16	52	20	30	19	69	4	11	5	20	2	10	10	22
(g) GMMs with segmentation—MFCC_Pitch_E_D_A	44	11	10	65	11	30	21	62	1	10	8	19	0	6	11	17
(h) Proposed algorithm with segmentation	45	10	12	67	10	31	19	60	1	11	9	21	0	5	10	15
(i) Proposed alg. with segmentation and pitch adaptation	46	14	11	71	10	35	23	68	0	6	4	10	0	2	12	14

The direct comparison of achieved results with other combined age and gender acoustic classification systems is difficult, as experiments were not conducted on the same speech databases (type and amount of speech, language), and also the evaluation conditions differed. A general comparison for the male, female, and child speaker classifications shows that accuracy in previous work [29] was 90.39%, while the proposed system achieved 92.25%, which is a statistically significant improvement. The gap in results between adults and child classes is, in the case of [29], as high as ~35% (classification success: child (60.96%) compared to female (94.50%) or male (96.09%)), while there is a gap in the case of the proposed system i) of between ~10% and ~15% (recall: child (83.5%) compared to female (93.1%) or male (99.2%)). It can be concluded that the inclusion of pitch values improved the classification modeling balance between the child and adult categories.

We performed additional analyses because we wanted to find out how many digits were in the recording when there was an error in the speaker's gender and age classification. Table 5 shows the average number of digits in the audio recordings when the gender and age of the speaker were classified incorrectly. If we compare Tables 4 and 5, we can see that, for 163 speakers, in most cases, errors occurred in 1 to 10 recordings. The number of digits that appeared in these incorrectly classified recordings was, on average, 1.64. In other words, 1 to 2 digits were pronounced in these recordings. The conclusion is that the maximum number of errors occurs in recordings that have small speech content.

Table 5. The average number of digits in the recordings when the gender and age of the speaker were classified incorrectly.

The gender and age of the speaker were classified incorrectly in 1 to 10 recordings.	1.63
The gender and age of the speaker were classified incorrectly in 11 to 20 recordings.	2.38
The gender and age of the speaker were classified incorrectly in 21 to 77 recordings.	3.12

The use of such gender and age speaker classification, based on the acoustic detection of the speaker's presence in the room, is intended primarily for use in intelligent environments of smart homes. The objective is to adapt and personalize services and content to particular user classes. If such a gender and age classification is used in the embedded system, energy consumption is also important. Therefore, we suggest using such a detector, in combination with a PIR motion detection sensor, to turn on the proposed system when a person enters the room. Once gender and age speaker classification, based on acoustic detection, has confirmed the gender or age of the speaker in the room with a high probability, the system can be switched off automatically. Of course, there is still the question of how to act if more people (e.g., an adult and a child) are present in the room. If the acoustic presence detector detects two persons in the room, belonging to different classes (e.g., one is an adult and the other is a child), it is not the task of the acoustic presence detector to define how the smart home environment should react in this case. The issue is resolved at a higher level of the decision support system in the smart home environment, which is not part of the focus of this paper.

6. Conclusions

The presented acoustic presence detection system can be applied in a smart home environment, either as a stand-alone solution or in combination with a PIR motion detection sensor. In this paper, we presented a method for gender and age classification of the speaker, which is based on three different methods completed in two steps. In the first step, the gender and age classification is based on GMMs. Basically, it counts the frames and calculates which frame has a greater probability of belonging to one of the gender and age (male, female, or child) classifications. If the difference between the highest two counted frames belonging to a male, female, or child speaker is less than 4, the second step of gender and age classification is performed, whereby two additional gender and age classification procedures are carried out. The first is based on the count of the frames with normalized pitch values, and the second is based on the sum of the frames with normalized pitch values, which belong to one of the speakers. If all three, or at least two, of the decisions match, then we choose the gender and age that is in the majority. However, if all three decisions are different, we adopt the classification based on GMMs.

Comparative experiments carried out in this paper have shown that algorithms with a large number of different features (some of which are also computationally complex) and more advanced modeling techniques provide slightly better results than in the presented gender and age classification algorithm. However, the proposed classification algorithm was developed for use in a smart home environment, where only simple and efficient classification algorithms are acceptable.

When analyzing the results, we came to the important conclusion that most of the incorrect classifications of the speaker's gender and age occurred in cases where we had a small amount of speech material to analyze. This was, in our case, when only one or two words were captured in the audio recording. We also proposed a procedure that allows us to quickly adapt the gender and age classification algorithm to the frequent users of such a system in smart home environments. The proposed adaptation procedure further improved the performance of speaker gender and age classifications. After performing an extensive set of experiments, we can infer that the proposed method for gender and age classification with adaptations to users could be a potential candidate for integration into real-life smart home environments.

In future work, we will further improve the classification accuracy for children's speech using other low-complexity feature extraction methods, as we aim to use embedded systems for smart home environments.

Author Contributions: Conceptualization, D.V. and A.Z.; methodology, D.V. and A.Z.; validation, D.V. and A.Z.; resources, D.V. and A.Z.; writing—original draft preparation, D.V. and A.Z.; writing—review and editing, D.V. and A.Z.; visualization, D.V.; supervision, A.Z. All authors have read and agreed to the published version of the manuscript.

Funding: This work was funded by the Slovenian Research Agency, under Contract No. P2-0069, Research Program "Advanced Methods of Interaction in Telecommunication".

Data Availability Statement: The TIDIGITS speech database is available via LDC: https://doi.org/10.35111/72xz-6x59 (accessed on 22 November 2022).

Acknowledgments: The authors thank Stavros Ntalampiras, for providing us with the source code of the Perceptual Wavelet Packets algorithm. The authors also thank Mirjam Sepesy Maučec, for her valuable comments and suggestions during the writing of this paper.

Conflicts of Interest: The authors declare no conflict of interest. The funders had no role in the design of the study; in the collection, analyses, or interpretation of data; in the writing of the manuscript; or in the decision to publish the results.

References

1. United Nations. *World Population to 2300*; Department of Economic and Social Affairs, Population Division: New York, NY, USA, 2004.
2. Mukhamediev, R.I.; Popova, Y.; Kuchin, Y.; Zaitseva, E.; Kalimoldayev, A.; Symagulov, A.; Levashenko, V.; Abdoldina, F.; Gopejenko, V.; Yakunin, K.; et al. Review of Artificial Intelligence and Machine Learning Technologies: Classification, Restrictions, Opportunities and Challenges. *Mathematics* **2022**, *10*, 2552. [CrossRef]
3. Astapov, S.; Gusev, A.; Volkova, M.; Logunov, A.; Zaluskaia, V.; Kapranova, V.; Timofeeva, E.; Evseeva, E.; Kabarov, V.; Matveev, Y. Application of Fusion of Various Spontaneous Speech Analytics Methods for Improving Far-Field Neural-Based Diarization. *Mathematics* **2021**, *9*, 2998. [CrossRef]
4. Giannoulis, P.; Tsiami, A.; Rodomagoulakis, I.; Katsamanis, A.; Potamianos, G.; Maragos, P. The Athena-RC system for speech activity detection and speaker localization in the DIRHA smart home. In Proceedings of the 2014 4th Joint Workshop on Hands-free Speech Communication and Microphone Arrays (HSCMA), Nancy, France, 12 May 2014; pp. 167–171. [CrossRef]
5. Solaimani, S.; Keijzer-Broers, W.; Bouwman, H. What we do–and don't–know about the Smart Home: An analysis of the Smart Home literature. *Indoor Built Environ.* **2015**, *24*, 370–383. [CrossRef]
6. Koo, J.H.; Cho, S.W.; Baek, N.R.; Lee, Y.W.; Park, K.R. A Survey on Face and Body Based Human Recognition Robust to Image Blurring and Low Illumination. *Mathematics* **2022**, *10*, 1522. [CrossRef]
7. Childers, D.G.; Wu, K.; Bae, K.S.; Hicks, D.M. Automatic recognition of gender by voice. In Proceedings of the ICASSP-88, International Conference on Acoustics, Speech, and Signal Processing, New York, NY, USA, 1 January 1988; pp. 603–604. [CrossRef]
8. Wu, K.; Childers, D.G. Gender recognition from speech. Part I: Coarse analysis. *J. Acoust. Soc. Am.* **1991**, *90*, 1828–1840. [CrossRef]
9. Gurgen, F.S.; Fan, T.; Vonwiller, J. On the Analysis of Phoneme Based Features for Gender Identification with Neural Networks. SST. Available online: https://assta.org/proceedings/sst/SST-94-Vol-1/cache/SST-94-VOL1-Chapter9-p8.pdf (accessed on 25 December 2022).
10. Gauvain, J.L.; Lamel, L. Identification of non-linguistic speech features. In Proceedings of the Workshop Held at Plainsboro, Plainsboro, NJ, USA, 21–24 March 1993. [CrossRef]
11. Li, M.; Han, K.J.; Narayanan, S. Automatic speaker age and gender recognition using acoustic and prosodic level information fusion. *Comput. Speech Lang.* **2013**, *27*, 151–167. [CrossRef]
12. Schuller, B.; Steidl, S.; Batliner, A.; Burkhardt, F.; Devillers, L.; Müller, C.; Narayanan, S. Paralinguistics in speech and language—State-of-the-art and the challenge. *Comput. Speech Lang.* **2013**, *27*, 4–39. [CrossRef]
13. Gaikwad, S.; Gawali, B.; Mehrotra, S.C. Gender Identification Using SVM with Combination of MFCC. *Adv. Comput. Res.* **2012**, *4*, 69–73.
14. Yücesoy, E.; Nabiyev, V.V. Gender identification of a speaker using MFCC and GMM. In Proceedings of the 2013 8th International Conference on Electrical and Electronics Engineering (ELECO), Bursa, Turkey, 28 November 2013; pp. 626–629. [CrossRef]
15. Zeng, Y.M.; Wu, Z.Y.; Falk, T.; Chan, W.Y. Robust GMM based gender classification using pitch and RASTA-PLP parameters of speech. In Proceedings of the 2006 International Conference on Machine Learning and Cybernetics, Dalian, China, 13–16 August 2006; pp. 3376–3379. [CrossRef]
16. Müller, C. Automatic Recognition of Speakers' Age and Gender on the Basis of Empirical Studies. In Proceedings of the Ninth International Conference on Spoken Language Processing, Pittsburgh, PA, USA, 17–21 September 2006; Available online: https://www.isca-speech.org/archive/interspeech_2006/muller06_interspeech.html (accessed on 25 December 2022).
17. Islam, M.A. GFCC-based robust gender detection. In Proceedings of the 2016 International Conference on Innovations in Science, Engineering and Technology (ICISET), Dhaka, Bangladesh, 28 October 2016; pp. 1–4. [CrossRef]
18. Meinedo, H.; Trancoso, I. Age and gender detection in the I-DASH project. *ACM Trans. Speech Lang. Process. (TSLP)* **2011**, *7*, 1–6. [CrossRef]
19. Ranjan, S.; Liu, G.; Hansen, J.H. An i-vector plda based gender identification approach for severely distorted and multilingual darpa rats data. In Proceedings of the 2015 IEEE Workshop on Automatic Speech Recognition and Understanding (ASRU), Scottsdale, AZ, USA, 13–17 December 2015; pp. 331–337. [CrossRef]

20. Bhavana, R.J.; Swati, P.; Mayur, A. Identification of Age and Gender Using HMM. *Int. J. Comput. Sci. Inf. Technol.* **2015**, *6*, 1643–1647.
21. Ntalampiras, S.; Potamitis, I.; Fakotakis, N. Acoustic detection of human activities in natural environments. *J. Audio Eng. Soc.* **2012**, *60*, 686–695.
22. Ntalampiras, S. A novel holistic modeling approach for generalized sound recognition. *IEEE Signal Process. Lett.* **2013**, *20*, 185–188. [CrossRef]
23. Bocklet, T.; Maier, A.; Bauer, J.G.; Burkhardt, F.; Noth, E. Age and gender recognition for telephone applications based on gmm supervectors and support vector machines. In Proceedings of the 2008 IEEE International Conference on Acoustics, Speech and Signal Processing, Las Vegas, NV, USA, 31 March–4 April 2008; pp. 1605–1608. [CrossRef]
24. Dehak, N.; Kenny, P.J.; Dehak, R.; Dumouchel, P.; Ouellet, P. Front-end factor analysis for speaker verification. *IEEE Trans. Audio Speech Lang. Process.* **2010**, *19*, 788–798. [CrossRef]
25. Abumallouh, A.; Qawaqneh, Z.; Barkana, B.D. Deep neural network combined posteriors for speakers' age and gender classification. In Proceedings of the 2016 Annual Connecticut Conference on Industrial Electronics, Technology & Automation (CT-IETA), Bridgeport, CT, USA, 14–15 October 2016; pp. 1–5. [CrossRef]
26. Qawaqneh, Z.; Mallouh, A.A.; Barkana, B.D. Deep neural network framework and transformed MFCCs for speaker's age and gender classification. *Knowledge-Based Syst.* **2017**, *115*, 5–14. [CrossRef]
27. Costantini, G.; Parada-Cabaleiro, E.; Casali, D.; Cesarini, V. The Emotion Probe: On the Universality of Cross-Linguistic and Cross-Gender Speech Emotion Recognition via Machine Learning. *Sensors* **2022**, *22*, 2461. [CrossRef]
28. Schuller, B.; Steidl, S.; Batliner, A.; Burkhardt, F.; Devillers, L.; Müller, C.; Narayanan, S. The INTERSPEECH 2010 paralinguistic challenge. In Proceedings of the INTERSPEECH 2010, Makuhari, Japan, 26–30 September 2010; pp. 2794–2797.
29. Yücesoy, E.; Nabiyev, V.V. A new approach with score-level fusion for the classification of a speaker age and gender. *Comput. Electr. Eng.* **2016**, *53*, 29–39. [CrossRef]
30. Meinedo, H.; Trancoso, I. Age and gender classification using fusion of acoustic and prosodic features. In Proceedings of the Eleventh Annual Conference of the International Speech Communication Association, Makuhari, Japan, 26–30 September 2010.
31. Bisio, I.; Delfino, A.; Lavagetto, F.; Marchese, M.; Sciarrone, A. Gender-driven emotion recognition through speech signals for ambient intelligence applications. *IEEE Trans. Emerg. Top. Comput.* **2013**, *1*, 244–257. [CrossRef]
32. Brutti, A.; Ravanelli, M.; Omologo, M. Saslodom: Speech activity detection and speaker localization in domestic environments. In *SASLODOM: Speech Activity Detection and Speaker LOcalization in DOMestic Environments*; Fondazione Bruno Kessler: Povo, Italy, 2014; pp. 139–146.
33. Guerrieri, A.; Braccili, E.; Sgrò, F.; Meldolesi, G.N. Gender Identification in a Two-Level Hierarchical Speech Emotion Recognition System for an Italian Social Robot. *Sensors* **2022**, *22*, 1714. [CrossRef]
34. Tursunov, A.; Choeh, J.Y.; Kwon, S. Age and gender recognition using a convolutional neural network with a specially designed multi-attention module through speech spectrograms. *Sensors* **2021**, *21*, 5892. [CrossRef]
35. Kwasny, D.; Hemmerling, D. Gender and age estimation methods based on speech using deep neural networks. *Sensors* **2021**, *21*, 4785. [CrossRef]
36. Vlaj, D.; Žgank, A.; Kos, M. Effective Pitch Value Detection in Noisy Intelligent Environments for Efficient Natural Language Processing. In *Recent Trends in Computational Intelligence*; Sadollah, A., Sinha, T.S., Eds.; IntechOpen: London, UK, 2019. [CrossRef]
37. *ETSI Standard ES 201 108 v1.1.1*; Speech Processing, Transmission and Quality aspects (STQ), Distributed Speech Recognition, Front-End Feature Extraction Algorithm, Compression Algorithm. ETSI: Valbonne, France, 2000.
38. Gender and Age Classification Source Code. Available online: https://github.com/dvlaj/FeatureGenderAgeClassification (accessed on 14 December 2022).
39. Anderson, S.R.; Lightfoot, D.W. Describing linguistic knowledge. In *The Language Organ: Linguistics as Cognitive Physiology*; Cambridge University Press: Cambridge, UK, 2002; pp. 92–110.
40. Young, S.; Evermann, G.; Gales, M.; Hain, T.; Kershaw, D.; Liu, X.; Moore, G.; Odell, J.; Ollason, D.; Povey, D.; et al. *The HTK Book*; Cambridge University Engineering Department: Cambridge, UK, 2002; Volume 3, p. 12.
41. Leonard, R. A database for speaker-independent digit recognition. In Proceedings of the ICASSP'84, IEEE International Conference on Acoustics, Speech, and Signal Processing, San Diego, CA, USA, 19 March 1984; Volume 9, pp. 328–331. [CrossRef]
42. Hirsch, H.G.; Pearce, D. The Aurora experimental framework for the performance evaluation of speech recognition systems under noisy conditions. In Proceedings of the ASR2000-Automatic Speech Recognition: Challenges for the New Millenium ISCA Tutorial and Research Workshop (ITRW), Paris, France, 18–20 September 2000.
43. Ntalampiras, S.; Potamitis, I.; Fakotakis, N. Exploiting temporal feature integration for generalized sound recognition. *EURASIP J. Adv. Signal Process.* **2009**, *2009*, 807162. [CrossRef]

Disclaimer/Publisher's Note: The statements, opinions and data contained in all publications are solely those of the individual author(s) and contributor(s) and not of MDPI and/or the editor(s). MDPI and/or the editor(s) disclaim responsibility for any injury to people or property resulting from any ideas, methods, instructions or products referred to in the content.

 *mathematics*

Article
BroadBand-Adaptive VMD with Flattest Response

Xizhong Shen * and Ran Li

School of Electrical and Electronical Engineering, Shanghai Institute of Technology, Shanghai 201418, China
* Correspondence: xzshen@yeah.net; Tel.: +86-133-9133-9836

Abstract: A mixed signal with several unknown modes is common in the industry and is hard to decompose. Variational Mode Decomposition (VMD) was proposed to decompose a signal into several amplitude-modulated modes in 2014, which overcame the limitations of Empirical Mode Decomposition (EMD), such as sensitivity to noise and sampling. We propose an improved VMD, which is simplified as iVMD. In the new algorithm, we further study and improve the mathematical model of VMD to adapt to the decomposition of the broad-band modes. In the new model, the ideal flattest response is applied, which is derived from the mathematical integral form and obtained from different-order derivatives of the improved modes' definitions. The harmonics can be treated via synthesis in our new model. The iVMD algorithm can decompose the complex harmonic signal and the broad-band modes. The new model is optimized with the alternate direction method of multipliers, and the modes with adaptive broad-band and their respective center frequencies can be decomposed. the experimental results show that iVMD is an effective algorithm based on the artificial and real data collected in our experiments.

Keywords: mode decomposition; spectral decomposition; variational problem; augmented Lagrangian; Fourier transform

MSC: 40B05; 68W01; 94D99

Citation: Shen, X.; Li, R. Broad Band-Adaptive VMD with Flattest Response. *Mathematics* **2023**, *11*, 1858. https://doi.org/10.3390/math11081858

Academic Editors: Grigoreta-Sofia Cojocar, Adriana-Mihaela Guran and Laura-Silvia Dioşan

Received: 28 February 2023
Revised: 27 March 2023
Accepted: 10 April 2023
Published: 13 April 2023

Copyright: © 2023 by the authors. Licensee MDPI, Basel, Switzerland. This article is an open access article distributed under the terms and conditions of the Creative Commons Attribution (CC BY) license (https:// creativecommons.org/licenses/by/ 4.0/).

1. Introduction

With the development of science and technology, nonstationary signal processing and its applications in engineering are gaining more and more attention. During recent decades, scholars have developed many approaches to process single-channel nonstationary signals, or even multi-channel ones, which are not discussed in this paper. Short-Time Fourier Transform (STFT) [1] and Wavelet Transform (WT) [2] are two of the most popular algorithms used to perform time–frequency (TF) transform on nonstationary signals. These transform methods exhibit limited TF resolutions [3], and cannot separate a multi-component signal into mono-components. These sometimes suffer from the consequences of the Heisenberg uncertainty principle. However, data-driven signal decomposition methods can decompose a multi-component signal into several modes—for example, Empirical Mode Decomposition (EMD) [4], and Variational Mode Decomposition (VMD) [5]. We develop a new signal decomposition method here.

Variational Mode Decomposition (VMD) [5] and Variational Nonlinear Chirp Mode Decomposition (VNCMD) [6] are proposed to adaptively extract a set of modes, which are called Intrinsic Mode Functions (IMFs). VMD is a non-recursive algorithm method to decompose a signal into several modes with quasi-orthogonality, intrinsics, and adaptivity [7]. VMD can concurrently look for the IMFs and their respective center frequencies. Each IMF is compact at a particular band. Unlike the EMD-based methods, VMD is built on well-founded mathematical theories.

Several other VMD-based algorithms have emerged. Due to the difficulty of selecting the mode number, successive VMDs (SVMD) [8] need not predefine the mode number K. The adaptive chirp mode pursuit (ACMP) [9] is proposed to recursively extract the nonlinear chirp modes. However, VNCMD and ACMP require high-limited instantaneous frequency (IF) initialization [6,9], and VMD and SVMD suffer from the narrowband assumption of IMFs.

The VMD was proposed as a one-dimensional algorithm [5], and a two-dimensional algorithm was later published [10,11]. Then, multivariate VMD (MVMD) [12] was developed to achieve a better performance than the direct use of univariate VMD in a channel-by-channel method. However, MVMD still suffered from the limited narrowband assumption, and the VMD-based developed algorithms could not decompose signals composed of wideband multivariate IMFs (MIMFs). A multivariate nonlinear chirp mode decomposition (MNCMD) and its improved version, multivariate intrinsic chirp mode decomposition (MICMD) [13], were developed. These two algorithms could process multichannel signals involving wideband MIMFs.

The VMD has attracted a broad variety of time–frequency analysis applications, such as signal decomposition in multivariate time–frequency analysis [3], speech signal processing [14,15], emotional speech classification [7,16], system identification [17], medicine [18], fault diagnosis [19], seismic signal analysis [20], and so on.

VMD suffers from the narrow band-limited mode, which has a center frequency, and VMD cannot decompose a complex signal with harmonics, in theory [21]. In this paper, we further develop a more adaptive variation method by augmenting the concept of flattest response in the mathematical model with extra adaptive bandwidth, and we also consider the high-order harmonics of the decomposed mode.

The rest of this paper is organized as follows: Section 2 reviews VMD primarily on the definition of the mode and the model of VMD; Section 3 introduces our idea for improving VMD mainly on the concept of the flattest response and bandwidth; Section 4 presents our improved model and its solution; Section 5 contains our rich experiments and results; and Section 6 concludes the discussion on iVMD.

2. Review of VMD

2.1. Mode Definition

Until now, there have been two definitions of mode.

Definition 1 of the Intrinsic mode function [2] is as follows: Intrinsic mode function (IMF), as the original IMF definition, is an amplitude-modulated and frequency-modulated (AMFM) signal, which is defined as

$$u_k(t) = a_k(t)\cos(\phi_k(t)). \tag{1}$$

Here, the phase $\phi_k(t)$ is a nondecreasing function, while $\phi'_k(t) \geq 0$, and $\phi'_k(t)$ are the instantaneous frequencies. The envelope is a non-negative, $a_k(t) \geq 0$. The maximum frequency contained in $a_k(t)$ and $\phi'_k(t)$ is much smaller than that in $\phi_k(t)$ [2].

The original IMF is a signal whose number of local extreme and zero-crossings differ at most by one [4]. IMFs are decomposed by VMD, and VMD IMFs [5] by VMD. The definition of VMD IMF is slightly more strict than the original IMF definition. VMD IMF has a central frequency, ω_k, with limited bandwidth, B_k, which is the total practical IMF bandwidth.

Definition 2 on the total practical IMF bandwidth (VMD bandwidth definition) [5] is as follows: total bandwidth of an IMF is defined as

$$B_k = 2(\Delta f + f_{\text{FM}} + f_{\text{AM}}). \tag{2}$$

Here, Δf is one half of the variation range of the instantaneous frequency, while f_{FM} is the excursion of the mode according to Carson's rule, and f_{AM} is the highest frequency of the envelope $a_k(t)$.

We offer a newer definition of each decomposed mode, whose bandwidths are decided via the flattest response filter. Details are given in the next sections. In those sections, we derive the adaptive bandwidth which is achieved via the flattest response filter.

2.2. VMD Model

We set a real valued input signal $x(t)$, which includes K modes, noted as $u_k(t), k = 1, \cdots, K$. The goal of VMD [5] is to decompose $x(t)$ into $u_k(t), k = 1, \cdots, K$. The modes $u_k(t)$ have specific sparsity properties, and thus the modes are fully quasi-orthogonal. The constrained variational problem of the VMD algorithm is

$$\min_{\{u_k,\omega_k\}} \left\{ \sum_k \left\| \frac{\partial}{\partial t} \left[\left(\left(\delta(t) + \frac{j}{\pi t} \right) * u_k(t) \right) e^{-j\omega_k t} \right] \right\|_2^2 \right\} \quad (3)$$
$$\text{st.} \sum_k u_k(t) = x(t).$$

VMD and its related algorithms solve the inverse problem by decomposing a signal into a given number K of modes with limited bandwidth [6,9], either exactly or in a least square sense. A classical ADMM approach [22] is applied to solve the variational problem. All the parameters, including the modes themselves, are updated directly in the Fourier domain.

2.3. Wiener Filtering of VMD

Consider the AM–FM signal $x(t)$, contaminated by an additive zero-mean Gaussian noise. The observed signal $x_0(t)$ is,

$$x_0(t) = x(t) + \eta \quad (4)$$

Recovering the unknown signal $x(t)$ is a typical ill-posed inverse problem [23], classically addressed using the Tikhonov regularization [24],

$$\min_x \left\{ \|x - x_0\|_2^2 + \alpha \|\partial_t x\|_2^2 \right\} \quad (5)$$

of which the Euler–Lagrange equations are easily obtained and typically solved in the following Fourier domain,

$$\hat{x}(\omega) = \frac{\hat{x_0}}{1 + \alpha \omega^2} \quad (6)$$

Here $\hat{x}(\omega) = \mathcal{F}\{x(\cdot)\}(\omega) = \frac{1}{2\pi} \int_{\mathbb{R}} x(t) e^{-j\omega t} dt$, with $j = \sqrt{-1}$, and α is the coefficient. K. Dragomiretskiy and D. Zosso [5] took the mode in (4) and its solution (6) as Wiener filter, and applied it in the VMD mathematical model (3).

3. Ideas for Improving VMD

In this section, we briefly propose a few ideas for improving VMD. These ideas constitute the building blocks of our improved VMD, which is simply abbreviated to iVMD.

3.1. The Flattest Response

VMD can recover an AM–FM mode with a low-pass, narrow-band selection of the input signal. The form in (6) was taken as a Wiener filter, and thus the recovered mode had a lowpass power spectrum. Based on the heuristic method of the filtering concept in (5) and (6), we rewrite the differential part $\frac{\partial}{\partial t} x$ of the model in (3) as a time differential equation to solve the model in (3), and generalize it as

$$\sum_{p=0}^{P} \beta_n \partial_t^p x(t) = x_0(t) \quad (7)$$

Here, $\partial_t^p \triangleq \frac{\partial^p}{\partial t^p}, p = 0, \cdots, P$ is the p-th derivative operator with $P \geq 1$, the highest derivative order, and $\partial_t^0 x(t) \triangleq x(t)$. We have noted that β_p is the coefficient of $\partial_t^p x(t)$ and $\beta_0 = 1$.

Therefore, we can obtain the corresponding frequency domain form of (7),

$$\hat{x}(\omega) = \frac{\hat{x}_0(\omega)}{1 + \sum_{p=1}^{P} \beta_p (j\omega)^p} \tag{8}$$

We set the ratio of $\frac{\hat{x}(\omega)}{\hat{x}_0(\omega)} = H_P(\omega)$ as the filter system; therefore,

$$H_P(\omega) = \frac{1}{1 + \sum_{p=1}^{P} \beta_p (j\omega)^p} \tag{9}$$

When $P = 1, 2, 3$, their amplitude spectra are, respectively,

$$\begin{aligned} \hat{x}_1(\omega) &= \frac{\hat{x}_0(\omega)}{1 + \beta_1 j\omega}, \\ \hat{x}_2(\omega) &= \frac{\hat{x}_0(\omega)}{1 - \beta_2 \omega^2 + \beta_1 j\omega}, \\ \hat{x}_3(\omega) &= \frac{\hat{x}_0(\omega)}{1 - \beta_2 \omega^2 + j(\beta_1 \omega - \beta_3 \omega^3)} \end{aligned} \tag{10}$$

and thus,

$$\begin{aligned} |H_1(\omega)| &= \frac{1}{\sqrt{1 + (\beta_1 \omega)^2}}, \\ |H_2(\omega)| &= \frac{1}{\sqrt{(1 - \beta_2 \omega^2)^2 + (\beta_1 \omega)^2}}, \\ |H_3(\omega)| &= \frac{1}{\sqrt{(1 - \beta_2 \omega^2)^2 + (\beta_1 \omega - \beta_3 \omega^3)^2}} \end{aligned} \tag{11}$$

Table 1 provides the coefficients of the different lowpass filters, and Figure 1 shows the squared amplitude frequency characteristic, $|H_P(\omega)|^2$. The system is a lowpass filter expressed by $H_P(\omega)$, with its coefficients carefully selected via many methods of filter designing from Butterworth, Chebyshev, etc. Here, we design the filter as a Butterworth filter [25], which has the flattest response in the frequency as depicted in Figure 1. The parameters of the Butterworth filter are calculated in the following equations:

$$P = \left[\frac{1}{2} \frac{\lg\left(\frac{10^{\frac{\alpha_s}{10}} - 1}{10^{\frac{\alpha_p}{10}} - 1}\right)}{\lg\left(\frac{\omega_s}{\omega_p}\right)}\right], \omega_c = \frac{\omega_p}{\left(10^{\frac{\alpha_p}{10}} - 1\right)^{\frac{1}{2P}}} \tag{12}$$

Here, $[\cdot]$ is meant to take the maximum integer and add 1, while α_p, α_s are the band pass and stop attenuations, respectively, and ω_p, ω_s are the responding frequencies. Certainly, other filter-type designs can also be applied here.

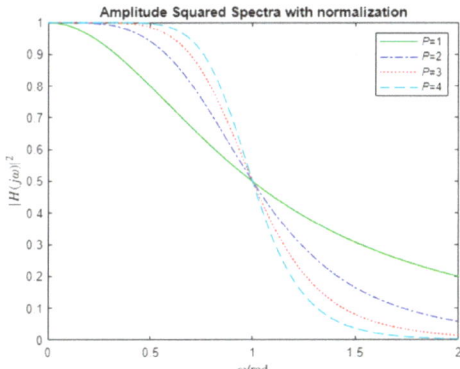

Figure 1. Amplitude Spectra of different order P with normalization.

Table 1. Coefficient of the lowpass Butterworth filter in the model (7).

P	β_1	β_2	β_3	β_4	β_5	β_6
1	1					
2	$\sqrt{2}$	1				
3	2	2	1			
4	2.61312593	3.41421356	2.61312593	1		
5	3.23606798	5.23606798	5.23606798	3.23606798	1	
6	3.86370331	7.46410162	9.14162017	7.46410162	3.86370331	1

Note that $\beta_0 = 1$.

3.2. To Set the Bandwidth

In the design of the lowpass Butterworth filter, we can adjust the bandwidth by normalizing the frequency. We set the normalized frequency as $\frac{\omega}{\omega_c}$, and thus we can set the lowpass bandwidth as $B = \omega_c$. Figure 1 shows the bandwidth is normalized by dividing with B, where the cutoff frequency is 1 kHz.

From (9), we rewrite the system function as

$$H_p\left(\frac{\omega}{B}\right) = \frac{1}{1 + \sum_{p=1}^{P} \beta_p \left(j\frac{\omega}{B}\right)^p} \tag{13}$$

Based on the property of the Fourier transform, if denormalization means ω is divided by B in the frequency domain, then the time domain response is $Bh_p(Bt)$, where $h_p(t)$ is the inverse Fourier transform of $H_p(\omega)$. We obtain the denormalized version of the filter as

$$\sum_{p=0}^{P} \beta_n B \partial_t^p f(Bt) = f_0(t) \tag{14}$$

3.3. Harmonics

Continuous periodic signal (mode), $u_k(t)$, may have multiple harmonic components with its base frequency of ω_k, each of which has a gradually attenuated amplitude a_m with the harmonic frequency $m\omega_k, m = 1, 2, \cdots, M_k$. We find that M_k is the highest order of harmonic frequency. In theoretical application, $M \to \infty$. That is,

$$u_k(t) = \sum_m a_m e^{jm\omega_k t}. \tag{15}$$

Therefore, the composite signal may consist of one harmonic mode with maximum harmonic order at M_k, and the center frequencies of the harmonic mode are $m\omega_k$, $m = 1, 2, \cdots, M_k$.

4. Improved VMD

4.1. Improved Optimal Problem

In this section, we introduce our improved mathematical model for the variational mode decomposition based on the VMD idea [5] and the previous section.

The new model is similar to the model found in (3), except in a few aspects. The sparsity in each mode is chosen to be its bandwidth, $2B$, in the spectral domain. Each mode without the harmonical frequencies, u_k, is compact around a center pulsation, ω_k, which is to be determined among the decomposition. Each mode with the harmonical frequencies is compact around the harmonical frequencies, $m\omega_k, m = 1, 2, \cdots$. Here, the sparsity also indicates full quasi-orthogonality.

We propose the following improved idea to decompose the signal $x(t)$: (1) for each mode, u_k, that has an adaptive bandwidth of $2B$, we design the flattest response lowpass filter which permits the mode to pass through; (2) for each mode, u_k, we shift the mode's harmonic frequencies spectrum with the baseband, by multiplying it with an exponential, $e^{-jm\omega_k t}$, which is tuned to the respective estimated center frequency, $m\omega_k$.

We set the analytical signal of $u_k(t)$ as,

$$a_k(t) = \left(\delta(t) + \frac{j}{\pi t}\right) * u_k(t) \qquad (16)$$

Here, $*$ is the convolution operator. The resulting constrained variational problem is

$$\min_{\{u_k,\omega_k,B_k\}} \left\{ \sum_k \sum_m \|\partial_t^P [B_k a_k(B_k t) e^{-jm\omega_k t}]\|_2^2 \right\} \\ \text{st.} \sum_k u_k(t) = x(t) \qquad (17)$$

where $u_k, k = 1, \cdots, K$ is the mode to be decomposed, where K is the given number of the modes, where B_k is the basic bandwidth of the mode u_k, and where ω_k is the center frequency corresponding with the mode u_k.

4.2. Solution to the Problem

The constraint optimal problem (17) can be solved via the augmented Lagrangian method. Lagrangian multipliers $\lambda(t)$ are set with a quadratic penalty term to render the problem unconstrained. The weight α_k of the penalty term is set as the factor of each mode u_k.

First, we project the minimization problem (17) into solving the extreme point of the augmented Lagrangian equation [26], which is

$$\mathcal{L}(u_k, \omega_k, B_k, \lambda) = \alpha_k \sum_k \sum_m \|\partial_t [B_k a_k(B_k t) e^{-jm\omega_k t}]\|_2^2 + \left\| x(t) - \sum_k u_k(t) \right\|_2^2 + \langle \lambda(t), x(t) - \sum_k u_k(t) \rangle \qquad (18)$$

The augmented Lagrangian (18) is in a sequence of alternate direction methods of multipliers (ADMM) [27]. Next, we detail how the respective sub-problems can be solved.

4.3. Minimization w.r.t u_k

To update the modes u_k, the problem (18) is rewritten as the following unconstraint goal function for u_k:

$$\mathcal{L}_{u_k} = \alpha_k \sum_m \|\partial_t [B_k a_k(B_k t) e^{-jm\omega_k t}]\|_2^2 + \left\| x(t) - \sum_k u_k(t) + \frac{\lambda(t)}{2} \right\|_2^2 \qquad (19)$$

This was achieved via Parseval–Plancherel Fourier isometry [28], and we take $\frac{\omega + m\omega_k}{B_k} \to \omega$ in the first term; then,

$$\mathcal{L}_{\hat{u}_k} = \alpha_k \sum_m \left\| \sum_{p=1}^{P} \beta_p (jB_k\omega - jm\omega_k)^p [(1 + \text{sgn}(\omega))\hat{u}_k(\omega)] \right\|_2^2 + \left\| \hat{x}(\omega) - \sum_k \hat{u}_k(\omega) + \frac{\hat{\lambda}(\omega)}{2} \right\|_2^2 \qquad (20)$$

By exploiting the Hermitian symmetry of the real signals,

$$\mathcal{L}_{\hat{u}_k} = \int_0^{+\infty} \left\{ 4\alpha_k \sum_m \left| \sum_{p=1}^{P} \beta_p (B_k\omega - m\omega_k)^p \hat{u}_k(\omega) \right|^2 + 2\left| \hat{x}(\omega) - \sum_k \hat{u}_k(\omega) + \frac{\hat{\lambda}(\omega)}{2} \right|^2 \right\} d\omega \qquad (21)$$

Letting the first variation vanish, i.e., $\frac{\delta}{\delta u_k}\mathcal{L}_{u_k} = 0$, for the positive frequencies. Thus,

$$\hat{u}_k(\omega) = \frac{\hat{x}(\omega) - \sum_{i \neq k} \hat{u}_i(\omega) + \frac{\hat{\lambda}(\omega)}{2}}{1 + 2\alpha_k \sum_m \sum_{p=1}^{P} \beta_p^2 |B_k\omega - m\omega_k|^{2p}} \qquad (22)$$

When $M = 1$, $P = 1$, $B_k = 1$, and $\beta_1 = 1$, which is taken from Table 1, then the above equation is simplified as,

$$\hat{u}_k(\omega) = \frac{\hat{x}(\omega) - \sum_{i \neq k} \hat{u}_i(\omega) + \frac{\hat{\lambda}(\omega)}{2}}{1 + 2\alpha_k |\omega - \omega_k|^2} \quad (23)$$

If we set $\alpha_k = 1$, $M = 1$, $P = 1$, and $\beta_1 = 1$ in Equation (22), then,

$$\hat{u}_k(\omega) = \frac{\hat{x}(\omega) - \sum_{i \neq k} \hat{u}_i(\omega) + \frac{\hat{\lambda}(\omega)}{2}}{1 + 2B_k^2 \left|\omega - \frac{\omega_k}{B_k}\right|^2}. \quad (24)$$

When $M = 1$, $P = 2$, and β_p which is taken from Table 1, then Equation (22) is,

$$\hat{u}_k(\omega) = \frac{\hat{x}(\omega) - \sum_{i \neq k} \hat{u}_i(\omega) + \frac{\hat{\lambda}(\omega)}{2}}{1 + 2\alpha_k \sum_m \left(\sqrt{2}|B_k\omega - m\omega_k|^2 + |B_k\omega - m\omega_k|^4\right)} \quad (25)$$

When $\alpha_k = 1$ and $M = 1$, Equation (25) is clearly identified as a Butterworth filtering of the current residual.

4.4. Minimization w.r.t ω_k

The center frequency ω_k is solved via the optimization of the following goal function,

$$\mathcal{L}_{\omega_k} = \sum_m \|\partial_t [B_k a_k(B_k t)] e^{-jm\omega_k t}\|_2^2 \quad (26)$$

As described previously, the minimization of (26) can work in the Fourier domain; that is,

$$\mathcal{L}_{\omega_k} = \frac{2}{\pi} \int_0^{+\infty} \sum_m \left|\sum_{p=1}^{P} \beta_p (B_k\omega - m\omega_k)^p\right|^2 |\hat{u}_k(\omega)|^2 d\omega \quad (27)$$

We also take the derivative of $\mathcal{L}_{\omega_k}$ to ω_k, and set it to be zero; then,

$$\sum_m \sum_{p=1}^{P} \sum_{p'=1}^{P} mp'\beta_{p'}\beta_p \int_0^{+\infty} (B_k\omega - m\omega_k)^{p+p'-1} |\hat{u}_k(\omega)|^2 d\omega = 0 \quad (28)$$

Applying the binomial theorem, we get,

$$\sum_{p=1}^{P} \sum_{p'=1}^{P} \sum_{i=0}^{p+p'-1} \left[(-1)^{p+p'-i} s_m^{p+p'-i} p'\beta_{p'}\beta_p C_{p+p'-1}^i B_k^i \overline{\omega^i}\right] \omega_k^{p+p'-1-i} = 0 \quad (29)$$

Here, we find that $C_n^i = \frac{n!}{i!(n-i)!}$, $\overline{\omega^n} = \int_0^{+\infty} \omega^n |\hat{u}_k(\omega)|^2 d\omega$, and $s_m^n = \sum_{m=1}^{M} m^n$. Equation (29) is a polynomial $2P$-power equation about ω_k. We rewrite (29) as

$$\sum_{n=0}^{2P-1} c_n \omega_k^n = 0 \quad (30)$$

Here, c_n is the n-power coefficient, and

$$c_n = \sum_{\substack{n=p+p'-1-i \\ p,p'=1,2,\ldots,P \\ i=0,1,\ldots,p+p'-1}} (-1)^{p+p'-i} s_m^{p+p'-i} p'\beta_{p'}\beta_p C_{p+p'-1}^i B_k^i \overline{\omega^i} \quad (31)$$

Solving the above equation in (30), we can obtain the solution of ω_k via the Newton–Raphson method, or others. Since Equation (28) is complex, it is not easy to obtain the solution. In fact, we find that M, P are not large, so we provide the different possible values of M, P, and obtain the corresponding solutions. Table 2 shows the different solutions of ω_k under M, P, and shows that ω_k should be selected via the conditions, (1) $\omega_k > 0$; (2) ω_k being a real number. Additionally, the solution exists in practice, which can be clearly proven since the power order is odd.

Table 2. The different solutions of $\omega_k(M, N)$.

P	M	$\omega_k(M,P)$
1	1	$c_1 = \overline{\omega^0}$, $c_0 = -B_k\overline{\omega}$ $\omega_k = B_k \dfrac{\int_0^{+\infty} \omega|\hat{u}_k(\omega)|^2 d\omega}{\int_0^{+\infty} |\hat{u}_k(\omega)|^2 d\omega}$
1	2	$\omega_k = B_k \dfrac{3\int_0^{+\infty} \omega|\hat{u}_k(\omega)|^2 d\omega}{5\int_0^{+\infty} |\hat{u}_k(\omega)|^2 d\omega}$
1	m	$\omega_k = B_k \dfrac{\sum_m m \int_0^{+\infty} \omega|\hat{u}_k(\omega)|^2 d\omega}{\sum_m m^2 \int_0^{+\infty} |\hat{u}_k(\omega)|^2 d\omega}$
2	m	Here, $c_3\omega_k^3 + c_2\omega_k^2 + c_1\omega_k + c_0 = 0$ $c_3 = 2\overline{\omega^0}s_m^4$ $c_2 = [-2\sqrt{2}\overline{\omega^0} - \sqrt{2}\overline{\omega^0} - 6B_k\overline{\omega^1}]s_m^3$ $c_1 = \left[2\overline{\omega^0} + 4\sqrt{2}B_k\overline{\omega^1} + 2\sqrt{2}B_k\overline{\omega^1} + 6B_k^2\overline{\omega^2}\right]s_m^2$ $c_0 = \left[-2B_k\overline{\omega^1} - 2\sqrt{2}B_k^2\overline{\omega^2} - \sqrt{2}B_k^2\overline{\omega^2} - 2B_k^3\overline{\omega^3}\right]s_m^1$
3	m	Here, $c_5\omega_k^5 + c_4\omega_k^4 + c_3\omega_k^3 + c_2\omega_k^2 + c_1\omega_k + c_0 = 0$ $c_5 = +3\overline{\omega^0}s_m^6$ $c_4 = \left(-15B_k\overline{\omega^1} - 10\overline{\omega^0}\right)s_m^5$ $c_3 = \left(+30B_k^2\overline{\omega^2} + 40B_k\overline{\omega^1} + 16\overline{\omega^0}\right)s_m^4$ $c_2 = \left(-30B_k^3\overline{\omega^3} - 60B_k^2\overline{\omega^2} - 48B_k\overline{\omega^1} - 12\overline{\omega^0}\right)s_m^3$ $c_1 = \left(+15B_k^4\overline{\omega^4} + 40B_k^3\overline{\omega^3} + 48B_k^2\overline{\omega^2} + 24B_k\overline{\omega^1} + 4m\overline{\omega^0}\right)s_m^2$ $c_0 = \left(-3B_k^5\overline{\omega^5} - 10B_k^4\overline{\omega^4} - 16B_k^3\overline{\omega^3} - 12B_k^2\overline{\omega^2} - 4B_k\overline{\omega^1}\right)s_m^1$

4.5. Minimization w.r.t B_k

The Bandwidth, B_k, is solved via optimization of the following goal function:

$$\mathcal{L}_{B_k} = \sum_m \|\partial_t[B_k a_k(B_k t)]e^{-jm\omega_k t}\|_2^2 \tag{32}$$

The minimization of (32) can be completed in the Fourier domain; that is,

$$\mathcal{L}_{B_k} = \frac{2}{\pi} \int_0^{+\infty} \sum_m \left|\sum_{p=1}^P \beta_p(B_k\omega - m\omega_k)^p\right|^2 |\hat{u}_k(\omega)|^2 d\omega \tag{33}$$

We also take the derivative of $\mathcal{L}_{B_k}$ to B_k, and set it to be zero; that is, $\frac{\partial}{\partial B_k}\mathcal{L}_{B_k} = 0$, then, via the binomial theorem, we get,

$$\sum_{p=1}^{P} \sum_{i=0}^{2p-1} p(-1)^i \overline{\omega^{i+1}} s_m^{2p-1-i} \beta_p^2 C_{2p-1}^i \omega_k^{2p-1-i} B_k^{\,i} = 0 \tag{34}$$

Here, we still rewrite (34) as

$$\sum_{i=0}^{2P-1} d_{2P-1-i} B_k^i = 0 \tag{35}$$

Here, d_i is the i-power coefficient, and

$$d_{2P-1-i} = (-1)^i \overline{\omega^{i+1}} \sum_{p=1}^{P} p s_m^{2p-1-i} \beta_p{}^2 C_{2p-1}^i \omega_k{}^{2p-1-i} \tag{36}$$

When $P = 1$, then

$$\begin{aligned} d_0 &= \overline{\omega^2} M \\ d_1 &= \overline{\omega^1} s_m^1 \omega_k \end{aligned} \tag{37}$$

And

$$B_k = \omega_k \frac{s_m^1 \overline{\omega^1}}{M \overline{\omega^2}} \tag{38}$$

As in the previous section, when solving the above equation in (35), we can obtain the solution of B_k via the Newton–Raphson method, or others.

4.6. Complete Algorithm

The Lagrangian multiplier $\lambda(t)$ is updated with the following equation [5]:

$$\lambda^{n+1}(t) = \lambda^n(t) + \tau \left(x(t) - \sum_k u_k(t) \right) \tag{39}$$

As well as in the frequency domain,

$$\hat{\lambda}^{n+1}(\omega) = \hat{\lambda}^n(\omega) + \tau \left(\hat{x}(\omega) - \sum_k \hat{u}_k(\omega) \right) \tag{40}$$

Here, n is the iterative number, and τ is the update parameter.

We directly optimize in the Fourier domain, and then we obtain the complete algorithm for iVMD in Algorithm 1.

Algorithm 1: Complete optimization of iVMD

Initialize $\{\hat{u}_k^1\}$, $\{\omega_k^1\}$, $\{B_k^1\}$, $\hat{\lambda}^1$, $n \leftarrow 1$
Repeat
$$n \leftarrow n + 1$$
    For $k = 1 : K$ do
        Update $\hat{u}_k$ for all $\omega \geq 0$:
$$\hat{u}_k^{n+1}(\omega) \leftarrow \frac{\hat{x}(\omega) - \sum_{i<k} \hat{u}_i^{n+1}(\omega) - \sum_{i>k} \hat{u}_i^n(\omega) + \frac{\hat{\lambda}^n(\omega)}{2}}{1 + 2\alpha \sum_m \sum_p^P \beta_p^2 \left| B_k(\iota) - m(\iota)_k^n \right|^{2n}}$$
        Update ω_k:
$$\omega_k^{n+1} \leftarrow \omega_k(M, N) \text{ in Table 2}$$
$$B_k^{n+1} \leftarrow Solving\ (35)$$
    End for
    Update Lagrangian multiplier for all $\omega \geq 0$:
$$\hat{\lambda}^{n+1}(\omega) = \hat{\lambda}^n(\omega) + \tau \left(\hat{x}(\omega) - \sum_k \hat{u}_k^{n+1}(\omega) \right)$$
Until convergence
$$\sum_k \frac{\|\hat{u}_k^{n+1} - \hat{u}_k^n\|^2}{\|\hat{u}_k^n\|^2} < \varepsilon$$

4.7. Reconstruction versus Denoising

The role of the Lagrangian multiplier [5] $\lambda(t)$ is the same in iVMD as in VMD, which serves to enforce the constraint, while the quadratic penalty α_k improves convergence.

The iVMD algorithm adds the extra bandwidth B_k, and it acts as a penalty factor, as detailed in Equation (24). Both the penalty factor and the bandwidth improve convergence, and we can initially set the factor and leave the bandwidth adaptively undated. If we set the bandwidth as $B_k = 1$, the penalty factor of iVMD acts as the VMD.

5. Experiments and Results

To demonstrate the effectiveness of the iVMD algorithm, we consider the same test signals that were previously suggested [2,5] with the purpose of increased comparability.

5.1. Example 1 with Linear Trend

The first signal is

$$x_{\text{Sig1}}(t) = 6t + \cos 8\pi t + \frac{1}{2}\cos 40\pi t. \tag{41}$$

The signal composes three parts, detailed in (41). The linear growth term in (41) has higher-order harmonics, which spread over the whole spectrum. Figure 2 shows the effective partition of the input spectra via iVMD, and we compare it with the results run via the VMD in Figure 3. The results are almost identical.

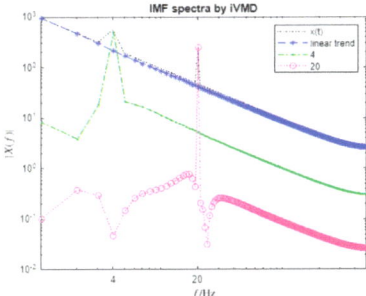 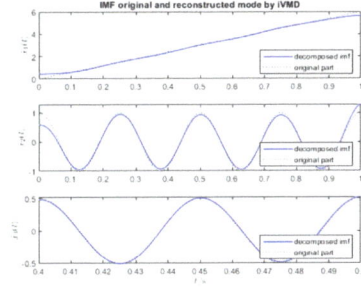

Figure 2. iVMD decomposition of $x_{\text{Sig1}}(t)$. The left shows the IMF's spectra, and the right shows the reconstructed modes. In the left figure, legend $x(t)$ expresses the spectrum of $x_{\text{Sig1}}(t)$, and legend 4 and 20, respectively, express the spectra of the components at 4 Hz and 20 Hz.

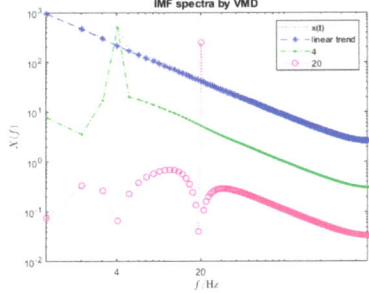 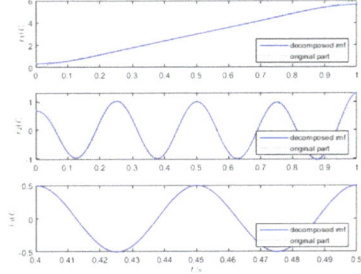

Figure 3. VMD decomposition of $x_{\text{Sig1}}(t)$.

5.2. Example 2 with a Piecewise Signal

The second signal is

$$x_{\text{Sig2}}(t) = 6t^2 + \cos\left(10\pi t + 10\pi t^2\right) + \begin{cases} \cos 60\pi t & t \leq 0.5 \\ \cos(80\pi t - 10\pi) & t > 0.5 \end{cases} \tag{42}$$

We set $K = 4$ in the iVMD algorithm, thus assigning each half of the piecewise-constant frequency signal to a separate mode. Both iVMD and VMD achieve effective convergence with the expected center frequencies after carefully tuning the parameters of the respective algorithms. For details, see Figures 4 and 5. When comparing the peaks in frequencies at 30, 40 Hz, the results run via iVMD show slightly better results.

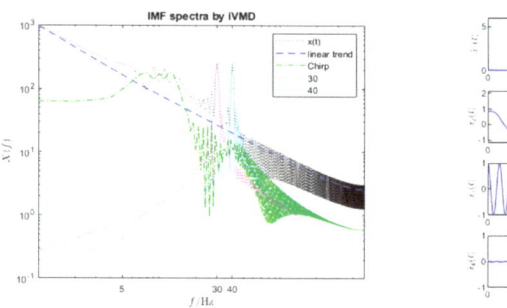 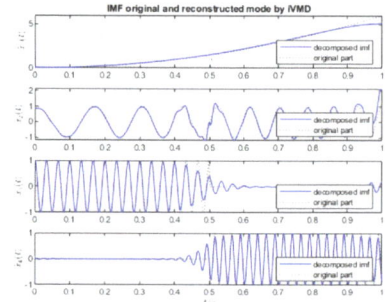

Figure 4. iVMD decomposition of $x_{\text{Sig2}}(t)$ run via iVMD. The left figure shows the IMF's spectra, and the right shows the reconstructed modes.

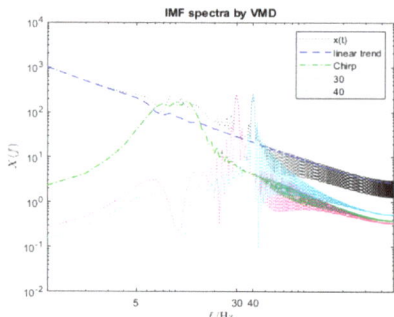 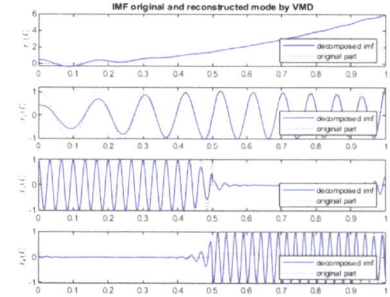

Figure 5. VMD decomposition of $x_{\text{Sig2}}(t)$.

5.3. Example 3: Intrawave Frequency Modulation

The third signal is

$$x_{\text{Sig3}}(t) = \frac{1}{1.2 + \cos(2\pi t)} + \frac{\cos(32\pi t + 0.2\cos(64\pi t))}{1.5 + \sin(2\pi t)} \tag{43}$$

The iVMD and VMD results are almost identical, as illustrated in Figures 6 and 7. In fact, the second term in (43) quickly converges with the correct main frequency of 16 Hz.

5.4. Example 4: Sawtooth Signal

The fourth signal is

$$x_{\text{Sig4}}(t) = x_{41}(t) + x_{42}(t). \tag{44}$$

The components x_{41}, x_{42} are sawtooth signals of different center frequencies, 10 Hz and 80 Hz, and amplitudes at 2. Figure 8, run via iVMD, shows the decomposition of the two sawtooth composite signals. The iVMD algorithm can obtain effective decomposition with the relatively small-value difference curve between the raw sawtooth and the estimated sawtooth. The two are compared by running at different settings of harmonical order—M, $M = [1; 3; 5]$—the bigger M is taken to allow more harmonical components, and the difference is smaller.

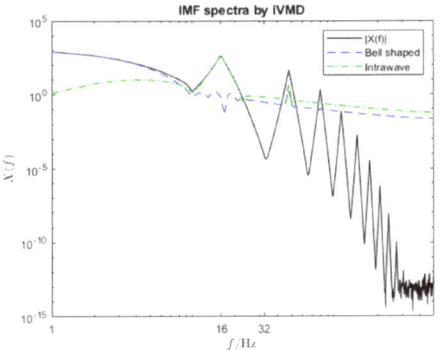
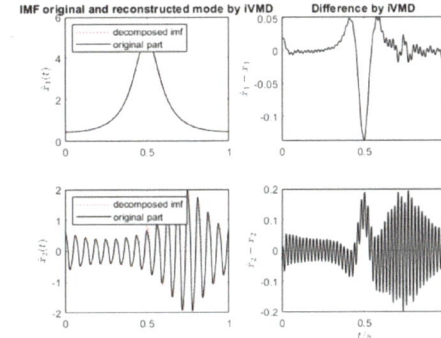

Figure 6. iVMD decomposition of $x_{\text{Sig3}}(t)$ run via iVMD. The left shows the IMF's spectra, and the right shows the reconstructed modes. In the reconstructed modes, we show four figures. The left two are the IMFs, and the right two show the differences between the estimated IMF and the original.

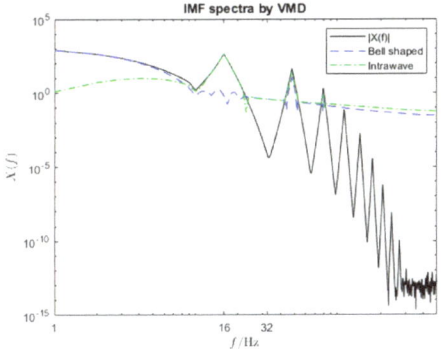
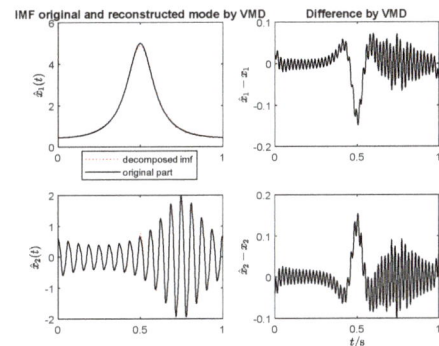

Figure 7. VMD decomposition of $x_{\text{Sig3}}(t)$.

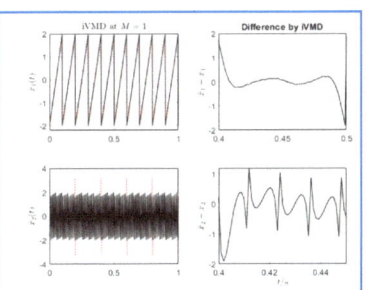
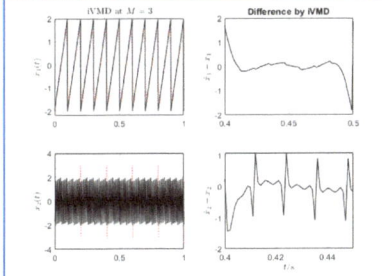
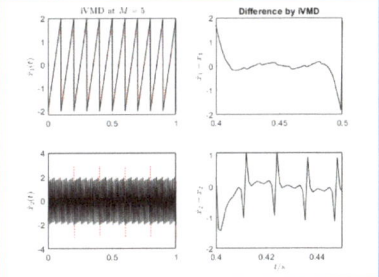

Figure 8. iVMD decomposition of $x_{\text{Sig4}}(t)$ run via iVMD. The algorithm iVMD is run at $M = [1; 3; 5]$, the figures of which are noted in the titles. Each figure has four sub-figures, with the left two being decomposed IMFs and the originals, while the right two are the correspondence differences.

For comparison, we still provide the results run by the VMD with the same aspect, which is depicted in Figure 9. The difference between the original and decomposed signal is relatively smoother in the iVMD results.

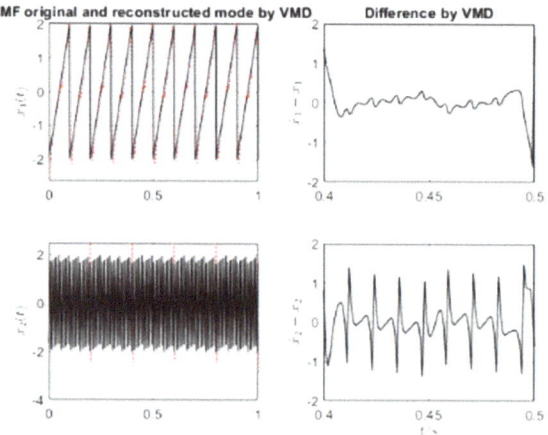

Figure 9. VMD decomposition of $x_{Sig4}(t)$.

5.5. Example 5: An Electrocardiogram

The fifth signal, $x_{Sig5}(t)$, is an electrocardiogram (ECG). The data are shared by [2]. The data present numerous components in which there exists an oscillating low-frequency pattern, and a noise with a high frequency. Figure 10 illustrates the spectra and the results run via iVMD. A high number of 12 modes is detected. The center frequencies are effectively detected, which converges with ECG spectral peaks. The first mode represents the baseline oscillation, and the last mode represents the high-frequency noise.

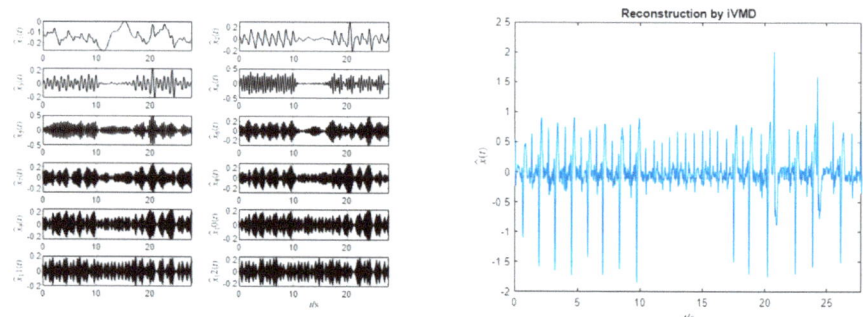

Figure 10. iVMD decomposition of $x_{Sig5}(t)$. We set $K = 12$. The left figure shows the IMFs, and the right shows the reconstructed ECG signal, where the first and last modes are discarded.

6. Conclusions and Outlook

We further developed the algorithm of VMD as iVMD from three points: (1) flattest response, (2) harmonic, and (3) bandwidth. The flattest response is applied in iVMD and thus, we can set the higher differential order P with respect to time, which results in the added weighting coefficient which can be obtained via Butterworth filter designing. As the harmonics may exist in the input signal, the mathematical model of VMD is further studied and modified via the harmonic order M, and the improved version can support M-order harmonical center frequency, $m\omega_k$. Each mode may have its adaptive bandwidth, and we set it in the model in (13) and (17). Through the above three points, we developed the algorithm iVMD.

In our experiments, iVMD works effectively with the same abilities as VMD and achieves a better performance than VMD.

The assumption of iVMD is the same as VMD, except that we can set the differential order and harmonic order with adjustable bandwidth, B_k. We explain the reasons behind decomposing the two sawtooth composite signals, and it is due to setting the M-order harmonics in the mathematical model.

The algorithm iVMD is now being further extended with two-dimension decomposition, and we expect further challenges to decompose more complex composite signals.

Author Contributions: Conceptualization, methodology, software, validation, formal analysis, investigation, resources, writing—original draft preparation, writing—review and editing, visualization, supervision, project administration, X.S.; data curation, R.L. All authors have read and agreed to the published version of the manuscript.

Funding: This research received no external funding.

Data Availability Statement: No new data were created, and the data are unavailable due to privacy restrictions.

Acknowledgments: The authors would like to thank Xizhi Shi for his kindness and encouragement on further studying VMD.

Conflicts of Interest: The authors declare no conflict of interest.

References

1. Crochiere, R. A weighted overlap-add method of short-time Fourier analysis/synthesis. *IEEE Trans. Acoust. Speech Signal Process.* **1980**, *28*, 99–102. [CrossRef]
2. Gilles, J. Empirical wavelet transform. *IEEE Trans. Signal Process.* **2013**, *61*, 3999–4010. [CrossRef]
3. Liu, S.; Yu, K. Successive multivariate variational mode decomposition based on instantaneous linear mixing model. *Signal Process.* **2022**, *190*, 108311. [CrossRef]
4. Huang, N.E.; Shen, Z.; Long, S.R.; Wu, M.C.; Shih, H.H.; Zheng, Q.; Yen, N.C.; Tung, C.C.; Liu, H.H. The empirical mode decomposition and the Hilbert spectrum for nonlinear and non-stationary time series analysis. *Proc. R. Soc. London Ser. A Math. Phys. Eng. Sci.* **1998**, *454*, 903–995. [CrossRef]
5. Dragomiretskiy, K.; Zosso, D. Variational Mode Decomposition. *IEEE Trans. Signal Process.* **2014**, *62*, 14. [CrossRef]
6. Chen, S.; Dong, X.; Peng, Z.; Zhang, W.; Meng, G. Nonlinear chirp mode decomposition: A variational method. *IEEE Trans. Signal Process.* **2017**, *65*, 6024–6037. [CrossRef]
7. Deb, S.; Dandapat, S.; Krajewski, J. Analysis and classification of cold speech using variational mode decomposition. *IEEE Trans. Affect. Comput.* **2020**, *11*, 296–307. [CrossRef]
8. Nazari, M.; Sakhaei, S.M. Successive variational mode decomposition. *Signal Process.* **2020**, *174*, 107610. [CrossRef]
9. Chen, S.; Yang, Y.; Peng, Z.; Dong, X.; Zhang, W.; Meng, G. Adaptive chirp mode pursuit: Algorithm and applications. *Mech. Syst. Signal Process.* **2019**, *116*, 566–584. [CrossRef]
10. Dragomiretskiy, K.; Zosso, D. Two-Dimensional Variational Mode Decomposition. In *Energy Minimization Methods in Computer Vision and Pattern Recognition*; Springer: Cham, Switzerland, 2015.
11. Zosso, D.; Dragomiretskiy, K.; Bertozzi, A.L.; Weiss, P.S. Two-Dimensional Compact Variational Mode Decomposition. *J. Math. Imaging Vis.* **2017**, *58*, 294–320. [CrossRef]
12. Ur Rehman, N.; Aftab, H. Multivariate variational mode decomposition. *IEEE Trans. Signal Process.* **2019**, *67*, 6039–6052. [CrossRef]
13. Chen, Q.; Lang, X.; Xie, L.; Su, H. Multivariate intrinsic chirp mode decomposition. *Signal Process.* **2021**, *183*, 108009. [CrossRef]
14. Stanković, L.; Brajović, M.; Daković, M.; Mandic, D. On the decomposition of multichannel nonstationary multicomponent signals. *Signal Process.* **2020**, *167*, 107261. [CrossRef]
15. Liu, W.; Hu, W.; Fu, D. Frequency Shifting-based Variational Mode Decomposition Method for Speech Signal Decomposition [Z]. In Proceedings of the 2022 International Conference on Automation, Robotics and Computer Engineering (ICARCE), Wuhan, China, 16–17 December 2022.
16. Dendukuri, L.S.; Hussain, S.J. Emotional speech analysis and classification using variational mode decomposition. *Int. J. Speech Technol.* **2022**, *25*, 457–469. [CrossRef]
17. Bagheri, A.; Ozbulut, O.E.; Harris, D.K. Structural system identification based on variational mode decomposition. *J. Sound Vib.* **2018**, *417*, 182–197. [CrossRef]
18. Chang, L.; Wang, R.; Zhang, Y. Decoding SSVEP patterns from EEG via multivariate variational mode decomposition-informed canonical correlation analysis. *Biomed. Signal Process. Control.* **2022**, *71*, 103209. [CrossRef]
19. Li, G.; Tang, G.; Luo, G.; Wang, H. Underdetermined blind separation of bearing faults in hyperplane space with variational mode decomposition. *Mech. Syst. Signal Process.* **2019**, *120*, 83–97. [CrossRef]

20. Zhang, X.; Chen, Y.; Jia, R.; Lu, X. Two-dimensional variational mode decomposition for seismic record denoising. *J. Geophys. Eng.* **2022**, *19*, 433–444. [CrossRef]
21. Guo, Y.; Zhang, Z. Generalized Variational Mode Decomposition: A Multiscale and Fixed-Frequency Decomposition Algorithm. *IEEE Trans. Instrum. Meas.* **2021**, *70*, 1–13. [CrossRef]
22. Rockafellar, R.T. A dual approach to solving nonlinear programming problems by unconstrained optimization. *Math. Program.* **1973**, *5*, 354–373. [CrossRef]
23. Bertero, M.; Poggio, T.A.; Torre, V. Ill-posed problems in early vision. *Proc. IEEE* **1988**, *76*, 869–889. [CrossRef]
24. Morozov, V.A. Linear and nonlinear ill-posed problems. *J. Math. Sci.* **1975**, *2*, 706–736. [CrossRef]
25. Butterworth, S. On the theory of filter amplifires. *Exp. Wirel.* **1930**, *7*, 536–541.
26. Bertsekas, D.P. Multiplier methods: A. survey. *Automatica* **1976**, *12*, 133–145. [CrossRef]
27. Bertsekas, D.P. *Constrained Optimization and Lagrange Multiplier Methods*; Academic Press: Boston, MA, USA, 1982.
28. Oppenheim, A.V.; Schafer, R.W.; Buck, J.R. *Discrete-Time Digital Signal Processing*; Prentice Hall, Inc.: Hoboken, NJ, USA, 1998.

Disclaimer/Publisher's Note: The statements, opinions and data contained in all publications are solely those of the individual author(s) and contributor(s) and not of MDPI and/or the editor(s). MDPI and/or the editor(s) disclaim responsibility for any injury to people or property resulting from any ideas, methods, instructions or products referred to in the content.

Article

Investigating Feature Selection Techniques to Enhance the Performance of EEG-Based Motor Imagery Tasks Classification

Md. Humaun Kabir [1], Shabbir Mahmood [1], Abdullah Al Shiam [2], Abu Saleh Musa Miah [3], Jungpil Shin [3,*] and Md. Khademul Islam Molla [4,*]

1. Department of Computer Science and Engineering, Bangamata Sheikh Fojilatunnesa Mujib Science & Technology University, Jamalpur 2012, Bangladesh
2. Department of Computer Science and Engineering, Sheikh Hasina University, Netrokona 2400, Bangladesh
3. School of Computer Science and Engineering, The University of Aizu, Aizuwakamatsu 965-8580, Japan
4. Department of Computer Science and Engineering, University of Rajshahi, Rajshahi 6205, Bangladesh
* Correspondence: jpshin@u-aizu.ac.jp (J.S.); khademul.cse@ru.ac.bd (M.K.I.M.)

Abstract: Analyzing electroencephalography (EEG) signals with machine learning approaches has become an attractive research domain for linking the brain to the outside world to establish communication in the name of the Brain-Computer Interface (BCI). Many researchers have been working on developing successful motor imagery (MI)-based BCI systems. However, they still face challenges in producing better performance with them because of the irrelevant features and high computational complexity. Selecting discriminative and relevant features to overcome the existing issues is crucial. In our proposed work, different feature selection algorithms have been studied to reduce the dimension of multiband feature space to improve MI task classification performance. In the procedure, we first decomposed the MI-based EEG signal into four sets of the narrowband signal. Then a common spatial pattern (CSP) approach was employed for each narrowband to extract and combine effective features, producing a high-dimensional feature vector. Three feature selection approaches, named correlation-based feature selection (CFS), minimum redundancy and maximum relevance (mRMR), and multi-subspace randomization and collaboration-based unsupervised feature selection (SRCFS), were used in this study to select the relevant and effective features for improving classification accuracy. Among them, the SRCFS feature selection approach demonstrated outstanding performance for MI classification compared to other schemes. The SRCFS is based on the multiple k-nearest neighbour graphs method for learning feature weight based on the Laplacian score and then discarding the irrelevant features based on the weight value, reducing the feature dimension. Finally, the selected features are fed into the support vector machines (SVM), linear discriminant analysis (LDA), and multi-layer perceptron (MLP) for classification. The proposed model is evaluated with two benchmark datasets, namely BCI Competition III dataset IVA and dataset IIIB, which are publicly available and mainly used to recognize the MI tasks. The LDA classifier with the SRCFS feature selection algorithm exhibits better performance. It proves the superiority of our proposed study compared to the other state-of-the-art BCI-based MI task classification systems.

Keywords: BCI; automatic feature selection; CFS; mRMR; SRCFS; CSP; MI classification; SVM; LDA; MLP

MSC: 68T10

1. Introduction

Brain-Computer Interface (BCI) is a promising technology mainly used to help the neuromuscular disorders of paralyzed patients and in motor rehabilitation centres. It also established a linking channel and control capabilities to transform messages between the electronic devices and the brain [1–3]. In recent decades, BCI-related systems have gained exponential importance due to the numerous applications in different sectors, specifically in

Citation: Kabir, M.H.; Mahmood, S.; Al Shiam, A.; Musa Miah, A.S.; Shin, J.; Molla, M.K.I. Investigating Feature Selection Techniques to Enhance the Performance of EEG-Based Motor Imagery Tasks Classification. *Mathematics* 2023, 11, 1921. https://doi.org/10.3390/math11081921

Academic Editors: Grigoreta-Sofia Cojocar, Adriana-Mihaela Guran and Laura-Silvia Dioşan

Received: 10 March 2023
Revised: 15 April 2023
Accepted: 17 April 2023
Published: 19 April 2023

Copyright: © 2023 by the authors. Licensee MDPI, Basel, Switzerland. This article is an open access article distributed under the terms and conditions of the Creative Commons Attribution (CC BY) license (https://creativecommons.org/licenses/by/4.0/).

the neuro-engineering and neuroscience fields. It has encouraged to use of neuroplasticity in brain stroke patients. In addition, it has made a huge contribution to people with disabilities to help them communicate with other people using emotion [4,5], event-related potential detection [6], and sleep detection [7]. Furthermore, it can collaborate with other individuals with disabilities to articulate their needs, ideas, and thoughts and assist in operating their assistive devices, such as wheelchairs. It also aids in the execution of daily tasks without physical movement by detecting emotions. BCI applications span from communication and rehabilitation to entertainment. Recently, researchers have integrated BCI with artificial intelligence (AI) and created adaptable BCI systems that enable the control of various robotic equipment through brain activity. For example, brain-controlled home automation, robotic arms, and prosthetic arms [3–5,8]. The main reason for using a robotic or prosthetic arm is that brain activity and thinking commands cannot pass through the muscle and peripheral nerves. At the same time, we collect the signal through the electroencephalogram (EEG) sensor and translate it into a digital command to control the assistive devices for locked-in people.

There are various ways to measure and capture brain activity in a non-alive approach: EEG, magnetoencephalogram (MEG), and functional magnetic response imaging (fMRI) are most of them. Among them, the BCI system with EEG signal is the most cost-effective and can be implemented with minimal clinical risk because the non-invasive approach does not require any operation; however, it needs some electrodes on the scalp [9–11]. Here, the person needs to imagine a specific muscle movement or limb movement without any patient action (motor action). That imagination makes a great oscillatory action with rhythmic tremors which is known as different kinds of event-related function ERD or ERS, which can be recognized with a machine learning algorithm [12,13]. The main goal of the BCI-based application is to identify actual human activity during the MI task aiming to translate human thinking to the corresponding digital command, which can be controlled by different kinds of machines. To implement the goal, researchers have been working to extract effective features and search the compatible machine learning algorithm for classification.

Various feature extraction methods have been applied to the EEG signal for motor imagery (MI) task classification; among them, common spatial pattern (CSP) is one of the most used feature extraction algorithms [14]. The main concept of the CSP method is to employ the optimal spatial filter on the training EEG datasets, which produces the weight matrix for each electrode and measures the electrode information's significance. Later, researchers replaced the spatial pattern of the CSP with common patterns such as frequency domain, time domain, or combined time-frequency domain to produce the effective features for the MI-based EEG signals [15]. The primary issue with these methods is that they employ Common Spatial Pattern (CSP) on a broad frequency range, such as 1–30 Hz. Due to the intricate nature of the EEG signal, narrow-band signals perform better than full-band frequencies. Researchers have proposed that the EEG signal is composed of various types of rhythms and bands, such as delta, theta, alpha, beta, gamma, and mu. Among these, alpha, beta, and gamma exhibit significant rhythmic properties of the EEG signals [16–18]. Luo et al. first applied a subband-based feature extraction technique with the CSP to include the narrow-band rhythmic properties in the system [19]. The primary issue with this study is that it has increased the computational complexity exponentially due to the multiband increase in the number of signals, which is virtually n times. Additionally, initially, researchers collected the imagination data with a minimum number of electrodes, which could be 1, 2, or 3. However, recently researchers have collected signals with many electrodes, creating a challenging situation for implementing a portable, inexpensive, and fast BCI system for daily activities. Furthermore, this large amount of electrode information produces redundant and noisy data, which adds significant computational complexity [20]. So the feature selection procedure is inevitable for the EEG-based MI classification task; however, no one used the following work [16–19].

As we said, the multiband processed features have been extracted from the individual band and combined to produce the final features; thus, it derived a very higher dimension [21] and it affected the classification algorithm by reducing the performance [22]. Various kinds of supervised and unsupervised feature selection algorithms are available in data science and other machine learning-related research domains [23]. Molla et al. employed a supervised-based feature selection algorithm, neighbourhood component analysis (NCA). They extracted spatial features by using the CSP and then combined the four band features, resulting in a large dimension of features. Finally, they used NCA to select the potential number of features that are less than or equal to 50% of the original feature. The main drawback of their concept is that they selected the feature based on the weighted value and less than or equal to 50%, which may result in difficulties in producing high performance because of the inefficiency of the feature.

To overcome the problems mentioned above, we proposed CFS, mRMR, and SRCFS feature selection approaches along with the SVM, LDA, and MLP classifiers where the LDA and SRCFS-based MI tasks classification system outperforms using EEG signals. The main idea of the SRCFS method is to divide the features into multi-subspace and produce a Laplacian score, which is considered a weight value for each channel using the multi k nearest neighbour technique. Based on the Laplacian score, we selected features from 50% of the original number of features here. We have also implemented the traditional feature selection methods such as f-test, random forest, and logistic lasso and it is proved that our proposed system is far better than the traditional methods.

2. Related Works

There are numerous studies that have been conducted to develop MI classification systems based on the EEG signal. In the year 1875, the first EEG signal was collected by Richard Caton from the animal brain, and later, in 1929, the EEG signal was collected from the human brain first by Hans Berger [24]. Recently, steady-state visual-evoked potential (SSVEP)-based BCI has been developed to assist paralyzed patients by recognizing SSVEP-based commands [25]. EEG mainly records the biological electrical activity of the human brain using many electrodes that are essential for many human-oriented applications to make life easier, especially for people with complete paralysis or extreme disability [26].

To classify the EEG-based classification, Pfurtscheller et al. first applied LDA with adaptive autoregressive (AAR) for classifying left- and right-hand MI-EEG [27]. Many researchers have employed the common spatial pattern (CSP) as an optimal spatial filter to extract a weighted score of each electrode based on a significant score that proves the importance of each electrode [17,18]. The main drawback of these methods is that they consider only a broader range of frequencies in EEG signals, but a narrow signal is more effective compared to a broader signal. Usually, researchers divide the broader EEG signal into different subbands, namely mu, beta, alpha, beta, and gamma rhythm [28]. Pfurtscheller et al. showed that narrowband frequency, specifically the mu and beta rhythms, contain essential information for voluntary movement, and these two rhythms should be considered when implementing the EEG-based MI task classification [16,29]. There are many methodologies that have been proposed for considering each narrow band rhythm such as subband CSP, discriminant filter bank with CSP [30,31], sparse filter-band CSP, and filter bank CSP [21]. However, combining multiband features into a feature yields a large feature vector size, increasing the computational complexity and reducing the system's performance.

To solve the problem, it is inevitable to reduce feature dimension and size to improve performance. Both supervised, and unsupervised algorithms are mainly used to select the effective feature from the large feature dimension [22]. All features in the feature vector might not be relevant and important for the MI task classification, which can be considered a garble for the classification algorithm and degrades the method's performance [32]. Molla et al. divided the EEG signal into multiple sub-bands and then extracted features from each subband, producing large feature dimensions. Lastly, they employed Graph Eigen Decomposition (GED) to reduce the dimensionality of the feature vector to improve the performance and achieved 99.39% accuracy for epileptic seizer detection [33]. Siuly et al. proposed a Logistic Regression with a cross-correlation technique for classifying the EEG-based MI tasks [34]. In the procedure, they first extracted features with the CSP and then reduced the feature dimension with the hybrid unsupervised feature selection technique. Ali et al. proposed a CSP approach to extract the feature and then rank that feature with the mutual information score. Finally, they applied LDA to classify the MI task and achieved good performance [35]. Kevrich et al. applied empirical mode decomposition, wavelet packet decomposition, and discrete wavelet transforms to generate the narrowband of the EEG signal from a broader frequency [36]. They converted the feature vector into a group of features to justify the performance of the specific set of features. Finally, they claimed that the multiscale principal component analysis (PCA) feature achieved better performance accuracy, which was produced by the highest averaging technique.

Siuly et al. employed an updated CC-LR algorithm to improve the MI tasks classification accuracy where they focused on the specific electrode features and evaluated their method with the BCI III dataset [37]. Song et al. applied a supervised feature selection algorithm that included regression and classification as a unified framework [38]. Goldberger et al. employed a supervised-based neighbourhood component analysis (NCA) feature selection algorithm [39].

Chen et al. proposed a feature selection approach called conditional covariance minimization (CCM) which employs kernel-based measures of independence to find a subset of covariates that is maximally predictive of the response. They carried out numerous experiments using synthetic and real-world data and found that it outperforms other state-of-the-art approaches including Minimum Redundancy Maximum Relevance (mRMR), Backward Elimination Hilbert-Schmidt Independence Criterion (BAHSIC), and Mutual Information (MI) [40]. Constantinopoulos et al. presented a Bayesian method for mixture model training that addresses the feature selection and the model selection problems at the same time. This approach combines a mixture model formulation considering the saliency of the features and a Bayesian approach to mixture learning that can automatically determine the number of components and the saliency of features. Authors proved that this algorithm outperforms the MML-based approaches [41]. A deep learning-based method—Graph Convolutional Network Feature Selector (GRACES) has been implemented to select important features for the high-dimensional and low-sample size (HDLSS) data in [42]. Chen et al. demonstrated empirical evidence that GRACES can achieve a superb and stable performance on both synthetic and real-world HDLSS datasets by utilizing GCN along with different overfitting-reducing strategies including multiple dropouts, the introduction of Gaussian noises, and F-correction.

Molla et al. employed a CSP feature extraction approach and then used a nearest-neighbour-based discriminative features selection method to select the potential feature and discard the garble feature to improve MI classification using multichannel EEG signal [43]. Finally, they applied a machine learning algorithm SVM and evaluated their method with the BCI Competition III dataset IIIB, and IVA obtained superior performance compared to the recently developed algorithms. Based on their algorithm, they selected 50% of the feature from the extracted feature. To overcome the lacking, we proposed an unsupervised-based sequential feature selection algorithm, which is able to achieve higher accuracy than the existing performance available in the literature.

3. Dataset Description

To evaluate our model, we used two benchmark datasets for MI classification. These are BCI Competition III Dataset IVA, and BCI Competition III Dataset IIIB are described in Sections 3.1 and 3.2 consequently.

3.1. BCI Competition III Dataset IVA

In this study, we consider conducting experiments using publicly available MI data, which is available online with a detailed description that can be found at [44]. This recorded signal was collected from 5 healthy people, namely aa, al, av, aw, and ay where 118 EEG electrodes were used to record the signal. Each person performed four tasks which are considered here MI tasks, namely right foot, right hand, left hand, and limb. In this study, we have considered only binary classifications, which are left and right classes. The electrodes are placed on the scalp of the subject by following the instruction of the international 10–20 system. The subject is in a relaxed mode during the signal recording, and the subject is asked to imagine specific motor imagery tasks: left and right-hand movements. Each trial is recorded in intervals of 1.25 s to 2.25 s. The recorded signals were filtered with a filter, namely a bandpass filter in the frequency range from 0.05 Hz to 200 Hz, and digitized at 1000 Hz with 16-bit precision. After that, the filtered signal is downsampled at 100 Hz and used in the experiment for the duration of 0.5 s to 3 s in each cue.

3.2. BCI Competition III Dataset IIIB

Another dataset we used here to evaluate our model, BCI competition III dataset IIIB is recorded from the three subjects, namely O3, S4, and X11. This dataset was recorded with the three electrodes which are placed on the subject scalp based on the international 10–20 system. A trial signal consists of a seven-second duration recorded signal. Different trials are collected from the different subjects, such as 320 trials collected from the O3 subjects, and 1080 trials collected from S4 and X11, respectively. This recorded signal was sampled with a ratio of 125 Hz then it was filtered with a notch filter in the range of 0.5 to 30 Hz [45]. Since the experiment was conducted in the virtual reality (VR) paradigm for the O3 subject, we have discarded this subject for performance evaluation of our proposed method (see the Figure 1).

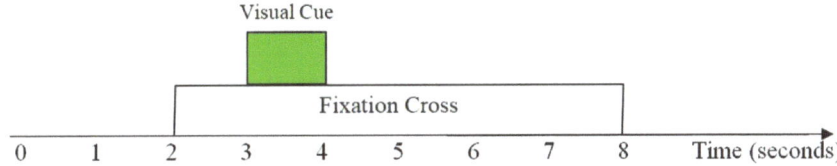

Figure 1. The timing sequence of BCI experiments when only the MI section from each dataset is used.

4. Proposed Method

The working flow architecture of the proposed method is given below in Figure 2, where we included the key contributions of this research and the implementation sequence of the study.

Step-1 Preprocessing of multichannel EEG signal
Step-2 Decompose each trial of EEG signal into subbands through filter bank analysis
Step-3 Extract the spatial from each subband by applying CSP
Step-4 Combine the features obtained from the individual subband to derive a feature vector
Step-5 Potential features are selected with feature selection algorithms named CFS, mRMR, and SRCFS, which are used as the final reduced feature vector for the classifier
Step-6 SVM, LDA and MLP classifiers are employed for the reduced features to distinguish the activities of MI EEG signals

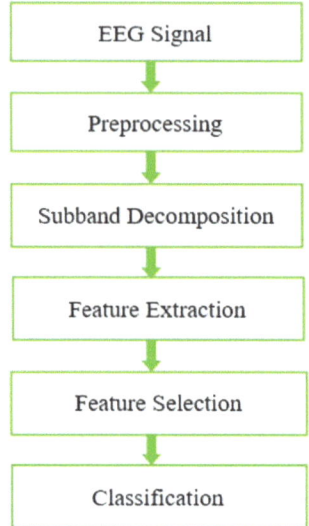

Figure 2. Working flow architecture of the proposed study.

4.1. Preprocessing

We applied a bandpass filter to remove noise from the raw EEG signal because raw EEG usually consists of different kinds of artefacts like eye blinking, sudden sound, muscle movement, body movement, environmental noises, etc. Furthermore, some narrowband EEG signal components are more sensitive to specific MI tasks. As a result, it is not surprising that using sub-bands rather than the entire EEG bandwidth results in more accurate MI task classification. According to a related study, the majority of brain activity associated with MI tasks occurs between 7 Hz and 36 Hz [46,47]. This study divides the broader 8–35 Hz frequency band EEG signal into multiple narrowband signals to calculate the exact feature information of the EEG signal. We have mainly decomposed the signal into four equivalent narrowband signals, namely Mu-band (8–13 Hz), low-beta (13–22 Hz), high-beta (22–35 Hz), and full-band (8–35 Hz) for our experimental purposes [43].

4.2. Feature Extraction

In this study, to extract the effective features from the narrowband signals, we have employed a well-known feature extraction method in multichannel EEG-based BCI the CSP [14,48,49]. The main concept of the algorithm is to minimize the variance among the intra-class features and maximize the variance among the inter-class. In addition, the CSP method finally projects the high-dimensional data into a low dimension, which is known as spatial feature subspace, by using a projection matrix. We have used the CSP algorithm as a spatial filter for making high-variance features between the right-hand and right-foot classes, resulting in peak variances between those classes. Let $E_{c_1}{}^i$ and $E_{c_2}{}^i$ be EEG signal of ith trial, c_1 and c_2 represent the class 1 and class 2. The projection matrix W_{CSP} is computed by first calculating the normalized spatial covariance matrix for both classes as follows in Equations (1) and (2).

$$C_L = \frac{E_{c_1} E_{c_1}{}'}{trace(E_{c_1} E_{c_1}{}')} \tag{1}$$

$$C_R = \frac{E_{c_2} E_{c_2}{}'}{trace(E_{c_2} E_{c_2}{}')} \tag{2}$$

where E' is the transpose of E. The averaged normalized covariances $\bar{C}_L$ and $\bar{C}_R$ are then computed by averaging all segments within each class. Equation (3) denotes the total composite spatial covariance.

$$C_c = \bar{C}_L + \bar{C}_R \qquad (3)$$

The following is the factorization of this covariance matrix into its eigenvalues and eigenvectors.

$$C_c = U_c \lambda_c U'_c \qquad (4)$$

Here, the eigenvector matrix and diagonal eigenvalue matrix are denoted by U_c and λ_c, respectively, which are organized in descending order. Following the above formula, we can calculate the whitening transformation using the following Equation (5).

$$P = \sqrt{\lambda_c^{-1}} U'_c \qquad (5)$$

where whitening transformation is denoted by P. The covariance matrices of the two classes are transformed by Equation (5). The projection matrix W_{CSP} is defined by

$$W_{CSP} = P'B = [w_1, w_2, \ldots, w_{(ch-1)} w_{ch}] \in R^{(ch \times ch)} \qquad (6)$$

where ch is the channel and B is an orthonormal matrix.

A matrix $W_{CSP} = [w_1, w_2, \ldots, w_{2m}] \in R^{(2 \times k)}$, including the spatial filters, represents k largest and smallest eigenvalues formed by the eigenvectors by solving the Equation (6). The final feature can be written as $f = [f_1, f_2, \ldots, f_{2k}]$.

$$f_j = \log(var(W'_{CSP}E), j = 1, 2, \ldots, 2k \qquad (7)$$

Here, variance is represented by $var(.)$, and $\log$ transformation is used for normalizing the elements of f_j.

4.3. Feature Selection

Since EEG signals are complex and collected using multiple electrodes, they often contain irrelevant information. Discarding such information is one of the most crucial steps in BCI. Features have a direct impact on how well a BCI system performs, and recent studies have focused on improving currently used methods or creating new ones. The extracted multiband feature dimensions are large and contain less effective features, which is not helpful for classification and increases computational complexity, resulting in reduced performance. In fact, machine learning algorithm performance is typically diminished by specific features. Feature selection techniques are divided into two groups: filter approaches and wrapper approaches [37]. Feature selection techniques can be divided into two groups: filter approaches and wrapper approaches. Filter approaches rely on predetermined criteria and are independent of the learning criteria. They create subsets that are assessed using a search algorithm. Wrapper approaches, on the other hand, require the use of a learning algorithm, and the performance of the selected feature subsets is evaluated using this algorithm.

In this study, we investigated three feature selection approaches: CFS, mRMR, and SRCFS. These methods have been recently developed and successfully applied in MI classification. We found that SRCFS outperformed the other two methods in terms of classification accuracy. In addition, the HSIC Lasso [50] and three conventional feature selection schemes named f-test, random forests, and logistic lasso have been investigated to evaluate the performance of our proposed system.

4.3.1. Correlation-Based Feature Selection (CFS)

The working idea of the CFS algorithm is to calculate a subset of the feature by following the initial hypothesis, which is mainly correlated with the output classes not correlated with themselves [22]. The usefulness of the features in class prediction and their connection with other features serve as the validation criteria. The subset calculation process of this algorithm can be written as the following formula,

$$CFS_s = \frac{f(\bar{r}_{tq})}{\sqrt{f + f(f-1)\bar{r}_{qq}}} \qquad (8)$$

Here, the mean of correlation among the inter-class and the mean of correlation among the intra-class are denoted by $\bar{r}_{tq}$ and $\bar{r}_{qq}$, respectively. In addition, the heuristic merit of each subset is denoted by f. The denominator measures the degree of redundancy among the features that make up the feature subset, and the numerator measures how predictive the feature subset is. The technique thus detects aspects that are superfluous or redundant. The search algorithm we utilized included backward exclusion and forward selection, and it was called Best First.

4.3.2. Minimum Redundancy and Maximum Relevance (mRMR)

A heuristic resembling CFS is used by the lowest redundancy and maximum relevance algorithm. The metric employed in this instance to verify the significance of the features is mutual information, which leads to a ranking of the features based on how well they cooperate with other features and the class. The most pertinent feature shares the least mutual information with the other features and the most with the class. This is achieved by increasing the value of the following expression,

$$F_{mRMR} = \frac{\frac{1}{n_f}\sum I(c,f)}{\frac{1}{n_f^2}\sum I(f_1,f_2)}. \qquad (9)$$

Here, the number of features, the mutual information between two classes, and the mutual information between two features are denoted by n_f, $\sum I(c,f)$, and $\sum I(f_1,f_2)$, respectively. After the ranking phase, this approach creates a subset with a varying number of features and orders it with the ranking score [51]. The machine learning algorithms finally validate these feature groups based on the ranking score.

4.3.3. Multi-Subspace Randomization and Collaboration-Based Unsupervised Feature Selection (SRCFS)

The SRCFS is a powerful framework for unsupervised feature selection in huge datasets where this algorithm conceals the original high-dimensional feature in several sub-groups [38,52]. Primarily, this algorithm creates a huge number of random subgroup features and after scoring each subspace it concatenated all the subgroups into a single feature vector based on the score of each group. Suppose, the feature partition variable is denoted with $F^{(i)}$ for the ith basic feature partition, and random subspace for j^{th} position can be denoted with $F^{(i,j)}$ of the $F^{(i)}$ partition. We can express the feature partition formula according to the following Equation (10). Then $F^{(i)}$ can be represented as follows,

$$F^{(i)} = \left\{F^{(i,1)}, F^{(i,2)}, \ldots, F^{(i,z)}\right\}. \qquad (10)$$

Here, $F^{(i)}$, and $F^{(i,1)}$ denote the feature partition and subspace in the partition, respectively. The quantity of random subspaces in F is given by z where an ideal condition would be for all subspaces to have the same size because the three must be equal to all random subspaces. Individual feature partition is created repeatedly, which can form a composed feature which is known as a final feature F and can be expressed with the following Equation (11).

$$F = \left\{ F^{(1)}, F^{(2)}, \ldots, F^{(g)} \right\}. \tag{11}$$

The total number of basic partitions and i^{th} basic partition are denoted with g and $F^{(i)}$, respectively. In each partition, there is an unknown number of subspaces which can be denoted with $g.z$, but the number of subspaces in each partition must be equal. It actually calculates g number of Laplacian scores where every partition must produce an individual score, which produced a final Laplacian score vector. The average Laplacian score can be calculated using the following formula which is the average of the Laplacian score for the basic partition F.

$$L_z(f) = \frac{1}{g} \sum_{i=1}^{g} L_s(F) \tag{12}$$

Here, $L_z(f) \in \mathbb{R}$ represents the full Laplacian score vector that be obtained by concatenating the Laplacian score vectors for all of its z random subspaces. To reflect the structure information of all $g.z$ numbers of random subspaces, we build $g.z$ numbers of KNN graphs. The combining information of the KNN Graph and the local preserving power of each subspace can lastly be used to compute the main score which is used to rank the feature and selected potential features called Laplacian scores of the features in each subspace.

4.4. Classification Using LDA, SVM and MLP

In this study, we used three well-known and mature machine learning-based classification algorithms, namely LDA, SVM, and MLP, to classify the left-hand and right-hand human motor imagery EEG signal. The goal is to find out and evaluate which one can be produced the best outcomes. LDA, also known as the Fisher linear discriminant, is a simple and well-known technique for categorizing BCI data. A linear binary classifier maps a p-dimensional input vector x to a hyperplane that divides the input space into two half spaces, each of which denotes a class (+1 or −1). The SVM is a relatively new classification method developed by Vapnik. It has a strong mathematical base in statistical learning theory and has demonstrated great performance in a variety of practical issues, particularly in BCI. To translate a higher-dimension row of training data, it uses a nonlinear map. Within this new dimension, it looks for the linear optimal dividing hyperplane (also known as a "choice border" separating the tuples of one class from another). A proper nonlinear mapping can always be used to split data from two classes into a suitably large dimension via a hyperplane. Support vectors are used by the SVM to find this hyperplane ("essential" training tuples) and margins (identified by the support vectors). SVM classifier with radial basis function (RBF) kernel is used to assess the proposed technique. A detailed description of these two methods can be found in [53,54]. MLP is a popular machine learning algorithm and a powerful tool for classifying brain activities. The inputs to the MLP are typically features extracted from EEG or other neuroimaging data. These features are then passed through multiple layers of interconnected nodes, with each node performing mathematical calculations on the input data. The output layer of the MLP represents the predicted class label for the input data. During training, the MLP's weights are changed to minimize the difference between the expected and actual output using techniques such as backpropagation. Their performance, however, is heavily influenced by the quality and significance of the input data, as well as the size and complexity of the MLP architecture [55,56]. The size of the hidden layers used in our experiment is ten.

5. Results and Discussion

To evaluate the model, we used here two well-known publicly available EEG-based MI task datasets. For each of the trials of the dataset, we decomposed into four narrowband signals to extract the exact information contained in the signal. The CSP approach is used to extract features from each narrow band and combine each feature to produce a final feature vector which generates a high-dimensional feature vector. The discriminative features are chosen using the CFS, mRMR, and SRCFS-based techniques. As a result, the collected features are utilized to train three classifiers, SVM, LDA, and MLP, separately. Then test data are used to assess the performance of the classifiers. Each 2.5 second trial for every person is taken out of the EEG data. Each frequency band is subjected to the CSP in order to extract the spatial information. From each subband, four pairs of spatial filters producing eight features are chosen from dataset BCI III-IVA and two pairs of spatial filters are chosen from BCI III-IIIB. For each trial, 32 (4 × 8) and 8 (4 × 2) dimensional feature vectors are created by combining the CSP features collected from each of the four bands from dataset BCI III-IVA and BCI III-IIIB, respectively. The high-dimensional feature space is then subjected to the CFS, mRMR, and SRCFS-based feature selection techniques. They give each feature a weight based on the label of the training data. The features are ranked based on the weights established by each of the feature selection approaches. The number of top-ranked features is chosen for classification.

5.1. Experimental Setting

We evaluated the proposed model with 5-fold cross-validation formula where we took the individual subject dataset feature and randomly divided the feature into five folded. After that, we randomly trained the model with four folded and tested the model with the rest one-fold features and preserved the accuracy for the first fold feature. We repeatedly preserved the accuracy five times and finally, we average the performance score and produced the final average performance score. We computed the accuracy (%) matrix using the following formula, which is also known as a best performance calculation procedure.

$$Accuracy = \frac{T_p + T_n}{T_p + T_n + F_p + F_n} \times 100 \qquad (13)$$

where, $T_p, T_n, F_p,$ and F_n represents true positive, true negative, false positive, and false negative, respectively. The accuracy values from the several experiments conducted mainly show the effectiveness of the proposed approach. Two different feature selection methods CFS, and mRMR have been employed and the result was compared with the SRCFS-based feature selection method. To evaluate the classifier performance, SVM and MLP are employed along with LDA. We have also calculated some statistical performance metrics like AUROC, F1 scores, and computational time of different subjects on two datasets to ensure the robustness and effectiveness of the proposed approach.

5.2. Performance Result with BCI Competition III Dataset IVA

Figure 3 demonstrates the performance comparison of different feature selection methods where SVM, LDA, and MLP are used, respectively. These figures proved that the SRCFS feature selection method's performance is better in most cases than others.

Figure 4 demonstrates that SRCFS with LDA outperforms the other for dataset BCI III-IVA. The result also showed that the feature selection technique has certain benefits in terms of enhancing classification performance. Without feature selection, the mean accuracy (across all subjects) is substantially lower than the other approaches that use feature selection methods. The method without feature selection uses extra features that are irrelevant and lowers the classifier's performance as a result.

Figure 5 compares the accuracy of the proposed method with different combinations of feature selection and classifier as a function of the number of selected features. It has been found that utilizing 16 well-chosen features from dataset BCI III-IVA enables the classification of objects with the highest degree of accuracy.

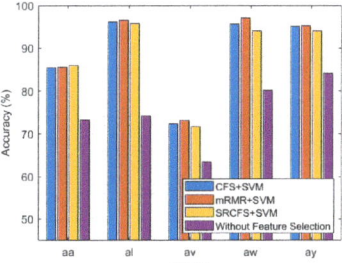 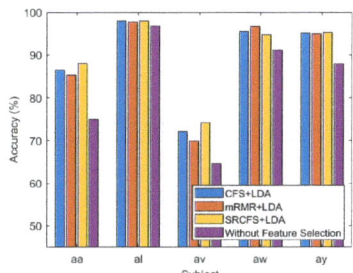 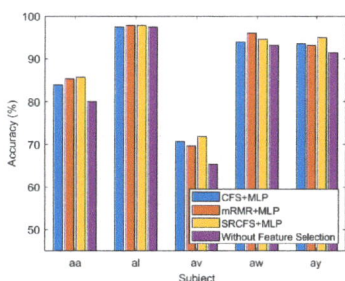

Figure 3. The motor imagery (MI) classification performance comparison among CFS, mRMR, SRCFS feature selection methods and without feature selection. The left, middle, and right subplots represent the accuracies of different subjects for the BCI III-IVA dataset, where SVM, LDA, and MLP classifier has been used, respectively.

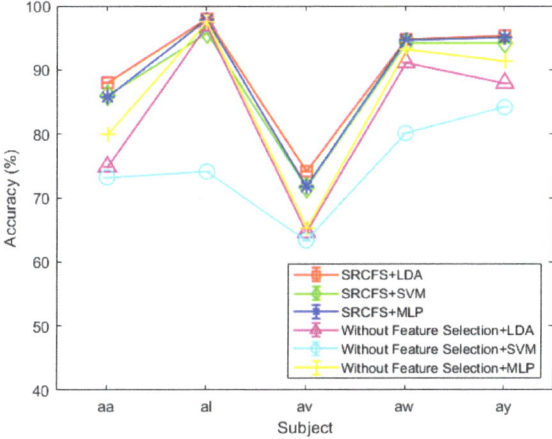

Figure 4. The motor imagery classification performance comparison between LDA, SVM, and MLP classifier using SRCFS feature selection method and without feature selection. The figure represents the accuracies of different subjects for the BCI III-IVA dataset.

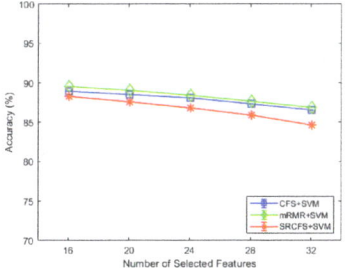 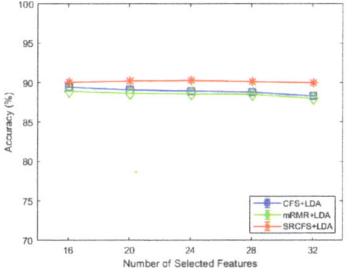 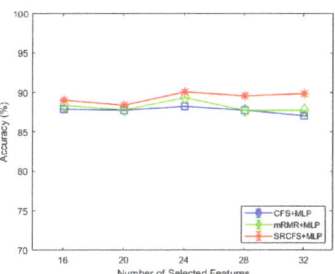

Figure 5. The motor imagery classification performance comparison using CFS, mRMR, and SRCFS feature selection methods with SVM, LDA, and MLP classifiers for different numbers of selected features. The left, middle, and right subplots represent the accuracies of the BCI III-IVA dataset for different numbers of features (50% to 100%) selected by the feature selection algorithm where SVM, LDA and MLP classifiers have been used.

5.3. Performance Result with BCI Competition III Dataset IIIB

Figure 6 demonstrates the performance comparison of different feature selection methods with SVM, LDA, and MLP classifiers, respectively. These figures show that the SRCFS feature selection method's performance is stable. This dataset has been used to verify the extensive generalizability property of our proposed method.

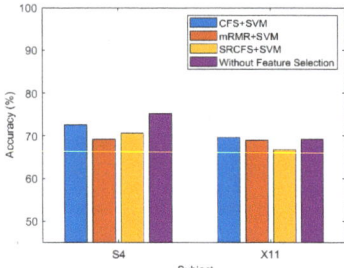 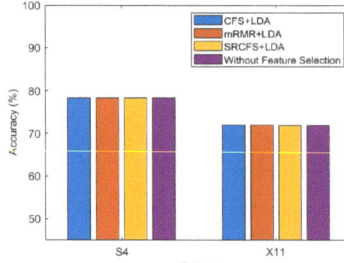 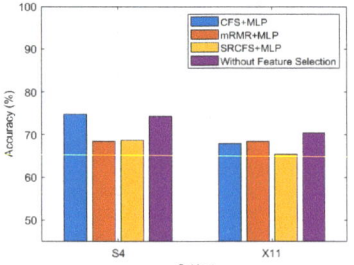

Figure 6. The motor imagery (MI) classification performance comparison among CFS, mRMR, SRCFS feature selection methods and without feature selection. The left, middle, and right subplots represent the accuracies of different subjects for the BCI III-III B dataset, where SVM, LDA and MLP classifier has been used, respectively.

Figure 7 demonstrates that without feature selection and SRCFS-based feature selection have similar accuracy for the dataset BCI III-III B. Due to the fewer number of channels, the dataset BCI-IIIB produced two pairs of spatial filters resulting in eight features. For low feature dimensions, SRCFS with LDA can not overcome the accuracy without feature selection. However, selecting features reduces classification complexity.

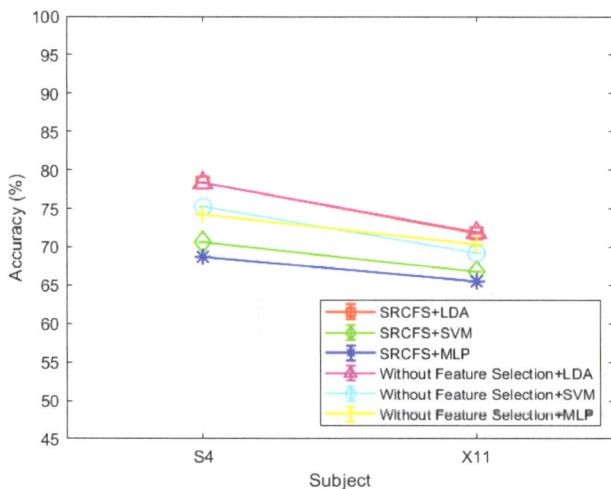

Figure 7. The motor imagery classification performance comparison between SVM, LDA, and MLP classifier using SRCFS feature selection method and without feature selection. The figure represents the accuracies of different subjects for the BCI III-IIIB dataset.

Figure 8 compares the accuracy of the proposed method with different combinations of feature selections and classifiers as a function of the number of selected features. It has been found that utilizing four well-chosen features from dataset BCI-IIIB enables the classification of objects with the highest degree of accuracy.

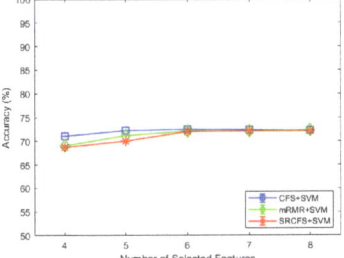 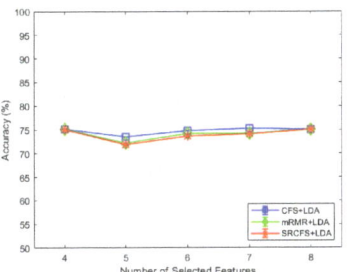 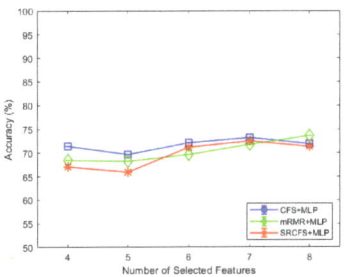

Figure 8. The motor imagery classification performance comparison using CFS, mRMR, and SRCFS feature selection methods with SVM, LDA, and MLP classifiers for different numbers of selected features. The left, middle, and right subplots represent the accuracies of for BCI III-IIIB dataset for different numbers of features (50% to 100%) selected by the feature selection algorithm where SVM, LDA, and MLP classifiers have been used.

Moreover, different statistical performance evaluation metrics have been calculated to validate the performance of our proposed method. Table 1 demonstrated the state-of-the-art comparison of the proposed model where our study achieved superiority over the competitive models. In addition,Tables 2–4 show the performance of the area under the ROC, F1 score, and computational time, respectively, of different subjects on BCI competition III dataset IVA. On the other hand, Table 5 shows the performance of AUROC, F1 score, and computational time, respectively, of different subjects on BCI competition III dataset IIIB. Here, the computational time is measured in seconds (s) and it represents the time required for training and classification of a single fold required by the classifier in a five-fold cross-validation technique. Moreover, some traditional feature selection methods like f test, random forests, and logistic lasso have also been studied. But, the performance of these methods is not further compared because of their high computational cost and low MI recognition rate. In addition, they are rarely used for MI task classification in BCI.

Furthermore, we have tested another feature selection technique named HSIC Lasso for 07 (seven) different kernels with LDA classifier using BCI competition III dataset IVA and IIIB. Since the LDA classifier performed best for our proposed method and other studied methods, we have considered this classifier for testing HSIC Lasso feature selection method in terms of AUROC, F1 score, computational time, and accuracy performance metrics. From our experimental results, it is shown that the performance of the HSIC Lasso with the best kernel ADMM is almost similar to mRMR for BCI Competition III dataset IVA, the accuracy of both HSIC Lasso and mRMR is 88.93 % and the performance of the mRMR is better than HSIC Lasso for BCI Competition III dataset IIIB, the accuracy of the mRMR and HSIC Lasso are 75.17% and 69.91%, respectively, in this case. Since the overall performance of HSIC Lasso is almost similar on BCI Competition III dataset IVA and slightly lower on BCI Competition III dataset IIIB compared to the proposed and other studied feature selection methods, the performance of this method is not further compared with others.

5.4. State of the Art Comparison with Previous Methods

Table 1 compares and contrasts the suggested method's classification accuracy results with those of recently developed algorithms. The proposed method's overall average classification accuracy is 90.05%. The performance of the proposed method is compared with the methods CSP-R-MF [57], R-MDRM [58], MKELM [59], and so on. It is observed that the average classification accuracy of the proposed method outperforms the other recently developed algorithm, as shown in Table 1. Table 1 demonstrated that for subjects aa, aw, and ay, the proposed method achieved the best performance.

Table 1. Performance comparison in terms of classification accuracy on BCI competition III dataset IVA of the proposed method with state-of-the-art works. The highest accuracy is marked in boldface.

Studies	Methods	Subjects					Mean ± SD
		aa	al	av	aw	ay	
Belwafi et al. [32]	WOLA-CSP	66.07	96.07	52.14	71.43	50.00	67.29
Dai et al. [38]	TKCSP	68.10	93.88	68.47	88.40	74.93	79.17
She et al. [39]	H-ELM	63.39	98.39	64.08	85.67	85.16	79.33
Park et al.[60]	SSS-CSP	74.11	**100**	67.78	90.07	89.29	84.46
Jian et al. [57]	CSP-R-MF	81.43	92.41	70.00	83.57	85.00	82.48
Selim et al. [61]	AM-BA-SVM	86.61	**100**	66.84	90.63	80.95	85.00
Singh et al. [58]	SR-MDRM	79.46	**100**	73.46	89.28	88.49	86.13
Zhang et al. [59]	MKELM	83.30	98.50	71.40	91.30	93.30	87.50
Singh et al. [62]	R-MDRM	81.25	**100**	**76.53**	87.05	91.26	87.21
Proposed Method	**SRCFS + LDA**	**88.03**	97.98	74.17	**94.76**	**95.31**	**90.05 ± 9.60**

Table 2. Performance of different studied methods in terms of area under the receiver operating characteristic curve (AUROC) on BCI competition III dataset IVA for each of the five subjects, the best result is marked in boldface.

Feature Selection Methods and Classifiers	AUROC				
	aa	al	av	aw	ay
CFS + SVM	0.9306	0.9922	0.8297	0.9836	0.9826
mRMR + SVM	0.9205	0.9936	0.7916	0.9921	0.9796
SRCFS + SVM	0.9242	0.9881	0.7513	0.9717	0.9823
CFS + LDA	0.9030	0.9911	0.7743	0.9914	0.9821
mRMR + LDA	0.9363	**0.9968**	0.7530	0.9929	0.9838
SRCFS + LDA	**0.9356**	0.9918	0.8072	**0.9905**	**0.9861**
CFS + MLP	0.9135	0.9944	0.8115	0.9802	0.9731
mRMR + MLP	0.9192	0.9892	0.7664	0.9795	0.9621
SRCFS + MLP	0.9263	0.9972	**0.8137**	0.9864	0.9844

Table 3. Performance of different studied methods in terms of F1 score on BCI competition III dataset IVA for each of the five subjects, the best result is marked in boldface.

Feature Selection Methods and Classifiers	F1 Score				
	aa	al	av	aw	ay
CFS + SVM	0.8593	0.9638	0.7287	0.9534	0.9534
mRMR + SVM	0.8364	0.9712	0.7015	0.9606	**0.9568**
SRCFS + SVM	0.8571	0.9562	0.6512	0.9187	0.9391
CFS + LDA	0.8470	0.9825	0.7000	0.9568	0.9373
mRMR + LDA	0.8582	0.9788	0.7254	**0.9677**	0.9373
SRCFS + LDA	**0.8633**	0.9789	0.7317	0.9496	0.9489
CFS + MLP	0.8443	0.9753	0.7092	0.9386	0.9353
mRMR + MLP	0.8520	0.9788	0.6886	0.9603	0.9304
SRCFS + MLP	0.8592	0.9787	0.7285	0.9458	0.9500

From Tables 1–4, it is clearly depicted that the SRCFS and LDA-based MI tasks classification system is robust and effective in terms of the performance metrics: accuracy, AUROC, F1 score, and computational time for BCI competition III dataset IVA. On the other hand, Table 5 shows that the computational time of the SRCFS and LDA-based system is low compared to others for the BCI competition III dataset IIIB dataset. It is also observed that the MLP classifier is more computationally costly than the others. From the above discussion, we can conclude that the SRCFS feature selection method with LDA classifier is undoubtedly a robust and effective system for MI tasks classification using EEG signal.

Table 4. Performance of different studied methods in terms of computational time on BCI competition III dataset IVA for each of the five subjects, the best result is marked in boldface.

Feature Selection Methods and Classifiers	Computational Time (s)				
	aa	al	av	aw	ay
CFS + SVM	0.1804	0.0133	0.0085	0.0082	0.0090
mRMR + SVM	0.1582	0.0137	0.0091	0.0087	0.0089
SRCFS + SVM	0.1573	0.0154	0.0087	0.0088	0.0087
CFS + LDA	0.1857	0.0133	**0.0074**	0.0101	0.0096
mRMR + LDA	0.1683	**0.0127**	0.0080	0.0082	0.0077
SRCFS + LDA	**0.1642**	0.0134	0.0079	**0.0075**	**0.0073**
CFS + MLP	0.7557	0.1970	0.1480	0.1629	0.2056
mRMR + MLP	0.8339	0.3850	0.1699	0.1936	0.2653
SRCFS + MLP	0.7235	0.2497	0.1937	0.2041	0.2471

Table 5. Performance of different studied methods in terms of AUROC, F1 score, and computational time (Com. Time) on BCI competition III dataset IIIB for each of the two subjects, the best result is marked in boldface.

Feature Selection Methods and Classifiers	Evaluation Metrics					
	AUROC		F1 Score		Com. Time (s)	
	S4	X11	S4	X11	S4	X11
CFS + SVM	**0.8379**	0.7567	0.7430	0.6640	0.2093	0.0149
mRMR + SVM	0.7670	0.7488	0.6863	0.6402	0.1819	0.0143
SRCFS + SVM	0.7916	0.7236	0.7188	0.6439	0.1866	0.0147
CFS + LDA	0.7811	**0.7638**	0.6965	**0.6992**	0.2040	0.0115
mRMR + LDA	0.7384	0.7481	0.6704	0.6732	0.1860	0.0115
SRCFS + LDA	0.8054	0.7552	0.7431	0.6922	**0.1675**	**0.0108**
CFS + MLP	0.8216	0.7482	0.7395	0.6614	0.8545	0.1718
mRMR + MLP	0.7276	0.7298	0.6756	0.6654	0.7804	0.1800
SRCFS + MLP	0.7509	0.7119	0.6922	0.6504	0.8262	0.1709

6. Conclusions

Supervised and Unsupervised feature selection methods are investigated in this paper to classify motor imagery-based EEG signals. The experiment is evaluated using two publicly available BCI Competition III Dataset IVA and BCI Competition III Dataset IIIB. The multichannel EEG signal is decomposed into four subbands. Features are extracted from each subband. Then the extracted features are combined to make a high-dimensional feature vector. Not all features are important for classification. The irrelevant feature may degrade the performance of the system. The performance of the classification is improved by properly removing redundant and irrelevant characteristics from the feature vector, which increases the feature vector's discriminative power. With the given class label, the unsupervised feature selection outperforms the supervised feature selection, as demonstrated in Table 1. The key benefit of using an unsupervised feature selection method is that each sample of a feature vector does not need to have its labels provided. It chooses features by taking the relationship between feature dimensions into account. It is clear that when the feature selection method has been applied, the accuracy is increased. The combination of features also plays a vital role. As shown in Table 1, the proposed combination of full band and subband signals and the use of the feature selection strategy improve the MI classification accuracy. It can be expanded to include multiclass MI classification issues in the BCI paradigm and we will study more feature selection methods and classifiers in future work.

Author Contributions: Conceptualization, M.H.K., S.M. and A.A.S.; methodology, M.H.K. and S.M.; software, M.H.K. and S.M.; validation, M.H.K. and S.M.; formal analysis, M.H.K., A.S.M.M., J.S. and M.K.I.M.; investigation, M.H.K. and S.M.; data curation, M.H.K., S.M. and A.S.M.M.; writing—original draft preparation, M.H.K., S.M. and A.A.S.; writing—review and editing, M.H.K.; A.S.M.M., J.S. and M.K.I.M.; visualization, M.H.K. and S.M.; supervision, M.K.I.M. and J.S.; funding acquisition, J.S. All authors have read and agreed to the published version of the manuscript.

Funding: This work was partly supported by the Competitive Research Fund of The University of Aizu, Japan.

Data Availability Statement: The proposed model is evaluated with two benchmark datasets, namely BCI Competition III dataset IVA and dataset IIIB, which are publicly available. The dataset links are provided below, https://www.bbci.de/competition/iii/#data_set_iva; https://www.bbci.de/competition/iii/#data_set_iiib.

Acknowledgments: This paper is a part of a project supported by Bangamata Sheikh Fojilatunnesa Mujib Science & Technology University, Jamalpur 2012, Bangladesh.

Conflicts of Interest: The authors declare no conflict of interest.

Abbreviations

BCI	Brain-Computer Interface
EEG	Electroencephalography
MEG	Magnetoencephalogram
fMRI	Functional Magnetic Response Imaging
MI	Motor Imagery
SSVEP	Steady-State Visual-Evoked Potential
SVM	support vector machines
MLP	Multi-layer Perceptron
LDA	Linear Discriminant Analysis
AAR	Adaptive Autoregressive
CSP	Common Spatial Pattern
NCA	Neighbourhood Component Analysis
PCA	Principal Component Analysis
CSP	Common Spatial Pattern
CFS	Correlation-Based Feature Selection
mRMR	Minimum Redundancy and Maximum Relevance
SRCFS	Multi-Subspace Randomization and Collaboration-Based Unsupervised Feature Selection
GCN	Graph Convolutional Network
GRACES	Graph Convolutional Network Feature Selector

ERD	Event-Related Desynchronization
ERS	Event-Related Synchronization
GED	Graph Eigen Decomposition
HSIC	Hilbert-Schmidt Independence Criterion
Lasso	Least Absolute Shrinkage and Selection Operator
BAHSIC	Backward Elimination Hilbert-Schmidt Independence Criterion
CCM	Conditional Covariance Minimization
MML	Meta Machine Learning
VR	Virtual Reality
HDLSS	High-Dimensional and Low-Sample Size

References

1. Molla, M.K.I.; Saha, S.K.; Yasmin, S.; Islam, M.R.; Shin, J. Trial regeneration with subband signals for motor imagery classification in BCI paradigm. *IEEE Access* **2021**, *9*, 7632–7642. [CrossRef]
2. Yang, L.; Song, Y.; Ma, K.; Xie, L. Motor imagery EEG decoding method based on a discriminative feature learning strategy. *IEEE Trans. Neural Syst. Rehabil. Eng.* **2021**, *29*, 368–379. [CrossRef] [PubMed]
3. Stegman, P.; Crawford, C.S.; Andujar, M.; Nijholt, A.; Gilbert, J.E. Brain-Computer Interface Software: A Review and Discussion. *IEEE Trans. Hum.-Mach. Syst.* **2020**, *50*, 101–115. [CrossRef]
4. Miah, A.S.M.; Shin, J.; Islam, M.M.; Molla, M.K.I.; Abdullah. Natural Human Emotion Recognition Based on Various Mixed Reality (MR) Games and Electroencephalography (EEG) Signals. In Proceedings of the 2022 IEEE 5th Eurasian Conference on Educational Innovation (ECEI) IEEE, Taipei, Taiwan, 10–12 February 2022; pp. 408–411.
5. Miah, A.S.M.; Shin, J.; Hasan, M.A.M.; Molla, M.K.I.; Okuyama, Y.; Tomioka, Y. Movie Oriented Positive Negative Emotion Classification from EEG Signal using Wavelet transformation and Machine learning Approaches. In Proceedings of the 2022 IEEE 15th International Symposium on Embedded Multicore/Many-Core Systems-on-Chip (MCSoC) IEEE, Penang, Malaysia, 19–22 December 2022; pp. 26–31.
6. Miah, A.S.M.; Mouly, M.A.; Debnath, C.; Shin, J.; Bari, S.S. Event-Related Potential Classification based on EEG data using xDWAN with MDM and KNN. In Proceedings of the Computing Science, Communication and Security: Second International Conference, COMS2 2021, Gujarat, India, 6–7 February 2021; Revised Selected Papers; Springer: Berlin/Heidelberg, Germany, 2021; pp. 112–126.
7. Zobaed, T.; Ahmed, S.R.A.; Miah, A.S.M.; Binta, S.M.; Ahmed, M.R.A.; Rashid, M. Real time sleep onset detection from single channel EEG signal using block sample entropy. *IOP Conf. Ser. Mater. Sci. Eng.* **2020**, *928*, 032021. [CrossRef]
8. Wang, Y.; Nakanishi, M.; Zhang, D. EEG-based brain-computer interfaces. In *Neural Interface: Frontiers and Applications*; Springer: Singapore, 2019; pp. 41–65.
9. Sun, B.; Zhang, H.; Wu, Z.; Zhang, Y.; Li, T. Adaptive spatiotemporal graph convolutional networks for motor imagery classification. *IEEE Signal Process. Lett.* **2021**, *28*, 219–223. [CrossRef]
10. Georgiadis, K.; Adamos, D.A.; Nikolopoulos, S.; Laskaris, N.; Kompatsiaris, I. A graph-theoretic sensor-selection scheme for covariance-based Motor Imagery (MI) decoding. In Proceedings of the 2020 28th European Signal Processing Conference (EUSIPCO) IEEE, Amsterdam, The Netherlands, 18–21 January 2021; pp. 1234–1238.
11. Akter, M.S.; Islam, M.R.; Tanaka, T.; Iimura, Y.; Mitsuhashi, T.; Sugano, H.; Wang, D.; Molla, M.K.I. Statistical features in high-frequency bands of interictal iEEG work efficiently in identifying the seizure onset zone in patients with focal epilepsy. *Entropy* **2020**, *22*, 1415. [CrossRef] [PubMed]
12. Nuyujukian, P.; Fan, J.M.; Kao, J.C.; Ryu, S.I.; Shenoy, K.V. A high-performance keyboard neural prosthesis enabled by task optimization. *IEEE Trans. Biomed. Eng.* **2014**, *62*, 21–29. [CrossRef] [PubMed]
13. Lotte, F.; Bougrain, L.; Cichocki, A.; Clerc, M.; Congedo, M.; Rakotomamonjy, A.; Yger, F. A review of classification algorithms for EEG-based brain–computer interfaces: A 10 year update. *J. Neural Eng.* **2018**, *15*, 031005. [CrossRef]
14. Miah, A.S.M.; Islam, M.R.; Molla, M.K.I. EEG classification for MI-BCI using CSP with averaging covariance matrices: An experimental study. In Proceedings of the 2019 International Conference on Computer, Communication, Chemical, Materials and Electronic Engineering (IC4ME2) IEEE, Rajshahi, Bangladesh, 11–12 July 2019; pp. 1–5.
15. Higashi, H.; Tanaka, T. Common spatio-time-frequency patterns for motor imagery-based brain machine interfaces. *Comput. Intell. Neurosci.* **2013**, *2013*, 8. [CrossRef]
16. McFarland, D.J.; Miner, L.A.; Vaughan, T.M.; Wolpaw, J.R. Mu and beta rhythm topographies during motor imagery and actual movements. *Brain Topogr.* **2000**, *12*, 177–186. [CrossRef]
17. Dornhege, G.; Blankertz, B.; Curio, G.; Muller, K.R. Boosting bit rates in noninvasive EEG single-trial classifications by feature combination and multiclass paradigms. *IEEE Trans. Biomed. Eng.* **2004**, *51*, 993–1002. [CrossRef] [PubMed]
18. Ramoser, H.; Muller-Gerking, J.; Pfurtscheller, G. Optimal spatial filtering of single trial EEG during imagined hand movement. *IEEE Trans. Rehabil. Eng.* **2000**, *8*, 441–446. [CrossRef] [PubMed]
19. Luo, J.; Wang, J.; Xu, R.; Xu, K. Class discrepancy-guided sub-band filter-based common spatial pattern for motor imagery classification. *J. Neurosci. Methods* **2019**, *323*, 98–107. [CrossRef] [PubMed]

20. Udhaya Kumar, S.; Hannah Inbarani, H. PSO-based feature selection and neighborhood rough set-based classification for BCI multiclass motor imagery task. *Neural Comput. Appl.* **2017**, *28*, 3239–3258. [CrossRef]
21. Dy, J.G.; Brodley, C.E. Feature selection for unsupervised learning. *J. Mach. Learn. Res.* **2004**, *5*, 845–889.
22. Song, L.; Smola, A.; Gretton, A.; Borgwardt, K.M.; Bedo, J. Supervised feature selection via dependence estimation. In Proceedings of the 24th International Conference on Machine Learning, Corvalis, OR, USA, 20–24 June 2007; pp. 823–830.
23. Goldberger, J.; Hinton, G.E.; Roweis, S.; Salakhutdinov, R.R. Neighbourhood components analysis. In *Advances in Neural Information Processing Systems 17*; NeurIPS: San Diego, CA, USA, 2004.
24. Zifkin, B.G.; Avanzini, G. Clinical neurophysiology with special reference to the electroencephalogram. *Epilepsia* **2009**, *50*, 30–38. [CrossRef]
25. Mahmood, S.; Shin, J.; Farhana, I.; Islam, M.R.; Molla, M.K.I. Frequency Recognition of Short-Time SSVEP Signal Using CORRCA-Based Spatio-Spectral Feature Fusion Framework. *IEEE Access* **2021**, *9*, 167744–167755. [CrossRef]
26. Wolpaw, J.R.; Birbaumer, N.; Heetderks, W.J.; McFarland, D.J.; Peckham, P.H.; Schalk, G.; Donchin, E.; Quatrano, L.A.; Robinson, C.J.; Vaughan, T.M.; et al. Brain-computer interface technology: A review of the first international meeting. *IEEE Trans. Rehabil. Eng.* **2000**, *8*, 164–173. [CrossRef]
27. Pfurtscheller, G.; Neuper, C.; Schlogl, A.; Lugger, K. Separability of EEG signals recorded during right and left motor imagery using adaptive autoregressive parameters. *IEEE Trans. Rehabil. Eng.* **1998**, *6*, 316–325. [CrossRef]
28. Joy, M.M.H.; Hasan, M.; Miah, A.S.M.; Ahmed, A.; Tofha, S.A.; Bhuaiyan, M.F.I.; Zannat, A.; Rashid, M.M. Multiclass MI-Task Classification Using Logistic Regression and Filter Bank Common Spatial Patterns. In Proceedings of the Computing Science, Communication and Security, Gujarat, India, 26–27 March 2020; pp. 160–170.
29. Pfurtscheller, G.; Da Silva, F.L. Event-related EEG/MEG synchronization and desynchronization: basic principles. *Clin. Neurophysiol.* **1999**, *110*, 1842–1857. [CrossRef]
30. Pfurtscheller, G.; Pregenzer, M.; Neuper, C. Visualization of sensorimotor areas involved in preparation for hand movement based on classification of μ and central β rhythms in single EEG trials in man. *Neurosci. Lett.* **1994**, *181*, 43–46. [CrossRef] [PubMed]
31. Ang, K.K.; Chin, Z.Y.; Zhang, H.; Guan, C. Filter bank common spatial pattern (FBCSP) in brain-computer interface. In Proceedings of the 2008 IEEE International Joint Conference on Neural Networks (IEEE World Congress on Computational Intelligence) IEEE, Padua, Italy, 18–23 July 2008; pp. 2390–2397.
32. Belwafi, K.; Romain, O.; Gannouni, S.; Ghaffari, F.; Djemal, R.; Ouni, B. An embedded implementation based on adaptive filter bank for brain–computer interface systems. *J. Neurosci. Methods* **2018**, *305*, 1–16. [CrossRef] [PubMed]
33. Molla, M.K.I.; Hassan, K.M.; Islam, M.R.; Tanaka, T. Graph eigen decomposition-based feature-selection method for epileptic seizure detection using electroencephalography. *Sensors* **2020**, *20*, 4639. [CrossRef] [PubMed]
34. Siuly; Li, Y.; Wen, P. Identification of motor imagery tasks through CC–LR algorithm in brain computer interface. *Int. J. Bioinform. Res. Appl.* **2013**, *9*, 156–172. [CrossRef]
35. Ali, S.; Ferdous, J.; Hamid, E.; Molla, K.I. A novel features selection approach with common spatial pattern for EEG based brain–computer interface implementation. *IETE J. Res.* **2022**, *68*, 1757–1771. [CrossRef]
36. Kevric, J.; Subasi, A. Comparison of signal decomposition methods in classification of EEG signals for motor-imagery BCI system. *Biomed. Signal Process. Control* **2017**, *31*, 398–406. [CrossRef]
37. Chaudhary, S.; Taran, S.; Bajaj, V.; Siuly, S. A flexible analytic wavelet transform based approach for motor-imagery tasks classification in BCI applications. *Comput. Methods Programs Biomed.* **2020**, *187*, 105325. [CrossRef]
38. Dai, M.; Zheng, D.; Liu, S.; Zhang, P. Transfer kernel common spatial patterns for motor imagery brain-computer interface classification. *Comput. Math. Methods Med.* **2018**, *2018*, 9871603. [CrossRef]
39. She, Q.; Chen, K.; Ma, Y.; Nguyen, T.; Zhang, Y. Sparse representation-based extreme learning machine for motor imagery EEG classification. *Comput. Intell. Neurosci.* **2018**, *2018*, 9593682. [CrossRef]
40. Chen, J.; Stern, M.; Wainwright, M.J.; Jordan, M.I. Kernel feature selection via conditional covariance minimization. In *Advances in Neural Information Processing Systems 30*; NeurIPS: San Diego, CA, USA, 2017.
41. Constantinopoulos, C.; Titsias, M.K.; Likas, A. Bayesian feature and model selection for Gaussian mixture models. *IEEE Trans. Pattern Anal. Mach. Intell.* **2006**, *28*, 1013–1018. [CrossRef]
42. Chen, C.; Weiss, S.T.; Liu, Y.Y. Graph Convolutional Network-based Feature Selection for High-dimensional and Low-sample Size Data. *arXiv* **2022**, arXiv:2211.14144.
43. Molla, M.K.I.; Al Shiam, A.; Islam, M.R.; Tanaka, T. Discriminative feature selection-based motor imagery classification using EEG signal. *IEEE Access* **2020**, *8*, 98255–98265. [CrossRef]
44. Blankertz, B.; Muller, K.R.; Curio, G.; Vaughan, TM.; Schalk, G.; Wolpaw, JR.; Schlogl, A.; Neuper, C.; Pfurtscheller, G.; Hinterberger, T.; Schroder, M. The BCI competition 2003: Progress and perspectives in detection and discrimination of EEG single trials *IEEE Trans. Biomed. Eng.* **2004**, *51*, 1044–1051. [CrossRef] [PubMed]
45. Galán, F.; Oliva, F.; Guàrdia, J., III. BCI Competition III. Dataset V: Algorithm Description. 2005. Available online: http://www.bbci.de/competition/iii/results/martigny/FerranGalan_desc.pdf (accessed on 13 October 2018).
46. Miah, A.S.M.; Ahmed, S.R.A.; Ahmed, M.R.; Bayat, O.; Duru, A.D.; Molla, M.K.I. Motor-Imagery BCI task classification using riemannian geometry and averaging with mean absolute deviation. In Proceedings of the 2019 Scientific Meeting on Electrical-Electronics & Biomedical Engineering and Computer Science (EBBT) IEEE, Istanbul, Turkey, 24–26 April 2019; pp. 1–7.

47. Miah, A.S.M.; Islam, M.R.; Molla, M.K.I. Motor imagery classification using subband tangent space mapping. In Proceedings of the 2017 20th International Conference of Computer and Information Technology (ICCIT) IEEE, Dhaka, Bangladesh, 22–14 December 2017; pp. 1–5.
48. Gaur, P.; Gupta, H.; Chowdhury, A.; McCreadie, K.;Pachori, R.B. A Sliding Window Common Spatial Pattern for Enhancing Motor Imagery Classification in EEG-BCI. *IEEE Trans. Instrum. Meas.* **2021**, *70*, 1–9. [CrossRef]
49. Saha, S.K.; Sarker, P.K.; Abdullah Al Shiam, M.; Rahoman, M. Motor Imagery EEG Signal Classification Using MWT-CSP for Online BCI Implementation. *Int. J. Comput. Sci. Inf. Secur. (IJCSIS)* **2020**, *18*, 124–130.
50. Yamada, M.; Jitkrittum, W.; Sigal, L.; Xing, E.P.; Sugiyama, M. High-dimensional feature selection by feature-wise kernelized lasso. *Neural Comput.* **2014**, *26*, 185–207. [CrossRef]
51. Zhao, Z.; Anand, R.; Wang, M. Maximum relevance and minimum redundancy feature selection methods for a marketing machine learning platform. In Proceedings of the 2019 IEEE International Conference on Data Science and Advanced Analytics (DSAA) IEEE, Washington, DC, USA, 5–8 October 2019; pp. 442–452.
52. Liu, T.; Jiang, H.; Chen, Q. Input features and parameters optimization improved the prediction accuracy of support vector regression models based on colorimetric sensor data for detection of aflatoxin B1 in corn. *Microchem. J.* **2022**, *178*, 107407. [CrossRef]
53. Hearst, M.A.; Dumais, S.T.; Osuna, E.; Platt, J.; Scholkopf, B. Support vector machines. *IEEE Intell. Syst. Their Appl.* **1998**, *13*, 18–28. [CrossRef]
54. Izenman, A. Linear Discriminant Analysis. In *Modern Multivariate Statistical Techniques*; Springer: New York, NY, USA, 2013; pp. 237–280.
55. Sánchez-Reolid, R.; García, A.S.; Vicente-Querol, M.A.; Fernández-Aguilar, L.; López, M.T.; Fernández-Caballero, A.; González, P. Artificial neural networks to assess emotional states from brain-computer interface. *Electronics* **2018**, *7*, 384. [CrossRef]
56. He, Y.; Lu, Z.; Wang, J.; Ying, S.; Shi, J. A Self-Supervised Learning Based Channel Attention MLP-Mixer Network for Motor Imagery Decoding. *IEEE Trans. Neural Syst. Rehabil. Eng.* **2022**, *30*, 2406–2417. [CrossRef]
57. Feng, J.K.; Jin, J.; Daly, I.; Zhou, J.; Niu, Y.; Wang, X.; Cichocki, A. An optimized channel selection method based on multifrequency CSP-rank for motor imagery-based BCI system. *Comput. Intell. Neurosci.* **2019**, *2019*, 8068357. [CrossRef] [PubMed]
58. Singh, A.; Lal, S.; Guesgen, H.W. Reduce calibration time in motor imagery using spatially regularized symmetric positives-definite matrices based classification. *Sensors* **2019**, *19*, 379. [CrossRef] [PubMed]
59. Zhang, Y.; Wang, Y.; Zhou, G.; Jin, J.; Wang, B.; Wang, X.; Cichocki, A. Multi-kernel extreme learning machine for EEG classification in brain-computer interfaces. *Expert Syst. Appl.* **2018**, *96*, 302–310. [CrossRef]
60. Park, Y.; Chung, W. BCI classification using locally generated CSP features. In Proceedings of the 2018 6th International Conference on Brain-Computer Interface (BCI) IEEE, Gangwon, Republic of Korea, 15–17 January 2018; pp. 1–4.
61. Selim, S.; Tantawi, M.M.; Shedeed, H.A.; Badr, A. A csp\am-ba-svm approach for motor imagery bci system. *IEEE Access* **2018**, *6*, 49192–49208. [CrossRef]
62. Singh, A.; Lal, S.; Guesgen, H.W. Small sample motor imagery classification using regularized Riemannian features. *IEEE Access* **2019**, *7*, 46858–46869. [CrossRef]

Disclaimer/Publisher's Note: The statements, opinions and data contained in all publications are solely those of the individual author(s) and contributor(s) and not of MDPI and/or the editor(s). MDPI and/or the editor(s) disclaim responsibility for any injury to people or property resulting from any ideas, methods, instructions or products referred to in the content.

Article

Generating Representative Phrase Sets for Text Entry Experiments by GA-Based Text Corpora Sampling

Sandi Ljubic [1,2,*] **and Alen Salkanovic** [1,2,]

[1] University of Rijeka, Faculty of Engineering, Vukovarska 58, HR-51000 Rijeka, Croatia; alen.salkanovic@riteh.hr

[2] Center for Artificial Intelligence and Cybersecurity, University of Rijeka, R. Matejcic 2, HR-51000 Rijeka, Croatia

* Correspondence: sandi.ljubic@riteh.hr

Abstract: In the field of human–computer interaction (HCI), text entry methods can be evaluated through controlled user experiments or predictive modeling techniques. While the modeling approach requires a language model, the empirical approach necessitates representative text phrases for the experimental stimuli. In this context, finding a phrase set with the best language representativeness belongs to the class of optimization problems in which a solution is sought in a large search space. We propose a genetic algorithm (GA)-based method for extracting a target phrase set from the available text corpus, optimizing its language representativeness. Kullback–Leibler divergence is utilized to evaluate candidates, considering the digram probability distributions of both the source corpus and the target sample. The proposed method is highly customizable, outperforms typical random sampling, and exhibits language independence. The representative phrase sets generated by the proposed solution facilitate a more valid comparison of the results from different text entry studies. The open source implementation enables the easy customization of the GA-based sampling method, promotes its immediate utilization, and facilitates the reproducibility of this study. In addition, we provide heuristic guidelines for preparing the text entry experiments, which consider the experiment's intended design and the phrase set to be generated with the proposed solution.

Keywords: text entry; phrase sets; text corpus sampling; genetic algorithm; Kullback–Leibler divergence

MSC: 68W50

Citation: Ljubic, S.; Salkanovic, A. Generating Representative Phrase Sets for Text Entry Experiments by GA-Based Text Corpora Sampling. *Mathematics* **2023**, *11*, 2550. https://doi.org/10.3390/math11112550

Academic Editors: Grigoreta-Sofia Cojocar, Adriana-Mihaela Guran and Laura-Silvia Dioşan

Received: 20 March 2023
Revised: 23 May 2023
Accepted: 30 May 2023
Published: 1 June 2023

Copyright: © 2023 by the authors. Licensee MDPI, Basel, Switzerland. This article is an open access article distributed under the terms and conditions of the Creative Commons Attribution (CC BY) license (https://creativecommons.org/licenses/by/4.0/).

1. Introduction

Text entry has been a significant area of research in human–computer interaction (HCI) since its inception, driven by the increasing need for office automation. This trend has continued in modern mobile computing, where text entry occurs on various devices using different interaction techniques. Touchscreen-based technology is now a platform of particular interest, as it enables the development of innovative software-based keyboard solutions. Various keyboard customizations, automatic adjustments, character layouts, and input assistance methods are being introduced to enhance convenience, reduce errors, improve efficiency, and ensure accessibility for all users.

New text entry methods are usually evaluated in controlled user experiments that focus on input speed and error rates as output metrics. In such an experimental approach, text-copy tasks requiring that users transcribe the provided phrases are favored over text-creation tasks, which assume the free input of arbitrary text [1].

While preselected phrases are commonly used as control stimuli in text entry experiments, there is currently no formally standardized phrase set that can serve as a reference. Kristensson and Vertanen [2] argue that choosing an appropriate phrase set may be important not only for the internal validity of the experimental research but also for its reproducibility, the heterogeneity of the study, and the external validity of the results.

Different ad hoc generated phrase sets make systematic review and comparison with the previously published results of text entry studies difficult. External validity requires conclusions that can be generalized to contexts outside the laboratory. This is difficult to achieve if the phrase sets do not adequately represent the domain or language in question.

There have been some notable attempts to create commonly accepted phrase sets. While we mention the major efforts in Section 1.1, this paper focuses on creating a representative phrase set from a single, presumably large, and pre-existing text corpus.

Predictive modeling is another way to evaluate text entry methods. It is an alternative to the empirical approach, which does not necessitate explicit testing with real users. Soukoreff and MacKenzie [3] presented a quantitative prediction technique that combines both a motion and a linguistic model:

$$WPM_{max} = \frac{1}{\sum_{i \in \mathbb{C}} \sum_{j \in \mathbb{C}} (P_{ij} \cdot MT_{ij})} \cdot \frac{60}{5} \tag{1}$$

While the movement model aims to predict the time MT_{ij} required to enter a character j preceded by a previously entered character i, the linguistic model uses digram frequencies in a given language (with the character set $\mathbb{C}$), resulting in computed occurrence probabilities P_{ij} for each digram. These models are combined to develop a prediction for the average number of characters entered per second, and thus for the theoretical upper limit of text entry speed WPM_{max} (WPM here stands for words per minute). This approach generally uses a variation of the Fitts's law [4] to predict the movement time between two consecutive keys, leading to the following formalization:

$$MT_{ij} = a + b \cdot \log_2 \left(\frac{A_{ij}}{W_j} + 1 \right) \tag{2}$$

Equation (2) shows that the predicted time MT_{ij} depends on A_{ij}—the distance between the center of key i and the center of key j; and W_j—the width of the target key. The coefficients a and b are constants obtained by linear regression.

The predictive modeling of text entry efficiency based on Fitts's law and the digram probability distribution has been successfully applied in several domains, including the development of various keyboards and input devices [3,5,6] and in target languages other than English [7,8]. This approach proved particularly important for modeling text entry methods that rely on a single pointing device.

The practical utility of Fitts's law in modeling text input is why we focus on the digram-based statistical properties of input text. Namely, predictive modeling results are often compared to the empirically obtained outcomes in text entry research. In this context, it is helpful to use the digram distribution to develop representative phrase sets for experiments since, as shown above, the same digram statistics are also used in the predictive modeling process. Therefore, our main goal is to develop an efficient method for extracting phrase sets from existing large corpora with the following subtasks:

- When searching for the "most representative" phrase set by sampling from a text corpus of a given language, representativeness should be considered as a function of the digram probability distribution;
- The proposed sampling procedure should outperform existing methods;
- A proof-of-concept should be demonstrated for several different languages.

1.1. Related Work

This subsection describes publicly available phrase sets that have already been considered a resource in text entry research. The main features are described for each phrase set, and the development process in those cases where the design procedure is known.

MacKenzie and Soukoreff [9] published a phrase set of 500 English sentences described as "moderate in length, easy to remember, and representative of the target language". As a metric for representativeness, the authors used the correlation coefficient between the distribution of individual letters in their phrase set and the letter frequencies previously derived by Mayzner and Tresselt [10]. Thus, the representativeness of this phrase set is derived from an outdated source of 20,000 words, which is an undersized sample compared to contemporary text corpora. Nonetheless, the corresponding phrase set has been used by many researchers, even in the mobile text entry domain. However, the phrases provided are unlikely to match well with text written in actual mobile messaging.

The AAC Research Group at the University of Nebraska [11] published several vocabulary lists and context-specific messages. The latter represents a collection of short conversational phrases suggested by AAC specialists that can be used as stimuli in text entry experiments. The phrases are categorized according to context, e.g., conversation control phrases, communication repairs/corrections, location markers, temporal markers, and social comments. It seems reasonable to use this set when a text entry experiment replicates a particular context of a written conversation. However, the representativeness of the language was not considered in the development of this phrase set.

Paek and Hsu [12] presented a method for generating phrase sets by randomly selecting n-grams, i.e., phrases with n words, from a large corpus, choosing the set with the digram probability distribution closest to the digram probability distribution of the source corpus. Hence, they proposed "a more mathematically principled method" based on the notion of representativeness on information theory. To compare the digram probability distributions between the source corpus and the target phrase set, they used relative entropy—also known as Kullback–Leibler divergence (KLD):

$$D(p||q) = \sum_{x \in \mathbb{C} \times \mathbb{C}} \left(p(x) \cdot \log_2 \frac{p(x)}{q(x)} \right) \quad (3)$$

In Equation (3), $p(x)$ gives the probability distribution of character digrams for a sample phrase set, and $q(x)$ is the probability distribution of character digrams for the source corpus. At the same time, $\mathbb{C}$ represents the set of characters in a given language. Paek and Hsu, in interpreting relative entropy, state that it is not a true "distance metric" since it is neither symmetric nor satisfies the triangle inequality [13]. However, since it is always non-negative and only equals zero when $p(x)$ and $q(x)$ are identical, one can argue that the phrase set is more representative of the source corpus when the relative entropy is closer to zero. The single sampling trial from the authors' proposed procedure is shown in Figure 1.

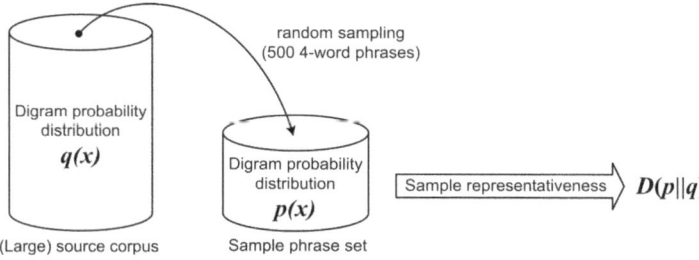

Figure 1. A phrase set sampling method by Paek and Hsu [12]. The sample is randomly generated from the source corpus, and its representativeness is calculated using the relative entropy based on the respective digram distributions.

Paek and Hsu used a predetermined number of random samples to find the most representative phrase set. They targeted four-word phrases only, regardless of whether they formed a meaningful sentence. In addition, phrase duplicates were allowed to remain in the phrase set. The phrase set generated from the Enron Email corpus [14] was made publicly available.

Vertanen and Kristensson [15] focused on mobile text entry and the memorability of the provided phrases. Their primary text resource was the Enron Email corpus, but only messages written on mobile devices were used for further analysis. The authors enriched each phrase in this dataset with memorability, expected input speed, and error rate information. This information was obtained empirically by conducting crowdsourcing experiments in which actual users performed text-memorization and text-copy tasks. The authors published five sets of 40 phrases for evaluations where memorable text was required. In addition, they created four phrase sets that are recommended when representativeness is desired instead. In their search for representative phrase sets, they used the procedure described by Paek and Hsu [12]. However, they modified it slightly to discard n-grams in the middle of the sentence, thus only obtaining intelligible phrases. They restricted their phrase sets to sentences with 3–9 words.

In their continued effort to provide phrase sets for mobile text entry, Kristensson and Vertanen [2] analyzed the NUS SMS corpus [16]—a publicly available collection of actual SMS messages. Since the source corpus contained noise due to many meaningless messages with poor grammar, it was first appropriately filtered. The authors demonstrated that selecting a particular phrase set as a stimulus for text entry experiments makes a difference. Namely, the SMS-based phrase set proved to be significantly more error-prone due to the "strange language, abbreviations, and sentence fragments". On the other hand, using the AAC phrase set resulted in significantly higher input rates, likely due to "simple, short, and familiar phrases that avoided proper names, unusual vocabulary, and difficult grammar".

Leiva and Sanchis-Trilles [17] focused on generating sets of memorable phrases while trying to preserve the language representativeness. In doing so, they decided to model the character error rate (CER) as a function of several language-independent features to predict memorability. Statistical analysis was performed on the corpus from which the phrases were taken to ensure representativeness. The final score is assigned to each candidate phrase, favoring low CER (i.e., high memorability) and high representativeness. The proposed approach requires two different corpora: one large enough to describe the target language and one from which the phrases are selected. This method was successfully applied in [18], wherein a collection of 30 datasets for ten major languages was obtained.

Yi et al. [19] proposed a phrase set sampling procedure that emphasizes a word clarity metric based on probability theory, which indicates how likely the word is to be confused with other words. The proposed method additionally considers digram frequency and memorability. However, the proof-of-concept phrase sets were not developed from a large-text corpus but from a phrase set developed by MacKenzie and Soukoreff.

Gaines and Vertanen [20] developed a 5000-phrase set from comments on the Reddit web forum. Each phrase in this set is assigned a difficulty rating from 1 to 10. The difficulty rating is based on the character error rate, which was determined by simulations of text input. In their research, however, the authors did not consider the representativeness of a target phrase set.

Abbot et al. [21] utilized text-to-speech systems to synthesize the audio clips of all phrases from the set of MacKenzie and Soukoreff. They provided a set of 92 phrases that could be transcribed without comprehension errors. Although representativeness was not considered in this study, it is still interesting because it shows that a phrase set does not have to be strictly in the form of the text as an experimental stimulus in a text entry experiment.

In general, related work suggests that three different sampling approaches can be automated with the goal of producing phrase sets that are comparable across languages and domains:

- The random selection of phrases from available text corpora where representativeness is not explicitly targeted.
- Random selection of phrases, where phrase sets with better representativeness are selected [12].

- Specific methods that consider the representativeness of a phrase set but focus on other metrics such as memorability [17] or word clarity [19] and analyze the aggregated metrics accordingly.

Table 1 summarizes the features of the phrase sets described in the related work.

Table 1. Available phrase sets for text entry empirical research.

Phrase Set	Source Corpus	Development Procedure	Representativeness	Main Statistics
MacKenzie and Soukoreff [9]	N/A	"Randomly" collected phrases	Normalized letter frequency correlated to Mayzner and Tresselt [10]	500 phrases 2712 words 14,304 characters
AAC	N/A	Phrases suggested by AAC specialists; context-specific	N/A	928 phrases 3771 words 17,221 characters
Paek and Hsu [12]	Enron Email	Random sampling of n-word phrases; searching for the representative sample	Relative entropy between the target phrase set and the source corpus (KLD)	500 phrases 2000 words 11,275 characters
Vertanen and Kristensson [15]	Enron Email (filtered)	Metadata tagging; filtering; random sampling for representative datasets	Relative entropy between the target phrase set and the source corpus (KLD)	600 phrases 3730 words 19,211 characters
Kristensson and Vertanen [2]	NUS SMS (filtered)	Filtering based on phrase length and existing dictionary lists	N/A	769 phrases 5442 words 25,261 characters
Sanchis-Trilles and Leiva [18]	OpenSubtitles 2011, Wikipedia	Modeling over language-independent features; statistical analysis of the corpus from which phrases are selected	Weighting phrases with a probability density function over several phrase features	Language-specific; see [18] for details
Yi et al. [19]	MacKenzie and Soukoreff	Combined analysis of word clarity, digram frequency, and memorability	Relative entropy between the target phrase set and the source corpus (KLD)	Four sets with 20, 40, 80, and 160 phrases; see [19] for details
Gaines and Vertanen [20]	Reddit (2005–2019)	Computing character error rates and assigning difficulty ratings	N/A	5000 phrases (full set), 1000 phrases (recommended set)
Abbot et al. [21]	MacKenzie and Soukoreff	Synthesizing audio clips; targeting phrases with no comprehension errors	N/A	96 audio clips

1.2. Contributions and Structure

In the context of research on representative phrase sets, we want to develop a new method that: (1) targets phrase set representativeness; (2) outperforms typical random sampling; (3) can work with multiple languages; and (4) requires a single-large-text corpus. We consider KLD a metric for representativeness because digram probability is essential for curating phrase sets and the predictive modeling of text entry (see Equation (1)). Our method is directly motivated by the work described in [12]; however, we attempt to provide a more efficient method of corpus sampling and more representative phrase sets. Although we are not targeting the memorability feature, we want to design the proposed method to use many different parameters, including the desired thresholds for the number of words in a phrase. Since the most memorable phrases are those with the fewest words, memorability could be targeted in this, albeit trivial, way.

To the best of our knowledge, no method has been proposed that uses (heuristic) optimization techniques (or the like) to exclusively target representativeness metrics, intending to find such a small phrase set from a single-large-text corpus that matches both the digram statistics of the original corpus and the intended design of the text-entry experiment. Therefore, we aim to provide this method not only as a proof-of-concept but, more importantly, as an out-of-the-box implementation that all text entry experimenters can use immediately and adapt as needed. In addition, we want to propose heuristic guidelines for preparing and running a text entry experiment, which would include generating a phrase set to be utilized in its entirety (which is often not the case).

In line with the above, the main contributions of this paper are as follows:

- A novel method for sampling text corpora using the GA approach aiming to achieve near-optimal representativeness of the phrase set;
- An open source implementation of the proposed method that can be readily used regardless of the target language, available corpora, target character set, number of words in the phrases, size of the phrase set, and choice of GA parameters;
- A set of heuristic guidelines for preparing text entry experiments that consider the experiment's intended design and the set of phrases to be generated by the proposed solution.

This paper is structured as follows. Section 2 describes our proposal for generating representative phrase sets from available text corpora, focusing on mapping the domain problem into a GA implementation. The results of the initial comparison with the random sampling method, GA tuning, and application of the solution for different languages are presented in Section 3. The discussion of the obtained results is presented in Section 4, and Section 5 brings the final conclusions.

2. Materials and Methods

Finding the most representative phrase set from the large source corpus is a search problem with a wide range of possible solutions. To better understand the size of such a typical search space, we can consider a hypothetical text corpus with 50,000 phrases, a moderate volume from today's point of view. We can further assume that the desired number of phrases in the target phrase set is 200. If we want to evaluate the representativeness of all possible phrase sets that can be derived by corpus sampling (with no duplicates allowed), the number of available combinations in our case increases to $C(50K, 200) = 5.297e + 564$. Of course, an exhaustive search would be both time-consuming and resource intensive in terms of computational power. As mentioned earlier, Paek and Hsu [12] used a predetermined number of samples in their method, i.e., they searched for the best solution out of 100 samples. They argued that the number of sample phrase sets researchers want to analyze depends on how much time they can spend collecting and evaluating candidates. Nevertheless, such an approach leaves much of the search space unexplored.

Proposing an alternative sampling method requires a benchmark to evaluate its efficiency. Therefore, we implemented our version of Paek and Hsu's method and named it "brute force" sampling (BF). The BF method is shown in Figure 2.

First, for a given source corpus (SC), the probability distribution $q(ij)$ of character digrams is computed. Here, ij represents a general term of the character digram, where both i and j must be elements of a previously defined target character set. For example, if only a lowercase English text without punctuation and non-alphabetic symbols other than the space character is considered, the total number of digrams is $27 \times 27 = 729$. After computing $q(ij)$, the source corpus is filtered to extract only n-grams, and thus condensed to the reduced corpus (RC). Unlike the original procedure of Paek and Hsu, we selected candidates from the RC that contain formed sentences with exactly n words (where n is a user-defined value). The sampling procedure of RC itself is quite simple and consists of a predefined number of trials (TRIALS) where the best of the observed solutions is retained. The single sampling trial involves: (i) generating the phrase set candidate (PSC) by randomly selecting it from RC; (ii) computing the digram probability distribution $p(ij)$ for the generated PSC; (iii) computing the Kullback–Leibler divergence (KLD); and (iv) declaring the current PSC as the target phrase set (TPS) if the associated KLD has the lowest value so far. Since the described procedure leads to finding the best-of-TRIALS phrase set, whose digram distribution is closest to the digram distribution over the entire SC, we declare the final TPS as the "most representative" phrase set determined by BF sampling.

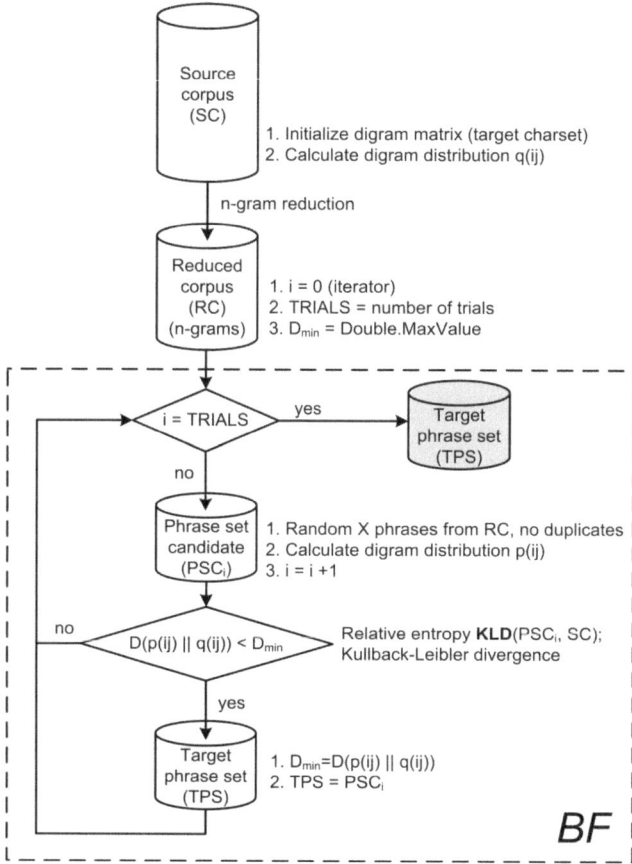

Figure 2. Procedure for finding representative phrase sets using the source corpus BF sampling.

Our case is obviously a typical mathematical optimization problem in which a suboptimal solution is sought in a large search space. To explore this search space of possible phrase sets more efficiently than BF, we propose a meta-heuristic approach using a genetic algorithm (GA). The basic idea of the corresponding method is shown in Figure 3.

As can be seen, the initial operations remain the same as in the BF sampling approach: based on the input target character set, the digram probability distribution $q(ij)$ is computed for the SC. At the same time, the n-gram reduction is performed to obtain the RC dataset. The main difference is that the genetic algorithm handles the process of actual sampling and sample evaluation. As a heuristic routinely used to generate solutions for optimization and search problems by mimicking the process of natural selection, a genetic algorithm seems a logical choice for our case. For now, we can consider GA as a black box that can generate a target phrase set that is likely to be more representative compared to the BF approach. However, this needs to be supported by actual data, so the GA parameters such as population, chromosome length, fitness function, termination criteria, and operators such as mutation, crossover, and elitism need to be appropriately applied to the problem domain.

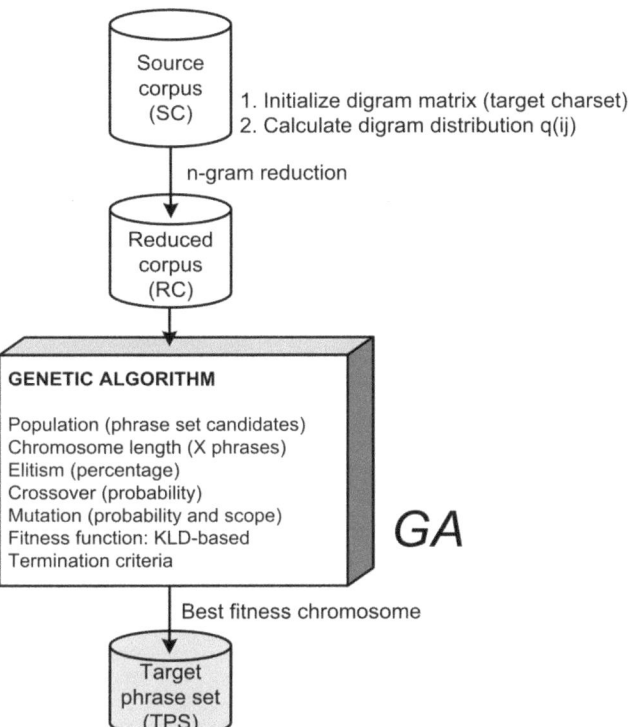

Figure 3. Procedure for finding representative phrase sets using the source corpus GA sampling.

2.1. Mapping the GA to the Problem Domain

Although a huge amount of literature deals with the theoretical foundations of genetic algorithms, only the basic principles and notations are briefly explained here. The implementation of a GA starts with a population of candidate solutions, usually randomly selected and declared as chromosomes. The population then enters an evolutionary process, representing one generation in a single iteration. Within a given generation, each chromosome is evaluated against a defined fitness function, usually corresponding to the main criteria for solving the problem. Chromosomes that represent a better solution to the target problem are then given more chances to "reproduce", i.e., they are subjected to crossover and random mutation after the intermediate selection process. As such, a new generation of candidate solutions is formed for the next iteration. Various termination criteria can be used to terminate the genetic algorithm, such as the specified maximum number of generations, the desired level of fitness, or the number of generations that do not increase fitness. More information on the computational behavior of GAs and how they support complex search problems can be found in [22].

Making an initial random population within our problem domain is illustrated in Figure 4.

Individual phrases from the reduced corpus represent genes in terms of the genetic algorithm. The phrases are randomly selected and grouped to form a single phrase set candidate (PSC) corresponding to a single chromosome. The number of phrases in the PSC (chromosome length) is a user-defined value. Our implementation does not allow for phrase duplicates to be present in a given chromosome. The number of PSCs we want to analyze iteratively represents a population size, which is also an arbitrary parameter.

Once the initial population of PSCs is created, their evolution towards better solutions can begin.

Each PSC from the population is evaluated using the fitness function, which in our case, is represented by the Kullback–Leibler divergence. The relative entropy between a given PSC and the SC can indicate how representative the phrase set in question is, i.e., how "good" the corresponding chromosome is. Concerning the KLD, chromosomes whose associated value is closer to zero are considered fitter.

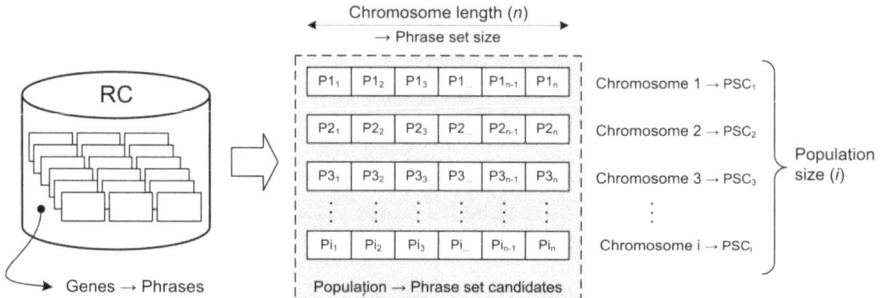

Figure 4. Population, chromosomes, and genes representation in the text corpus sampling problem domain.

One of the basic principles of GA assumes that the best candidates should be retained and bred to produce even better solutions for the next generation. Choosing chromosomes for a potential crossover operation represents a selection process, and several methods provide this functionality in GA. Simple truncation selection, for example, eliminates a fixed percentage of the weakest candidates and is considered less sophisticated because weaker solutions may not survive at all. Weaker solutions can sometimes be an advantage in the crossover process since there is always some chance of obtaining genes that might prove useful. Therefore, we opted for fitness selection, also known as roulette wheel selection, in which the probability of an individual being selected for a crossover increases with the fitness of the individual in question. We used the two-point technique for the crossover method, in which two parent chromosomes are combined to generate two new child chromosomes (see Figure 5).

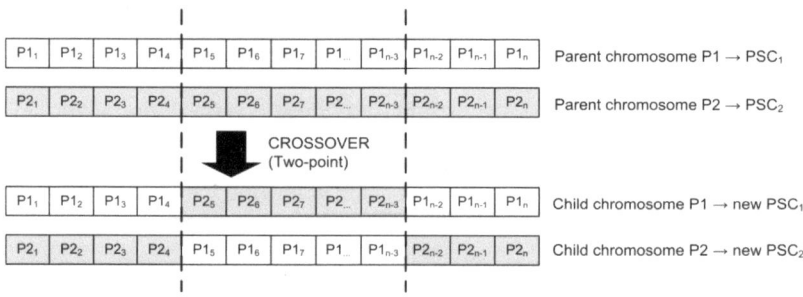

Figure 5. Two-point crossover swaps the text phrases between the parent chromosomes, based on the positions of two points, resulting in the generation of two new PSCs.

The resulting offspring replace the parent chromosomes in the current population, thus performing a generational change. The main advantage of such an approach is its ease of implementation; however, the obvious disadvantage is that highly fit individuals are not guaranteed to pass unchanged into the next generation. For this reason, our implementation includes an additional elitism operator. Elitism allows a certain percentage of the best candidates (elitism percentage) to be included in the next generation without being modified beforehand, ensuring that future generations do not lack quality.

Finally, we had to account for genetic diversity by including the mutation operator. Unlike the binary crossover operator, the unary mutation operator acts on a single chromosome by changing one or more gene values. While crossover directly supports convergence to a local optimum, the mutation operator is, in turn, used to cause divergence by adding new genetic information. Mutation occurs with a user-defined mutation probability, usually set relatively low. However, setting the best value for the mutation rate is highly problem-specific, as this value defines the desired trade-off between the exploration and exploitation capabilities of the GA.

A custom mutation operator is proposed and implemented to support specific requirements within the problem domain. Along with the mutation probability, we introduced an additional parameter—a number of phrases to be altered in a mutating PSC. In our case, the mutation probability represents the chance that a given PSC will undergo the mutation process. When such a mutation is eventually triggered, a predefined number of phrase swaps are made at random positions within the PSC. The corresponding mutation process is shown in Figure 6.

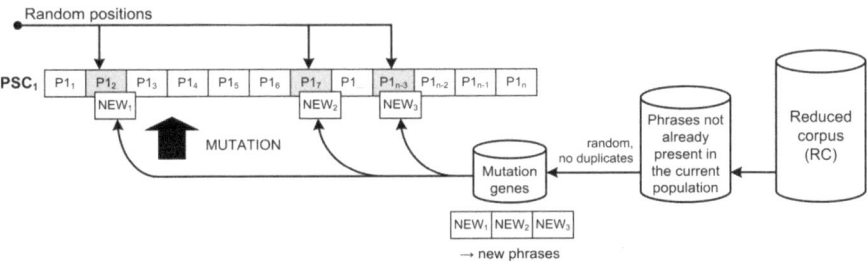

Figure 6. The mutation operator used in our implementation.

Each single mutation session consists of three basic operations: (i) based on the predefined number of gene modifications, phrases to be randomly replaced within the respective chromosome are determined; (ii) the same number of new phrases are randomly extracted from the subset of RC; and (iii) the determined current phrases are swapped with the new ones. In Figure 6, the number of mutations is assumed to be 3. Phrases $P2$, $P7$, and P_{n-3} are swept and become part of the RC subset in the next generation if they are not already contained in one of the remaining chromosomes.

The design of our mutation operator, in which several phrases (genes) in a set (chromosome) can be changed simultaneously, retains all the essential features of a typical mutation operator. This facilitates the exploration by including diversity even in cases where a representative set with a large number of phrases is required. When introducing multiple mutations, avoiding excessive population disruption is important. Care must be taken to ensure that the number of changed phrases in a set is reasonable and does not lead to chaotic or unpredictable behavior. In addition, our mutation operator ensures that diversity is maintained in the population, as it only replaces existing phrases with those not yet present in the entire population. Even though our operator allows a kind of "fast" mutation within a generation, combinations of phrases that have previously shown a good fit are protected from mutation by the elitism operator. Thus, the additional parameterization of the mutation operator allows further adaptation to our domain problem and the properties of the target phrase set. After all, the proposed GA method can be used to set the number of target genes for mutation in the described operator to 1, effectively turning our mutation operator into the default one.

Figure 7 shows the structure of the GA process pipeline used in our implementation.

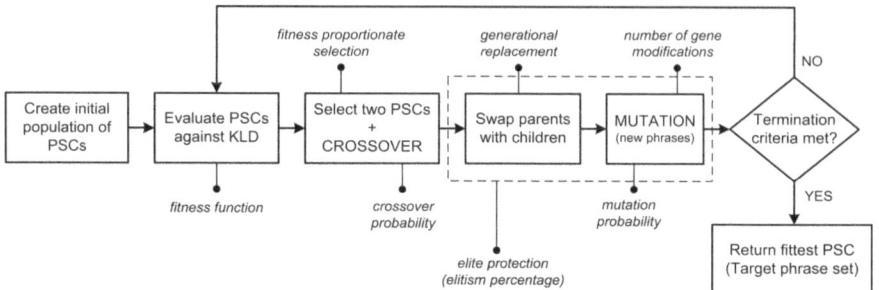

Figure 7. GA process pipeline utilized for corpus sampling.

2.2. Implementation of GA-Based Text Corpora Sampling

The proposed procedure for sampling a text corpus using a genetic algorithm is implemented in C# within the .NET platform. To support the functionality of GA, we used the freely available genetic algorithm framework (GAF)—the single multi-thread assembly that provides programming resources for many types of genetic algorithms [23]. While the most common genetic operators are built into GAF, external operators can also be developed and added to the standard GA process pipeline. No problems were encountered in mapping the properties of the problem domain to the appropriate programming structures, and implementing our custom mutation operator was quite straightforward.

As a final result of our project development phase, we provided several C# classes with a number of useful methods for dealing with corpora sampling. Some of the functionalities provided by our implementation, which includes both BF and GA approaches, are as follows:

- Loading the corpus from a text file;
- Reducing the available source corpus to the dataset containing only n-word phrases;
- Computing the letter/digram probability distribution for the provided text corpus based on the defined target character set;
- Computing the relative entropy (KLD) between two digram probability distributions;
- Parameterized BF sampling;
- Setting GA by defining the basic parameters, the processing pipeline, and the input datasets (RC and the character set for a target language);
- Specific GA event handling (managing the completion of a single generation or a GA run).

We provide simple C# code snippets that perform all the necessary analysis and computation to demonstrate how easily the provided implementation can be used to obtain the phrase sets. As can be seen in Figure 8, corpus sampling can be invoked with just a few lines of code, regardless of whether the BF or GA approach is preferred. Furthermore, the corresponding methods are parameterized to allow the easy customization of the sampling process. For example, defining completely new GA parameters at one point is possible. This forms the basis for a simple GA parameter tuning in the later phase of the analysis of the results.

Other useful features of our implementation can be highlighted:

- The n-gram reduction from the SC is performed on sentence-based premises so that only meaningful phrases can be included in the further analysis;
- The RC does not contain duplicate phrases; consequently, each phrase set candidate, as well as the target phrase set, is duplicate-free;
- The probability distributions do not have to be recalculated, but can be loaded from the respective files with the previously computed digram/letter frequencies (this is especially useful while working with large text corpora);

- The methods are designed in such a way that large text corpora can be analyzed independently of the available hardware resources: file processing is implemented using byte streams so that large text files do not have to be entirely loaded into memory;
- The whole sampling procedure depends on a defined target character set (which can be easily changed), while the algorithm itself is not language-specific since corpora can be sampled by analyzing the whole or restricted alphabet of a given language, with or without punctuation and additional characters;
- The sampling steps are recorded in the corresponding log file, including all relevant parameters and intermediate results, so that the performance of both BF and GA can be checked in detail.

BF sampling

```
CorpusTextSampler.BruteForceCorpusSampling_FromScratch
(
        "SC.txt",              // source corpus file (SC)
        100,                   // number of random sampling trials
        500,                   // number of phrases in the target phrase set
        new[]{4},              // number of words in phrases
        "charset.txt",         // character set for a given language
        "RC.txt",              // source corpus limited to n-grams only (RC)
        "TPS.txt",             // OUTPUT: target phrase set (TPS)
        "SC-letters.csv",      // OUTPUT: letter probability distribution for SC
        "TPS-letters.csv",     // OUTPUT: letter probability distribution for TPS
        "SC-digrams.csv",      // OUTPUT: digram probability distribution for SC
        "TPS-digrams.csv",     // OUTPUT: digram probability distribution for TPS
        "log.csv"              // OUTPUT: log file for the analysis of the BF sampling
);
```

GA sampling

```
Distribution corpusDist = new Distribution("SC.txt", "charset.txt", true, new[]{4}, "RC.txt");
HashSet<string> reducedCorpus = CorpusTextSampler.loadReducedDatasetFromFile("RC.txt");

GA myGA = new GA(
        "charset.txt",         // character set for a given language
        corpusDist,            // digram probability distribution for SC
        500,                   // number of phrases in the target phrase set
        reducedCorpus,         // source corpus limited to n-grams only (RC) - as Hashset
        100,                   // GA population size
        true, 5,               // elitism operator (true/false), elitism percentage
        0.8,                   // crossover probability
        0.1, 10,               // mutation probability, number of genes to be mutated
        1000,                  // maximum number of generations
        "TPS.txt",             // OUTPUT: target phrase set (TPS)
        "log.csv"              // OUTPUT: log file for the analysis of the GA sampling
);

myGA.Run();
```

Figure 8. Starting BF and GA sampling with the provided C# methods. In both cases, only two resources are required as input arguments: the source corpus (a file that presumably contains a large amount of text) and the target character set for a given language.

The implementation's source code is freely available as an open source project on GitHub [24]. Researchers can use this resource and experiment by "feeding" the provided methods with different text corpora and different sampling features to obtain representative phrase sets with the desired properties (language, character set, phrase set size, and phrase length). The result of the GA-based sampling procedure can be examined in more detail using different combinations of GA parameters and compared with the benchmark BF approach. In addition, the provided source code can be modified and/or adapted to support some specific domain problems and tackle performance issues. For example, a different way of handling unwanted characters in the source corpus can be considered, alternative BF sampling approaches can be used, a new version of the GA mutation operator can be developed, and so on. A completely different fitness function can even be introduced to analyze possible new metrics for phrase set representativeness.

3. Results

This section gives an overview of all the results obtained by applying the proposed solution. In doing so, we describe the initial tests and compare the effects of BF and GA on the available Croatian text corpus. The Croatian language was chosen for the reason that it is the native language of the authors of this work, and there are no representative phrase sets that could be used for the text entry experiments in this language. Then, we show the procedure and the results of tuning the GA, and finally, we present the results of applying the tuned algorithm to text corpora from several different languages. All results were obtained on the following computer PC configuration: CPU Intel i7-5600U @3.20 GHz, 12 GB RAM, 512 GB SSD.

3.1. Initial Assessment of BF and GA Sampling Effects

The proposed procedure was first tested for sampling the Croatian text corpus. As the main source corpus, we chose fHrWaC [25], a filtered version of the Croatian web corpus hrWaC, initially compiled by Ljubešić and Erjavec [26]. hrWaC is a web corpus collected from the *.hr* top-level domain, containing 1.2 billion tokens in its first version and distributed under the CC-BY-SA license. Since this resource was found to contain segments of non-textual content, such as code snippets and formatting structures, as well as some encoding errors and foreign language content, we decided to use the filtered version instead. The final filtered corpus contains 50,940,598 sentences, is licensed under CC-BY-SA 3.0, and can be downloaded from a website maintained by the Text Analysis and Knowledge Engineering Lab (TakeLab) [27] at the University of Zagreb.

A sampling of the fHrWaC corpus was initially conducted using the BF approach. It was decided that an analysis would be performed based on the character set consisting of the lowercase alphabet typically used in Croatian QWERTY layouts. This includes all 26 English characters as well as five additional Croatian diacritical marks: č, ć, đ, š, and ž. Except for the space character, no other punctuation characters were considered, so our digram matrix includes exactly $32 \times 32 = 1024$ records. As the first step of the sampling procedure, we derived the digram probability distribution for the source corpus. Table 2 shows the statistics for the ten most frequent digrams in the fHrWaC corpus.

Table 2. Ten most frequent digrams in the fHrWaC corpus (based on the used character set).

Character Digram	Number of Occurrences	Probability
a-space	215,614,936	0.032759789
e-space	190,822,444	0.028992904
i-space	155,658,921	0.023650279
je	152,481,601	0.023167528
space-s	115,031,757	0.017477528
o-space	110,503,789	0.016789564
u-space	107,987,401	0.016407233
space-p	105,068,195	0.015963699
na	87,110,973	0.013235341
space-n	80,275,325	0.012196756

Based on the calculated fHrWaC digram probability distribution $q(ij)$, it can be seen that digrams containing the blank are generally more frequently used, which is not surprising if we know that they represent the beginning and/or the end of words. As mentioned earlier, the sampling procedure should now search for a phrase set with its digram probability distribution $p(ij)$ being the most representative of the obtained $q(ij)$ with respect to the KLD.

We decided to retrieve the target phrase sets of exactly 200 phrases and focus on phrases of 3–15 words. Naturally, shorter phrases are the preferred stimuli in text entry experiments where the text to be typed must be memorized beforehand. In comparison, shorter and longer phrases can be used simultaneously in typical experimental text typing tasks. A total of 1000 trials were conducted, resulting in 13 different phrase sets whose representativeness values are shown in Figure 9. It can be seen that both the mean relative entropy and its minimum value decrease with increasing phrase length. Thus, we conclude that better representativeness is more difficult to achieve when the target set contains shorter phrases. Since most text entry experiments use short phrases, finding representative solutions becomes even more challenging.

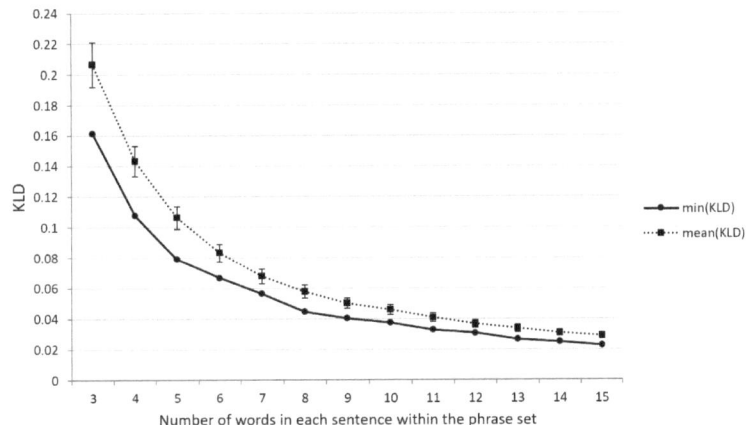

Figure 9. Sampling 200 phrase sets from an fHrWaC reduced to n words using the BF approach with 1000 random trials. In addition to the KLD mean value, the corresponding standard deviation is also shown.

We set the benchmark phrase length to five words for further analysis. According to the initial results from BF, the minimum value of relative entropy obtained for a phrase set containing 200 phrases of five words is 0.079179. Next, the effect of the phrase set size was assessed by an additional round of sampling with six different sizes. Again, 1000 random trials were used in each BF sampling run. The corresponding results are shown in Figure 10.

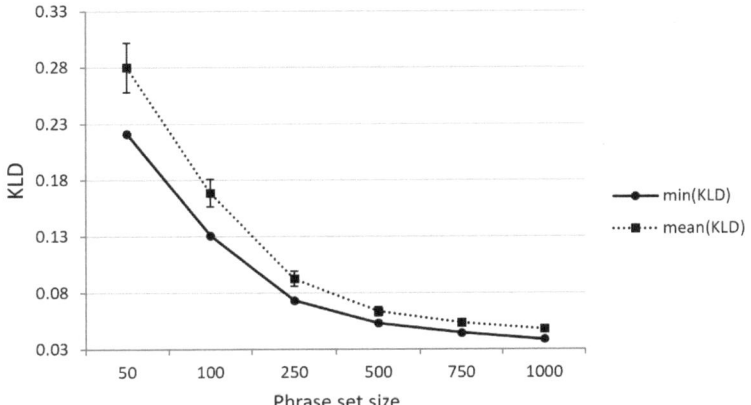

Figure 10. Sampling phrase sets with a variable size from a 5-word reduced fHrWaC using the BF approach with 1000 random trials. In addition to the KLD mean value, the corresponding standard deviation is also shown.

Again, the results show that relative entropy (both average and minimum values) generally decreases as the amount of text in the target phrase set increases. This confirms analogous results from Paek and Hsu [12], where the corresponding trend was attributed to smaller quantization effects for larger phrase sets. Thus, it has already been argued that "it is much more important to make sure that a sample phrase set is representative of the source corpus when there is a small number of phrases". Therefore, we decided to stick with 200-phrase sets for further analysis.

Finally, we wanted to analyze how the number of random trials in the BF procedure affects the best value of relative entropy. As mentioned earlier, this number significantly depends on how much time can be spent on BF sampling concerning the search space under investigation. We sampled the RC eight times, from a run with only ten random trials to the more time-consuming processes, the last of which involved half a million samples. The results obtained are shown in Figure 11.

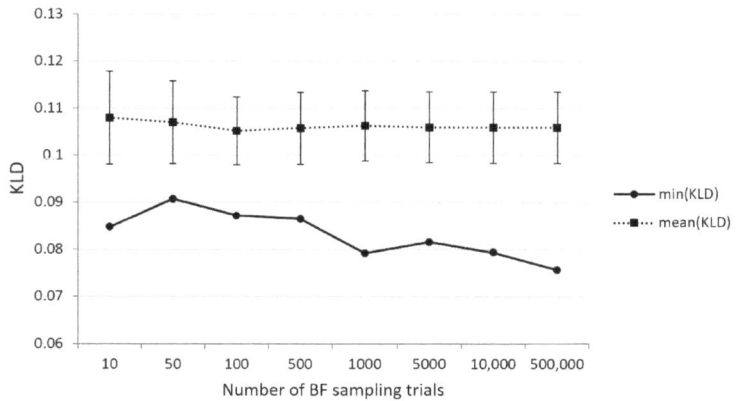

Figure 11. Sampling 200-sentence phrase sets from the 5-word reduced fHrWaC using the BF approach with a different number of random trials. In addition to the KLD mean value, the corresponding standard deviation is also shown.

No major differences were observed between the mean values of relative entropy (ranging from 0.105109 to 0.107923) and their respective standard deviations. However, the KLD minimum values associated with the most representative phrase sets found in each BF sampling procedure generally showed a negative trend. This is an understandable effect since a more extended search means a higher probability of finding a more appropriate phrase set. We can now be interested in the absolute gain in terms of relative entropy values: a BF run with 500,000 random trials yielded the best sample with $min(KLD) = 0.075669$. In contrast, the second best result was observed in a procedure with 1000 random trials with $min(KLD) = 0.079320$. The best value obtained serves as the final BF benchmark to be compared with the proposed GA sampling procedure.

After analyzing the effects of BF sampling, the next step was to test the support of GA. In line with the previous analysis, the proposed GA sampling procedure was used to obtain a representative set of 200 phrases with exactly five words. The reduced corpus was already available through the BF sampling procedure. The initial parameters of GA were set as follows: a population of 50 phrase sets (chromosomes), elitism of 2%, crossover probability of 0.65, mutation probability of 0.1, five new genes involved in each mutation process, and a maximum number of generations (500) as the criterion for GA termination. This preliminary GA run produced the results shown in Figure 12.

Within the initial population, the most representative phrase set of 50 randomly selected candidates had the corresponding KLD value of 0.086755. Further crossovers and mutations in the GA process pipeline resulted in the KLD value being more than halved after only 500 generations. Thus, even the first run of GA yielded a target phrase set which was more representative of the source corpus ($KLD = 0.032082$) than any phrase set previously obtained using the BF approach. This was somewhat surprising since the BF procedure had already involved a large number of trial runs without being able to derive a phrase set with a value even close to the KLD value obtained in the first run of GA. Thus, the most representative phrase set yet was easily obtained, but the next task was to experiment with the parameters of GA to search for possibly better solutions.

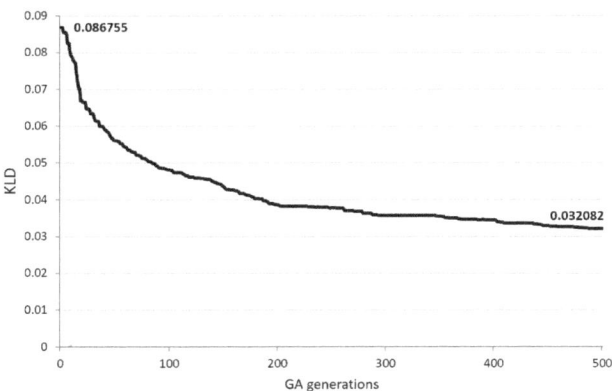

Figure 12. Sampling 200-sentence phrase sets from the 5-word reduced fHrWaC using the GA approach with initially set parameters.

3.2. GA Parameter Tuning

Determining the "right" parameters for the GA to solve a particular search problem is anything but a trivial task. Generally, this task can be divided into parameter tuning and parameter control. As explained in Eiben and Smit [28], parameter control assumes that parameter values change during a GA run, so initial parameter values must be fixed and appropriate tuning strategies must be used. On the other hand, parameter tuning is less complicated because no changes occur during a GA run, and only a single value per parameter is required. However, since there are a large number of options that can be manipulated, parameter tuning remains a serious issue. Considering that there are several possible approaches for tuning the GA parameters, a possible analysis of the respective tuning algorithms is beyond the scope of this paper. The existing tuning algorithms and their impact on GA-based corpus sampling, both in terms of performance improvements and computational costs, are viable options for future studies. The parameterized features of the provided implementation (including GAF support and our sampling methods) allow such an analysis without modifying the genetic algorithm.

Consequently, a more conservative approach to parameter tuning was adopted in our work. Values are selected by convention (general principles or rules of thumb such as "lower mutation rate"), ad hoc decisions (e.g., two-point crossover), and, most importantly, experimental comparisons with a limited number of parameter combinations. When experimenting with different parameter values, particular emphasis was placed on algorithm performance, convergence to the best solution, and final KLD values after a certain number of GA generations. Some parameters are directly related to the observed results, e.g., a larger population size and/or a higher number of generations increases the time required to complete GA. On the other hand, it is not immediately obvious how a particular combination of parameters, here including the probabilities of crossover and mutation, affects the outcomes of GA. Approximately 60 combinations were tested, resulting in a similar decreasing trend of the KLD value.

All tuning sessions showed a faster decline in KLD values in the first generations and a slower convergence to the best solution in the later stages of the GA run. Regarding the execution speed, a single GA run with 1000 generations and a population size in the range of 500–1500 was completed in less than an hour with the aforementioned PC configuration. Since we considered this time a reasonable cost for the investment in parameter tuning, and due to the similarity of the obtained KLD trends, it was decided that the final GA parameters should be selected according to the best obtained KLD value across all tuning runs with 1000 generations. As a result, the parameter values were set as follows: population size—500; elitism—5%; crossover probability—0.8; mutation probability—0.2; and number of genes involved in the mutation process—20.

When testing different values for the custom mutation operator, we observed a typical effect: for better results, the combination of a very high mutation rate and a large number of variable genes should be avoided, as well as a combination of a very low mutation rate and a small number of variable genes. Several aspects can explain the positive effects of a somewhat higher mutation rate in our case. First, the search space for representative phrase sets is very large, corresponding to the size of modern text corpora. The risk of premature convergence, where GA gets stuck in a suboptimal solution, is more pronounced in such a large domain. A higher mutation rate introduces additional randomness into the population, helping to explore different regions of the search space and avoid premature convergence by leaving local optima. In addition, a higher mutation rate promotes exploration by introducing more disruptive changes into candidate phrase sets. Such exploration can help discover new combinations of phrases that exhibit higher representativeness, even if they may initially be far from the optimum. Moreover, a higher mutation rate helps maintain diversity by introducing new phrases that are not yet present in the population, which is ensured by the design of our mutation operator. This diversity promotes the exploration of different linguistic patterns and increases the chances of finding more representative phrase sets.

Once the final parameters for GA were established, it was possible to formally compare the BF and GA sampling methods. Assuming that 500 solutions (GA population size) are evaluated in every single GA generation, a complete GA run with 1000 generations would include a total of 500 × 1000 = 500,000 evaluations. In this respect, comparing such a GA run with the BF procedure involving the same number of random sampling trials is fair. The result of this analysis is presented in Figure 13.

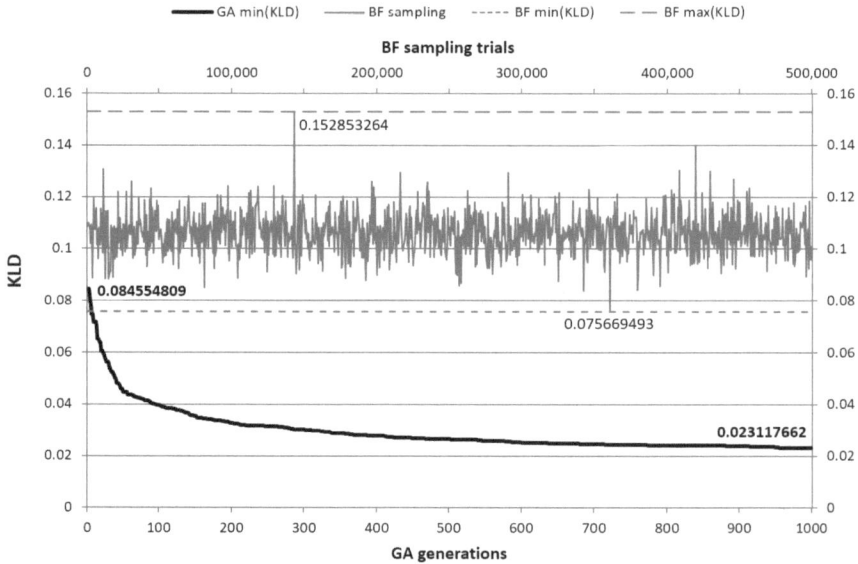

Figure 13. Comparison of sampling results between the BF procedure with 500,000 random trials and a GA with 1000 generations and a population size of 500 (200-sentence phrase sets from the 5-word reduced fHrWaC were sampled).

The ordinal number of BF trials can be tracked on the upper horizontal axis and is relevant for the highly variable KLD values obtained with the BF method (upper part of the graph). In contrast, the ordinal number of GA generation can be tracked on the lower horizontal axis and is relevant to the decreasing KLD values obtained with the GA approach (lower part of the graph).

The advantage of the GA approach is apparent in terms of the final solution and performance. The most representative phrase set found from the fHrWaC corpus reduced to five words using the BF procedure has the associated KLD value of 0.075669493. The phrase set with better representativeness was found within the first generations of the corresponding GA run. Moreover, the GA eventually resulted in a target phrase set with a considerably lower KLD, namely 0.023117662. In terms of execution speed, GA also outperforms BF sampling. However, this can be attributed to the multi-threading support in GA implementation, in contrast to the BF procedure, which relies on serial iterations with a sample-and-evaluate rate of almost 200 phrase set candidates per minute. Therefore, the results of BF shown in Figure 14 were obtained in no less than 40 h, which is significantly more compared to the GA approach.

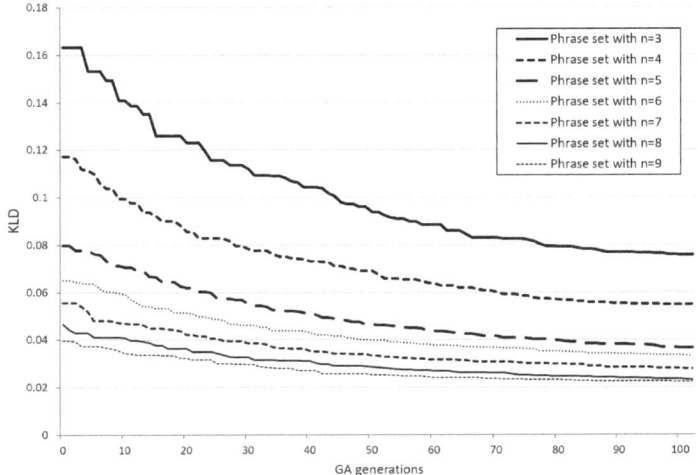

Figure 14. Final results of fHrWaC corpus GA-based sampling (only the first 100 generations are shown).

3.3. The Final Outcomes and a Multi-Language Context

In order to obtain representative phrase sets for the Croatian language, in a final step, we decided to target sets of exactly 200 phrases with seven different phrase lengths (3–9 words). We used the proposed GA sampling procedure, setting the parameters of GA as previously described. In addition, we configured GA to terminate after 10,000 generations to further improve the final solutions. Since all n-word reduced corpora ($n \in [3, \ldots, 9]$) were previously generated by BF sampling runs, additional n-word filtering was not required. Each GA run was then applied to the corresponding reduced corpus, and thus, the most representative phrase sets after 10,000 generations were found.

The results confirm that the relative entropy of the best solutions decreases when the target set contains phrases with more words. To see the differences between the seven KLD trends more clearly, we show the GA sampling results, but only within the first 100 GA generations, where the convergence speed is higher (see Figure 14).

The characteristics of the phrase sets obtained, the corresponding values of the KLD metric, and an example sentence from each phrase set (with an English translation) are given in Table 3.

Table 3. Characteristics of the most representative phrase sets sampled from the fHrWaC source corpus found using the proposed GA-based approach. Example phrases in Croatian are additionally translated into English (EN) for clarity.

Phrase Length	Phrase Set Characteristics	Example Phrase
3 words	200 phrases, 600 words 4.57 characters/word $KLD(fHrWaC)$: 0.035726331	*jako ih volim* EN: *I like them very much*
4 words	200 phrases, 800 words 4.87 characters/word $KLD(fHrWaC)$: 0.025814862	*tajna je u preljevu* EN: *the secret is in the dressing*
5 words	200 phrases, 1000 words 5.06 characters/word $KLD(fHrWaC)$: 0.020257031	*želim otići iz toga kaosa* EN: *I want to leave this chaos*
6 words	200 phrases, 1200 words 5.11 characters/word $KLD(fHrWaC)$: 0.019554355	*igra nije bila za visoku ocjenu* EN: *the game was not for high rating*
7 words	200 phrases, 1400 words 5.22 characters/word $KLD(fHrWaC)$: 0.014567244	*ostala sam jedan dan više u bolnici* EN: *I stayed one more day in the hospital*
8 words	200 phrases, 1600 words 5.25 characters/word $KLD(fHrWaC)$: 0.012153204	*za večeru pojedite pitu ili čips od jabuke* EN: *have apple pie or chips for dinner*
9 words	200 phrases, 1800 words 5.29 characters/word $KLD(fHrWaC)$: 0.011310758	*na njegovom posljednjem albumu ona je napisala osam pjesama* EN: *on their last album she wrote eight songs*

After completing the search for representative phrase sets using the GA procedure, a problem remains that needs to be addressed. Large web-scraped corpora usually contain, in addition to the inevitable spelling and grammatical errors, some parts with offensive language that are difficult to filter out automatically. The fHrWaC corpus is no exception in this respect, so there is a possibility that the obtained phrase sets contain some undesirable texts. Therefore, it is recommended that the phrase sets are manually checked by correcting possible errors and removing unwanted content. Such a modification of the obtained phrase sets inevitably leads to a change in their digram statistics and, consequently, their relative entropy. A minor change in the KLD value can be expected if only a few grammatical issues are involved. However, finding the correct replacements may become a larger problem if many phrases need to be completely removed. Therefore, it would be ideal to have large text corpora that have been adequately "cleaned" beforehand at disposal.

In order to prove the usefulness and effectiveness of the proposed method on a general level, we decided to apply it to different languages. It is important to generate representative sets of phrases for different languages because it has already been proven that language plays a significant role in text entry experiments and directly affects the efficiency of text input [29]. We additionally extended the method's capabilities to generate sets containing phrases with different word counts. In this way, it is left to the end user (the operator of the text entry experiment) to generate a representative set for the target language that best fits the intended design of the experiment. For example, if the goal is to test the input of memorable phrases, generating a set of phrases containing between 3 and 5 words is possible. On the other hand, if one wants to study the effects of transcribing a larger amount of text, the method can be used to generate a phrase set with longer sentences.

The proof of concept was carried out, in parallel with the native Croatian language (HR), for English (EN), Italian (IT), Spanish (ES), Russian (RU), Polish (PL), French (FR), and German (DE). For each of the above languages, a corresponding character set had to be defined—a set of all letters/graphemes that can form valid digrams in that language. Following common practice in text entry research, we limited phrases to lowercase letters without punctuation, such as commas and periods. We chose phrase sets with different numbers of phrases (150, 200, 250, 300) containing different numbers of words (3–5, 4–6, 5–6, 6–7). Sampling was performed for each language using the BF and GA methods, thus allowing the comparison with the baseline method. In doing so, we decided to make two GA runs for each language – with two thousand and three thousand generations.

We used the OpenSubtitles 2013 collection [30,31] as a resource for text corpora in different languages. It should be noted that the mentioned corpora are not filtered with respect to the possible presence of undesirable parts of the text. The results of the sampling methods applied to this resource, targeting eight different languages, are shown in Figure 15.

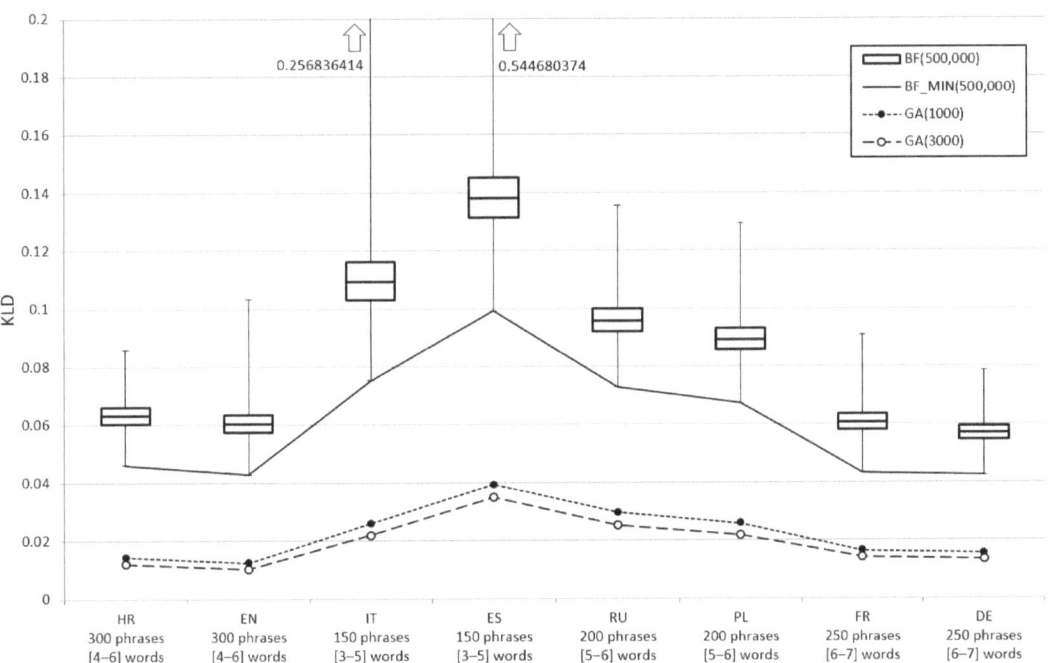

Figure 15. Results of applying the proposed method to several different languages from the OpenSubtitles 2013 corpora.

The upper part of the diagram shows box-and-whiskers plots illustrating the variability of the results of the separate experiments in which the BF approach was used (with 500,000 sample trials). In contrast, the lower part of the diagram shows the results of the GA approach—performed with a total of 1000 and 3000 generations. Since the best result of BF sampling is the one with the lowest KLD value, we connected all BF minima with a line. With this kind of visualization, we wanted to point out the following:

- The shape of the three lines shows that the final results of the different experiments (referring to different languages and target phrase sets) have a similar relationship, regardless of whether the BF or GA is used.
- The mutual distance between the three lines shows how effective GA is in finding better solutions, given the difference in the KLD values obtained.

As can be seen, it is once again shown that the proposed GA method outperforms the BF, this time in the context of different languages. Regardless of the target language, of how many phrases the target set contains, and of how many words phrases in the target set contain, the GA method is proven to be able to find a phrase set of higher linguistic representativeness. As expected, GA runs with 3000 generations yielded more appropriate solutions.

The details of the phrase sets obtained from sampling the corpora of different languages are given in Table 4.

Table 4. Characteristics of the most representative phrase sets sampled from the *OpenSubtitles 2013* (*OS*) source corpora found using the proposed GA-based approach with 3000 generations. Eight languages are selected for the analysis.

Language	Phrase Length	Phrase Set Characteristics	Example Phrases
Italian (IT)	3–5 words	150 phrases, 656 words 4.72 characters/word $KLD(OS-IT)$: 0.02193727	siete tutti sani prendila come un gioco hai chiamato a casa sua
Spanish (ES)	3–5 words	150 phrases, 679 words 4.45 characters/word $KLD(OS-ES)$: 0.034925941	prepare el carro me harté de llorar ofender no era mi intención
Croatian (HR)	4–6 words	300 phrases, 1490 words 4.50 characters/word $KLD(OS-HR)$: 0.012102423	to je samo sok bila sam jutros u banci ja ću ti paziti na opremu
English (EN)	4–6 words	300 phrases, 1567 words 4.08 characters/word $KLD(OS-EN)$: 0.010343915	go with the plan that goes for every man love is like taking a train
Russian (RU)	5–6 words	200 phrases, 1103 words 4.94 characters/word $KLD(OS-RU)$: 0.025255478	я вижу ты чтото знаешь я вернулся так скоро как смог
Polish (PL)	5–6 words	200 phrases, 1103 words 5.24 characters/word $KLD(OS-PL)$: 0.021751797	nie ma leków na amnezję przyjechałam tak szybko jak tylko usłyszałam
French (FR)	6–7 words	250 phrases, 1618 words 4.49 characters/word $KLD(OS-FR)$: 0.014245106	vous aurez votre chance cette nuit combien de fois vas tu regarder ça
German (DE)	6–7 words	250 phrases, 1622 words 4.87 characters/word $KLD(OS-DE)$: 0.013459111	niemals mehr will ich dich verlieren man muss den kunden bei laune halten

4. Discussion

Text entry is still a hot topic among the HCI community. Many novel text entry methods and solutions for various application domains have recently been introduced. These include text entry in immersive virtual environments [32,33] and augmented reality systems [34], speech-based text entry [35], and typing on passive surfaces [36,37]. All these work uses a common phrase set, namely that developed by MacKenzie and Soukoreff, whilst related experiments sometimes only use part of the set. This suggests that, while there are ways to generate phrase sets with better language representativeness, many researchers have not yet utilized them. The above work points to another problem: text entry is mostly tested in English, even though the experiments are not necessarily conducted with native English speakers. Evaluations of text entry methods in other languages are limited, and when English is not the focus, either ad hoc phrase sets are invented [38] or MacKenzie and Soukoreff's phrase set is translated [39]. These facts further contextualize the potential and the need for representative phrase sets.

Although GA can be considered an old technique, it continues to attract attention. In recent research efforts, it has been successfully applied in text analysis, particularly for text feature selection [40], text clustering [41], and text summarization [42].

Besides GA, other heuristic algorithms such as simulated annealing, particle swarm optimization, and ant colony optimization could also be considered to solve the observed problem. However, one of the main reasons for using the genetic algorithm was the interpretability of this method and its relation to the problem domain. Namely, the process of encoding phrases and their evolution by genetic operators allows the direct mapping of solutions to the problem domain. The set of phrases can be directly represented as a candidate chromosome, with each phrase representing a single gene. This representation is consistent with the nature of the problem and allows GA, with its crossover and mutation operators, to work directly with the units of interest. In addition, GAs are well suited for nonlinear optimization problems where the relationship between the input variables and the objective function is complex and may exhibit nonlinearity. In our phrase set selection, the fitness function is based on Kullback–Leibler divergence, which involves nonlinear relationships between character digrams, making GA a favorable choice for optimizing such an objective. Finally, since GAs have been extensively studied and implemented in various domains, numerous programming resources are available for implementing and tweaking GAs. Therefore, the proposed GA-based sampling method can be offered as a readily available resource for various platforms.

Although GA offers the above advantages, we recognize that the effectiveness of any optimization method depends on the specific problem and its characteristics and that it is important to also evaluate other algorithms. Implementing alternative optimization methods and comparisons with GA represents future research opportunities.

The current versions of all obtained phrase sets only include only lowercase phrases, as using only such phrases in HCI text entry experiments is common. If the inclusion of uppercase letters is preferred instead, corpora sampling without explicit lowercasing would be required, and the target character set would need to be defined differently. The same applies to including numbers, additional symbols, and punctuation marks. For example, suppose we want to add only simple punctuation (comma and period) to the current lowercase alphabet. In that case, the input charset file should be updated accordingly, e.g., for English, this would mean the following string: "abcdefghijklmnopqrstuvwxyz". In this case, the digram matrix would have the size $29 \times 29 = 841$, with the corresponding digram frequency values calculated in the first step of the sampling procedure. Once computed, this digram probability distribution can be readily used as a language model for predictive text input evaluation. Namely, it can be combined with previously derived motion models (e.g., the well-known Fitts's law in Equation (2)) to obtain predictions about text entry speed for a given input technique. At the same time, the digram probability distribution of the source corpus serves as a baseline for assessing the representativeness of the selected phrase set.

The proposed sampling procedure can be easily used to develop phrase sets with specific features that match the desired experimental design. The preferred source corpus, target language, associated character set, number of phrases, and phrase length can all be configured using input arguments from readily available programming methods. In this way, user-defined experimental stimuli can be generated without interfering with the proposed procedure's internal implementation logic. The parameters of GA can also be configured in this way, allowing the further analysis of the efficiency of the procedure under different combinations of crossover probability, mutation rate, and elitism percentage.

Besides using the GA sampling procedure by simply applying the already provided methods, it is possible to modify the implementation's source code to adapt GA sampling to more specific requirements. Here are some customization possibilities that can be performed, provided that some experience in .NET/C# programming has been acquired beforehand:

- A target phrase set could be generated according to a specific phrase length distribution (or average length);
- The use of a different language unit to evaluate the representativeness of a phrase set, e.g., a word-based KLD would include the relative entropy between the word probability distributions of the target phrase set and the SC;

- The initial preprocessing of the SC by removing phrases containing words from a list of known offensive terms;
- Introducing an adaptive mutation operator (e.g., with a phrase length-dependent number of genes involved in the mutation process).

Better source corpora will undoubtedly produce better target phrase sets. Therefore, it is desirable to obtain such text resources in which grammatical errors, rare dialect expressions, unpleasant content, and semantically meaningless phrases are rare. However, we must be aware that the language used in text entry is highly context-specific. For example, punctuation, grammar, and capitalization are largely ignored in today's mobile messaging. At the same time, abbreviations and contractions ("1drfl" for "wonderful"), as well as specific shortenings ("lol" for "laughing out loud") and pictograms ("i < 3 u" for "I love you"), are commonly used. Thus, if mobile text input is the subject of an experimental evaluation, it seems reasonable to use NUS SMS or public Facebook/Twitter feeds as the initial corpus for GA-based sampling, regardless of the potentially higher efforts required for initial filtering.

In empirical research on text entry, phrase sets should be used in such a way that the phrases they contain are evenly distributed among different tasks and participants so that the high linguistic representativeness of the sets supports the external validity of the results. In this context, the proposed method can either be used to generate a unique phrase set to standardize it for the target language or to create a customized phrase set corresponding to a specific experiment. For the latter case, we introduce the following heuristic guidelines to prepare the text entry experiment:

1. Select a high-quality and as large as possible text corpus for the target language and target domain of the text entry experiment;
2. Determine the number of test subjects to participate in the text entry experiment (N);
3. Determine how many unit tasks (typing different text phrases) the user must perform using the observed method (M);
4. If M is large (e.g., 100+ sentences), the proposed method can generate a representative set of M phrases, requiring participants to go through the entire set. On the other hand, if M is smaller (at the level of 10–20 sentences, which is common in text entry experiments), it is proposed to generate a set of $M \times N$ phrases, where each participant would type different M phrases from this set;
5. Report the statistics of the phrase set used, indicating the total number of phrases, the total number of words in the set, and the average number of characters in a word.

Conducting a text entry experiment with such a manipulation of phrase sets would help in standardization efforts, ensure the representativeness of the target language, and allow the valid comparison of results from different text entry studies.

Although it is known that target language and representativeness affect the efficiency of text input, we plan to study these effects in more detail in future work using phrase sets obtained with our method. In doing so, we plan to collaborate with researchers worldwide to organize experiments with participants who would write the text in both English and their native language.

5. Conclusions

Representative phrase sets play an essential role in empirical research on text entry, as they allow for a more accurate comparison of different text entry techniques. While Mackenzie and Soukoreff's phrase set has emerged as a de facto standard, there have been notable efforts to improve the quality and contextual appropriateness of phrase sets. Instead of indiscriminately collecting random phrases, a more rigorous approach involves sampling from large, trustworthy text corpora to select linguistically more representative sets.

To tackle the optimization challenge of finding a relatively small, highly representative phrase set within the vast search space of a single-text corpus, we proposed a GA-based approach that utilizes Kullback–Leibler divergence to evaluate candidate sets. As demonstrated in the paper, this method is highly customizable, outperforms typical random sampling, and exhibits language independence.

The implementation of the proposed method is readily available in the public GitHub repository [24], which promotes its immediate utilization and the reproducibility of this study. Researchers can quickly obtain representative phrase sets tailored to their designs of text entry experiments, considering factors such as the target language, source corpus, character set, phrase lengths, set size, and GA parameter values.

Finally, along with the proposed method and its source code, we provide heuristic guidelines for preparing and conducting text entry experiments. These guidelines include the generation of the target phrase set using the proposed method and its utilization in its entirety.

Author Contributions: Conceptualization, S.L.; methodology, S.L.; software, S.L.; validation, S.L. and A.S.; formal analysis, S.L. and A.S.; investigation, S.L. and A.S.; resources, S.L. and A.S.; data curation, S.L. and A.S.; writing—original draft preparation, S.L.; writing—review and editing, S.L. and A.S.; visualization, S.L.; supervision, S.L.; project administration, S.L.; funding acquisition, S.L. All authors have read and agreed to the published version of the manuscript.

Funding: This research received no external funding.

Data Availability Statement: Not applicable.

Conflicts of Interest: The authors declare no conflict of interest.

Abbreviations

The following abbreviations are used in this manuscript:

HCI	Human–Computer Interaction
GA	Genetic algorithm
KLD	Kullback–Leibler divergence
AAC	Augmentative and Alternative Communication
CER	Character Error Rate
BF	Brute Force (sampling)
SC	Source corpus
RC	Reduced corpus
PSC	Phrase set candidate
TPS	Target phrase set
GAF	Genetic Algorithm Framework

References

1. MacKenzie, I.S. *Human–Computer Interaction: An Empirical Research Perspective*, 1st ed.; Morgan Kaufmann Publishers Inc.: San Francisco, CA, USA, 2013.
2. Kristensson, P.O.; Vertanen, K. Performance Comparisons of Phrase Sets and Presentation Styles for Text Entry Evaluations. In Proceedings of the IUI '12, 2012 ACM International Conference on Intelligent User Interfaces, Lisbon, Portugal, 14–17 February 2012; Association for Computing Machinery: New York, NY, USA, 2012; pp. 29–32. [CrossRef]
3. Soukoreff, R.W.; MacKenzie, I.S. Theoretical upper and lower bounds on typing speed using a stylus and a soft keyboard. *Behav. Inf. Technol.* **1995**, *14*, 370–379. [CrossRef]
4. Fitts, P.M. The information capacity of the human motor system in controlling the amplitude of movement. *J. Exp. Psychol.* **1954**, *47*, 381–391. [CrossRef] [PubMed]
5. Mackenzie, I.S.; Zhang, S.X.; Soukoreff, R.W. Text entry using soft keyboards. *Behav. Inf. Technol.* **1999**, *18*, 235–244. [CrossRef]
6. Silfverberg, M.; MacKenzie, I.S.; Korhonen, P. Predicting Text Entry Speed on Mobile Phones. In Proceedings of the CHI '00, SIGCHI Conference on Human Factors in Computing Systems, The Hague, The Netherlands, 1–6 April 2000; Association for Computing Machinery: New York, NY, USA, 2000; pp. 9–16. [CrossRef]
7. Ilinkin, I.; Kim, S. Design and Evaluation of Korean Text Entry Methods for Mobile Phones. In Proceedings of the CHI EA '08, Extended Abstracts on Human Factors in Computing Systems, Florence, Italy, 5–10 April 2008; Association for Computing Machinery: New York, NY, USA, 2008; pp. 2853–2858. [CrossRef]
8. Liu, Y.; Räihä, K.J. Predicting Chinese Text Entry Speeds on Mobile Phones. In Proceedings of the CHI '10, SIGCHI Conference on Human Factors in Computing Systems, Atlanta, GA, USA, 10–15 April 2010; Association for Computing Machinery: New York, NY, USA, 2010; pp. 2183–2192. [CrossRef]

9. MacKenzie, I.S.; Soukoreff, R.W. Phrase Sets for Evaluating Text Entry Techniques. In Proceedings of the CHI EA '03, Extended Abstracts on Human Factors in Computing Systems, Ft. Lauderdale, FL, USA, 5–10 April 2003; Association for Computing Machinery: New York, NY, USA, 2003; pp. 754–755. [CrossRef]
10. Mayzner, M.S.; Tresselt, M.E. Table of single letter and digram frequency counts for various word-length and letter-position combinations. *Psychon. Monogr. Suppl.* **1965**, *1*, 13–32.
11. University of Nebraska, College of Education and Human Sciences. Augmentative and Alternative Communication (AAC). Available online: https://cehs.unl.edu/aac/ (accessed on 3 March 2023).
12. Paek, T.; Hsu, B.J.P. Sampling Representative Phrase Sets for Text Entry Experiments: A Procedure and Public Resource. In Proceedings of the CHI '11, SIGCHI Conference on Human Factors in Computing Systems, Vancouver, BC, Canada, 7–12 May 2011; Association for Computing Machinery: New York, NY, USA, 2011; pp. 2477–2480. [CrossRef]
13. Cover, T.M.; Thomas, J.A. *Elements of Information Theory (Wiley Series in Telecommunications and Signal Processing)*, 2nd ed.; Wiley-Interscience: New York, NY, USA, 2006.
14. Klimt, B.; Yang, Y. Introducing the Enron Corpus. In Proceedings of the CEAS '04, First Conference on Email and Anti-Spam, Mountain View, CA, USA, 30–31 July 2004.
15. Vertanen, K.; Kristensson, P.O. A Versatile Dataset for Text Entry Evaluations Based on Genuine Mobile Emails. In Proceedings of the MobileHCI '11, 13th International Conference on Human Computer Interaction with Mobile Devices and Services, Stockholm, Sweden, 30 August–2 September 2011; Association for Computing Machinery: New York, NY, USA, 2011; pp. 295–298. [CrossRef]
16. Chen, T.; Kan, M.Y. Creating a live, public short message service corpus: The NUS SMS corpus. *Lang. Resour. Eval.* **2013**, *47*, 299–335. [CrossRef]
17. Leiva, L.A.; Sanchis-Trilles, G. Representatively Memorable: Sampling the Right Phrase Set to Get the Text Entry Experiment Right. In Proceedings of the CHI '14, SIGCHI Conference on Human Factors in Computing Systems, Toronto, ON, Canada, 26 April–1 May 2014; Association for Computing Machinery: New York, NY, USA, 2014; pp. 1709–1712. [CrossRef]
18. Sanchis-Trilles, G.; Leiva, L.A. A Systematic Comparison of 3 Phrase Sampling Methods for Text Entry Experiments in 10 Languages. In Proceedings of the MobileHCI '14, 16th International Conference on Human–Computer Interaction with Mobile Devices & Services, Toronto, ON, Canada, 23–26 September 2014; Association for Computing Machinery: New York, NY, USA, 2014; pp. 537–542. [CrossRef]
19. Yi, X.; Yu, C.; Shi, W.; Bi, X.; Shi, Y. Word Clarity as a Metric in Sampling Keyboard Test Sets. In Proceedings of the CHI '17, 2017 CHI Conference on Human Factors in Computing Systems, Denver, CO, USA, 6–11 May 2017; Association for Computing Machinery: New York, NY, USA, 2017; pp. 4216–4228. [CrossRef]
20. Gaines, D.; Vertanen, K. A Phrase Dataset with Difficulty Ratings Under Simulated Touchscreen Input. In Proceedings of the MobileHCI '22, MobileHCI 2022 Workshop on Shaping Text Entry Research for 2030, Vancouver, BC, Canada, 28 September–1 October 2022.
21. Abbott, J.; Kaye, J.; Clawson, J. Identifying an Aurally Distinct Phrase Set for Text Entry Techniques. In Proceedings of the CHI '22, 2022 CHI Conference on Human Factors in Computing Systems, New Orleans, LA, USA, 29 April–5 May 2022; Association for Computing Machinery: New York, NY, USA, 2022. [CrossRef]
22. Whitley, D. A genetic algorithm tutorial. *Stat. Comput.* **1994**, *4*, 65–85. [CrossRef]
23. Newcombe, J. GAF—Genetic Algorithm Framework for .NET. Available online: https://www.nuget.org/packages/GAF (accessed on 3 March 2023).
24. Ljubic, S. Text Corpus Sampling. Available online: https://github.com/sljubic/text-corpus-sampling (accessed on 15 March 2023).
25. Šnajder, J.; Padó, S.; Agić, Ž. Building and Evaluating a Distributional Memory for Croatian. In Proceedings of the 51st Annual Meeting of the Association for Computational Linguistics, Sofia, Bulgaria, 4–9 August 2013; Association for Computational Linguistics: Sofia, Bulgaria, 2013; pp. 784–789.
26. Ljubešić, N.; Erjavec, T. hrWaC and slWac: Compiling Web Corpora for Croatian and Slovene. In Proceedings of the TSD '11, International Conference on Text, Speech and Dialogue, Pilsen, Czech Republic, 1–5 September 2011; Habernal, I., Matoušek, V., Eds.; Springer: Berlin/Heidelberg, Germany, 2011; pp. 395–402. [CrossRef]
27. TakeLab. fHrWaC—Filtered Croatian Web Corpus (hrWaC). Available online: https://takelab.fer.hr/data/fhrwac/ (accessed on 3 March 2023).
28. Eiben, A.E.; Smit, S.K. Evolutionary Algorithm Parameters and Methods to Tune Them. In *Autonomous Search*; Hamadi, Y., Monfroy, E., Saubion, F., Eds.; Springer: Berlin/Heidelberg, Germany, 2012; pp. 15–36. [CrossRef]
29. Isokoski, P.; Linden, T. Effect of Foreign Language on Text Transcription Performance: Finns Writing English. In Proceedings of the NordiCHI '04, Third Nordic Conference on Human–Computer Interaction, Tampere, Finland, 23–27 October 2004; Association for Computing Machinery: New York, NY, USA, 2004; pp. 109–112. [CrossRef]
30. Tiedemann, J. Parallel Data, Tools and Interfaces in OPUS. In Proceedings of the LREC '12, Eighth International Conference on Language Resources and Evaluation, Istanbul, Turkey, 23–25 May 2012; European Language Resources Association (ELRA): Istanbul, Turkey, 2012; pp. 2214–2218.
31. OPUS. OpenSubtitles2013. Available online: https://opus.nlpl.eu/OpenSubtitles2013.php (accessed on 3 March 2023).
32. Yanagihara, N.; Shizuki, B.; Takahashi, S. Text Entry Method for Immersive Virtual Environments Using Curved Keyboard. In Proceedings of the VRST '19, 25th ACM Symposium on Virtual Reality Software and Technology, Parramatta, Australia, 13–15 November 2019; Association for Computing Machinery: New York, NY, USA, 2019. [CrossRef]

33. He, Z.; Lutteroth, C.; Perlin, K. TapGazer: Text Entry with Finger Tapping and Gaze-Directed Word Selection. In Proceedings of the CHI '22, 2022 CHI Conference on Human Factors in Computing Systems, New Orleans, LA, USA, 29 April–5 May 2022; Association for Computing Machinery: New York, NY, USA, 2022. [CrossRef]
34. Lu, X.; Yu, D.; Liang, H.N.; Goncalves, J. IText: Hands-Free Text Entry on an Imaginary Keyboard for Augmented Reality Systems. In Proceedings of the UIST '21, 34th Annual ACM Symposium on User Interface Software and Technology, Virtual, 10–14 October 2021; Association for Computing Machinery: New York, NY, USA, 2021; pp. 815–825. [CrossRef]
35. Kimura, N.; Gemicioglu, T.; Womack, J.; Li, R.; Zhao, Y.; Bedri, A.; Su, Z.; Olwal, A.; Rekimoto, J.; Starner, T. SilentSpeller: Towards Mobile, Hands-Free, Silent Speech Text Entry Using Electropalatography. In Proceedings of the CHI '22, 2022 CHI Conference on Human Factors in Computing Systems, New Orleans, LA, USA, 29 April–5 May 2022; Association for Computing Machinery: New York, NY, USA, 2022. [CrossRef]
36. Streli, P.; Jiang, J.; Fender, A.R.; Meier, M.; Romat, H.; Holz, C. TapType: Ten-Finger Text Entry on Everyday Surfaces via Bayesian Inference. In Proceedings of the CHI '22, 2022 CHI Conference on Human Factors in Computing Systems, New Orleans, LA, USA, 29 April–5 May 2022; Association for Computing Machinery: New York, NY, USA, 2022. [CrossRef]
37. Zhang, M.R.; Zhai, S.; Wobbrock, J.O. TypeAnywhere: A QWERTY-Based Text Entry Solution for Ubiquitous Computing. In Proceedings of the CHI '22, 2022 CHI Conference on Human Factors in Computing Systems, New Orleans, LA, USA, 29 April–5 May 2022; Association for Computing Machinery: New York, NY, USA, 2022. [CrossRef]
38. Sandnes, F.E. Can Automatic Abbreviation Expansion Improve the Text Entry Rates of Norwegian Text with Compound Words? In Proceedings of the DSAI 2018, 8th International Conference on Software Development and Technologies for Enhancing Accessibility and Fighting Info-Exclusion, Thessaloniki, Greece, 20–22 June 2018; Association for Computing Machinery: New York, NY, USA, 2018; pp. 1–7. [CrossRef]
39. Ruan, S.; Wobbrock, J.O.; Liou, K.; Ng, A.; Landay, J.A. Comparing Speech and Keyboard Text Entry for Short Messages in Two Languages on Touchscreen Phones. In *Proceedings of the ACM on Interactive, Mobile, Wearable and Ubiquitous Technologies*; Association for Computing Machinery: New York, NY, USA, 2018; Volume 1. [CrossRef]
40. Labani, M.; Moradi, P.; Jalili, M. A multi-objective genetic algorithm for text feature selection using the relative discriminative criterion. *Expert Syst. Appl.* **2020**, *149*, 113276. [CrossRef]
41. Mustafi, D.; Mustafi, A.; Sahoo, G. A novel approach to text clustering using genetic algorithm based on the nearest neighbour heuristic. *Int. J. Comput. Appl.* **2022**, *44*, 291–303. [CrossRef]
42. Jain, A.; Arora, A.; Morato, J.; Yadav, D.; Kumar, K.V. Automatic Text Summarization for Hindi Using Real Coded Genetic Algorithm. *Appl. Sci.* **2022**, *12*, 6584. [CrossRef]

Disclaimer/Publisher's Note: The statements, opinions and data contained in all publications are solely those of the individual author(s) and contributor(s) and not of MDPI and/or the editor(s). MDPI and/or the editor(s) disclaim responsibility for any injury to people or property resulting from any ideas, methods, instructions or products referred to in the content.

Article

Deep Neural Network-Based Simulation of Sel'kov Model in Glycolysis: A Comprehensive Analysis

Jamshaid Ul Rahman [1,2], Sana Danish [2] and Dianchen Lu [1,*]

[1] School of Mathematical Sciences, Jiangsu University, 301 Xuefu Road, Zhenjiang 212013, China; jamshaid@mail.ustc.edu.cn
[2] Abdus Salam School of Mathematical Sciences, GC University, Lahore 54600, Pakistan; sana_danish_21@sms.edu.pk
* Correspondence: dclu@ujs.edu.cn

Abstract: The Sel'kov model for glycolysis is a highly effective tool in capturing the complex feedback mechanisms that occur within a biochemical system. However, accurately predicting the behavior of this system is challenging due to its nonlinearity, stiffness, and parameter sensitivity. In this paper, we present a novel deep neural network-based method to simulate the Sel'kov glycolysis model of ADP and F6P, which overcomes the limitations of conventional numerical methods. Our comprehensive results demonstrate that the proposed approach outperforms traditional methods and offers greater reliability for nonlinear dynamics. By adopting this flexible and robust technique, researchers can gain deeper insights into the complex interactions that drive biochemical systems.

Keywords: biochemical system; nonlinear dynamics; neural network; Sel'kov model; coupled differential equations

MSC: 97-04; 92B20

1. Introduction

The human body is an intricate system capable of exhibiting a range of behaviors, ranging from low complexity and seemingly disordered behavior to high complexity and unpredictable behavior [1]. The field of nonlinear dynamics [2] aims to comprehend the complex and frequently unforeseeable behavior of systems that adhere to nonlinear equations [3]. Nonlinear dynamics can be a valuable tool in comprehending the behavior of biological systems [4] within the human body, such as the nervous system [5], musculoskeletal [6], and circulatory systems [7]. Through studying the dynamics of these systems, we can gain a better understanding of the underlying mechanisms of various diseases and conditions, as well as potential solutions.

We are considering one of the nonlinear dynamical systems: a mathematical model that depicts the behavior of a biochemical reaction network [8] containing glycolysis [9], a crucial metabolic process [10] in living creatures, known as the Sel'kov glycolysis model [11,12], which was first put forth by Russian biochemist Anatolii Sel'kov in 1968. Due to the model's simplicity and capacity to grasp crucial aspects of glycolytic oscillations found empirically in yeast and other organisms, it has received extensive study and analysis in the field of systems biology. The Sel'kov model for glycolysis has been studied using a variety of methodologies, including analytical methods, numerical methods, data-driven approaches, and sensitivity analysis [11,13]. Moreover, finding the bifurcation points in a system is crucial for stability analysis in order to comprehend the system's dynamics and transition [14]. Researchers commonly combine several approaches to gain a deeper knowledge of the dynamics and behavior of the system.

Deep neural networks (DNNs) [15] have demonstrated great potential in the field of solving nonlinear dynamical systems because of their capacity to recognize intricate, non-

linear relationships between input and output factors [16]. DNNs have been particularly effective in modeling and predicting the behavior of complicated nonlinear systems. Traditional numerical methods [17] to solve complicated nonlinear differential equations [18] require high computational cost and simplification of the underlying system that might not always be suitable; the capacity of the DNN-based approach to approximate extremely complex and nonlinear relationships between input and output variables made them well suited for the solution of differential equations with complex dynamics. In summary, the application of deep neural networks (DNNs) has the potential to enhance the handling and prediction of complex nonlinear dynamical systems across a range of disciplines, including applied mathematics [19], engineering [20], and biology [21]. By providing a powerful tool for capturing nonlinear dynamics and bifurcation behavior, DNNs offer significant opportunities for advancing our understanding of complex systems and developing more effective approaches for managing and predicting their behavior.

2. Mathematical Model and Deep Neural Network

Sel'kov Glycolysis Model

The theories of nonlinear dynamics, or "the study of complexity," offer a strict, mathematical foundation for the description of living things. Consequently, both nonlinear dynamicists and biologists need to be knowledgeable about nonlinear dynamics. We considered the Sel'kov model in order to apply our proposed DNN-based approach to the simulation of nonlinear dynamics. Two nonlinear differential equations are used in the model to characterize the amounts of the two chemical species that are engaged in glycolysis. Its simplified version of temporal dynamics in mathematical form is given as follows:

$$\begin{cases} \frac{du}{dt} = -u + av + u^2v & (a) \\ \frac{dv}{dt} = b - av - u^2v & (b) \\ u(0) = 1, \ v(0) = 0 & \end{cases} \quad (1)$$

With the inclusion of both positive and negative feedback mechanisms, the Equation (1) reflects the dynamics of the two variables u and v over time.

The dependent variables u and v represent concentrations of adenosine diphosphate (ADP) [22] and fructose 6-phosphate (F6P) [23] in the process of glycolysis. Equation (1)(a) represents the rate of change in the concentration of ADP with respect to time. The term $-u$ indicates the decay of ADP, a ($a > 0$) is the rate of the constant for the production of F6P, the term av with a positive sign is responsible for the rate of production of ADP due to presence of v scaled by using parameter a, and u^2v is responsible for nonlinearity, implying that the concentration of u promotes its own production multiplied by the concentration of v.

Equation (1)(b) represents the rate of change in the concentration of fructose 6-phosphate. The term b ($b > 0$) is the rate constant for the decay of ADP and the term $-av$ is responsible for the rate of consumption of F6P due to the reaction of u and v. The product term u^2v indicates nonlinear interactions between two chemical species, suggesting that the concentration of u inhibits the production of v. Due to the squared components involving u^2v, the model shows nonlinearity, which can result in fascinating behaviors such as oscillations or the establishment of persistent steady states.

3. Methodology

For the simulation of the aforementioned problem, we took advantage of a DNN-based strategy to solve a set of nonlinear differential equations. The working rule that DNN follows to solve differential equations is that it codifies the differential equation [24] as a loss function [25,26] for optimization problems and then curtails the loss by adopting different optimization techniques. Here, a thorough explanation of how neural networks function and perform is offered.

3.1. Data Preparation

In approximating a dependent variable of a differential equation using DNN, the type of data typically consists of input features and corresponding dependent variable values. The parameters a and b in our system of differential equations serve as the input features. By input features, we mean the variables or parameters that are known in the situation at hand. We must select definite a and b values as well as the time period at which we wish to approximate. The dependent variable values $u(t)$ and $v(t)$ are the solutions of a given system of differential equations at a different time t; these are unknown and must be approximated by DNN. Pairs of input characteristics (a, b) with their associated values of $(u(t), v(t))$ at various time points t would make up the dataset.

The fully connected layer can estimate the dependent variable for new input configurations by utilizing this dataset to understand the underlying patterns and connections between the input characteristics and the dependent variable values. The dataset is divided into a training set and a testing set as per the setup of the Python package known as NeuroDiffEq [27].

3.2. Neural Network Architecture Design

As baseline architecture, we adopted a fully connected neural network (FCNN) to meet our task described in our proposed methodology.

For each dependent variable, the settings in our model that make the neural network architecture consist of one input layer, one output layer, and three fully connected hidden layers. The first two hidden layers each contain 64 units of neurons, and the third layer has 128 neurons. Before moving on to the next layer, the input is stimulated during the process by using an activation function. The activation function [28], which is in charge of activating neurons, aims to create nonlinearity between the levels. The activation function used in our setup, the Tanh function activation [29], is smooth and continuous. This characteristic of the Tanh activation function enables the network to have continuous and differentiable outputs, supporting gradient-based optimization techniques such as backpropagation. In this baseline architecture of DNN, we adjusted the hyperparameters including the learning rate, activation function, optimization technique, number of layers, and number of neurons per layer manually in the process of training a neural network. Figures 1 and 2 unveil the inner working of the neural network intended for use in the simulation of a given problem. There are several layers in the network, including input, hidden, and output layers, which are connected by weighted connections. To approximate the behavior of the glycolysis system, each layer carries out specialized computations.

3.3. Training of the Model

The model is trained by initializing random weights and biases after all structural settings have been completed. For the training loop, we set epochs to 30,000 and the learning rate to 0.01. The input data are sent forward over the network. After computing the weighted sum of the inputs in each layer, the activation function is applied and the output is propagated to the next layer. A specified threshold value is used by the activation function to determine whether or not a neuron should be stimulated to transfer output to the next layer. This loop keeps running until the output layer is reached. The activation function enhances the expressive power of the fully connected layer. Through this predicted output, the error or the loss is calculated using the appropriate loss function.

Mean squared error (MSE) [30], which is frequently used as a metric for regression problems [31], is adopted here to calculate the average difference between predicted and actual output values in order to measure the performance of the model during training. The mathematical form of *MSE* is given in Equation (2).

$$MSE = \frac{1}{n}\left(\sum_{i=1}^{n}(y_{i\_true} - y_{i\_predicted})^2\right) \qquad (2)$$

n = the number of sample points in the dataset,
y_i_true = true values of the ith sample
$y_i\_predicted$ = predicted values of the ith sample

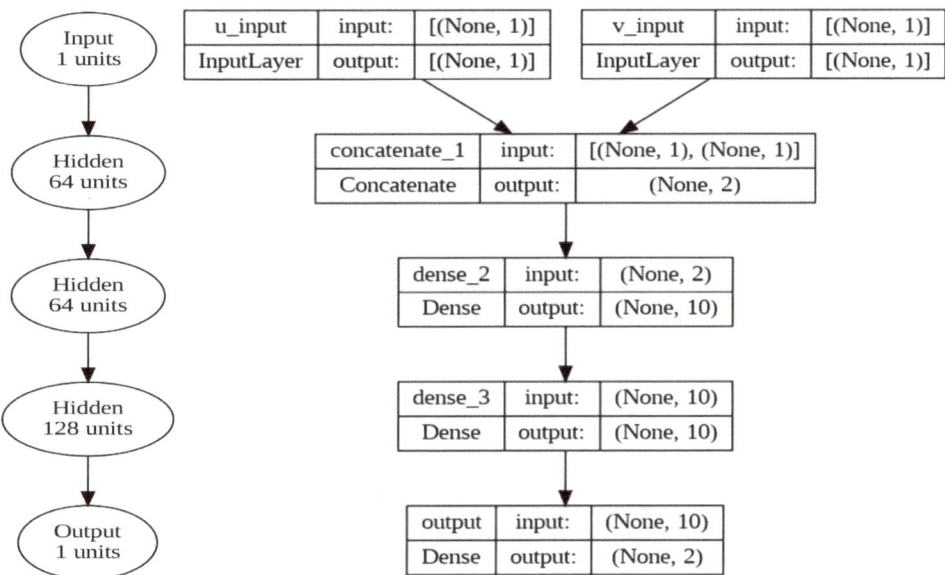

Figure 1. The figure visually encapsulates the in-depth exploration, unveiling the intricate inner workings of neural networks.

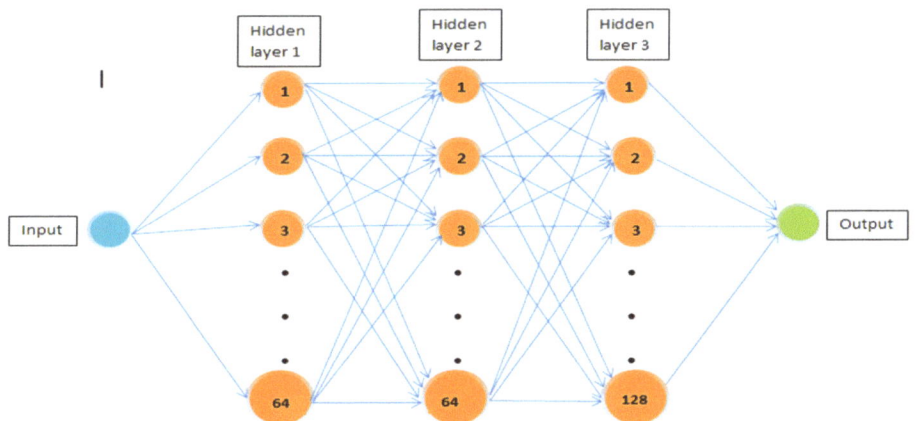

Figure 2. The complete neural architecture comprises hidden layers 1, 2, and 3, consisting of 64, 64, and 128 units respectively.

Using optimization techniques [32] in backpropagation [33], this loss is then minimized to update the model's parameters (weights and biases) and improve accuracy. The optimization technique we utilized is the integration of momentum and adaptive learning rate techniques; that is, the Adam (adaptive moment estimation) algorithm [34]. It is efficient because even with large datasets, it tends to converge rapidly. The working rule of the Adam algorithm can be summarized mathematically as follows:

$$\begin{cases} m_t = \beta_1 m_{t-1} + (1-\beta_1)(g_t)^2 \\ V_t = \sqrt{\beta_2 V_{t-1} + (1-\beta_2)(g_t)^2} \\ \theta_{t+1} = m_t - \eta \frac{\sqrt{(1-\beta_2)}}{(1-\beta_1)} \cdot \frac{m_t}{V_{t+\epsilon}} \end{cases} \quad (3)$$

The term m_t is the first-moment estimate and is the mean of the gradients calculated at each time step t, β_1 and β_2 are exponential decaying parameters, V_t is the second-moment estimate which is the variance of the gradients calculated at each time step, g_t is the gradient calculated at each time step t, η is the learning rate for regulating the step size in the parameter update, and θ_{t+1} is the updated parametric value at time $t+1$.

3.4. Analysis of the Model's Performance

Once the model is trained, we validated the model, which helps to improve the performance of the model by adjusting parameters [35] and hyperparameters such as the number of epochs and the learning rate, and then we test the model to see if it could handle new data points. As a final stage, the accuracy and loss of the suggested methodology were determined by comparing the findings to those of a conventional numerical method. We took advantage of the state-of-the-art programming language Python to simulate and visualize the results of our model of a system of a differential equation. The DNN-based technique is clearly illustrated in Figure 3, which makes it easier to analyze and comprehend the steps required in approximating a dependent variable with a DNN.

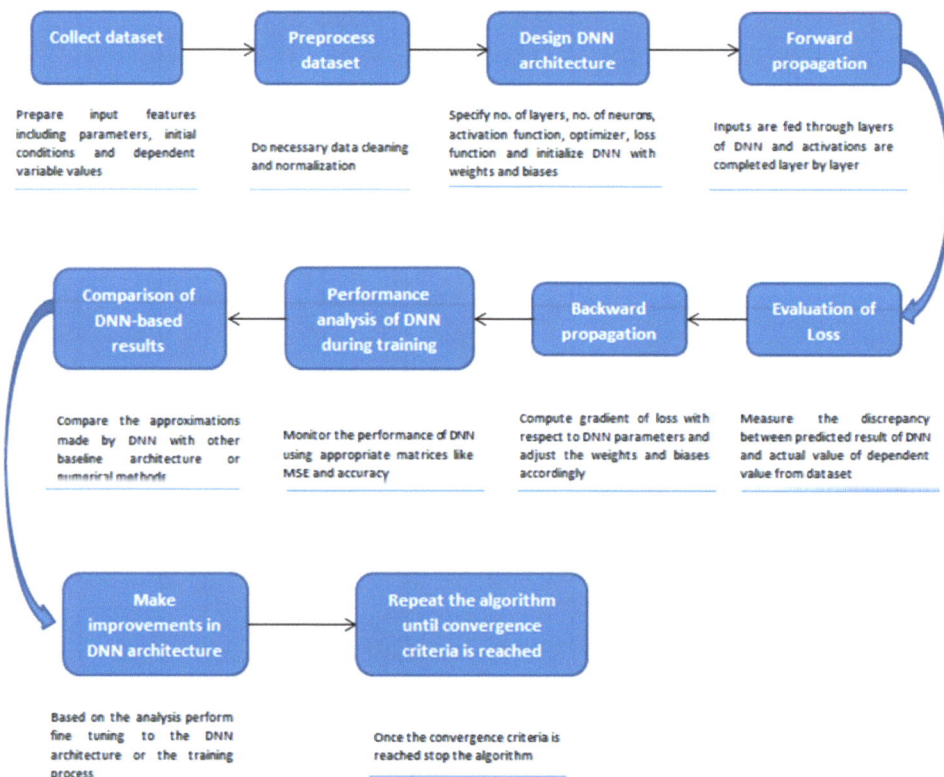

Figure 3. Description for the DNN-based model for the simulation of a nonlinear dynamical system.

4. Results and Discussion

This section will discuss the simulation results achieved using the suggested DNN-centered scheme. We carried out various experiments to observe how changes in the parametric values of the nonlinear temporal dynamical model provided in Equation (1) can affect the solution of a set of differential equations.

Figure 4 shows oscillations produced during the glycolysis process evaluated using a DNN-based method. We noticed impacts of various values of parameter "b" ranging from 0.10 to 0.95 on the oscillations while holding the parameter "a" fixed to a value of 0.08 as shown in all the graphs of Figure 4. In the second training run, these outcomes were attained. In Figure 4, the orange color represents the solution of Equation (1)(a) and the blue color represents the solution of Equation (1)(b). Figure 4 shows that as the value of "b" rises, there are a growing number of oscillations. For smaller values of b, the oscillations begin as tiny and the graphs for v show monotonic declines while graphs for u show abrupt increases that eventually achieve their maximum value. Oscillation values rise along with increasing values of b, and they abruptly shift after a while.

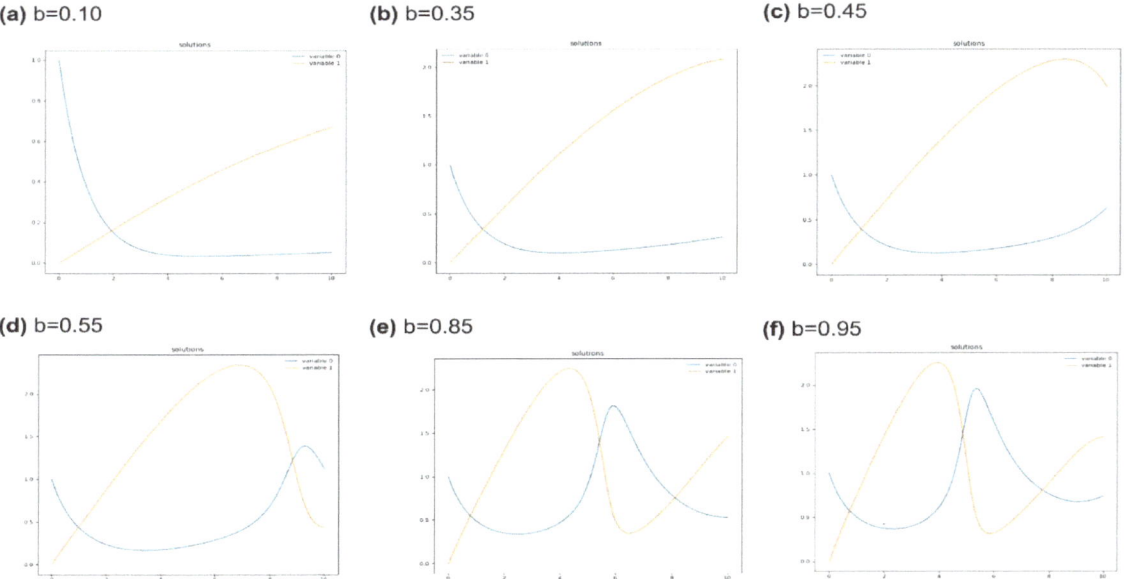

Figure 4. Representing the solutions of the Sel'kov glycolysis model for different values of kinetic parameters using a DNN-based approach.

A comparison between the DNN-based solutions and the solutions obtained from the numerical method (the Runge–Kutta method) are plotted in Figure 5. It is obvious from the graphical results how beautifully the neural network approximated the solution of the nonlinear dynamical system presented in Equation (1). Figure 5 shows plots with dotted lines for neural network approximation and solid lines for numerical method approximation that are very well matched with one another. Runge–Kutta and other numerical techniques can be computationally costly, especially for complicated systems or large-scale problems. Moreover, the cost of computation rises as more iterations are needed to reach a solution. DNN-based solutions can offer predictions or answers significantly faster than numerical approaches once they have been trained. The Runge–Kutta method is predicated on the assumptions and the underlying mathematical model; on the other hand, a DNN can potentially generalize to a wider range of problems once trained on diverse and representative data.

We performed an error analysis and documented the loss and accuracy of the desired model in order to verify the veracity of our suggested advanced DNN-based scheme, as is evident from the bar graph shown in Figure 6. It shows the loss and accuracy for both u and v. It is clear that, starting at b = 0.95, we have little loss but high accuracy, and that, for b = 0.85, accuracy temporarily decreases. However, for a decrease in the value of parameter b, we observed maximum accuracy in the case of b = 0.10. It is observed that the proposed architecture of the DNN outperformed the traditional numerical techniques for the nonlinear dynamical system, as it produces findings that are precise and effective.

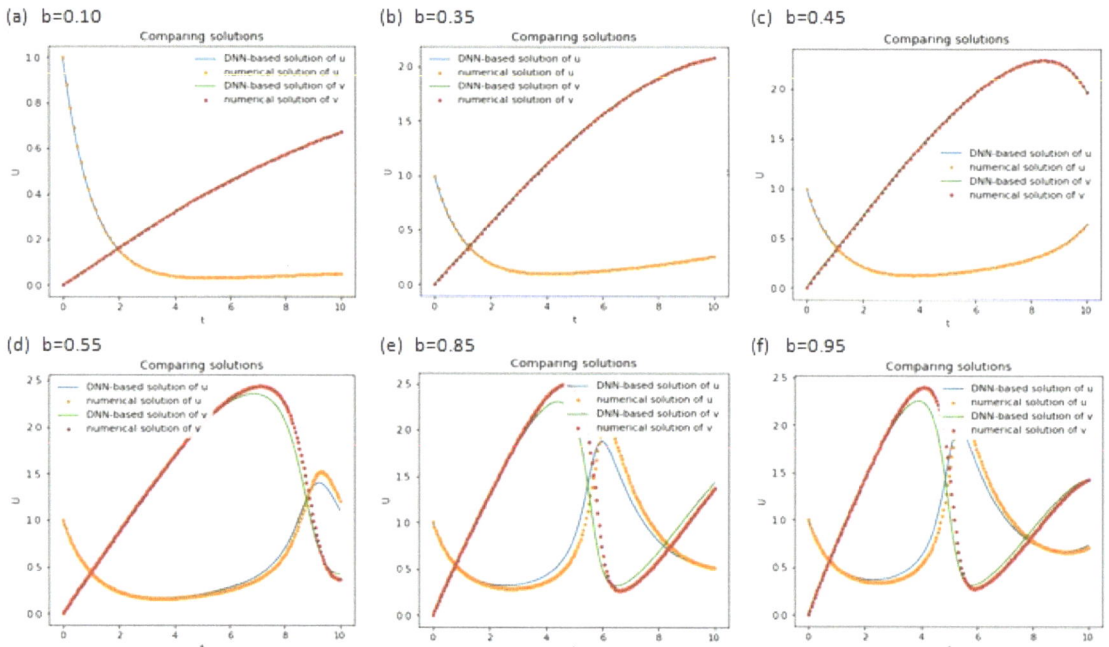

Figure 5. A comparison of DNN-based solutions and numerical solutions of the Sel'kov glycolysis model with different kinetic parameters.

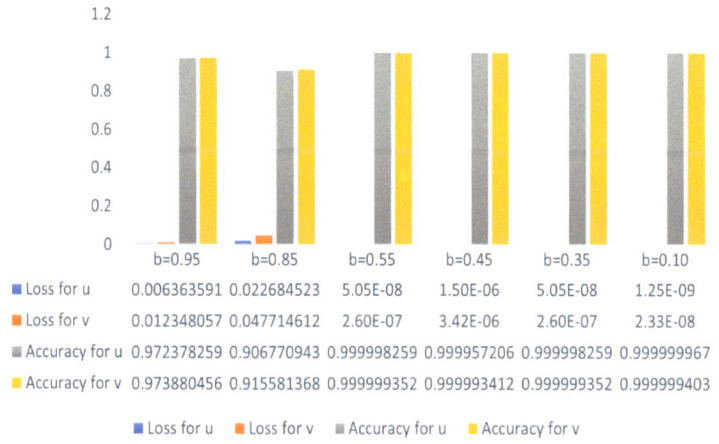

Figure 6. Error analysis of the Sel'kov glycolysis model with different kinetic parameters.

5. Conclusions

In conclusion, the proposed DNN-based strategy has proven to be a powerful tool for simulating the Sel'kov glycolysis model, which is a complex nonlinear dynamical system. Through a series of experiments, we have demonstrated that the DNN architecture is effective in capturing the system's nonlinear dynamics and bifurcation behavior, even when parametric values are changed. In an error analysis, it is helpful to visualize the effects of each parametric value on the dependent variable. The deviance and trends that the model identified are highlighted in the graphical findings. These findings suggest that the DNN-based approach can provide a valuable means for understanding and analyzing the concentration profiles of biochemical reactions. We are confident that our research will contribute to the development of more advanced and effective approaches to solving nonlinear dynamical systems, paving the way for new discoveries in this field. Overall, this study highlights the immense potential of the DNN-based approach in understanding complex systems and advancing scientific research. The proposed strategy can be integrated with recently proposed activation functions to optimize and better capture the complexities of nonlinear dynamical systems. Additionally, extending the proposed methodology to more complex biological models beyond Sel'kov and incorporating the oscillatory activation function [27,36] can offer new opportunities to investigate chemical reactions with vibratory structures.

Author Contributions: Conceptualization, J.U.R. and S.D.; Methodology, J.U.R. and S.D.; Software, S.D.; Validation, S.D. and D.L.; Formal analysis, J.U.R., S.D. and D.L.; Investigation, S.D.; Resources, D.L.; Data curation, D.L.; Writing—original draft, S.D.; Writing—review & editing, D.L.; Visualization, S.D. and D.L.; Supervision, D.L.; Project administration, D.L.; Funding acquisition, D.L. All authors have read and agreed to the published version of the manuscript.

Funding: This work is supported by the National Natural Science Foundation of China (Grant Nos. 12102148 and 11872189) and the Natural Science Research of Jiangsu Higher Education Institutions of China (Grant No. 21KJB110010).

Data Availability Statement: Not applicable.

Conflicts of Interest: The authors declare no conflict of interest.

References

1. El-Safty, A.; Tolba, M.F.; Said, L.A.; Madian, A.H.; Radwan, A.G. A study of the nonlinear dynamics of human behavior and its digital hardware implementation. *J. Adv. Res.* **2020**, *25*, 111–123. [CrossRef]
2. Peters, W.S.; Belenky, V.; Spyrou, K.J. Spyrou. Regulatory use of nonlinear dynamics: An overview. In *Contemporary Ideas on Ship Stability*; Elsevier: Amsterdam, The Netherlands, 2023; pp. 113–127.
3. Mahdy, A.M.S. A numerical method for solving the nonlinear equations of Emden-Fowler models. *J. Ocean. Eng. Sci.* 2022, in press. [CrossRef]
4. Yeongjun, L.; Lee, T.-W. Organic synapses for neuromorphic electronics: From brain-inspired computing to sensorimotor nervetronics. *Acc. Chem. Res.* **2019**, *52*, 964–974.
5. Adina, T.M.-T.; Shortland, P. *The Nervous System, E-Book: Systems of the Body Series*; Elsevier Health Sciences: Amsterdam, The Netherlands, 2022.
6. Money, S.; Aiyer, R. Musculoskeletal system. *Adv. Anesth. Rev.* **2023**, *341*, 152. [CrossRef]
7. Morris, J.L.; Nilsson, S. The circulatory system. In *Comparative Physiology and Evolution of the Autonomic Nervous System*; Routledge: London, UK, 2021; pp. 193–246.
8. Lakrisenko, P.; Stapor, P.; Grein, S.; Paszkowski; Pathirana, D.; Fröhlich, F.; Lines, G.T.; Weindl, D.; Hasenauer, J. Efficient computation of adjoint sensitivities at steady-state in ODE models of biochemical reaction networks. *PLOS Comput. Biol.* **2023**, *19*, e1010783. [CrossRef]
9. Fu, Z.; Xi, S. The effects of heavy metals on human metabolism. *Toxicol. Mech. Methods* **2020**, *30*, 167–176. [CrossRef]
10. Wu, G. Nutrition and metabolism: Foundations for animal growth, development, reproduction, and health. In *Recent Advances in Animal Nutrition and Metabolism*; Springer: Berlin/Heidelberg, Germany, 2022; pp. 1–24.
11. Basu, A.; Bhattacharjee, J.K. When Hopf meets saddle: Bifurcations in the diffusive Selkov model for glycolysis. *Nonlinear Dyn.* **2023**, *111*, 3781–3795. [CrossRef]
12. Dhatt, S.; Chaudhury, P. Study of oscillatory dynamics in a Selkov glycolytic model using sensitivity analysis. *Indian J. Phys.* **2022**, *96*, 1649–1654. [CrossRef]

13. Pankratov, A.; Bashkirtseva, I. Stochastic effects in pattern generation processes for the Selkov glycolytic model with diffusion. *AIP Conf. Proceeding* **2022**, *2466*, 090018.
14. Montavon, G.; Samek, W.; Müller, K.-R. Methods for interpreting and understanding deep neural networks. *Digit. Signal Process.* **2018**, *73*, 1–15. [CrossRef]
15. Ul Rahman, J.; Faiza, M.; Akhtar, A.; Sana, D. Mathematical modeling and simulation of biophysics systems using neural network. *Int. J. Mod. Phys. B* **2023**, 2450066. [CrossRef]
16. Rehman, S.; Akhtar, H.; Ul Rahman, J.; Naveed, A.; Taj, M. Modified Laplace based variational iteration method for the mechanical vibrations and its applications. *Acta Mech. Autom.* **2022**, *16*, 98–102. [CrossRef]
17. Zarnan, J.A.; Hameed, W.M.; Kanbar, A.B. New Numerical Approach for Solution of Nonlinear Differential Equations. *J. Hunan Univ. Nat. Sci.* **2022**, *49*, 163–170. [CrossRef]
18. Kremsner, S.; Steinicke, A.; Szölgyenyi, M. A deep neural network algorithm for semilinear elliptic PDEs with applications in insurance mathematics. *Risks* **2020**, *8*, 136. [CrossRef]
19. Li, Y.; Wei, H.; Han, Z.; Huang, J.; Wang, W. Deep learning-based safety helmet detection in engineering management based on convolutional neural networks. *Adv. Civ. Eng.* **2020**, *2020*, 9703560. [CrossRef]
20. Sahu, A.; Rana, K.P.S.; Kumar, V. An application of deep dual convolutional neural network for enhanced medical image denoising. *Med. Biol. Eng. Comput.* **2023**, *61*, 991–1004. [CrossRef] [PubMed]
21. Pan, G.; Zhang, P.; Chen, A.; Deng, Y.; Zhang, Z.; Lu, H.; Zhu, A.; Zhou, C.; Wu, Y.; Li, S. Aerobic glycolysis in colon cancer is repressed by naringin via the HIF1A pathway. *J. Zhejiang Univ. Sci. B* **2023**, *24*, 221–231. [CrossRef] [PubMed]
22. Chen, X.; Ji, Y.; Zhao, W.; Niu, H.; Yang, X.; Jiang, X.; Zhang, Y.; Lei, J.; Yang, H.; Chen, R.; et al. Fructose-6-phosphate-2-kinase/fructose-2, 6-bisphosphatase regulates energy metabolism and synthesis of storage products in developing rice endosperm. *Plant Sci.* **2023**, *326*, 111503. [CrossRef]
23. Hsu, S.-B.; Chen, K.-C. *Ordinary Differential Equations with Applications*; World Scientific: Singapore, 2022; Volume 23.
24. Tian, Y.; Su, D.; Lauria, S.; Liu, X. Recent advances on loss functions in deep learning for computer vision. *Neurocomputing* **2022**, *497*, 129–158. [CrossRef]
25. Ul Rahman, J.; Ali, A.; Ur Rehman, M.; Kazmi, R. A unit softmax with Laplacian smoothing stochastic gradient descent for deep convolutional neural networks. In Proceedings of the Intelligent Technologies and Applications: Second International Conference, INTAP 2019, Bahawalpur, Pakistan, 6–8 November 2019; Springer: Singapore, 2020; Revised Selected Papers 2.
26. Chen, F.; Sondak, D.; Protopapas, P.; Mattheakis, M.; Liu, S.; Agarwal, D.; Di Giovanni, M. Neurodiffeq: A python package for solving differential equations with neural networks. *J. Open Source Softw.* **2020**, *5*, 1931. [CrossRef]
27. Rahman, J.; Ul, F.M.; Dianchen Lu, D. Amplifying Sine Unit: An Oscillatory Activation Function for Deep Neural Networks to Recover Nonlinear Oscillations Efficiently. *arXiv*, 2023, arXiv:2304.09759.
28. Roy, S.K.; Manna, S.; Dubey, S.R.; Chaudhuri, B.B. LiSHT: Non-parametric linearly scaled hyperbolic tangent activation function for neural networks. In *International Conference on Computer Vision and Image Processing, Nagpur, India, 4–6 November 2022*; Springer Nature: Cham, Switzerland, 2022.
29. Qi, J.; Du, J.; Siniscalchi, S.M.; Ma, X.; Lee, C.-H. On mean absolute error for deep neural network based vector-to-vector regression. *IEEE Signal Process. Lett.* **2020**, *27*, 1485–1489. [CrossRef]
30. Tianle, C.; Gao, R.; Hou, J.; Chen, S.; Wang, D.; He, D. A gram-gauss-newton method learning overparameterized deep neural networks for regression problems. *arXiv* **2019**, arXiv:1905.11675.
31. Yong, H.; Huang, J.; Hua, X.; Zhang, L. Gradient centralization: A new optimization technique for deep neural networks. In Proceedings of the Computer Vision–ECCV 2020: 16th European Conference, Glasgow, UK, 23–28 August 2020; Springer International Publishing: Cham, Switzerland, 2020; Proceedings, Part I 16.
32. Wright, L.G.; Onodera, T.; Stein, M.M.; Wang, T.; Schachter, D.T.; Hu, Z.; McMahon, P.L. Deep physical neural networks trained with backpropagation. *Nature* **2022**, *601*, 549–555. [CrossRef] [PubMed]
33. Ariff, N.A.M.; Ismail, A.R. Study of adam and adamax optimizers on alexnet architecture for voice biometric authentication system. In Proceedings of the 2023 17th International Conference on Ubiquitous Information Management and Communication (IMCOM), Seoul, Republic of Korea, 3–5 January 2023; IEEE: Piscataway, NJ, USA, 2023.
34. Legaard, C.M.; Schranz, T.; Schweiger, G.; Drgoňa, J.; Falay, B.; Gomes, C.; Iosifidis, A.; Abkar, M.; Larsen, P.G. Constructing Neural Network Based Models for Simulating Dynamical Systems. *ACM Comput. Surv.* **2023**, *55*, 236. [CrossRef]
35. Hong, Z.; Lu, Y.; Liu, B.; Ran, C.; Lei, X.; Wang, M.; Wu, S.; Yang, Y.; Wu, H. Glycolysis, a new mechanism of oleuropein against liver tumor. *Phytomedicine* **2023**, *114*, 154770. [CrossRef] [PubMed]
36. Jamshaid Ul, R.; Makhdoom, F.; Lu, D. ASU-CNN: An Efficient Deep Architecture for Image Classification and Feature Visualizations. *arXiv* **2023**, arXiv:2305.19146.

Disclaimer/Publisher's Note: The statements, opinions and data contained in all publications are solely those of the individual author(s) and contributor(s) and not of MDPI and/or the editor(s). MDPI and/or the editor(s) disclaim responsibility for any injury to people or property resulting from any ideas, methods, instructions or products referred to in the content.

Article
Spectral Salt-and-Pepper Patch Masking for Self-Supervised Speech Representation Learning

June-Woo Kim [1], Hoon Chung [2] and Ho-Young Jung [1,*]

[1] Department of Artificial Intelligence, Kyungpook National University, Daegu 41566, Republic of Korea; kaen2891@knu.ac.kr
[2] Electronics and Telecommunications Research Institute, Daejeon 34129, Republic of Korea; hchung@etri.re.kr
* Correspondence: hoyjung@knu.ac.kr

Abstract: Recent advanced systems in the speech recognition domain use large Transformer neural networks that have been pretrained on massive speech data. General methods in the deep learning area have been frequently shared across various domains, and the Transformer model can also be used effectively across speech and image. In this paper, we introduce a novel masking method for self-supervised speech representation learning with salt-and-pepper (S&P) mask which is commonly used in computer vision. The proposed scheme includes consecutive quadrilateral-shaped S&P patches randomly contaminating the input speech spectrum. Furthermore, we modify the standard S&P mask to make it appropriate for the speech domain. In order to validate the effect of the proposed spectral S&P patch masking for the self-supervised representation learning approach, we conduct the pretraining and downstream experiments with two languages, English and Korean. To this end, we pretrain the speech representation model using each dataset and evaluate the pretrained models for feature extraction and fine-tuning performance on varying downstream tasks, respectively. The experimental outcomes clearly illustrate that the proposed spectral S&P patch masking is effective for various downstream tasks when combined with the conventional masking methods.

Keywords: self-supervised learning; speech representation learning; salt-and-pepper masking; spectrum patch masking

MSC: 68T10

1. Introduction

The majority of recent speech representation models typically depend on large Transformer neural networks [1] that are pretrained using self-supervised learning methods with thousands of hours of speech data. In general, self-supervised speech representation learning utilizes the structure of the input speech itself for the learning process without any annotations. Through speech representation pretraining with massive speech datasets, researchers have been able to achieve state-of-the-art performance on a diverse set of speech-related tasks, such as speech recognition (ASR), phoneme recognition, emotion recognition, and speaker verification [2–6]. Overall, the pretraining of large Transformer networks using self-supervised learning techniques has become a key strategy for advancing state-of-the-art speech processing technology.

Various promising outcomes of neural network models and sophisticated methodologies are often adapted to various other domains as well. Specifically, the Transformer network was first proposed in natural language processing (NLP) tasks such as machine translation and language modeling and has become popular in various domains, including computer vision, speech, and signal processing. Moreover, the masked language modeling for self-supervised learning introduced in BERT [7] has found extensive use in speech representation learning tasks [3,6,8–12]. Contrastive Predictive Coding (CPC) [13], a well-known technique for representation learning, is extensively applied in speech [2,4,10,14,15], NLP [16,17], and computer vision domains [18–20], even in a supervised setting [21].

Especially, speech spectrograms share similar data formats with images, and consequently, there has been a mutual influence between data preprocessing techniques and data training neural networks. For example, several applications of transfer learning from visual to audio tasks have been demonstrated to be effective [22,23]. The vision Transformer [24], derived from the Transformer for word sequences, has enabled patch embedding in audio streams [25,26].

SpecAugment [27] is a speech data augmentation technique inspired by "Cutout" [28], an augmentation method proposed in the computer vision domain. Within the domain of self-supervised speech representation learning, masking techniques based on SpecAugment are mainly used in reconstruction tasks [3,6,8–12]. Similar to image processing techniques, SpecAugment performs masking over continuous time–frequency regions of a given input spectrogram by drawing continuous blocks with zero values. By reconstructing these masked regions to their original forms, the pretrained model can learn more robust speech representations and has outperformed conventional techniques in several downstream tasks [3,6,8,9,11,12].

In the computer vision domain, salt-and-pepper (S&P) noise refers to a type of impulse contamination in an image, where random white and black dots appear. This kind of noise can often be eliminated by using techniques such as denoising autoencoders [29,30] and convolutional-neural-network-based median layers [31,32]. These denoising pretext tasks aim to remove or reduce the noise to improve their quality and make them more useful for downstream tasks.

Inspired by this, we introduce a novel self-supervised speech representation learning strategy that utilizes the S&P mask. The proposed masking method involves consecutive quadrilateral-shaped S&P patches that contaminate the speech spectrogram by a randomly determined percentage. The S&P noise in computer vision, however, cannot be effectively applied to the speech domain due to the difference in resolution or scale between the spectrograms and images. To cope with this problem, the proposed scheme uses the S&P mask modifying the standard S&P noise to make it suitable for the speech domain. Figure 1 presents the overall framework of this paper.

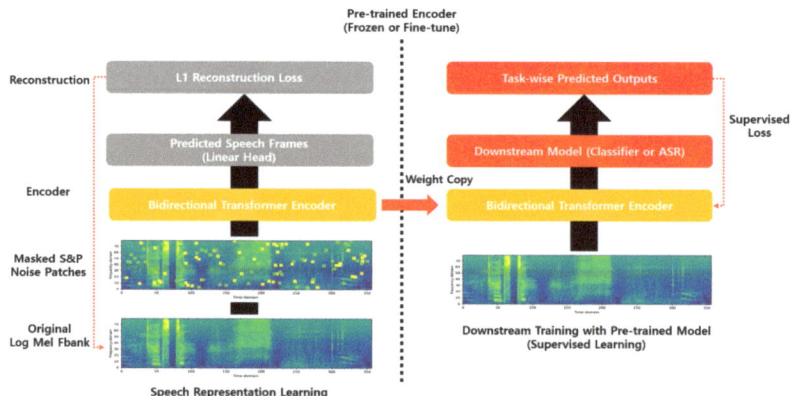

Figure 1. The overall framework of this paper consists of two parts. The left side illustrates the architecture of the speech representation model that uses the proposed spectral S&P patch masking for self-supervised learning. On the right side, labeled speech data are finally trained using the pretrained speech representation model. In other words, the pretrained encoder is connected to the downstream model, which can be used as a feature extraction (weight frozen) or fine-tuning (gradient flow) approach.

To assess the efficacy of the proposed spectral S&P patch masking method for self-supervised speech representation learning, pretraining experiments are performed separately in two languages: English [33] and Korean [34]. The pretrained model is then evaluated in two ways, namely feature extraction and fine-tuning, on several downstream tasks, which include speech recognition for both the English and Korean datasets, phoneme classification, keyword spotting, and speaker identification. Furthermore, a comparative analysis is conducted to determine the effectiveness of the spectral S&P patch masking method on its own, as well as in combination with other conventional masking approaches. Our findings confirm that the proposed spectral S&P patch masking, when utilized in conjunction with conventional masking techniques, yields superior results for various speech-related downstream tasks. These results indicate that the proposed method can serve as a valuable supplement to existing self-supervised learning techniques, potentially leading to improvements in speech representation learning.

The main contributions of this paper can be summarized as follows:

- We propose a straightforward and novel masking method for self-supervised speech representation learning with consecutive quadrilateral-shaped S&P patch blocks. S&P masking has not been attempted before for speech representation learning.
- Due to the difference in resolution or scale between the spectrogram and the image, applying S&P noise directly is not a useful method. To this end, we demonstrate that modifying S&P noise is more applicable for reconstruction objectives of self-supervised speech representation learning.
- We show that the combination of the proposed spectral S&P patch method with the conventional reconstruction-based speech representation learning approach is more effective in several speech downstream tasks compared with using the traditional masking methods alone.

The rest of this paper is organized as follows: A concise overview of related works on S&P noise and masking reconstruction for self-supervised speech representation learning is provided in Section 2. In Section 3, the details of the proposed spectral S&P patch masking and pretraining method are introduced. In Section 4, detailed information about the experimental setting is provided, including various downstream tasks such as feature extraction, fine-tuning, and the datasets used. In Section 5, extensive experimental results are presented to validate the effectiveness of the proposed method. Finally, the discussion and conclusion of this paper are given in Sections 6 and 7.

2. Related Work

In this section, we briefly review the S&P noise in the computer vision domain and the masking-based reconstruction method for self-supervised speech representation learning.

2.1. Salt-and-Pepper Noise

S&P noise is a common type of image distortion caused by impulse contamination in the field of computer vision, where white and black pixels are randomly caused throughout the image, resembling grains of salt and pepper. In the conventional approaches, the removal of this kind of noise involves using median filtering, which replaces each pixel in the image with the median value of the neighboring pixels [35,36] and CNN-based median layers [31,32]. Furthermore, recent approaches to the utilization of S&P noise as a pretext task for unsupervised learning have been demonstrated to be effective [30,37,38]. As a result, pretrained models are able to obtain improved performance in downstream tasks by learning to extract stable and consistent features, achieved through reconstructing the original input data from noisy and contaminated data. In contrast to existing research focused on the image domain, our study introduces a novel modification to the conventional pointwise S&P noise technique by transforming it into quadrilateral-shaped patch masking. This adaptation ensures its suitability for the speech domain, and we utilize it as a reconstruction objective for self-supervised speech representation learning. Furthermore, the pretrained speech representation model with the proposed spectral S&P patch masking demonstrates synergistic effects when combined with conventional masking approaches across various downstream tasks.

2.2. Masked Reconstruction for Self-Supervised Speech Representation Learning

Inspired by BERT [7], masking-based reconstruction is one of the most commonly used in self-supervised speech representation learning techniques [2–6,8,9,11,12]. The objective of the masking-based speech representation model is to restore the original speech frames from the masked ones using a reconstruction loss function. To this end, continuous time frames of the given spectrogram are randomly chosen and then masked by zero value or replaced with other frames. Similar to SpecAugment [27], a more recent method includes masking both time and frequency regions of spectrograms. This process enables the pretrained model to restore the contaminated input speech features while also acquiring robust speech representation. In this study, we introduce a straightforward spectral S&P patch masking method for self-supervised speech representation learning that randomly masks selected regions with consecutive quadrilateral-shaped S&P blocks, without any complex operations. Adding the proposed method to the previous studies [3,6,12] will demonstrate more effectiveness for various speech downstream tasks compared with conventional masking methods only.

3. Method

3.1. Modified S&P for Speech Representation Learning

Typically, image pixels usually have integer values between 0 to 255, where 0 and 255 represent black and white color in the image, respectively. S&P noise in computer vision refers to a type of impulse contamination that results in random white and black dots appearing in image pixels. Directly applying the S&P noise technique originally designed for image data in the computer vision domain to spectrograms would not yield effective results. This is primarily because of the inherent differences in data scales between spectrogram and image. Generally, spectrograms consist of floating-point values, while image data are represented using that of an integer. As a consequence, applying the S&P noise method to spectrograms as a masking strategy that operates on a different scale may lead to suboptimal outcomes when we perform self-supervised speech representation learning. Therefore, it is crucial to consider the specific characteristics and requirements of spectrogram data to enhance speech representation learning effectively. In this work, the proposal is made to modify S&P noise to enhance its suitability for speech samples.

Let $x_{f,t}$, for $(f,t) \in \mathcal{S} \equiv \{1, \ldots, F\} \times \{1, \ldots, T\}$, be the original F-by-T spectrogram x at pixel location (f,t) and $[v_{min}, v_{max}]$ be the dynamic vector range of x, i.e., $v_{min} \leq x_{f,t} \leq v_{max}$ for all $(f,t) \in \mathcal{S}$. Consequently, a noisy spectrogram is denoted as y. Therefore, the proposed S&P noise for speech samples at pixel location (f,t) is given by

$$y_{f,t} = \begin{cases} v_{max}, & \text{with probability } s \\ v_{min}, & \text{with probability } p \\ x_{f,t}, & \text{with probability } 1-p-s \end{cases} \qquad (1)$$

where s and p are the probability of salt and pepper noise, respectively, with α representing the noise level defined as the sum of s and p. In this work, we set s and p to 0.002, resulting in α being equal to 0.004. Note that the speech data are normalized with zero mean and unit variance before obtaining the salt values used for self-supervised learning.

3.2. Consecutive Quadrilateral-Shaped Spectral S&P Patch Masking for Self-Supervised Learning

Unlike image data, speech has continuous characteristics and is larger than the image in scale (time frames). Scale issues may prevent accurate self-supervised speech representation learning when the original S&P noise is applied to the masking strategy. Figure 2 shows the different point sizes of the S&P noise applied to masking the spectrograms. As shown in Figure 2b, the original point-shaped S&P noise (frame-level noise) is a very small portion of the given spectrogram. As a result, conventional point-shaped S&P noise is not very effective for self-supervised pretext tasks in the speech domain, since the single pointwise noise is a tiny fraction of the spectrogram (e.g., 10 s is 1000 frames and the pointwise 1 frame noise is 25 ms), that is, typically extracted with a window size of 25 ms.

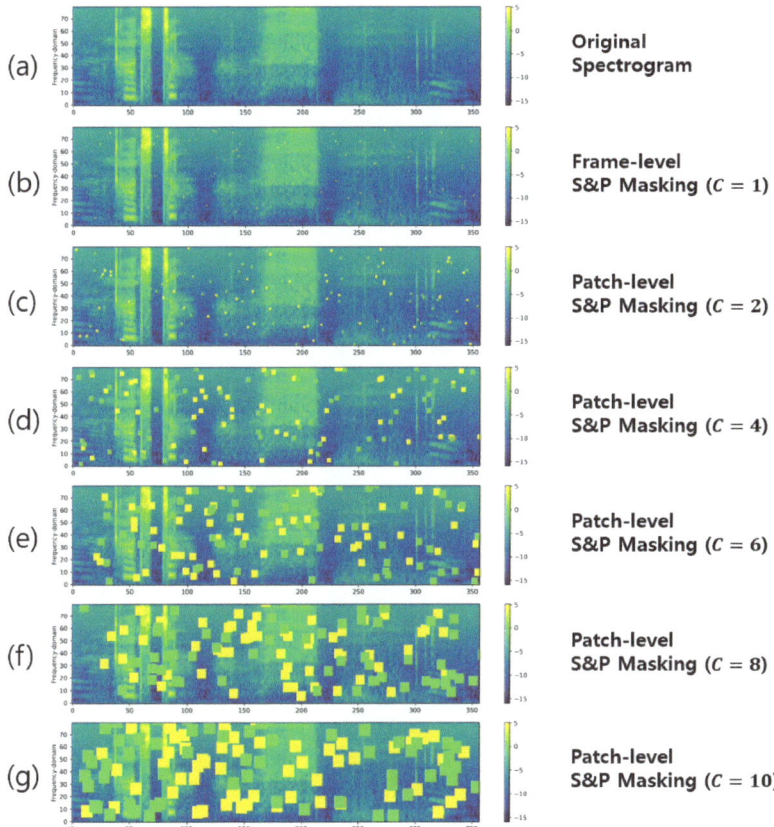

Figure 2. Illustration of the S&P patch masking on the spectrogram with various consecutive factor C but same total noise masking level $\alpha = 0.004$. (**a**) shows the input original spectrogram while (**b**–**g**) illustrates the masked spectrogram on different hyperparameters $C = 1, 2, 4, 6, 8, 10$, respectively.

To consider the specific scale characteristics of spectrogram data and improve the effectiveness of the masking strategy using S&P for speech representation learning, we propose a solution that substitutes consecutive quadrilateral-shaped patches for point-shaped noise, illustrated in Figure 2. To this end, a consecutive factor C is employed, which determines the number of frames to be masked during pretraining. This encourages the model to learn contextualized representations from the spectrogram structure. Specifically, the initial step of the process entails the random selection of a spectrum point denoted as $y_{f,t}$ according to Equation (1). Subsequently, a quadrilateral-shaped region with a side length of C is masked starting from the selected point, where C represents a certain value. For instance, if C is assigned a value of 3, the masking process involves 9 points within the square region, resulting in a square size of 9×9. The termination condition for each random point $y_{f,t}$ is when it intersects with either the endpoint of a horizontal or vertical point within the spectrogram or when it is moved by C.

When a larger value of C is used (Figure 2e,f), the model is encouraged to learn relationships between more distant parts of the spectrogram. This can be advantageous for capturing higher-level structures and dependencies that span across larger temporal contexts. On the other hand, when a smaller value of C is employed (Figure 2c,d), the model is focused more on local relationships within shorter temporal windows. This can be beneficial for capturing fine-grained details and local patterns within the spectrogram.

Using excessively small or large values of C, however, can lead to challenges in accurate speech representation learning. Extremely small values (Figure 2b) might overly constrain the model's ability to learn meaningful representations, limiting its capacity to capture the relevant information within the spectrogram. Conversely, excessively large values might (Figure 2f) hinder the model's capability to faithfully reconstruct the original input spectrogram. Therefore, finding an appropriate range for the value of C is crucial for ensuring accurate speech representation learning. We provide an exposition on how the consecutive factor C affects the learning of speech representation for its performance of downstream tasks in Section 5.

3.3. Pretraining with S&P Patch Masking for Self-Supervised Learning

To pretrain the speech representation model in self-supervision manner, the first step involves applying the proposed spectral S&P patch masking to the original input spectrogram. Figure 3 provides an overview of the masking process using the proposed spectral S&P patch.

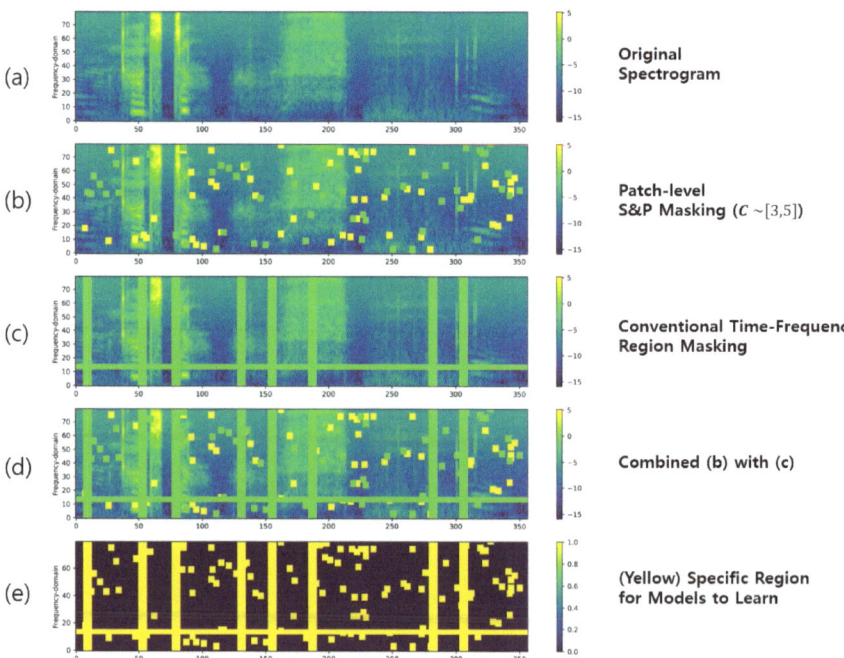

Figure 3. The overall process of the proposed spectral S&P patch masking with $\alpha = 0.004$ and $C \sim [3, 5]$. (**a**) shows the input original spectrogram while (**b**) and (**c**) demonstrate the spectrogram after being masked with the S&P patches and conventional time-frequency regions masking respectively, and (**d**) shows the combination of both (**b**) and (**c**). In (**d**), both the pepper and conventional masking regions (green) are masked with zero value and the salt (yellow) regions consist of the maximum value in the given spectrogram. (**e**) shows that the yellow area in the spectrogram denoted where the model will be learned during the reconstruction pretext tasks. The masked input spectrogram (**d**) is subsequently fed into the speech feature representation model. The model is trained with the objective of accurately reconstructing the masked spectrogram (**d**) to the original spectrogram (**a**) using the reconstruction loss.

Initially, the input original spectrogram (Figure 3a) is masked by applying S&P values. The process of setting the region masked by the S&P patch involves assigning a value of zero to half of the region and the maximum value of the given spectrogram to the other half, depending on the total masking value α. This ensures that half of the masked region contains no information (represented by a value of zero), while the other half retains the maximum value from the original spectrogram. This approach helps to introduce randomness and variability in the masked region, promoting robust feature learning during the self-supervised training process. In Figure 3b, the pepper and salt patch regions are depicted in green and yellow colors, respectively. We use a random value of C between 3 and 5 (denoted $C \sim [3, 5]$) with $\alpha = 0.004$ condition during pretraining to encourage the model to learn contextualized representations from spectrogram structure. Note that the quadrilateral-shaped spectral S&P patches can be rectangle or square and overlapped with each other.

In addition, the proposed spectral S&P patch masking approach can be easily integrated with other masking methods. Figure 3c depicts the conventional time–frequency region masking method [6], while Figure 3d illustrates the combination of Figure 3b,c. Note that the existing masking methods can be time, frequency, or time–frequency regions for reconstruction [3,6,12]. In Figure 3e, the yellow area in the spectrogram represents the specific region where the model focuses on reconstruction for pretraining tasks.

To reconstruct the masked spectrogram shown in Figure 3d back to its original form in Figure 3a, 3-layer bidirectional Transformer encoders with 768 hidden sizes and position encoding, 3072-dimensional feed-forward networks, and 12 multihead attentions are used. Speech sequence length is limited to under 1500 to fast model training, which is approximately 15 s. The proposed pretrained model utilizes the masked spectrogram as input and generates a reconstructed version using L1 loss as the objective function for minimizing between the original spectrogram and predicted outputs.

In order to perform the aforementioned process using the proposed spectral S&P patch masking, we use 80-dimensional log Mel Fbank (filter bank) features, which were extracted with a window size of 25 ms and an overlap size of 10 ms. These speech features are normalized with a mean of zero and a unit variance to use as input to the model. To optimize the pretrained model, the AdamW optimizer with a learning rate scheduler is used, which increases from 0 up to a maximum value of 0.0002 after 7% of the training steps have been completed and then decreases back to 0. In the pretraining experiments, 32 batch size and 4 gradient accumulation steps are used until 1,000,000 steps, which are approximately 100 epochs, to learn optimal model parameters that minimize the L1 loss for reconstruction. For reproducibility reasons, we use the same configuration as described in the S3PRL toolkit [39].

To summarize the pretraining stage, we aim to let the pretrained model learn representations that capture essential information from the masked spectrogram in Figure 3d in order to successfully reconstruct the original spectrogram in Figure 3a using the reconstruction loss.

3.4. Training Pretrained Model on Downstream Tasks

To evaluate the effectiveness of the pretrained model using the proposed S&P patch masking, there are two ways to measure several downstream tasks.

(1) Speech representation extraction: To obtain speech representations from the pretrained model, we extract the hidden states of the last layer of the model, which correspond to the deepest Transformer encoder layer. Subsequently, these extracted representations are utilized as inputs for the downstream model, effectively replacing the speech features (e.g., log Mel Fbank). By feeding the speech representations of the pretrained model to the downstream model, we enable it to leverage the rich and meaningful information encoded in the representations for performing various tasks. Note that when training the downstream tasks in this manner, the parameters of the pretrained model are frozen. In other words, the parameters of the pretrained model are not updated during the training process of the downstream tasks. This allows the pretrained model to serve as a fixed

speech feature extractor, providing stable and reliable representations for the downstream tasks. This method is represented as "feature extraction" in later experimental tables.

(2) *Fine-tuning*: Another approach for utilizing the pretrained model is through fine-tuning in conjunction with downstream models. In this method, the output of the pretrained model is connected to a downstream model, and the downstream model can be of any type, depending on the specific task at hand. Initially, while the pretrained model retains its learned knowledge, the parameters of the downstream model are randomly initialized. During fine-tuning, both the pretrained model and the downstream model are updated together. The fine-tuning process involves jointly optimizing the parameters of both models using task-specific training data. This method is denoted as "fine-tuning" in subsequent experimental tables.

4. Experimental Setup

In this section, a comprehensive evaluation of the proposed spectral S&P patch masking for self-supervised speech representation learning by performing six downstream tasks is conducted.

4.1. Dataset Description

We standardize the audio sampling rate to 16 kHz to ensure that all speech data used in the experiments have a consistent quality. Table 1 shows all the datasets used in this paper. Details of various datasets used in this paper are as below.

Table 1. Speech datasets summary used in the pretraining and downstream experiments in this paper. The symbols ✗ and ✓ denoted yes and no.

Dataset Specific		Used For	
Name	Hours	Pretraining	Downstream Task
LibriSpeech [33]	960	✓	Phoneme Classification (100 h) English ASR (100 h)
TIMIT [40]	5.4	✗	Phoneme Classification (All)
Speech Commands [41]	18	✗	Keyword Spotting (All)
VoxCeleb1 [42]	352	✗	Speaker Identification (All)
KsponSpeech [34]	1000	✓	Korean ASR (All)

(1) *LibriSpeech*: The LibriSpeech dataset [33] is one of the widely used benchmarks for speech recognition research. This dataset encompasses a large-scale collection of English speech recordings totaling approximately 960 h from audiobooks. The training set comprises three subsets: train-clean-100, train-clean-360, and train-other-500. The "clean" designation indicates the absence of noise, while "other" denotes the presence of noise. The numbers 100, 360, and 500 refer to the respective hour durations of the subsets. For evaluation purposes, the dataset includes the dev-clean, dev-other, test-clean, and test-other subsets. In our experiments, we utilize a total of 960 h from the LibriSpeech dataset for pretraining. For the downstream tasks, the train-clean-100 subset is used for training the phoneme classification and English ASR tasks, and the dev-clean and test-clean subsets are used for evaluation.

(2) *TIMIT*: The TIMIT [40] dataset is a well-known corpus used for speech recognition and acoustic–phonetic studies. This dataset consists of recordings from 630 American English speakers pronouncing phonetically rich sentences. In our experiments, we only use this dataset for conducting phoneme classification for downstream tasks. The TIMIT dataset is divided into three subsets: "train", "dev", and "test". During our experiments, we train the downstream tasks using the training set and determine the best-performing checkpoint on the dev set to assess the performance on the test set.

(3) Speech Commands: The Speech Commands [41] dataset is usually used in the field of keyword spotting, which is specifically designed to recognize and classify spoken commands of keywords. The dataset comprises recordings of short spoken commands from a diverse set of speakers, covering different categories such as "yes", "no", "up", "down", "left", "right", "stop", "go", and more. In our experiments, we train the keyword spotting downstream model using the training set and then evaluate the performance of the model on the development set and test set. Note that the Speech Commands dataset is not utilized for pretraining in our experiments.

(4) VoxCeleb1: The VoxCeleb1 [42] dataset is an audio–visual dataset that contains more than 100,000 utterances from 1251 celebrities. These utterances are extracted from videos on YouTube. The VoxCeleb1 dataset is widely used for tasks such as speech recognition and speaker identification. For conducting the speaker identification downstream task, we utilize the VoxCeleb1 training and test set split provided within the dataset itself. The VoxCeleb1 dataset is not used for pretraining in this paper.

(5) KsponSpeech: To explore the effectiveness of the proposed method in languages other than English, the KsponSpeech [34] dataset is used for both pretraining and ASR downstream tasks. By using a non-English dataset, we can evaluate the performance and generalizability of the proposed method in different linguistic contexts. This allows us to investigate the applicability and effectiveness of the method beyond the English language. The KsponSpeech dataset is widely used in the Korean ASR domain and comprises around 1000 h of speech from native Korean adult males and females, providing a total of 620,000 training examples. For pretraining, the speech samples that are shorter than 3 s were excluded, so only 517,144 samples were utilized for self-supervised learning with the proposed method. In contrast, all the KsponSpeech training samples were used to measure ASR performance in the downstream task. In the Korean ASR experiment, the ASR performance is reported on the KsponSpeech dev set.

4.2. Downstream Tasks Details

In this subsection, the respective six downstream tasks setup and training details are explained.

(1) LibriSpeech phoneme classification: The framewise phoneme prediction performance is evaluated using classifiers trained on the last hidden state of representations for both the feature extraction and fine-tuning stages. To ensure reproducibility, this downstream task follows previous work as described in [39]. For the phoneme classification task on the LibriSpeech [33] dataset, the train-clean-100 subset includes 41 possible phoneme classes used for training. To ensure consistency, we make use of aligned phoneme labels, train/test split, and the development set derived from 10% of the training set as provided in [39]. In evaluating the LibriSpeech phoneme classification task, the phoneme classification accuracy (%) on the development and test sets employing two measurement approaches are provided: *1-linear classifier* and *2-linear classifier*. In the 1-linear classifier approach, a single linear classifier is employed to evaluate the linear separability of phonemes. This setting is denoted as "1-linear classifier". Furthermore, the incorporated classifiers with a single hidden layer of 768 dimensions are referred to as the "2-linear classifier" setting. During training, the AdamW [43] optimizer with a learning rate of 0.0002 and a batch size of 32 is used. The training process continues until 500,000 steps.

(2) TIMIT phoneme classification: For the TIMIT [40] phoneme classification task, framewise phoneme predictions are estimated based on the manual phoneme transcriptions provided in the TIMIT dataset. To ensure reproducibility, the procedures outlined in previous work [39] are followed. In experiments, the phoneme classification task is conducted using the TIMIT training set, which comprises 39 phoneme classes, as described in [39,44]. The phoneme classification accuracy (%) on the test set is reported using three different measurement approaches: *conv-bank classifier*, *1-linear classifier*, and *2-linear classifier*. In the conv-bank classifier approach, a 64-dimensional hidden layer is utilized, along with three 1D-CNN layers with kernel sizes of [3, 5, 7] and channel sizes of [32, 32, 32]. This is

followed by a 96-dimensional hidden layer and a phoneme classifier. This specific setting is referred to as the "conv-bank classifier" approach. The structures of both the 1-linear classifier and the 2-linear classifier are equivalent to the phoneme classification setting used for the LibriSpeech task. For training, the AdamW optimizer is employed with a learning rate of 0.0002 and a batch size of 16. The training process for this task continues until 500,000 steps.

(3) Keyword spotting: To evaluate the quality of representations for the keyword spotting task in both the feature extraction and fine-tuning stages, the Speech Commands [41] dataset is used, following the setup employed in the S3PRL toolkit [39]. In this setup, keyword spotting is treated as a 12-class classification problem. A two 256-dimensional hidden layer feed-forward classifier is employed for this task. Prior to the output layer, mean pooling over time is applied to the representations, as described in [39]. The evaluation metric reported is the keyword classification accuracy (%) on the test set. This evaluation allows for the assessment of the pretrained model's representation transferability across different domains. During the keyword spotting training, the Adam optimizer [45] is used with a learning rate of 0.0001 and a batch size of 32. The training process for this task continues until 200,000 steps.

(4) Speaker identification: For evaluating the speaker identification task in both the feature extraction and fine-tuning stages, the VoxCeleb1 dataset [42] is used. A frame-wise linear transformation is applied, followed by mean-pooling across all sequences. This is then followed by another linear transformation with a cross-entropy loss for the utterance-level task. This setting is consistent with the approach described in [39,46]. The evaluation metric used for this task is accuracy (%), which measures the percentage of correctly identified speakers. During training, the Adam optimizer is utilized with a learning rate of 0.0001 and a batch size of 8. Additionally, 4 gradient accumulation steps are employed until reaching 200,000 training steps.

(5) English ASR: To evaluate the English Automatic Speech Recognition (ASR) downstream performance in both the feature extraction and fine-tuning stages, the LibriSpeech dataset [33] is utilized. Specifically, the train-clean-100, dev-clean, and test-clean subsets of LibriSpeech are used for training, validation, and testing, respectively. The performance of two types of deep neural network settings, BiGRU and BiLSTM, is measured as described in [39,46]. For both the BiGRU and BiLSTM settings, a 2-layer bidirectional GRU and bidirectional LSTM with a dimensionality of 1024 are used. The models are optimized using the Connectionist Temporal Classification [47] loss on 32 English characters. Once trained, the ASR models are decoded using the LibriSpeech official 4-gram language model performed by KenLM [48] and the Wav2letter toolkit [49]. The evaluation metric reported for English ASR modeling on the LibriSpeech dataset is the word error rate (WER, %) on the test-clean subset. During the training stage, the Adam optimizer is used with a learning rate of 0.0001, a batch size of 32, and a beam size of 5 until 200,000 steps.

(6) Korean ASR: To evaluate the performance of Korean ASR downstream performance for feature extraction, the KsponSpeech dataset [34] is employed. In order to compare the performance of feature extraction, the weights of various pretrained models are kept frozen. The speech representations are extracted from the hidden state of the final bidirectional Transformer encoder. These representations are then fed into the ASR model architecture described in [50]. Specifically, an ESPNet [51]-like Transformer model is used for ASR architecture, which includes 7-layer CNNs with 8 subsampling operations, followed by 3 Transformer encoder layers and 6 Transformer decoder layers. The maximum input length for the training set is set to 25 s, and no additional normalization or preprocessing is applied. During training, the AdamW optimizer is utilized with a learning rate of 0.001, and a Transformer learning rate scheduler [1] is employed. The model is trained using a total batch size of 64 on 4 TITAN RTX GPUs until 50 epochs. Label smoothing [52] is also applied during training.

Unlike English characters, the KsponSpeech dataset includes 2311 symbols, including special tokens such as "start", "end", "mask", "pad", and "unk". This makes the Korean ASR downstream task more challenging to predict accurately. To evaluate the performance of the Korean ASR downstream task, the character error rate (CER, %) is used as a commonly employed metric in Korean ASR. The CER is computed at the syllable level by measuring the Levenshtein distance [53] between the ASR-predicted results and the corresponding labels.

4.3. Software and Hardware Details

In all the experiments of this paper, the following software and hardware configurations are utilized. By using these specific versions of the software and libraries, the reproducibility and consistency of the experimental setup are ensured.

- Python version: 3.9.15
- GPU server: The pretraining and downstream experiments are conducted on an NVIDIA RTX A6000 GPU (48GB) server and TITAN RTX GPU (24GB) server running Ubuntu 18.04.6 LTS, respectively.
- Deep learning framework: PyTorch [54] version 1.12.1 with CUDA version 11.3 and CuDNN version 8.21. These libraries enable efficient GPU acceleration for training and inference.
- Speech preprocessing: For speech preprocessing tasks, we rely on the TorchAudio [55] library (version 0.12.1) for audio-related operations. Additionally, Numpy [56] (version 1.23.5) and SoundFile (version 0.11.0) are used for numerical computations and reading and writing audio files, respectively.
- English ASR downstream: For English ASR tasks, both KenLM [48] (Available online: https://github.com/kpu/kenlm, accessed on 14 June 2023) and Wav2letter++ [49] (Available online: https://github.com/flashlight/wav2letter, accessed on 14 June 2023) libraries are employed. KenLM is used for language modeling, while Wav2letter++ provides useful ASR functionality.
- Korean ASR downstream: In the case of Korean ASR tasks, the python-Levenshtein library (version 0.20.9) is utilized to compute the edit distance metric.

5. Results

In all the downstream tasks, the effectiveness of the proposed spectral S&P patch masking alone or combined with previous speech representations learning methods is compared.

Table 2 presents seven selected methods, including diverse self-supervised representation learning techniques (Fbank, APC [15], NPC [10], Mockingjay [3], Audio ALBERT [12], TERA [6], and the proposed spectral S&P Patch). Note that the Fbank refers to the input that is directly converted from the original speech without using any pretrained speech feature representation. These methods have been chosen to provide a comprehensive evaluation of the proposed S&P patch masking in relation to existing approaches. In Table 2, the designation of * models indicates the utilization of their pretrained weights from the S3PRL [39] toolkit, which are employed for our downstream tasks without modification. On the contrary, the † models listed in Table 2 signify the pretrained speech representation models that we implement ourselves using the S3PRL toolkit.

Furthermore, the experimental results are presented by integrating their approaches with contemporary self-supervision masking methods. In our experiments, note that these combined experiments exclusively focus on parallel network-type models that are composed of Transformer-based architectures [3,6,12], namely Mockingjay + Ours, Audio ALBERT + Ours, and TERA + Ours.

Table 2. Details of various self-supervised speech representation approaches. Nonparallel and Parallel denote the using Non-Transformer and Transformer-based neural network architecture for pretraining, respectively. * represents the pretrained model provided in the S3PRL toolkit. † denotes the pretrained model we implemented ourselves using the S3PRL toolkit.

Representations	Network Type	No. Model Paramaters
Fbank *	-	0
APC * [15]	Non-parallel	9,107,024
NPC * [10]	Non-parallel	19,380,560
Mockingjay * [3]	Non-parallel	22,226,928
Audio ALBERT * [12]	Non-parallel	7,805,264
TERA * [6]	Non-parallel	21,981,008
S&P Patch † (Ours)	Non-parallel	21,981,008
Combined with other representations		
Mockingjay + Ours †	Parallel	22,226,928
Audio ALBERT + Ours †	Parallel	7,805,264
TERA + Ours †	Parallel	21,981,008

5.1. LibriSpeech Phoneme Classification Results

Figure 4 demonstrates the performance of both feature extraction and fine-tuning for the LibriSpeech [33] phoneme classification task using various representations. All the pretrained models of these features are extracted from the final layer. For the feature extraction, all the pretrained model parameters are kept fixed when conducting the downstream task, and the representations are provided as input to the downstream model. In contrast to the feature extraction, all the pretrained model parameters are updated during the fine-tuning experiments on the downstream task.

In Figure 4a, the proposed method outperforms the Mockingjay [3], considering the average results from two methods: 1-linear classifier and 2-linear classifier. It is also observed that combining the proposed method with representations from previous parallel-based approaches yields better performance on average than when they are used alone. Notably, the relatively lower performance of Mockingjay is significantly improved when integrated with the proposed method (Mockingjay + Ours).

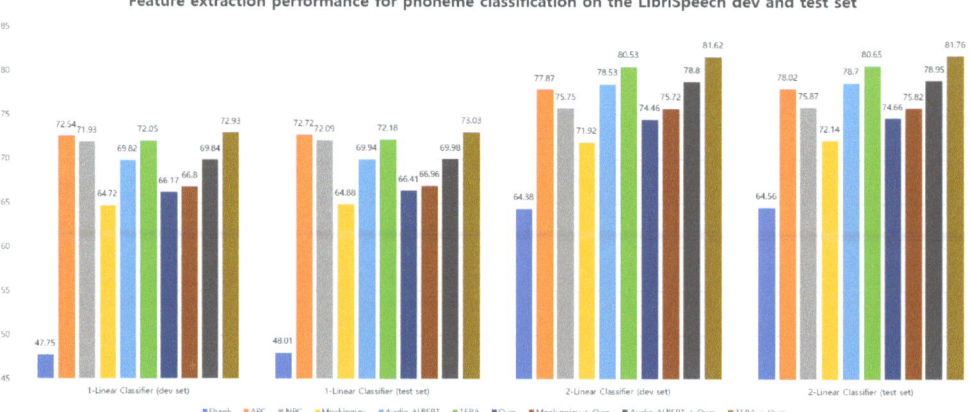

(**a**) Feature extraction performance.

Figure 4. *Cont.*

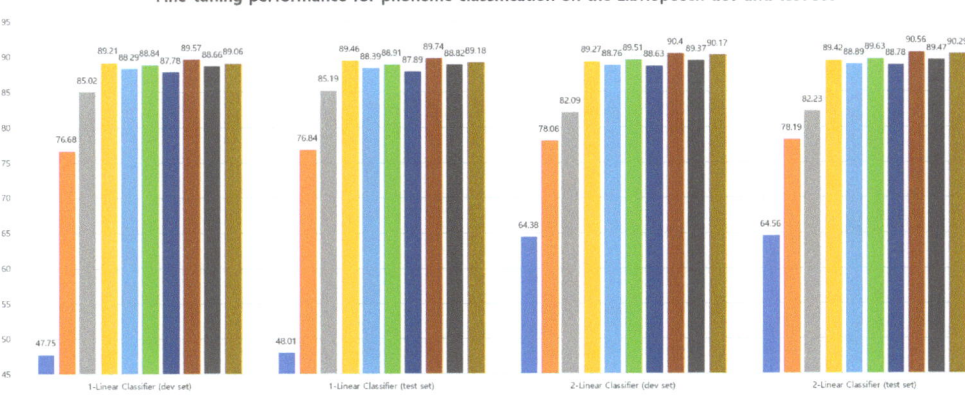

(**b**) Fine-tuning performance.

Figure 4. Feature extraction (**a**) and fine-tuning (**b**) performance on LibriSpeech [33] phoneme classification task between different representations. The higher the better.

According to the results presented in Figure 4, the fine-tuning performance (Figure 4b) of all representations surpasses the performance observed on the feature extraction performance (Figure 4a). Particularly, the proposed method demonstrates notable improvement when compared with its performance in the feature extraction stage when used alone. Furthermore, it is observed that the proposed method exhibits significant enhancement compared with feature extraction, outperforming the APC [15] and NPC [10] approaches in terms of average results from the 1-linear and 2-linear classifier. Additionally, it is discovered that the proposed method shows synergistic performance when combined with other methods for fine-tuning, similar to its performance in the feature extraction stage.

5.2. TIMIT Phoneme Classification Results

The performance of both feature extraction and fine-tuning for the TIMIT [40] phoneme classification task using different representations are presented in Figure 5. As mentioned previously, the conv bank classifier results for both the feature extraction and fine-tuning stages are added to Figure 5. Among the various pretrained representations, the proposed spectral S&P patch masking achieves the lowest performance among other pretraining approaches on the feature extraction performance (Figure 5a) but outperforms the APC on the fine-tuning performance (Figure 5b). However, when combined with other methods, it exhibits effective performance, resulting in improved overall performance. Particularly, it is found that when the pretrained models using the proposed method on the LibriSpeech dataset are applied to a downstream task with a different domain (TIMIT dataset), they still demonstrate a synergistic effect.

Furthermore, it is observed that all representations exhibit improved performance when used with a deeper downstream model, both in the context of feature extraction and fine-tuning. This can be a restricted labeled data environment, as observed in the TIMIT dataset. Specifically, the performance achieved with the 2-linear classifier outperforms that of the conv bank classifier and the 1-linear classifier for all representations. This observation suggests that the 2-linear classifier is capable of extracting more informative features compared with 1-linear classifier, leading to enhanced performance across all representations. As a result, it is worth noticing that the pretrained model combined with the proposed method and previous approaches for both feature extraction and fine-tuning, even with limited labeled data (TIMIT dataset), shows synergistically to further improve the overall performance.

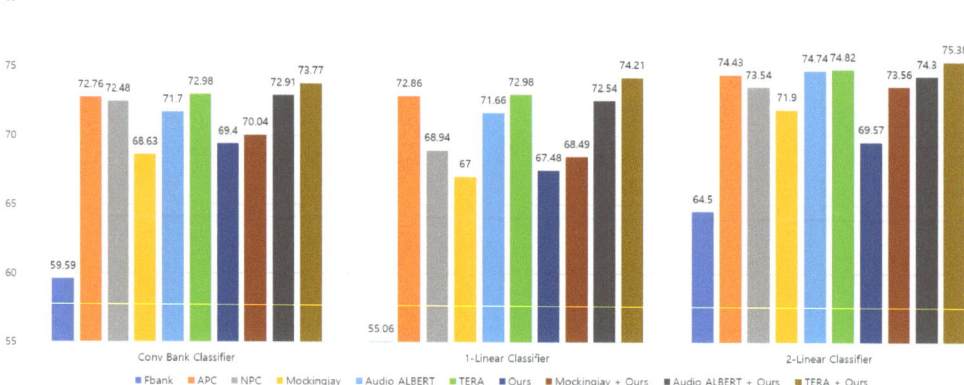

(**a**) Feature extraction performance.

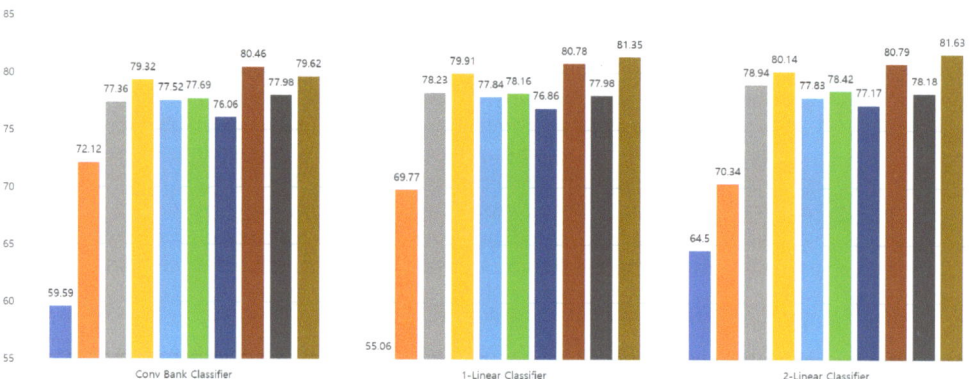

(**b**) Fine-tuning performance.

Figure 5. Feature extraction (**a**) and fine-tuning (**b**) performance on TIMIT [40] phoneme classification task between different representations. The higher the better.

5.3. Keyword Spotting Results

Figure 6 provides an overview of the keyword classification performance on the Speech Commands [41] dataset, considering both feature extraction and fine-tuning tasks. Overall, the results indicate that fine-tuning demonstrates higher performance compared with feature extraction. Interestingly, the proposed method achieves the lowest keyword spotting performance (80.40%) among the pretrained representations in the feature extraction but achieves 92.86% accuracy, which outperforms the APC [15] (90.45%) and NPC [10] (90.34%) methods when applied in the fine-tuning stage. Furthermore, a substantial improvement is noted when the proposed method is combined with other representations, compared with using them individually. Specifically, it is observed that the combination of the proposed method with TERA [6], Audio ALBERT [12], and Mockingjay [3] leads to an average performance boost, respectively, compared with using TERA, Audio ALBERT, and Mockingjay alone.

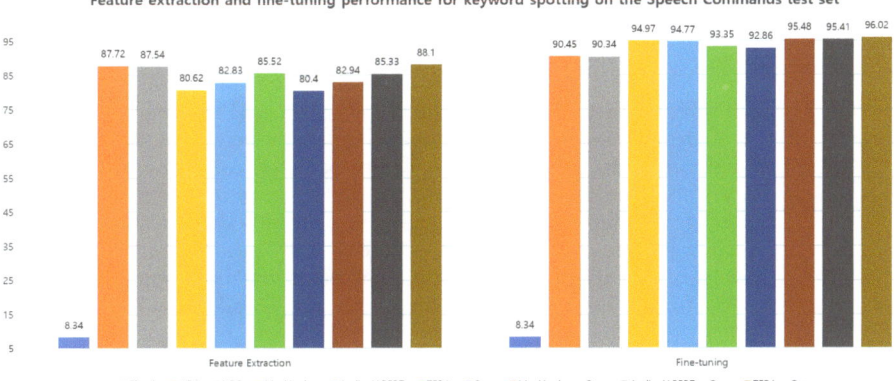

Figure 6. Feature extraction and fine-tuning performance for keyword spotting task on the Speech Commands [41] dataset between different representations, respectively. The higher the better.

5.4. Speaker Identification Results

Figure 7 summarizes the speaker identification results for the VoxCeleb1 [42] dataset across feature extraction and fine-tuning experiments. During feature extraction, the proposed spectral S&P patch masking showed significantly outperforms the non-parallel-based architectures of APC [15] and NPC [10]. Surprisingly, all representations exhibit performance degradation when fine-tuning is applied to speaker identification downstream tasks. Despite following the same settings as described in [39,46], it is conjectured that the chosen hyperparameters for fine-tuning may not be suitable. Interestingly, the fine-tuning performance using the proposed method outperforms that of NPC [10], as well as the parallel-based architectures of Mockingjay [3] and Audio ALBERT [12]. Moreover, experimental results indicate that combining the proposed method with other feature representations leads to improved overall performance. This suggests that the proposed spectral S&P patch masking can serve as simple yet effective self-supervised speech representation learning techniques for speaker identification tasks.

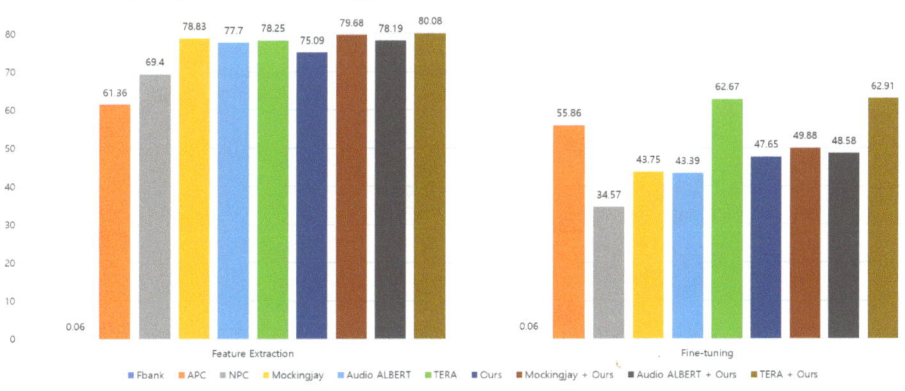

Figure 7. Feature extraction and fine-tuning performance for speaker identification task on the Voxceleb1 [42] dataset between different representations, respectively. The higher the better.

5.5. English ASR Results

In this section, the proposed method and the comparison results in terms of the Word Error Rate (WER) metric are presented. The ASR models are trained using feature extraction and fine-tuning approaches, respectively. All methods are pretrained with

960 h of the LibriSpeech [33] dataset. For decoding and rescoring, the setup described in Section 4.2 is employed for all representations, using both BiGRU and BiLSTM models as ASR architectures.

In Tables 3 and 4, a summary of the results obtained from the feature extraction and fine-tuning approaches using both BiGRU and BiLSTM frameworks is presented. These tables include results from previous literature, as well as the proposed method. Overall, when comparing the results from feature extraction and fine-tuning, it is consistently observed that fine-tuning yields superior performance compared with using the extracted speech feature representations for ASR downstream tasks. Similar to the findings in the LibriSpeech phoneme classification task described in Figure 4, a significant improvement in the performance of the proposed method is observed when transferring from feature extraction to fine-tuning, especially outperforming the non-parallel-based approaches [10,15].

Table 3. Feature extraction and fine-tuning performance on LibriSpeech [33] ASR downstream task using BiGRU network between different representations, respectively. The lower the better ($\downarrow$).

Representations	Feature Extraction ($\downarrow$)		Fine-Tuning ($\downarrow$)		Average ($\downarrow$)	
	WER	Rescore	WER	Rescore	WER	Rescore
Fbank	27.90	18.42	27.90	18.42	27.90	18.42
APC [15]	23.66	16.58	21.44	15.37	22.55	15.98
NPC [10]	24.18	16.25	21.20	14.55	22.69	15.40
Mockingjay [3]	26.45	17.59	19.48	14.43	22.97	16.01
Audio ALBERT [12]	24.32	16.14	19.16	14.27	21.74	15.21
TERA [6]	22.47	14.96	19.95	14.16	21.21	14.56
Ours	26.35	16.83	20.39	14.52	23.37	15.68
Combined with other representations						
Mockingjay + Ours	26.35	16.83	20.39	14.52	23.37	15.68
Audio ALBERT + Ours	26.23	17.30	19.25	14.05	22.74	15.68
TERA + Ours	21.74	14.04	17.78	13.03	19.76	13.54

Table 4. Feature extraction and fine-tuning performance on LibriSpeech [33] ASR downstream task using BiLSTM network between different representations, respectively. The lower the better ($\downarrow$).

Representations	Feature Extraction ($\downarrow$)		Fine-Tuning ($\downarrow$)		Average ($\downarrow$)	
	WER	Rescore	WER	Rescore	WER	Rescore
Fbank	22.89	15.35	22.89	15.35	22.89	15.35
APC [15]	21.94	15.32	19.18	13.26	20.56	14.29
NPC [10]	22.21	15.45	19.42	13.36	20.82	14.41
Mockingjay [3]	21.56	15.31	17.75	12.52	19.66	13.92
Audio ALBERT [12]	21.13	14.54	17.20	12.25	19.17	13.40
TERA [6]	19.90	13.33	17.18	12.06	18.54	12.70
Ours	22.03	15.89	17.88	13.02	19.96	14.46
Combined with other representations						
Mockingjay + Ours	21.22	15.06	17.31	12.42	19.27	13.74
Audio ALBERT + Ours	20.58	14.24	17.03	12.02	18.81	13.13
TERA + Ours	18.02	12.94	16.37	11.51	17.20	12.23

In conclusion, it is found that the overall performance of the BiLSTM-based ASR model in Table 3 exhibits notably better performance compared with the BiGRU model in Table 4. Furthermore, it is also observed that combining the proposed method with other approaches leads to increased ASR performance in both the feature extraction and fine-tuning stages.

5.6. Korean ASR Results

To measure the proposed spectral S&P patch masking on the Korean ASR downstream task, we compare previous works that were pretrained on the KsponSpeech [34] dataset. For training the Korean ASR downstream task, each pretrained model is utilized as a feature extractor for the respective ASR model. All the pretrained comparisons experimental results use the S3PRL toolkit [46]. We report the CER (%) on the KsponSpeech dev set.

Table 5 demonstrates the performance of feature extraction for the overall Korean ASR performance, including the proposed method. According to our experimental results, the ASR performance using the proposed spectral S&P patch masking alone achieves a 14.66% CER, which outperforms the NPC [10] (14.78%), Mockingjay [3] (17.25%), and Audio ALBERT [12] (16.95%), respectively. This indicates that the proposed spectral S&P patch can be simple yet effective for masking strategy, which can be useful for ASR downstream tasks.

Table 5. Feature extraction performance on Korean ASR downstream task. The lower the better ($\downarrow$).

Representations	CER ($\downarrow$)
Fbank	15.31
APC [15]	13.36
NPC [10]	14.78
Mockingjay [3]	16.95
Audio ALBERT [12]	17.25
TERA [6]	13.86
SVR1K [50]	12.32
Ours	14.66
Combined with other representations	
Mockingjay + Ours	14.83
Audio ALBERT + Ours	15.87
TERA + Ours	12.14

In addition, while the ASR performances of conventional Mockingjay [3], Audio ALBERT [12], and TERA [6] are 16.95%, 17.25%, and 13.86% of CER, respectively, each method combined with the proposed S&P patch masking obtain performances of 14.83%, 15.87%, and 12.14%, which implies a relative average improvement of 10%. In particular, when the proposed method was added to TERA (TERA + Ours), it outperformed the results of SVR1K [50], which had the best ASR performance among all speech representations. As a result, our results demonstrate that combining the proposed spectral S&P patch with conventional masking methods is a useful supplement to the existing self-supervised techniques for speech representation learning.

5.7. Ablation: Impact of Two S&P Patch Masking Hyperparameters

In this section, an ablation study is performed to further explore the effectiveness of the proposed spectral S&P patch masking for self-supervised speech pretraining. Specifically, we experiment and report on two hyperparameter factors: the total amount of the S&P patch α and the consecutive noise patches factor C. The goal is to investigate the contribution of quadrilateral-shaped noise patches in the speech domain. To this end, ablation studies are conducted on the LibriSpeech phoneme classification task for both feature extraction and fine-tuning, as well as on the Korean ASR task for the feature extraction task.

First, an investigation is conducted on six different values of α and eight different values of C in the TERA + Ours setting for the LibriSpeech phoneme classification tasks. According to the phoneme classification accuracy results obtained from the LibriSpeech test-clean set, as presented in Table 6a,b, our experimental findings indicate that when using the parameters $\alpha = 0.004$ and $C \sim [3,5]$, the most promising outcomes are achieved for both feature extraction and fine-tuning processes. In our findings, it is observed that there is no significant difference in the fine-tuning performance when varying the hyperparameters. However, a notable gap is noticed in the feature extraction performance across different hyperparameter settings, especially in C. This observation supports the hypothesis that a point-shaped S&P patch ($C = 1$) is not effective for learning speech feature representation.

Table 6. Ablation study on hyperparameters of the proposed S&P noise patches. The higher the better (↑). (**a**) LibriSpeech phoneme classification for both feature extraction and fine-tuning performance comparison according to the various α. (**b**) LibriSpeech phoneme classification for both feature extraction and fine-tuning performance comparison according to the various C. Bold denotes the best result.

(a)			
α	C	Feature Extraction (↑)	Fine-Tuning (↑)
0.001		68.91	88.06
0.002		70.29	88.46
0.004	$C \sim [3,5]$	**73.03**	**89.18**
0.006		71.07	88.85
0.008		69.97	88.75
0.01		69.02	88.14

(b)			
α	C	Feature Extraction (↑)	Fine-Tuning (↑)
	$C = 1$	70.84	87.89
	$C \sim [1,3]$	71.82	88.13
	$C = 3$	71.70	88.49
0.004	$\mathbf{C \sim [3,5]}$	**73.03**	**89.18**
	$C \sim [3,8]$	72.10	88.87
	$C = 5$	71.59	88.49
	$C \sim [1,10]$	68.85	88.44
	$C \sim [3,10]$	71.76	88.86

As shown in Table 7, we also explore five different values of α and four different values of C in the TERA + Ours setting for the Korean ASR downstream task. Similar to Table 6, the best ASR performance is obtained when using the $\alpha = 0.004$ and $C \sim [3,5]$ settings. In particular, it is observed that too small (point-shaped) or too large amounts of S&P patches are not suitable for self-supervised pretext tasks. Additionally, considering that the conventional pointwise ($C = 1$) S&P patch has a CER of 17.25%, the results provide evidence that the proposed spectral S&P patch masking is highly effective. These findings indicate that the consecutive patch masking factor C plays a crucial role in shaping the effectiveness of the spectral S&P patch masking for speech representation learning.

According to the ablation study results for English and Korean ASR presented in Tables 6 and 7, respectively, the optimal hyperparameter configuration that yielded the best performance is $\alpha = 0.004$ and $C \sim [3,5]$. Indeed, the results obtained from using the representations of the fixed pretrained model without any parameter updates provide support for the hypothesis that a point-shaped S&P patch with $C = 1$ is not effective for speech representation learning. We also highlight the importance of using the proposed quadrilateral-shaped patches to achieve effective speech feature representation learning.

Table 7. Ablation study on hyperparameters of the proposed spectral S&P patch masking. The lower the better (↓). (**a**) ASR performance comparison according to the various α. (**b**) ASR performance comparison according to the various C. **Bold** denotes the best result.

(a)		
α	C	CER (↓)
0.002		13.84
0.004		12.14
0.006	$C \sim [3, 5]$	13.58
0.008		13.75
0.01		13.34
(b)		
α	C	CER (↓)
	$C \sim [1, 3]$	17.25
0.004	$C \sim [\mathbf{3, 5}]$	12.14
	$C \sim [3, 8]$	13.51
	$C \sim [3, 10]$	15.82

6. Discussion

The primary goal of this paper is to successfully apply the spectral S&P patch masking method for self-supervised speech representation learning. To the best of our knowledge, this study is the first attempt to utilize the S&P patch as a masking strategy for self-supervised speech representation learning. To address the difference in resolution or scale between speech and image data, we have introduced the novel salt value and consecutive quadrilateral-shaped patches for masking, which allows for the useful extraction of continuous information from the speech input.

In our experiments, we conducted an extensive investigation of a diverse range of speech downstream tasks using the proposed method. Firstly, we obtained two pretrained speech representation models on both English and Korean datasets. To ensure a fair comparison of the proposed method, various pretrained weights (models) available in the S3PRL toolkit were directly utilized, and the performance gap across different downstream tasks was reported. As a result, the proposed method achieved similar performance to other recent approaches when used alone for various downstream tasks. Furthermore, we have shown that combining the proposed spectral S&P patch masking with conventional methods for self-supervised speech representation learning leads to effective results in various downstream tasks.

The primary limitation of our study lies in the fact that the proposed spectral S&P patch masking method can only be utilized or combined with masking-based speech representation learning approaches. To gain a more profound understanding of speech representation pretraining, further research is required to extend the proposed method, such as investigating its applicability to directly extracting speech using CNNs like wav2vec 2.0 [2] and HuBERT [5]. Second, in our study, we limited the pretraining to 960 h of the LibriSpeech [33] dataset for the English ASR downstream task. To ensure fair comparisons with other conventional masking-based approaches, we utilized the S3PRL framework using 960 h of LibriSpeech dataset, as described in TERA and SUPERB. However, the amount of data used for pretraining has a significant impact on the performance of models in various downstream tasks. Even when using a large-scale speech dataset such as 60,000 h of Libri-Light [57], further validation is required so verify whether the proposed method shows reliable results. This will enable us to estimate the method's scalability and its potential to yield robust results under more data-rich conditions. Third, we observed that keeping the pretrained weights frozen worked better than fine-tuning them during the training of the Korean ASR model. In the future, we plan to concentrate on addressing these limitations and potentially striving to improve the performance further.

In conclusion, our findings demonstrated that the proposed spectral S&P patch masking shows reasonable performance on several downstream tasks, but it significantly enhanced effectiveness particularly when combined with other conventional approaches. We believe that the proposed methods can be extended to various benchmarks and downstream tasks.

7. Conclusions

In this paper, we introduced simple yet effective spectral S&P patch masking for self-supervised speech representation learning. In order to handle the difference in resolution or scale between spectrograms and images, we also suggested consecutive quadrilateral-shaped patches that extract the continuous information from spectrograms. Experimental results demonstrate the effectiveness of the proposed method on several speech downstream tasks and show it can be a useful supplement to existing self-supervised techniques for speech representation learning.

In our experiments, we observed that keeping the pretrained weights frozen worked better than fine-tuning them during the training of the Korean ASR model. Moreover, further studies are required to ensure that the proposed spectral S&P method can surpass masking-based approaches and encompass direct waveform extraction using CNNs or pretraining with quantizers. In the future, we plan to focus on these issues and potentially improve the performance further.

Author Contributions: Conceptualization, J.-W.K.; methodology, J.-W.K.; software, J.-W.K.; validation, J.-W.K., H.C., and H.-Y.J.; formal analysis, J.-W.K.; investigation, J.-W.K.; resources, J.-W.K. and H.-Y.J.; data curation, J.-W.K.; writing—original draft preparation, J.-W.K.; writing—review and editing, J.-W.K. and H.-Y.J.; visualization, J.-W.K.; supervision, J.-W.K. and H.-Y.J.; project administration, J.-W.K., H.C., and H.-Y.J.; funding acquisition, H.C. and H.-Y.J. All authors have read and agreed to the published version of the manuscript.

Funding: This work was supported in part by the National Research Foundation (NRF), Korea, under project BK21 FOUR, in part by the MSIT (Ministry of Science and ICT), Korea, under the ITRC (Information Technology Research Center) support program (IITP-2023-2020-0-01808) supervised by the IITP (Institute of Information & Communications Technology Planning & Evaluation), and in part by IITP grant funded by the Korea government (MSIT) (2019-0-00004, Development of semi-supervised learning language intelligence technology and Korean tutoring service for foreigners).

Institutional Review Board Statement: Not applicable.

Informed Consent Statement: Not applicable.

Data Availability Statement: The LibriSpeech dataset is available at [33], the TIMIT dataset is available at [40], the Speech Commands dataset is available at [41], the VoxCeleb1 dataset is available at [42], and the KsponSpeech dataset is available at [34].

Conflicts of Interest: The authors declare no conflicts of interest.

References

1. Vaswani, A.; Shazeer, N.; Parmar, N.; Uszkoreit, J.; Jones, L.; Gomez, A.N.; Kaiser, Ł.; Polosukhin, I. Attention is all you need. *Adv. Neural Inf. Process. Syst.* **2017**, *30*.
2. Baevski, A.; Zhou, Y.; Mohamed, A.; Auli, M. wav2vec 2.0: A framework for self-supervised learning of speech representations. *Adv. Neural Inf. Process. Syst.* **2020**, *33*, 12449–12460.
3. Liu, A.T.; Yang, S.w.; Chi, P.H.; Hsu, P.c.; Lee, H.y. Mockingjay: Unsupervised speech representation learning with deep bidirectional transformer encoders. In Proceedings of the ICASSP 2020–2020 IEEE International Conference on Acoustics, Speech and Signal Processing (ICASSP), Barcelona, Spain, 4–8 May 2020; pp. 6419–6423.
4. Chung, Y.A.; Zhang, Y.; Han, W.; Chiu, C.C.; Qin, J.; Pang, R.; Wu, Y. W2v-bert: Combining contrastive learning and masked language modeling for self-supervised speech pre-training. In Proceedings of the 2021 IEEE Automatic Speech Recognition and Understanding Workshop (ASRU), Cartagena, Colombia, 13–17 December 2021; pp. 244–250.
5. Hsu, W.N.; Bolte, B.; Tsai, Y.H.H.; Lakhotia, K.; Salakhutdinov, R.; Mohamed, A. Hubert: Self-supervised speech representation learning by masked prediction of hidden units. *IEEE/ACM Trans. Audio Speech Lang. Process.* **2021**, *29*, 3451–3460. [CrossRef]

6. Liu, A.T.; Li, S.W.; Lee, H.y. Tera: Self-supervised learning of transformer encoder representation for speech. *IEEE/ACM Trans. Audio Speech Lang. Process.* **2021**, *29*, 2351–2366. [CrossRef]
7. Kenton, J.D.M.W.C.; Toutanova, L.K. BERT: Pre-training of Deep Bidirectional Transformers for Language Understanding. In Proceedings of the NAACL-HLT, Minneapolis, MN, USA, 2–7 June 2019; pp. 4171–4186.
8. Ling, S.; Liu, Y.; Salazar, J.; Kirchhoff, K. Deep contextualized acoustic representations for semi-supervised speech recognition. In Proceedings of the ICASSP 2020–2020 IEEE International Conference on Acoustics, Speech and Signal Processing (ICASSP), Barcelona, Spain, 4–8 May 2020; pp. 6429–6433.
9. Wang, W.; Tang, Q.; Livescu, K. Unsupervised pre-training of bidirectional speech encoders via masked reconstruction. In Proceedings of the ICASSP 2020–2020 IEEE International Conference on Acoustics, Speech and Signal Processing (ICASSP), Barcelona, Spain, 4–8 May 2020; pp. 6889–6893.
10. Liu, A.H.; Chung, Y.A.; Glass, J. Non-Autoregressive Predictive Coding for Learning Speech Representations from Local Dependencies. *Proc. Interspeech 2021* **2021**, 3730–3734. [CrossRef]
11. Ling, S.; Liu, Y. Decoar 2.0: Deep contextualized acoustic representations with vector quantization. *arXiv* **2020**, arXiv:2012.06659.
12. Chi, P.H.; Chung, P.H.; Wu, T.H.; Hsieh, C.C.; Chen, Y.H.; Li, S.W.; Lee, H.y. Audio albert: A lite bert for self-supervised learning of audio representation. In Proceedings of the 2021 IEEE Spoken Language Technology Workshop (SLT), Shenzhen, China, 19–22 January 2021; pp. 344–350.
13. Oord, A.v.d.; Li, Y.; Vinyals, O. Representation learning with contrastive predictive coding. *arXiv* **2018**, arXiv:1807.03748.
14. Schneider, S.; Baevski, A.; Collobert, R.; Auli, M. wav2vec: Unsupervised Pre-Training for Speech Recognition. *Proc. Interspeech 2019* **2019**, 3465–3469. [CrossRef]
15. Chung, Y.A.; Hsu, W.N.; Tang, H.; Glass, J. An Unsupervised Autoregressive Model for Speech Representation Learning. *Proc. Interspeech 2019* **2019**, 146–150.
16. Gunel, B.; Du, J.; Conneau, A.; Stoyanov, V. Supervised Contrastive Learning for Pre-trained Language Model Fine-tuning. *arXiv* **2020**, arXiv:2011.01403.
17. Kim, T.; Yoo, K.M.; Lee, S.g. Self-Guided Contrastive Learning for BERT Sentence Representations. *arXiv* **2021**, arXiv:2106.07345.
18. Chen, T.; Kornblith, S.; Norouzi, M.; Hinton, G. A simple framework for contrastive learning of visual representations. In Proceedings of the International conference on machine learning, PMLR, Virtual, 13–18 July 2020; pp. 1597–1607.
19. He, K.; Fan, H.; Wu, Y.; Xie, S.; Girshick, R. Momentum contrast for unsupervised visual representation learning. In Proceedings of the IEEE/CVF Conference on Computer Vision and Pattern Recognition, Seattle, WA, USA, 13–19 June 2020; pp. 9729–9738.
20. Grill, J.B.; Strub, F.; Altché, F.; Tallec, C.; Richemond, P.; Buchatskaya, E.; Doersch, C.; Avila Pires, B.; Guo, Z.; Gheshlaghi Azar, M.; et al. Bootstrap your own latent-a new approach to self-supervised learning. *Adv. Neural Inf. Process. Syst.* **2020**, *33*, 21271–21284.
21. Khosla, P.; Teterwak, P.; Wang, C.; Sarna, A.; Tian, Y.; Isola, P.; Maschinot, A.; Liu, C.; Krishnan, D. Supervised contrastive learning. *Adv. Neural Inf. Process. Syst.* **2020**, *33*, 18661–18673.
22. Palanisamy, K.; Singhania, D.; Yao, A. Rethinking CNN models for audio classification. *arXiv* **2020**, arXiv:2007.11154.
23. Gong, Y.; Chung, Y.A.; Glass, J. Psla: Improving audio tagging with pretraining, sampling, labeling, and aggregation. *IEEE/ACM Trans. Audio Speech Lang. Process.* **2021**, *29*, 3292–3306. [CrossRef]
24. Dosovitskiy, A.; Beyer, L.; Kolesnikov, A.; Weissenborn, D.; Zhai, X.; Unterthiner, T.; Dehghani, M.; Minderer, M.; Heigold, G.; Gelly, S.; et al. An Image is Worth 16x16 Words: Transformers for Image Recognition at Scale. *arXiv* **2020**, arXiv:2010.11929.
25. Gong, Y.; Chung, Y.A.; Glass, J. AST: Audio Spectrogram Transformer. *Proc. Interspeech 2021* **2021**, 571–575. [CrossRef]
26. Gong, Y.; Lai, C.I.; Chung, Y.A.; Glass, J. Ssast: Self-supervised audio spectrogram transformer. *AAAI Conf. Artif. Intell.* **2022**, *36*, 10699–10709. [CrossRef]
27. Park, D.S.; Chan, W.; Zhang, Y.; Chiu, C.C.; Zoph, B.; Cubuk, E.D.; Le, Q.V. SpecAugment: A Simple Data Augmentation Method for Automatic Speech Recognition. *Proc. Interspeech 2019* **2019**, 2613–2617. [CrossRef]
28. DeVries, T.; Taylor, G.W. Improved regularization of convolutional neural networks with cutout. *arXiv* **2017**, arXiv:1708.04552.
29. Vincent, P.; Larochelle, H.; Lajoie, I.; Bengio, Y.; Manzagol, P.A.; Bottou, L. Stacked denoising autoencoders: Learning useful representations in a deep network with a local denoising criterion. *J. Mach. Learn. Res.* **2010**, *11*, 3371–3408.
30. Agostinelli, F.; Anderson, M.R.; Lee, H. Adaptive multi-column deep neural networks with application to robust image denoising. *Adv. Neural Inf. Process. Syst.* **2013**, *26*.
31. Lehtinen, J.; Munkberg, J.; Hasselgren, J.; Laine, S.; Karras, T.; Aittala, M.; Aila, T. Noise2Noise: Learning Image Restoration without Clean Data. *arXiv* **2018**, arXiv:1803.04189.
32. Liang, L.; Deng, S.; Gueguen, L.; Wei, M.; Wu, X.; Qin, J. Convolutional neural network with median layers for denoising salt-and-pepper contaminations. *Neurocomputing* **2021**, *442*, 26–35. [CrossRef]
33. Panayotov, V.; Chen, G.; Povey, D.; Khudanpur, S. Librispeech: An asr corpus based on public domain audio books. In Proceedings of the 2015 IEEE International Conference on Acoustics, Speech and Signal Processing (ICASSP), South Brisbane, QLD, Australia, 19–24 April 2015; pp. 5206–5210.
34. Bang, J.U.; Yun, S.; Kim, S.H.; Choi, M.Y.; Lee, M.K.; Kim, Y.J.; Kim, D.H.; Park, J.; Lee, Y.J.; Kim, S.H. Ksponspeech: Korean spontaneous speech corpus for automatic speech recognition. *Appl. Sci.* **2020**, *10*, 6936. [CrossRef]
35. Chan, R.H.; Ho, C.W.; Nikolova, M. Salt-and-pepper noise removal by median-type noise detectors and detail-preserving regularization. *IEEE Trans. Image Process.* **2005**, *14*, 1479–1485. [CrossRef]

36. Esakkirajan, S.; Veerakumar, T.; Subramanyam, A.N.; PremChand, C. Removal of high density salt and pepper noise through modified decision based unsymmetric trimmed median filter. *IEEE Signal Process. Lett.* **2011**, *18*, 287–290. [CrossRef]
37. Erhan, D.; Courville, A.; Bengio, Y.; Vincent, P. Why does unsupervised pre-training help deep learning? In Proceedings of the Thirteenth International Conference on Artificial Intelligence and Statistics, JMLR Workshop and Conference Proceedings, Sardinia, Italy, 13–15 May 2010; pp. 201–208.
38. Glorot, X.; Bordes, A.; Bengio, Y. Deep sparse rectifier neural networks. In Proceedings of the Fourteenth International Conference on Artificial Intelligence and Statistics, JMLR Workshop and Conference Proceedings, Ft. Lauderdale, FL, USA, 11–13 April 2011; pp. 315–323.
39. S3PRL Speech Toolkit (S3PRL). Github. Available online: https://github.com/s3prl/s3prl (accessed on 9 June 2023).
40. Garofolo, J.S.; Lamel, L.F.; Fisher, W.M.; Fiscus, J.G.; Pallett, D.S. DARPA TIMIT acoustic-phonetic continous speech corpus CD-ROM. NIST speech disc 1-1.1. *NASA STI/Recon Tech. Rep. N* **1993**, *93*, 27403.
41. Warden, P. Speech Commands: A Public Dataset for Single-Word Speech Recognition. Available online: http://download.tensorflow.org/data/speech_commands_v0 (accessed on 9 June 2023).
42. Nagrani, A.; Chung, J.S.; Xie, W.; Zisserman, A. Voxceleb: Large-scale speaker verification in the wild. *Comput. Speech Lang.* **2020**, *60*, 101027. [CrossRef]
43. Loshchilov, I.; Hutter, F. Decoupled Weight Decay Regularization. *arXiv* **2017**, arXiv:1711.05101.
44. Lee, K.F.; Hon, H.W. Speaker-independent phone recognition using hidden Markov models. *IEEE Trans. Acoust. Speech Signal Process.* **1989**, *37*, 1641–1648. [CrossRef]
45. Kingma, D.P.; Ba, J. Adam: A method for stochastic optimization. *arXiv* **2014**, arXiv:1412.6980.
46. wen Yang, S.; Chi, P.H.; Chuang, Y.S.; Lai, C.I.J.; Lakhotia, K.; Lin, Y.Y.; Liu, A.T.; Shi, J.; Chang, X.; Lin, G.T.; et al. SUPERB: Speech Processing Universal PERformance Benchmark. *Proc. Interspeech 2021* **2021**, 1194–1198. [CrossRef]
47. Graves, A.; Fernández, S.; Gomez, F.; Schmidhuber, J. Connectionist temporal classification: Labelling unsegmented sequence data with recurrent neural networks. In Proceedings of the 23rd International Conference on Machine Learning, Pittsburgh, PA, USA, 25–29 June 2006; pp. 369–376.
48. Heafield, K. KenLM: Faster and smaller language model queries. In Proceedings of the Sixth Workshop on Statistical Machine Translation, Edinburgh, UK, 30–31 July 2011; pp. 187–197.
49. Pratap, V.; Hannun, A.; Xu, Q.; Cai, J.; Kahn, J.; Synnaeve, G.; Liptchinsky, V.; Collobert, R. Wav2letter++: A fast open-source speech recognition system. In Proceedings of the ICASSP 2019-2019 IEEE International Conference on Acoustics, Speech and Signal Processing (ICASSP), Brighton, UK, 12–17 May 2019; pp. 6460–6464.
50. Kim, J.W.; Chung, H.; Jung, H.Y. Unsupervised Representation Learning with Task-Agnostic Feature Masking for Robust End-to-End Speech Recognition. *Mathematics* **2023**, *11*, 622. [CrossRef]
51. Watanabe, S.; Hori, T.; Karita, S.; Hayashi, T.; Nishitoba, J.; Unno, Y.; Enrique Yalta Soplin, N.; Heymann, J.; Wiesner, M.; Chen, N.; et al. ESPnet: End-to-End Speech Processing Toolkit. *Proc. Interspeech 2018* **2018**, 2207–2211. [CrossRef]
52. Müller, R.; Kornblith, S.; Hinton, G.E. When does label smoothing help? *Adv. Neural Inf. Process. Syst.* **2019**, *32*.
53. Yujian, L.; Bo, L. A normalized Levenshtein distance metric. *IEEE Trans. Pattern Anal. Mach. Intell.* **2007**, *29*, 1091–1095. [CrossRef]
54. Paszke, A.; Gross, S.; Massa, F.; Lerer, A.; Bradbury, J.; Chanan, G.; Killeen, T.; Lin, Z.; Gimelshein, N.; Antiga, L.; et al. Pytorch: An imperative style, high-performance deep learning library. *Adv. Neural Inf. Process. Syst.* **2019**, *32*.
55. Yang, Y.Y.; Hira, M.; Ni, Z.; Astafurov, A.; Chen, C.; Puhrsch, C.; Pollack, D.; Genzel, D.; Greenberg, D.; Yang, E.Z.; et al. Torchaudio: Building blocks for audio and speech processing. In Proceedings of the ICASSP 2022-2022 IEEE International Conference on Acoustics, Speech and Signal Processing (ICASSP), Singapore, 23–27 May 2022; pp. 6982–6986.
56. Harris, C.R.; Millman, K.J.; Van Der Walt, S.J.; Gommers, R.; Virtanen, P.; Cournapeau, D.; Wieser, E.; Taylor, J.; Berg, S.; Smith, N.J.; et al. Array programming with NumPy. *Nature* **2020**, *585*, 357–362. [CrossRef]
57. Kahn, J.; Rivière, M.; Zheng, W.; Kharitonov, E.; Xu, Q.; Mazaré, P.E.; Karadayi, J.; Liptchinsky, V.; Collobert, R.; Fuegen, C.; et al. Libri-light: A benchmark for asr with limited or no supervision. In Proceedings of the ICASSP 2020-2020 IEEE International Conference on Acoustics, Speech and Signal Processing (ICASSP), Barcelona, Spain, 4–8 May 2020; pp. 7669–7673.

Disclaimer/Publisher's Note: The statements, opinions and data contained in all publications are solely those of the individual author(s) and contributor(s) and not of MDPI and/or the editor(s). MDPI and/or the editor(s) disclaim responsibility for any injury to people or property resulting from any ideas, methods, instructions or products referred to in the content.

Article

Machine-Learning-Based Approaches for Multi-Level Sentiment Analysis of Romanian Reviews

Anamaria Briciu [1,*], Alina-Delia Călin [1,*], Diana-Lucia Miholca [1,*], Cristiana Moroz-Dubenco [1], Vladiela Petrașcu [1] and George Dascălu [2]

[1] Department of Computer Science, Babeș-Bolyai University, 1 M. Kogalniceanu Street, 400084 Cluj-Napoca, Romania; cristiana.moroz@ubbcluj.ro (C.M.-D.); vladiela.petrascu@ubbcluj.ro (V.P.)
[2] T2 S.R.L., 35 Ceauș Firică Street, 145100 Roșiori de Vede, Romania; george.dascalu@t-2.srl
* Correspondence: anamaria.briciu@ubbcluj.ro (A.B.); alina.calin@ubbcluj.ro (A.-D.C.); diana.miholca@ubbcluj.ro (D.-L.M.)

Abstract: Sentiment analysis has increasingly gained significance in commercial settings, driven by the rising impact of reviews on purchase decision-making in recent years. This research conducts a thorough examination of the suitability of machine learning and deep learning approaches for sentiment analysis, using Romanian reviews as a case study, with the aim of gaining insights into their practical utility. A comprehensive, multi-level analysis is performed, covering the document, sentence, and aspect levels. The main contributions of the paper refer to the in-depth exploration of multiple sentiment analysis models at three different textual levels and the subsequent improvements brought with respect to these standard models. Additionally, a balanced dataset of Romanian reviews from twelve product categories is introduced. The results indicate that, at the document level, supervised deep learning techniques yield the best outcomes (specifically, a convolutional neural network model that obtains an AUC value of 0.93 for binary classification and a weighted average F1-score of 0.77 in a multi-class setting with 5 target classes), albeit with increased resource consumption. Favorable results are achieved at the sentence level, as well, despite the heightened complexity of sentiment identification. In this case, the best-performing model is logistic regression, for which a weighted average F1-score of 0.77 is obtained in a multi-class polarity classification task with three classes. Finally, at the aspect level, promising outcomes are observed in both aspect term extraction and aspect category detection tasks, in the form of coherent and easily interpretable word clusters, encouraging further exploration in the context of aspect-based sentiment analysis for the Romanian language.

Keywords: sentiment analysis; latent semantic indexing; machine learning; deep learning; CNN; dense embedding layer; aspect term extraction; aspect category detection; Romanian language

MSC: 68T50

1. Introduction

The increased prevalence of digital communication in recent years has amplified the importance of automatically extracting and assessing sentiment in textual data, with organizations and researchers engaged in exploration of models with this capability, that allow them to gain insights into customer preferences and pinpoint emerging trends. An especially relevant application domain for sentiment analysis (SA) research revolves around the examination of consumer product reviews, which have evolved into an integral component of the purchasing process. Given that reviews inherently consist of opinions and evaluations of products and often employ subjective language, there is significant potential for sentiment identification at multiple textual levels. This includes the assessment of overall product evaluations (document-level SA), finer-grained analysis that aims to capture shifts in sentiment within a document (sentence-level SA), and the exploration of targeted sentiment, which involves identifying pairs of product features and the specific sentiments expressed in relation to these features (aspect-level SA).

This work presents an extensive examination of SA approaches for texts in Romanian, proposing an in-depth analysis at the document, sentence, and aspect levels, with the objective of filling a gap in the existing literature, which lacks multi-level investigation of datasets that hold commercial value for the Romanian language. Thus, the primary goal of this study is to assess the appropriateness of current machine learning and deep learning models for sentiment analysis in the context of the Romanian language, in order to acquire a comprehensive understanding of their viability for practical implementation in various business scenarios.

The original contributions of our study are as follows: (1) an in-depth exploration of SA models' performance at multiple textual levels for Romanian-language documents; (2) the introduction of a balanced dataset of Romanian reviews (structured in twelve different product categories), with five automatically assigned labels; and (3) improvements that we bring with respect to the standard models.

Below, we summarize the research questions we aim to answer within this paper.

RQ1 Is latent semantic indexing (LSI) in conjunction with conventional machine learning classifiers suitable for sentiment analysis of documents written in Romanian?

RQ2 Can deep-learned embedding-based approaches improve the performance of document- and/or sentence-level sentiment analysis, as opposed to classical natural language processing (NLP) embedding-based deep learning approaches?

RQ3 What is the relevance of different textual representations in the task of sentence polarity classification, and what impact do additional preprocessing steps have in this task?

RQ4 In terms of aspect extraction, is it feasible for a clustering methodology relying on learned word embeddings to delineate groups of words capable of serving as aspect categories identified within a given corpus of documents?

RQ5 How can the aspect categories discussed within a document be identified, if an aspect category is given through a set of words?

The rest of this paper is structured as follows. Section 2 includes a succinct description of the tasks addressed in this paper. A literature review on sentiment analysis models for the Romanian language and other related aspects is provided in Section 3. Section 4 is dedicated to the description of the methodology employed, while Section 5 presents the results we obtained. Additionally, we include a comparison of our approach with existing works in the literature and an analysis of the obtained results in Section 6. The last section, Section 7, contains conclusions and directions for future work.

2. Sentiment Analysis

Sentiment analysis is the area of research concerned with the computational study of people's opinions, sentiments, emotions, moods, and attitudes [1], and it involves a number of different tasks and perspectives. In this section, we include descriptions of the specific tasks from the sentiment analysis domain we have addressed in the present study.

2.1. Document-Level Sentiment Analysis (DLSA)

At the document level, sentiment analysis systems are concerned with identifying the overall sentiment from a given text. The assumption this task is based on is that a single opinion is expressed in the entire document. The advantage of simplicity in the definition of the problem has encouraged a substantial amount of work, especially in the early stages of exploration within the field.

In a machine learning and deep learning context, the DLSA task can be viewed as a classic text classification problem, in which the classes are represented by the sentiments/polarities [1]. The task can be formalized as a binary classification problem, in which the two classes are represented by the positive and negative polarities. There are various multi-class formulations of the sentiment analysis task in the literature. Most commonly, a third neutral class is considered besides the positive and negative ones to define a three-class classification problem [2,3]. In cases in which finer-grained sentiment labels are available, the targeted classes are, usually, strongly negative, negative, neutral, positive, and strongly positive [4–6]. In this context, any features or models used in the traditional text classification tasks may be applied, or new, explicit sentiment-oriented features, such as the occurrence of words from a sentiment lexicon, may be introduced.

However, a main disadvantage of DLSA refers to the assumption that a document, regardless of its length, contains a single opinion, and, consequently, a single overarching sentiment is expressed. Evidently, this does not always hold. Thus, researchers have progressively shifted their focus towards more fine-grained types of analysis.

2.2. Sentence-Level Sentiment Analysis (SLSA)

The objective of sentence-level sentiment analysis is to ascertain the sentiment conveyed in a specific sentence [7].

The motivation behind SLSA stems from the recognition that a single document can contain diverse opinions with varying polarities. This is particularly evident in texts like reviews, where users may make positive evaluations and negative evaluations in the same review. For example, a review with an average number of stars in a defined rating system is almost guaranteed to comprise both. Additionally, it is not uncommon for reviews to include neutral and objective statements of fact. This task thus serves as a connection between DLSA and aspect-level sentiment analysis. It aims to offer a more comprehensive view of the sentiment expressed in a document, without the intention of identifying the exact entities and aspects that the sentiment is directed towards. When considering the level of complexity, it can be observed that, although sentences may be regarded as short documents (and, thus, the problem can be formalized in an identical manner as for DLSA), they possess significantly less content compared to full-length documents. Consequently, the process of categorization becomes more challenging [8].

2.3. Aspect-Based Sentiment Analysis (ABSA)

While it is crucial to obtain an understanding of user opinion through analysis at the document level, and decompose it further into a study at the sentence level, in reviews, users often make evaluations with respect to different aspects of a given product, where an aspect refers to a characteristic, behavior, or trait of a product or entity [9]. For instance, for mobile phones, aspect categories of interest to users, generally, are battery life, photo and video quality, sound, and performance. Thus, creating a system that provides a summary of opinion polarity with regard to each of these aspects would be of great use for both users, who could benefit from customized recommendations aligned with their preferences and priorities, and for businesses, who could pinpoint areas of improvement in their products or services and make targeted changes to enhance product quality and customer satisfaction.

Aspect-based sentiment analysis is defined as the problem of identifying aspect and sentiment elements from a given text (usually a sentence) and the dependencies between them, either separately or simultaneously [10]. There are four fundamental elements of ABSA: aspect terms (words or expressions that are explicitly included in the given text, and that refer to an aspect that is the target of an opinion), aspect categories (a unique aspect of the given entity that usually belongs to a small list of predefined characteristics that are of interest), opinion terms (expressions through which a sentiment is conveyed towards the targeted aspect), and sentiment polarity (generally, positive, negative, or neutral).

Separate tasks can be defined to identify each of these elements and their dependencies: aspect term extraction (ATE), aspect category detection (ACD), opinion term extraction (OTE), and aspect sentiment classification (ASC). The ATE task aims to identify the explicit expressions used to refer to aspects that are evaluated in a text [10]. If formulated as a supervised classification task, then the goal is to label the tokens of a sentence as referring to an aspect or not. Since this implies the existence of annotated data, which is scarce for most languages besides English, a significant number of works employ unsupervised approaches. In recent years, this type of approach has involved the use of word embeddings in various self-supervised techniques enhanced with attention mechanisms to learn vector representations of aspects [11,12].

As for ACD, which aims to identify the discussed aspect categories for a given sentence, most state-of-the-art approaches formalize the task as a supervised text classification problem where a generally small set of predefined, domain-specific aspect categories represent the classes [13]. Unsupervised formulations often involve two steps: first extracting candidate aspect terms (the ATE task), and then grouping or mapping these terms to corresponding aspect categories. Manual assignment of labels to the obtained groups is a common practice in such approaches [11,14], but recent works [12,15] have proposed various methods to automate the process.

3. Related Work

This section presents an overview of recent SA approaches found in the literature, structured according to the distinct levels of sentiment analysis addressed by our study (document, sentence, and aspect) and focusing on those targeting the Romanian language.

With respect to sentiment analysis (and NLP tasks, in general), Romanian is known as an under-resourced language, with few comprehensive, publicly available datasets or corpora, as well as dedicated tools. As indicated by the LiRo benchmark and leaderboard platform [16], LaRoSeDa [17] is, to date, the only publicly available large corpus for sentiment analysis in Romanian. It consists of 15,000 positive and negative product reviews, extracted from an electronic commerce platform, that have been automatically labeled based on the number of associated stars. Although perfectly balanced (out of the total number of reviews, half being positive and the other half negative), the dataset is highly polarized, the great majority of positive reviews being rated five stars, while most of the negative ones, one star. Moreover, the authors admit that the labeling process is sub-optimal (as stars' numbers do not always faithfully reflect the associated polarity of a review), mentioning manual labeling or noise removal as future improvement tasks.

Regarding models, in recent years, transformer-based ones (both multi- and monolingual) have become the de facto standard within the NLP domain. BERT (bidirectional encoder representations from transformers) has been adopted as the baseline for transformer models, providing state-of-the-art results for various NLP tasks. For Romanian sentiment analysis, there are multi-lingual (mBERT [18], XML-RoBERTa [19]), and dedicated BERT-models available (Romanian BERT [20], RoBERT [21]), with the ones in the latter category performing better, due to their training on comprehensive language-specific datasets. In addition, approaches aimed at achieving higher performance on domain-specific analysis (such as JurBERT [22]) or at adapting the large-scale pretrained Romanian BERTs to computationally constrained environments (such as DistilBERT [23] or ALR-BERT [24]) have also been reported. When it comes to speed and efficiency, the multi-lingual, lightweight fastText [25] (also covering Romanian) is a popular alternative to multi-lingual BERTs, with the latter being more suited though for complex, data-intensive tasks.

In addition to the previously mentioned approaches, several research papers (detailed in the following) have reported the usage, improvement, or comparison of various classical and deep learning models, with the purpose of achieving similar or better results for SA in Romanian. As resulted from our investigation, most of the existing work has targeted the document level, with only a few studies explicitly covering the sentence- and aspect-based ones.

3.1. DLSA for Romanian

The papers mentioned in this subsection report experimenting with either only classical machine learning (ML) approaches, only deep learning (DL) ones, or both.

Within the first category, the work of Burlăcioiu et al. [26] aims to capture users' perceptions with respect to telecommunications and energy services, by analyzing 50,000 scraped reviews of mobile applications, offered by Romanian providers in these fields. They compare the results of five well-known SA models (logistic regression (LR), decision trees (DT), k-nearest neighbors (kNN), support vector machines (SVM), and naïve Bayes (NB)) on a balanced, automatically labeled version of the dataset, using term frequency–inverse document frequency (TF-IDF) encoding [27]. The best accuracy is obtained by employing DT and SVM (79.5% on average for the two models), with the former achieving better time performance. Russu et al. [28] provide a solution for sentiment analysis at the document and aspect levels, considering unstructured documents written in Romanian. They employ two different methods for sentiment polarity classification: one using SentiWordnet [29] as a lexical resource, and one based on the use of the Bing search engine. The experiments are conducted on a perfectly balanced corpus, consisting of 1000 movie reviews written in Romanian (500 positive and 500 negative), manually extracted from several blogs and websites. The documents have been manually labeled, based on the individual scores assigned by the user (in the range [1–10]). To identify document-level polarity, the authors experiment with random forest (RF), kNN, NB, and SVM, the maximum precision values obtained being 81.8% (using SentiWordnet) and 79.2% (using Bing queries).

Regarding DL approaches, the authors of LaRoSeDa, Tache et al. [17], propose using self-organizing maps (SOM), instead of the classical k-means algorithm, for clustering word embeddings generated by either word2vec [30] or Romanian BERT. The top accuracy rate reported on test data is 90.90%, by employing BERT-bag of word embedding (BERT-BOWE). Echim et al. [31] aim to optimize well-known NLP models (convolutional neural network (CNN), long short-term memory (LSTM), bi-LSTM, gated recurrent unit (GRU), Bi-GRU) with the aid of capsule networks and adversarial training, the new approaches being used for satire detection and sentiment analysis in Romanian. For the latter task, they use the LaRoSeDa dataset, the best accuracy (99.08%) being obtained using the Bi-GRU model with RoBERT encoding and dataset augmentation.

Belonging to the category of combined ML approaches, there is the work of Neagu et al. [32], whose general purpose is building a multinomial classifier (negative/positive/neutral) to be used for inferring the polarity of Romanian tweets in a video-surveillance context. By using both classical (Bernoulli NB, SVM, RF, LR) and deep learning approaches (deep neural network (DNN), CNN, LSTM), together with different types of encodings (TF-IDF/doc2vec for classical ML and DNN, word2vec for CNN and LSTM), they argue that, by adapting the NLP pipeline to the specificity of the data, good results can be achieved even in the absence of a comprehensive Romanian dataset (their dataset consists of 15,000 tweets, translated from English). The best obtained accuracy (78%) has resulted from using Bernoulli NB with TF-IDF encoding, while the state-of-the-art value (81%) is provided by the multi-lingual BERT, with a training time penalty though. Istrati and Ciobotaru [33] report on creating a framework aimed at brands' monitoring and evaluation, based on the analysis of Romanian tweets, that includes an SA binomial classifier trained and tested on a corpus labeled by the authors. The data are preprocessed using four proposed pipelines, the resulting sets being used to train and test various ML models, both classical and modern. The best accuracy and F1-scores are achieved by using a neural network with fastText [25], that being the model chosen for the framework classifier. Coita et al. [34] use SA in order to assess the attitude of Romanian taxpayers towards the fiscal system. In this respect, they try to predict the polarity of each of the answers provided by around 700 respondents to a 3-item questionnaire, using a BERT model pretrained and tested on a corpus of around 38,000 movie and product reviews in Romanian. BERT is chosen, as it provides maximum accuracy (98%) among several compared models, namely itself, recurrent neural network (RNN), and three classical ML approaches: LR, DT, and SVM.

3.2. SLSA for Romanian

Buzea et al. [35] introduce a novel sentence-level SA approach for Romanian, using a semi-supervised ML system based on a taxonomy of words that express emotions. Three classes of emotions are taken into account (positive, negative, and neutral). The obtained results are compared to those provided by classical ML algorithms, such as DT, SVM, and NB. Experiments are conducted using a corpus of around 26,000 manually annotated news items from Romanian online publishers and more than 42,000 labeled words from the Romanian dictionary. In terms of F1-score, the proposed system outperforms the three classical algorithms for the neutral and negative classes, while for the positive class, the highest metric value is achieved by DT.

Using a custom-made application, Roșca and Ariciu [36] aim to evaluate the performance of the Azure Sentiment Analysis service at sentence level for five languages, including Romanian. With this purpose, they generate 100 sentences per language, half positive and the other half negative. Although the service performs SA using three sentiment classes (positive, negative, and neutral), their evaluation only considers the first two, assuming any neutral label as incorrect. Classification accuracy is computed for three types of sentences: shorter than 100 characters, in the range of 100–250 characters, and longer. The reported accuracies are 83% for the first and last categories and 90% for the middle one.

3.3. Aspect Term Extraction (ATE) and Aspect Category Detection (ACD)

The only work that proposes a complete ABSA system for the Romanian language is that of Russu et al. [28], who also aim to identify sentiment at the document level, as described in Section 3.1. In this paper, the authors use seven syntactic rules to identify aspect terms and opinion words in a set of movie reviews. The polarity associated with the discovered entity is computed either using SentiWordnet or a search engine, using a set of seed words.

In this context, we provide a succinct description of unsupervised approaches for the ATE and ACD tasks, which are the two ABSA tasks we address in this paper.

For the task of aspect term extraction, early unsupervised approaches were generally based on rules [37–39]. For instance, Hu and Liu [37] use an association mining approach to identify product features and a WordNet-based approach to predict the orientation of opinion sentences. Other works propose analyzing the syntactic structure of a sentence at the word or phrase level to identify aspects and aspect-word/sentiment-word relations [39]. Such rule-based approaches are also frequently employed for aspect category detection. Hai et al. [40] attempt to find features (aspects) expressed implicitly in text through a two-step co-occurrence association rule mining approach. In the first phase, the co-occurrence is computed for opinion words and explicit features, extracted from a set of cell phone reviews in Chinese, and they refer to verbs and adjectives, and nouns and noun phrases, respectively. Additional constraints based on syntactic dependencies are applied for the extraction. In the second step, a k-means clustering algorithm is applied to the identified rule consequences, which are the explicit aspects, to generate more robust rules that can be then used for implicit aspect identification. Schouten et al. [41] propose a similar co-occurrence-based approach, but their unsupervised model uses a set of seed words for the considered aspect categories.

Another type of unsupervised approach to these tasks is represented by variants of classic topic modeling techniques. Titov and McDonald [42], for example, propose a multi-grain topic model (MG-LDA), which aims to capture two types of topics, global and local, and pinpoint rateable aspects to be modeled by the latter, the local topics. Brody and Elhadad propose the use of a standard LDA algorithm, but treat each sentence as a separate document to guide the model towards aspects of interest to the user, rather than global topics present in the corpus [43]. A topic modeling approach is also proposed by García-Pablos et al. [44], but it is a hybrid one, also making use of word embeddings and a Maximum Entropy classifier to tackle ABSA tasks.

In terms of neural models, He et al. [11] rely on word embeddings in the context of an attention-based approach, through which aspect embeddings are learned by a neural network similar to an auto-encoder. Tukens and van Cranenburgh [15] propose a simple two-step technique for aspect extraction, which first selects candidate aspects in the form of nouns with the help of a part-of-speech (PoS) tagger, and then employs contrastive attention to select aspects.

While there are approaches that rely mainly on clustering techniques, they are less frequent. An example of a clustering-based approach is that of Ghadery et al. [45], who use k-means clustering on representations of sentences obtained by averaging word2vec embeddings and a soft cosine similarity measure, to determine the similarity between a sentence and an aspect category, represented by a set of seed words.

As far as word clustering is concerned, the identification of semantically meaningful groups in a vocabulary has been a topic of interest for decades. Recent approaches either focus on using word clustering to detect topics in a document [46–48], or use it as a technique to enhance the performance of classifiers by means of improved document representations [17]. Sia et al. [46] explore the ability of embedding-based word clusters to summarize relevant topics from a corpus of documents. Different types of word embeddings are examined, both contextualized and non-contextualized, along with a number of hard (k-means, spherical k-means, k-medoids) and soft (Gaussian mixture models and von Mises–Fisher Models) clustering techniques to identify topics in documents. CluWords, the model proposed in [47], is shown to advance the state-of-the-art in topic modeling by exploiting neighborhoods in the embedding space to obtain sets of similar terms (i.e., meta-words/CluWords), which, in turn, are used in document representations with a novel TF-IDF strategy designed specifically for weighting the meta-words.

4. Methodology

4.1. Case Study

This section describes the dataset used in our study, a new dataset comprising reviews written in Romanian. We start by providing a brief summary of the data collection process and our motivation in creating the RoProductReviews dataset, and then we present a detailed description of its content, highlighting its suitability for the proposed tasks.

4.1.1. Data Collection

The reviews that make up the RoProductReviews dataset were manually collected from a highly popular Romanian e-commerce website. Specifically, the gathered information consists of the text of the review, the title, and the associated number of stars, which ranges between 1 and 5, and can be viewed as a numerical representation of customers' satisfaction with the reviewed product. In this context, assigning 1 star to a review represents complete dissatisfaction, while a 5-star evaluation indicates complete satisfaction with the product. Reviews were collected for a total of 12 product categories of electronics and appliances. The only criteria used in selecting reviews were the number of associated stars and the length of the text: the first, in terms of having a balanced dataset on the whole with respect to positive and negative sentiment, as we planned to use supervised learning techniques for the task of sentiment analysis, and the second, with the ABSA task in mind, reviews with longer texts were sought out to be included along with short, one-sentence reviews, since, generally, in the longer reviews, discussions about specific aspects of the product are included.

Through this data collection process, we built a balanced dataset with reviews written between 2014 and 2023 that is representative of the various modes of expression encountered in e-commerce product evaluations. To prevent the introduction of bias, ten individuals with diverse backgrounds collected the data. Clear guidelines outlining the purpose and intended structure of the dataset were provided to ensure consistency.

4.1.2. Dataset Description

Table 1 presents the number of reviews in the dataset associated with each number of stars, as well as the number of sentences they consist of. Additionally, the total number of tokens, the number of unique tokens, and unique lemmas are included for each category, as well as the average sentence length, computed as the average number of words in a sentence.

Table 1. RoProductReviews statistics.

	Number of Reviews	Number of Sentences	Average Sentence Length	Number of Tokens	Number of Unique Tokens	Number of Unique Lemmas
1 star	1357	3574	16.51	67,188	7669	5547
2 stars	1152	3873	18.39	81,120	9152	6840
3 stars	1280	4014	18.54	84,997	9691	6984
4 stars	1309	3621	17.43	72,305	8671	6203
5 stars	1336	2869	14.03	46,282	6123	4436

The RoProductReviews dataset is utilized in its entirety, as presented in Table 1, for the document-level sentiment analysis tasks. The classification labels for this dataset consist of either the assigned number of stars (for multi-class classification) or a positive/negative label derived from aggregating the higher- and lower-rated reviews, respectively (i.e., reviews with ratings of 1 and 2 stars are considered negative, while reviews associated with 4 and 5 stars are deemed positive; reviews with a 3-star rating are discarded in this setting). Although there is a possibility that the labels as obtained do not always faithfully reflect the sentiment expressed in the review [17], we consider them sufficient in terms of the intended experiments at the document level.

Nevertheless, when it comes to classifying sentiment at the sentence level, the rating assigned to the review that contains the sentences is an inaccurate predictor of the sentiment being communicated. Hence, a manual annotation procedure was utilized for a specific subset of RoProductReviews. A total of 2067 short reviews, consisting of single sentences, were annotated by 5 annotators who were only presented with the text of the review, but not the number of stars associated with it. A sentiment label was assigned if it was agreed upon by the majority; otherwise, the instance was discarded. Limitations exist in the annotation process, primarily inherent to sentiment annotation. Specifically, we emphasize the challenge of accurately identifying sentiment in extremely short sentences lacking explicit sentiment words or featuring ambiguous language. Additionally, annotators may delineate between neutral, positive, and negative sentiment differently, resulting in conflicting label assignments for the same sentence. To address these limitations, the annotation process incorporates majority voting, mitigating the impact of these challenges.

The reviews were chosen due to the fact that they did not require any additional processing in terms of sentence segmentation. The annotators utilized a labeling system that consisted of three categories: negative, neutral, and positive. As a consequence, a subset consisting of 804 reviews (sentences) annotated with the label negative was obtained. Additionally, there were 171 reviews annotated with the label neutral and 1092 reviews annotated with the label positive. A series of examples from this subset of RoProductReviews is included in Table 2.

Generally, RoProductReviews is characterized by a relatively equitable distribution among the various rating categories, with the exception of the 2-star category, which shows a lower level of representation. This under-representation of reviews in the 2-star category can be attributed to data availability constraints. During the data collection process, there was a noticeable scarcity of 2-star ratings, with a significant portion of unfavorable reviews predominantly attributed to a 1-star rating. It is plausible that customers articulating adverse sentiments may encounter challenges in acknowledging positive aspects of the reviewed product, which, in turn, might result in a milder form of negative evaluation, namely, a 2-star rating.

Table 2. Examples of manually annotated one-sentence reviews.

Review Text	Product Category	Number of Stars	Label
Asa cum m-am asteptat...face treaba pt birou As expected...it does the job for the office.	Monitor	5	Positive
Funcționează bine, mulțumit deocamdată de el It works well, satisfied with it for now.	Smartwatch	5	Positive
E un router ok It's an ok router	Router	4	Positive
NU E ULTRA SUPER CALITATE DAR E BUN It's not ultra-super quality, but it's good	Speakers	4	Positive
Este doar bună pentru jocuri și desene, pozele ies ca pe telefoanele mai vechi It's only good for games and drawings; the photos come out like on older phones	Tablet	3	Neutral
Sunt acceptabile la redarea sunetului, dar la convorbiri nu prea se aude microfonul They are acceptable for sound playback, but the microphone is not very audible during calls	Headphones	3	Neutral
Mi s-a blocat de nenumărate ori și pierdea des semnalul It has frozen numerous times, and it often lost the signal	Smartphone	2	Negative
Nu ține deloc bateria, după nici 12 ore de la încărcarea completă (100%) s-a descărcat complet The battery doesn't hold at all; after not even 12 h from a full (100%) charge, it completely discharged	Fitness bracelet	1	Negative
Cel mai silențios mouse, dar conexiune prin infraroșu mediocră, se întrerupe non-stop The quietest mouse, but with a mediocre infrared connection, it keeps disconnecting non-stop	Mouse	1	Negative
Procesor slab rău Terribly weak processor	Laptop	1	Negative

Regarding sentence length, we can observe that sentences in the rating categories that do not indicate complete satisfaction or dissatisfaction with the reviewed product (i.e., 2-, 3-, and 4-star categories) tend to be longer. This is intuitive, as in these cases, customers are more likely to provide detailed accounts of both the strengths and weaknesses of the product to justify their assigned rating. This is especially evident in reviews associated with 3 stars, an evaluation customers generally make after careful analysis of a series of positive and negative aspects of the reviewed product. Alternatively, 1-star and 5-star reviews may only consist of short sentences such as *"Nu recomand/Don't recommend"*, *"Calitate proasta/Bad quality"*, *"Slab/Weak"* and *"Super/Super"*, *"Tableta excelentă/Excellent tablet"*, *"Multumit de achizitie/Content with my purchase"*, respectively.

Table 3 presents analogous statistics, this time segmented by product category. The dataset exhibits diversity in terms of the number of reviews gathered for each category. For instance, there is a nearly threefold difference in the number of reviews collected for *smartphones* compared to *routers*. This diversity is essential for creating a realistic evaluation scenario for various sentiment analysis models directed toward specific product categories (e.g., aspect-based sentiment analysis), reflecting the real-world scenario where certain product types enjoy more popularity and consequently accumulate more reviews than others.

Table 3. RoProductReviews dataset description per category.

Product Category	Number of Reviews	Number of Sentences	Average Sentence Length	Total Number of Tokens	Number of Unique Tokens	Number of Unique Lemmas
Headphones	409	984	16.54	18,480	2990	2205
Fitness bracelets	599	1578	16.45	29,500	4117	2967
Keyboard	899	2522	17.71	51,160	5856	4249
Laptop	404	1313	16.70	25,005	4070	3038
Monitor	419	971	15.98	17,852	3061	2328
Mouse	395	1062	16.69	20,383	3157	2298
Router	300	853	17.25	16,785	2919	2248
Smartphone	897	2348	17.16	45,906	6432	4882
Smartwatch	577	1469	17.38	29,213	4285	3109
Speakers	455	1429	18.59	30,240	4325	3163
Tablet	680	1753	15.59	31,445	4440	3291
Vacuum cleaner	400	1669	18.88	35,923	4842	3418
TOTAL	6434	17,951	17.08	351,892	21,430	15,311

We note that, despite this imbalance across product categories, the distribution of reviews in each star rating category is preserved. With a few exceptions (*monitor, tablet, smartphone*), the sets are almost perfectly balanced in this respect.

Additionally, we present a series of statistics that further support the use of the RoProductReviews dataset for the sentiment analysis tasks addressed in this study. Specifically, to provide context for the aspect identification task, which relies on the identification and grouping of nouns, we computed the part-of-speech distribution within each product category with the help of the NLP-Cube Part of Speech Tagging Tool [49]. We found that nouns represent approximately 20% of all tokens for every category. The percentage of adjectives ranges from 0.04 to 0.06, with *vacuum cleaner* reviews having the smallest proportion and *monitors*, the highest. Alternatively, *vacuum cleaner* reviews are the richest in terms of verbs (0.14), while reviews about peripherals, like *monitors* and *keyboards*, have the smallest proportion of verbs, along with *routers* (0.11). Similarly, small differences are observed with respect to adverbs: the highest percentage of adverbs can be found in *headphones* reviews (0.12), with *router* at the other end (0.09). The notable presence of nouns in reviews provides a favorable foundation for our proposed approach to aspect identification, which relies on noun clustering, but underscores the necessity of devising an effective method for discerning the most relevant nouns. As for adjectives, a part-of-speech traditionally linked with sentiment, we note that their relatively low presence may be due to users often expressing sentiment with regard to products by stating what works and what does not (e.g., *I can't run multiple applications simultaneously*), or by providing domain-specific clues (e.g., *the refresh rate is 144 Hz, and it shows*). Nonetheless, out of all adjectives, between 38% and 50% are valenced across categories (as identified by the lexicon RoEmoLex [50]), which lends credit to the possibility of exploring dependency-based approaches to associating sentiment with the aspect terms discovered through nouns. Interestingly, around 20–25% of verbs in each category are also found in the sentiment lexicon, while only about 13–17% of nouns and 5–6% of adverbs are used to express sentiment directly.

In view of this analysis, we consider that the proposed dataset is suitable for a case study that aims to examine the appropriateness of different machine learning and deep learning models for sentiment analysis for the Romanian language.

4.2. Theoretical Models

This section includes the formalization of the sentiment analysis tasks at each level, which target $\mathcal{D}$, a collection of documents that, in our case study, refers to the RoProductReviews dataset. Each $doc \in \mathcal{D}$, where $doc = \{w_1, w_2, \ldots, w_N\}$ represents a document from the collection comprising N words, and w_i with $1 \leq i \leq N$ is a word in the document. Let $\mathcal{V}$ be the vocabulary used in this collection, defined as:

$$\mathcal{V} = \bigcup_{doc \in \mathcal{D}} doc \quad (1)$$

Additionally, we denote by $\mathcal{D}_c$ the collection of documents in a given product category c.

4.2.1. Document-Level Sentiment Analysis

The task of sentiment analysis at the document level assumes that the document doc (for example, a movie review or, as in our case, a product review) expresses an opinion regarding a specific (single) entity e. In this context, document sentiment classification aims to determine the overall sentiment s expressed related to the entity e, which can be positive or negative (in binary classification). The sentiment options, however, can be extended to a range, in our case, the five stars ranging from 1 (strongly negative) to 5 (strongly positive), leading to a multi-class classification problem [1].

4.2.2. Sentence-Level Sentiment Analysis

Sentence-level sentiment analysis assumes that each sentence st expresses a single opinion, oriented towards a single known entity e. Therefore, the goal of classification at the sentence level is to identify the sentiment s expressed in sentence st regarding the entity e. Since reviews, by definition, express opinions about a product or service, it is expected that at least one of the multiple sentences in a document expresses a positive or negative opinion. This is why document-level analysis can ignore the neutral class, but sentence-level analysis cannot: a sentence within a review can be objective, which means that it does not express any sentiment or opinion and is therefore neutral [1].

4.2.3. Aspect Term Extraction and Aspect Category Detection

We address the aspect term extraction task through an examination of word embeddings and their subsequent properties in the learned vector space. We build on previous research that indicates that aspects are explicitly referred to in texts through nouns [15,37,40], and employ a clustering algorithm to obtain groups of similar words, particularly nouns, that are interpreted as aspect categories. This analysis serves as an initial step for addressing the ABSA task, which currently lacks extensive exploration in the context of the Romanian language. We also provide a method to estimate the presence of an aspect in a document (sentence/review), thus addressing the aspect category detection task, highlighting its potential for application at both the document and sentence levels.

Let $\mathcal{N}_c$ be the set of nouns used in a category c. A clustering algorithm is applied on the set $E_c = \{embedding_w | embedding_w = f_{model}(w), w \in \mathcal{N}_c\}$, which contains the embeddings obtained through embedding model f_{model} for the nouns used throughout documents in category c. A partition $\mathcal{P}$ of set E_c is thus generated, with $\mathcal{A} \in \mathcal{P}$ a set of similar embeddings, where for similarity, a suitable metric is chosen.

The sets $\mathcal{A}_w, \mathcal{A}_w = \{w | embedding_w \in \mathcal{A}\}$ represent candidate aspect categories and their members, candidate aspect terms. To obtain the most relevant aspects from each product category, we apply the following heuristic: we eliminate from consideration sets $\mathcal{A}$ for which $|\mathcal{A}| < 3$ and $|\mathcal{A}| > 10$, where $|\mathcal{A}|$ represents the number of elements in set $\mathcal{A}$. We based this decision on the potential interpretability of such word groups: less than three words might not provide sufficient information for identifying an overarching aspect category, while a group of more than ten words will most likely contain miscellaneous terms with respect to semantic information, especially when considering the restricted vocabulary of only nouns. Then, we rank the remaining sets $\mathcal{A}$ to obtain the most representative groups with respect to the considered product category. Each set $\mathcal{A}_w$ is associated with a value defined as $score_{freq} = \sum_{w \in \mathcal{A}_w} \sum_{doc \in \mathcal{D}_c} freq(w, doc)$, which considers the overall frequency of the nouns in set $\mathcal{A}$ in the considered reviews $doc \in \mathcal{D}_c$ from a given product category c. We also experimented with a ranking based on the number of documents covered by the words in the obtained sets, with $score_{coverage} = |\bigcup_{w \in \mathcal{A}_w} \{doc | w \in doc, doc \in \mathcal{D}_c\}|$, and obtained similar results. Then, according to the ranking given by one of these scores, the top t percent groups are considered the most relevant aspect categories, as, according to the ranking, these are the most frequently discussed in the given category. A short, descriptive label is assigned manually to each of these clusters based on its content.

4.3. Data Representation

4.3.1. Preliminaries: Data Preparation and Preprocessing

This section describes the preprocessing steps taken for each of the proposed analyses.

In all cases, a preprocessing step was performed, which involved the transformation of the text to lowercase and the removal of URL links. For stop word removal, the list provided with the advertools library version 0.13.5 (https://github.com/eliasdabbas/advertools (accessed on 20 January 2024)) was used, from which the words that may express opinions or sentiments, such as *bine* (well), *bună* (good), or *frumos* (beautiful), were removed.

In the approach at the document level, the title of the review was concatenated at the beginning of the review text to be classified. Moreover, the stop words were not removed, to avoid loss of information relevant to the model and to be able to perform a baseline comparison. Also, punctuation was not removed because there were several emoticons which were punctuation based (and not Unicode characters).

For the sentence-level approach, the title of the review was not taken into consideration, as it usually contains two or three words, summarizing the review without forming a sentence. Similar to the document-level approach, the punctuation was not removed, due to the possible existence of text emoticons. As for the stop words, experiments were run both with and without removing them, to assess their impact on the model performance.

In terms of analysis at the aspect level, a number of preprocessing steps were followed. Punctuation, stop words and URLs were also removed for this task, as they represented elements that either could not represent aspect terms or could not contribute to the definition of aspect categories. Additionally, lemmatization of the tokens was performed. Part-of-speech tagging was the last step in our preprocessing process, the result of which was only used at the clustering stage to identify the nouns in a given set of reviews.

4.3.2. TF-IDF Representation

Term frequency–inverse document frequency is a commonly used algorithm that transforms text into numeric representations (embeddings) to be used with machine learning algorithms. As its name suggests, this method combines two concepts: term frequency (TF)—the number of times a term w (word) appears in a document doc—and document frequency (DF)—the number of documents in which a term appears. For the SLSA case, we consider each sentence to be a document and, thus, compute the frequency with which a specific term appears in a sentence and the number of sentences that contain that specific term.

Term frequency can be simply defined as the number of times the term appears in a document, while inverse document frequency (IDF) works by computing the commonness of the term among the documents contained in the corpus.

By using the inverse document frequency, infrequent terms have a higher impact, leading to the conclusion that the importance of a term is inversely proportional to its corpus frequency. While the TF part of the TF-IDF algorithm contains information about a term's frequency, the IDF results in information about the rarity of a specific term.

4.3.3. LSI Representation

In addition to the TF-IDF representation described in the previous subsection, we also propose the examination of the relevance of features extracted by latent semantic indexing (LSI) [51] in a sentiment classification task for the Romanian language.

LSI is a count-based model for representing variable-length texts (in our case, documents and sentences containing reviews written in Romanian) as fixed-length numeric vectors. It builds a matrix of occurrences of words in documents and then uses singular-value decomposition to reduce the number of words while keeping the similarity structure between documents.

Therefore, each document doc is represented as a vector composed of numerical values corresponding to a set $\mathcal{F} = \{ft_1, ft_2, \ldots, ft_{size}\}$ of *size* features extracted from the review text directly using LSI.

- $doc^{LSI} = (doc_1^{LSI}, \cdots, doc_{size}^{LSI})$, where doc_i^{LSI} ($\forall 1 \leq i \leq size$) denotes the value of the i-th feature computed for the document doc in the documents dataset by using the LSI-based embedding.

As far as the experimental setup is concerned, for extracting the LSI-based embeddings for the documents, we used the implementation offered by Gensim [52]. We opted for $size = 30$ as the length of the embedding and for $num\_topics = 30$ as the number of latent dimensions that represents the number of topics in the given corpus. For the SLSA task, the $size$ was reduced to 10, since most of the sentences contain less than 30 terms even before reduction.

4.3.4. Deep-Learned Representation

An alternative to count-based feature extraction for machine learning approaches is represented by using neural models that can automatically generate features for the considered tasks.

In deep learning approaches, specific word-embedding techniques have been developed, which are actually based on neural network layers and dense vectors [30]. In our experiments, we used dense embedding in conjunction with four deep learning networks: CNN, global average pooling (GAP), GRU, and LSTM.

As far as the experimental setup is concerned, after following the general preprocessing step described in Section 4.3.1, we used word number encoding, considering a vocabulary of 15,000 words, and a padding for each review to 500 words These encoding parameters were chosen after performing a search of best parameters based on the characteristics of our dataset and literature findings. The embedding is performed in the first dense embedding layer of each machine learning model. The text document is encoded using a word-embedding dense layer, which is then processed by the network layers. Formally, given doc^{EM}, a text document embedded with a model of token sequences (in which a token could be a word or a letter), with N terms in the document, we have $doc^{EM} = x_1 x_2 \ldots x_N$, where $x_i = (x_i^1, x_i^2, \ldots, x_i^M) \in \mathbb{R}^M$ is a token embedding of size M. Next, the embedding is submitted to linear transformations (for the CNN model), average region functions (in the GAP model), or memory units and gates (in recurrent neural networks, such as LSTM and GRU).

4.3.5. Word Representations

As far as word representations are concerned, word2vec [30] embeddings are used, a type of representation learned through a neural network from a text corpus. The word2vec model, $f_{w2v} : \mathcal{V} \longrightarrow \mathbb{R}^{mw}$, is an embedding model that maps each word $w \in \mathcal{V}$ to a vector representation (embedding) that has size mw: $embedding_w = (em_1, em_2, \ldots, em_{mw})$, where em_i denotes the value of the i-th feature computed for the word w by the model f_{w2v}.

For the proposed tasks, the word2vec model was trained on the corpus of all reviews, with a number of preprocessing steps employed, as described in Section 4.3.1. Next, word embeddings for all lemmas in the vocabulary were learned. We experimentally determined the size of 150 for the word vectors to be the best performing.

4.4. Models

4.4.1. Supervised Classification

To assess the relevance of the TF-IDF and LSI-based embeddings when it comes to the automatic polarity classification for reviews written in Romanian, we trained and evaluated multiple standard machine learning classification models, such as SVM, RF, LR, NB, voted perceptron (VP), and multilayer perceptron (MLP).

The models used in deep learning approaches were configured using a dense embedding base layer, which assumes 500 as the embedding dimension, on top of which the particular model layers are added. The CNN model has a convolution 1D layer, a global max pooling 1D layer, and a hidden dense layer with output 24. For GRU, the hidden layers consist of a bidirectional GRU layer and a dense layer with 24 output units, while LSTM contains a bidirectional LSTM layer and a dense layer with 24 output units. The GAP model contains an average pooling layer and a dense one with 24 output units. The output dense layer (which is the same for all models) has one unit in the case of binary classification and five output units for multi-class classification. The activation function [53] for the hidden dense layer is the rectified linear unit (ReLU). For binary classification, the output dense layer is the *sigmoid* function, and the models are compiled using binary cross-entropy as the loss function and the adaptive movement estimation optimizer Adam [54]. In the case of multi-class classification with 3 or 5 classes, the models are compiled using the sparse categorical cross-entropy function, and for the output dense layer, we use the *softmax* function.

Each training session of a model was performed for at most 30 epochs, with early stopping after five epochs without any improvement on the loss function. The implementation was performed using the scikit-learn version 1.3.1 (https://scikit-learn.org/stable/ (accessed on 20 January 2024)) and keras version 2.14.0 (https://keras.io/ (accessed on 20 January 2024)) Python packages.

4.4.2. Unsupervised Analysis

As a clustering technique, we employ k-means and SOM. For similar tasks, k-means is the most frequently encountered [46,55], but SOM has shown better performance in recent studies [56]. Therefore, we aimed to examine the suitability of the two techniques in terms of a Romanian-language dataset. For both, the initial number of nodes/clusters was set at 200, value which was experimentally determined to generate the best results for our dataset. For k-means, the implementation from the scikit-learn library version 1.3.1 was used, with no additional parameters. For SOM, we used the implementation from the NeuPy version 0.6.5 (http://neupy.com/pages/home.html (accessed on 20 January 2024)) Python package, with the learning radius set at 1 and the step at 0.25. The distance used was cosine. The top 5% percent of the obtained aspect clusters are considered representative ($t = 0.05$).

4.5. Evaluation

4.5.1. Methodology

In order to reliably evaluate the performance of the proposed approaches, we performed 10 repetitions of 5-fold cross-validation in all the experiments carried out on our dataset, *RoProductReviews*.

During the cross-validation process, the confusion matrix for the classification task was computed for each testing subset. Based on the values from the confusion matrix, multiple performance metrics, as described in Section 4.5.2, were computed. For each metric, the values were averaged during the cross-validation process, and the 95% confidence interval (CI) of the mean values was calculated.

4.5.2. Performance Indicators

Supervised classification. Based on state-of-the-art views, the most used performance metrics in sentiment analysis are accuracy (*Accuracy*), F1-score (*F1*), precision (*Precision*), recall (*Recall*), specificity (*Specificity*), and area under the ROC curve (AUC). These can be calculated individually for every class in the dataset or as an arithmetic or weighted average for the entire model. To compute each metric, we require the resulting confusion matrix, a matrix that, in supervised learning, evaluates the performance of a model comparing the actual class of an entry versus the predicted class. In this sense, for a class k, we denote with TP_k the true positives of class k and with TN_k the true negatives of class k. TP_k is defined as the number of instances from class k correctly classified in class k, and TN_k is defined as the number of instances that are not in class k and have been correctly classified as a different class from k. FP_k denotes the false positives, meaning the number of instances that are not in class k but have been classified as being class k, and FN_k denotes the false negatives, meaning the number of instances that are in fact in class k but have been incorrectly classified to be a different class from k. In Equation (2), we define the accuracy of a class k, denoted by $Accuracy_k$. We present the definition for precision for a class k, denoted as $Precision_k$, in Equation (3). In Equation (4), the formula for computing the recall for a class k, denoted by $Recall_k$, is presented. The specificity for a class k, denoted as $Specificity_k$, is computed as in Equation (5).

$$Accuracy_k = \frac{TP_k + TN_k}{TP_K + FP_k + TN_K + FN_k} \quad (2)$$

$$Precision_k = \frac{TP_k}{TP_k + FP_k} \quad (3)$$

$$Recall_k = \frac{TP_k}{TP_k + FN_k} \quad (4)$$

$$Specificity_k = \frac{TN_k}{TN_k + FP_k} \quad (5)$$

The area under the ROC curve is generally employed for classification approaches that yield a single value, which is then converted into a class label using a threshold. For each threshold value, the point $(1 - Specificity, Recall)$ is represented on a plotm and the AUC value is computed as the area under this curve. For the approaches where the direct output of the classifier is the class label, there is only one such point, which is linked to the $(0, 0)$ and $(1, 1)$ points. The AUC measure represents the area under the trapezoid and is computed as in Equation (6).

$$AUC_k = \frac{Recall_k + Specificity_k}{2} \quad (6)$$

The last measure used, the F1-score for a class k, is defined in Equation (7).

$$F1_k = \frac{2 \times Precision_k \times Recall_k}{Precision_k + Recall_k} \quad (7)$$

All the previously mentioned performance evaluation measures range from 0 to 1. For better classifiers, larger values are expected.

For a binary classification in sentiment analysis, we have two classes (the positive class and the negative class); thus, we denote the metrics referring to positive predicted values (PPVs) for the precision of the positive class and negative predicted values (NPVs) for the precision of the negative class. In the general case of multi-class classification with NC classes, having calculated the performance indicators per each class with the above formulas, we define the overall weighted average for each performance metric $PI \in \{Accuracy, Precision, Recall, F1\}$ as in Equation (8).

$$PI = \sum_{k=1}^{NC} weight_k * PI_k, \quad (8)$$

where PI_k is the performance indicator for class k, and $weight_k$ is the weight of class k. The weight of a class k is computed as $weight_k = I_k/I_{NC}$, with I_k equal to the number of instances from class k in the dataset and I_{NC} the total number of instances for all classes in the dataset.

Unsupervised analysis. For the proposed unsupervised analysis, we used two evaluation measures, namely normalized pointwise mutual information (NPMI) [57] and a WordNet-based similarity measure. NPMI is the normalized variant of *pointwise mutual information*, a measure commonly used to evaluate association. This normalized variant has the advantage of a range of values with fixed interpretation.

$$NPMI(w_1; w_2) = \frac{\log\left(\frac{p(w_1,w_2)}{p(w_1)\cdot p(w_2)}\right)}{-\log p(w_1,w_2)} \qquad (9)$$

In Equation (9), the formula for computing the NPMI for two words is shown, where $p(w_1)$ and $p(w_2)$ represent the probabilities of occurrence of words w_1 and w_2, respectively, and $p(w_1, w_2)$ is the probability of the co-occurrence of the two. For an aspect cluster $\mathcal{A}_w = \{w_1, w_2, \ldots w_{N_a}\}$, containing N_a words denoted by w_i, $1 \leq i \leq N_a$, the NPMI value is computed as an average over the NPMI values obtained for every pair (w_i, w_j), $i < j$.

While it was defined in the context of collocation extraction, the NPMI measure has also been used in topic modeling literature to evaluate topic coherence [46,47], as it was found to reflect human judgment [58].

The NPMI bases the assessment on the co-occurrence of terms, while the proposed WordNet-based measure takes advantage of the hierarchy of noun and noun phrases in WordNet, in which *is-a* (hyponymy/hypernymy) relations, as well as *part-of* associations, are recorded. We are especially interested in the hierarchy determined by the *is-a* relationships between nouns, as we need to evaluate the ability of determined groups of nouns (aspect *terms*) to describe a more general concept (aspect *category*). Thus, we used a measure that describes how closely related two words are in this hierarchical structure of the WordNet lexical database: the Leacock and Chodorow (LCH) similarity [59]. We compute this metric as in Equation (10), using the Romanian WordNet (RoWordNet [60]).

$$LCH(synset_{w_1}, synset_{w_2}) = -\log_2 \frac{sp(synset_{w_1}, synset_{w_2}) + 1}{2 \cdot maxWNDepth} \qquad (10)$$

In Equation (10), the Leacock–Chodorow similarity is computed between the first senses of the two terms w_1 and w_2, which are encapsulated in RoWordNet *synsets*. Thus, we denote by $sp(synset_{w_1}, synset_{w_2})$ the shortest path length between the concepts represented by w_1 and w_2 in the WordNet hierarchy, while $maxWNDepth$ represents the maximum taxonomy depth.

The NPMI measure has the advantage of evaluating performance on an unseen test set, providing a realistic measure of the proposed approach. However, we argue that, while NPMI may be an informative measure with respect to the coherence of topics, which are defined as sets of words that co-occur, it is less suitable for measuring the coherence of groups of words meant to be interpreted as aspect terms which define an aspect category. Usually, when discussing an aspect of a product, the number of aspect terms from a given category used in the same sentence, and even review, is limited—in fact, these aspect terms are often used interchangeably. For NPMI, the range of values is $[-1, 1]$, with values of -1 characterizing words that occur separately, but not together, and values of 1 describing words that only occur together. As for LCH, the range of values is $(0, log(2 * maxWNDepth)]$, where the maximum RoWordNet depth in the hypernymy tree is 16. Considering that $sp(synset_{w_1}, synset_{w_2}) = 0$ when w_1 and w_2 have the same sense, a higher value for the LCH measure signifies increased relatedness between the concepts represented by w_1 and w_2.

5. Results

In this section, we present the results of our study, which aims to investigate the efficacy of machine learning techniques in sentiment analysis, specifically applied to a dataset of Romanian reviews. Results are provided for the three textual levels we addressed: document (as detailed in Section 5.1), sentence (outlined in Section 5.2), and aspect level (discussed in Section 5.3).

5.1. Document Level

The first embedding we evaluated in the context of sentiment analysis when using the RoProductReviews dataset is the one based on LSI.

The classifiers employed in evaluating the relevance of the LSI-based embedding for sentiment analysis were SVM, RF, LR, and a neural-network-based model (VP [61] for binary classification and MLP for multi-class classification).

The results obtained when classifying the RoProductReviews reviews on two classes of polarity, positive and negative, when representing the reviews as LSI-based embeddings, are given in Table 4. For each of the four models, we present the mean value and confidence interval calculated for each performance metric used in evaluation, methodology that was described in Section 4.5. We have obtained AUC values up to 0.894 and F1-score values up to 0.893. The best-performing classification model is LR, which is immediately followed by VP, for which AUC and F1-score values of 0.891 were obtained.

The performances obtained in the case of multi-class classification are given in Table 5. The conclusion that has been drawn for binary classification, regarding the relative performance of the classifiers, holds, the best-performing classifier remaining logistic regression. LR obtained a weighted average F1-score value of 0.690, while the second-best classifier is still the artificial neural network model, in particular the MLP that replaced the VP used for binary classification. A weighted average F1-score value of 0.676 was obtained by the MLP classifier.

Table 4. Results obtained for LSI-based binary classification with the RoProductReviews dataset. The highest value for each performance indicator is marked in bold.

Performance Indicator	SVM Mean	95% CI	RF Mean	95% CI	LR Mean	95% CI	VP Mean	95% CI
Accuracy	0.878	0.001	0.880	0.001	**0.893**	0.001	0.891	0.001
Precision PPV	**0.924**	0.001	0.903	0.002	0.911	0.001	0.897	0.002
Precision NPV	0.838	0.001	0.858	0.001	0.876	0.001	**0.885**	0.003
Average precision	0.881	0.001	0.881	0.001	**0.893**	0.001	0.891	0.002
Sensitivity/Recall—TPR	0.830	0.001	0.859	0.001	0.878	0.001	**0.890**	0.003
Specificity—TNR	**0.928**	0.001	0.902	0.002	0.909	0.001	0.892	0.003
AUC	0.879	0.001	0.881	0.001	**0.894**	0.001	0.891	0.001
F1-score Positive Class	0.875	0.001	0.881	0.001	**0.894**	0.001	0.893	0.001
F1-score Negative Class	0.881	0.001	0.880	0.001	**0.892**	0.001	0.889	0.001
Weighted F1-score	0.878	0.001	0.880	0.001	**0.893**	0.001	0.891	0.001

Table 5. Results obtained for LSI-based multi-class classification with the RoProductReviews dataset. The highest value for each performance indicator is marked in bold.

Performance Indicator		SVM Mean	95% CI	RF Mean	95% CI	LR Mean	95% CI	MLP Mean	95% CI
Accuracy	Avg	0.660	0.001	0.660	0.005	**0.689**	0.001	0.675	0.002
Precision	Class 1 Star	0.599	0.001	0.644	0.002	0.656	0.002	**0.660**	0.014
	Class 2 Stars	0.568	0.002	0.579	0.004	0.602	0.003	**0.604**	0.016
	Class 3 Stars	**0.733**	0.003	0.676	0.005	0.727	0.003	0.709	0.023
	Class 4 Stars	0.617	0.004	0.622	0.004	**0.650**	0.002	0.628	0.011
	Class 5 Stars	**0.858**	0.001	0.816	0.004	0.825	0.002	0.788	0.008
Recall	Class 1 Star	0.712	0.002	0.698	0.003	**0.714**	0.002	0.708	0.016
	Class 2 Stars	**0.607**	0.003	0.588	0.005	0.606	0.004	0.593	0.019
	Class 3 Stars	0.669	0.002	0.667	0.003	**0.698**	0.002	0.679	0.017
	Class 4 Stars	0.680	0.003	0.671	0.003	**0.696**	0.003	0.657	0.015
	Class 5 Stars	0.626	0.002	0.681	0.003	0.720	0.002	**0.728**	0.007
F1 Score	Class 1 Star	0.650	0.001	0.670	0.001	**0.684**	0.001	0.682	0.005
	Class 2 Stars	0.587	0.002	0.583	0.004	**0.604**	0.003	0.597	0.005
	Class 3 Stars	0.700	0.001	0.671	0.004	**0.712**	0.002	0.693	0.004
	Class 4 Stars	0.647	0.003	0.646	0.003	**0.672**	0.003	0.642	0.004
	Class 5 Stars	0.724	0.001	0.743	0.003	**0.769**	0.002	0.757	0.004
Precision	Weighted Avg	0.677	0.001	0.670	0.001	**0.694**	0.002	0.680	0.003
Recall	Weighted Avg	0.660	0.001	0.663	0.001	**0.689**	0.002	0.675	0.002
F1-Score	Weighted Avg	0.663	0.001	0.665	0.001	**0.690**	0.002	0.676	0.002

Table 6 shows the results obtained for binary classification on the RoProductReviews dataset using the deep learning models, while in Table 7, results for multi-classification with five classes are presented.

Table 6. Binary classification using deep learning models with the RoProductReviews dataset. The highest value for each performance indicator is marked in bold.

Performance Indicator	LSTM Mean	95% CI	GRU Mean	95% CI	CNN Mean	95% CI	GAP Mean	95% CI
Accuracy	0.918	0.007	0.920	0.006	**0.930**	0.005	0.918	0.005
Precision PPV	0.924	0.014	0.925	0.012	**0.930**	0.007	0.929	0.010
Precision NPV	0.912	0.010	0.915	0.010	**0.931**	0.006	0.908	0.011
Average precision	0.918	0.012	0.920	0.011	**0.931**	0.006	0.918	0.011
Sensitivity/Recall—TPR	0.915	0.011	0.919	0.011	**0.934**	0.006	0.910	0.013
Specificity—TNR	0.920	0.017	0.921	0.014	**0.926**	0.008	0.926	0.012
AUC	0.918	0.007	0.920	0.006	**0.930**	0.005	0.918	0.005
AUPRC	0.920	0.006	0.922	0.006	**0.932**	0.004	0.920	0.005
F1-score Positive Class	0.919	0.006	0.921	0.006	**0.932**	0.004	0.919	0.005
F1-score Negative Class	0.916	0.007	0.918	0.007	**0.928**	0.005	0.917	0.005
Average F1-score	0.918	0.007	0.920	0.006	**0.930**	0.005	0.918	0.005
Weighted F1-score	0.918	0.007	0.920	0.006	**0.930**	0.005	0.918	0.005

Table 7. Multi-class classification using deep learning models with the RoProductReviews dataset. The highest value for each performance indicator is marked in bold.

Performance Indicator		GAP Mean	95% CI	LSTM Mean	95% CI	GRU Mean	95% CI	CNN Mean	95% CI
Accuracy	Avg	0.652	0.013	0.722	0.011	0.739	0.009	**0.767**	0.005
Precision	Class 1 Star	0.699	0.036	0.738	0.030	0.732	0.025	**0.800**	0.026
	Class 2 Stars	0.527	0.039	0.626	0.027	0.645	0.026	**0.692**	0.023
	Class 3 Stars	0.624	0.039	0.698	0.033	0.726	0.022	**0.738**	0.021
	Class 4 Stars	0.637	0.026	0.727	0.024	**0.751**	0.022	0.750	0.019
	Class 5 Stars	0.805	0.040	0.833	0.022	0.846	0.022	**0.854**	0.014
Recall	Class 1 Star	0.714	0.040	0.713	0.042	0.722	0.031	**0.796**	0.023
	Class 2 Stars	0.557	0.064	0.646	0.039	0.665	0.030	**0.691**	0.029
	Class 3 Stars	0.607	0.041	0.712	0.028	**0.726**	0.020	0.718	0.023
	Class 4 Stars	0.605	0.047	0.713	0.031	0.750	0.023	**0.767**	0.019
	Class 5 Stars	0.758	0.043	0.815	0.026	0.825	0.023	**0.848**	0.017
F1 Score	Class 1 Star	0.702	0.018	0.721	0.021	0.725	0.017	**0.796**	0.009
	Class 2 Stars	0.533	0.032	0.633	0.022	0.653	0.021	**0.690**	0.012
	Class 3 Stars	0.610	0.021	0.702	0.012	0.725	0.010	**0.726**	0.008
	Class 4 Stars	0.617	0.025	0.718	0.015	0.750	0.014	**0.757**	0.009
	Class 5 Stars	0.776	0.016	0.822	0.012	0.834	0.014	**0.851**	0.009
Precision	Weighted Avg	0.663	0.014	0.727	0.010	0.743	0.009	**0.769**	0.006
Recall	Weighted Avg	0.652	0.013	0.722	0.011	0.739	0.009	**0.767**	0.005
F1-Score	Weighted Avg	0.652	0.014	0.722	0.011	0.740	0.009	**0.767**	0.005

The best results in the case of binary classification are obtained by the CNN model, with accuracy 0.930, average precision 0.931, recall 0.934, and F1-score 0.930. The other three models have a similar performance of accuracy 0.918 for LSTM, 0.920 for GRU, and 0.918 for GAP. We generally notice a slightly higher precision and F1-score for the positive class than the negative class (for example, GAP precision PPV is 0.929, and LSTM precision NPV is 0.908), which may be due to the slight imbalance of the dataset (2509 negative reviews and 2615 positive reviews), but not very significant, meaning it could also be the result of the random cross-validation experimental setup.

For multi-class classification, the best overall results are also obtained by the CNN model (accuracy 0.767, precision 0.769), followed by GRU (accuracy 0.739, precision 0.743), then LSTM (accuracy 0.722, precision 0.727), and the worst performance is obtained by GAP (accuracy 0.652, precision 0.669).

In terms of performance metric indicators per class, the best result is obtained by all models for Class 5, corresponding to five stars, with the highest value of 0.854 for precision using CNN. The next best value yielded by all models is for Class 1, corresponding to one-star evaluations, with values up to 0.800 for precision using CNN. The worst performance is obtained for class 2-star, for which the highest value is 0.692 for precision with CNN, and the lowest is 0.527 for precision with GAP. This result could be somewhat influenced by the slight imbalance of dataset classes (only 1152 instances of two-star reviews, while there are 1336 reviews with five stars). Moreover, the higher results for the classes with five stars and one star could be explained by the fact that they are the extremes of the rating scale. This means that the sentiment conveyed in the class 5-star and class 1-star reviews is more intense and clearly expressed as *positive* (when the customer is clearly satisfied) or *negative* (expressing customer dissatisfaction).

Consequently, the classifiers may also find it easier to identify sentiment patterns in these two rating categories, while for the classes with two, three, and four stars, the reviews may present reasons both in favor of and against the reviewed product, thus a mix of sentiment.

In terms of computation time, the CNN model required the least time for training and repeated cross-fold validation (approximately 8 h), as opposed to the other models, which required between 31 and 48 h on the same hardware device. However, while in this case, CNN proves to be the best choice among deep learning models, an important limitation remained for the execution time, which was much higher than that of classical approaches, for example, those based on LSI embedding and machine learning classifiers such as NB, RF, or SVM.

In the following, we have compared the results obtained by the LR model, which proved to be the best-performing classifier on the RoProductReviews dataset, with those obtained using CNN, which proved to be the best-performing of the deep learning models.

The comparison for binary classification is visually presented in Figure 1a, while Figure 1b depicts the comparison for multi-class classification, when the 95% confidence intervals of the weighted average performance indicators values for the five classes was considered. As Figure 1a,b show, CNN leads to consistent better performance.

We have also comparatively analyzed the results at the class level for both binary and multi-class classification. The comparison at the class level is shown in Figure 2a,b and, as it can be observed, it reinforces the conclusion that CNN behaves consistently better for classifying product reviews written in Romanian in classes of polarity.

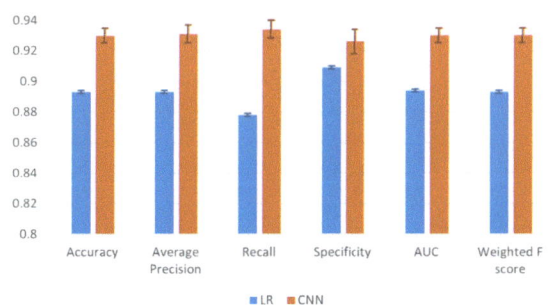

(**a**) Binary classification

Figure 1. *Cont.*

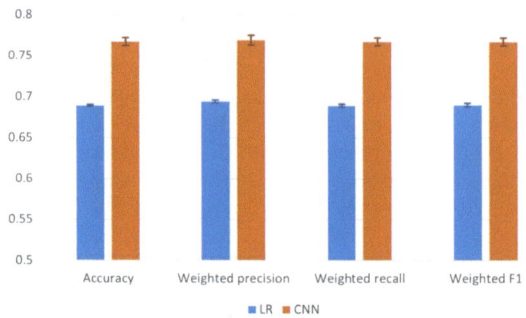

(**b**) Multi-class classification

Figure 1. Comparison between CNN and LR for binary and multi-class classification on the RoProductReviews dataset.

While for the binary classification CNN performs similarly for both positive and negative classes, LR presents small differences in performance for each class and measure. However, for the multi-class classification, there is a consistent behavior of the two models in which class 5 stars presents the best results, while class 2 stars presents the worst result. This shows that specific characteristics of the dataset are most probably responsible for the confusion in classification, namely the smaller number of reviews for two stars (1152) in comparison with the other classes.

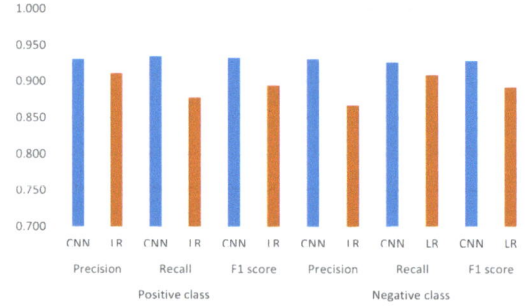

(**a**) Binary classification

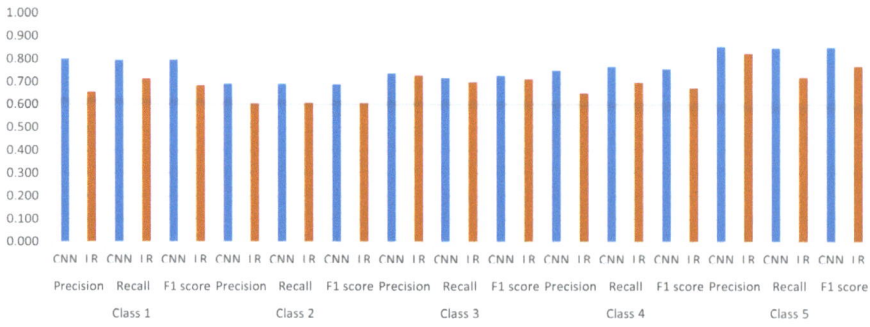

(**b**) Multi-class classification

Figure 2. Comparison between CNN and LR for binary and multi-class classification on the RoProductReviews dataset at class level.

5.2. Sentence Level

Tables 8 and 9 show the classification results obtained at sentence level for the RoProductReviews dataset, using the TF-IDF and LSI representations presented in Section 4.3, both by removing and not removing stop words, configurations which are denoted as "without", and "with", respectively. Specifically, Table 8 contains the results obtained for the TF-IDF representation and Table 9, the results obtained for the LSI representation. These experiments were performed with three goals in mind: (1) establishing whether the removal of stop words influences the classification results, (2) deciding which representation works best for the sentences from the RoProductReviews dataset, and (3) choosing the algorithm that is best suited for sentence-level sentiment classification.

In order to answer the first question, we have analyzed the results from each table individually, thus leading to a conclusion for each representation. For TF-IDF, almost all the averaged performance indicators (accuracy, precision, recall, and F1-score) are higher for the case when stop words are not removed, with the exceptions of precision for NB. However, if we are to look at the percentage difference, which is 0.4%, we can state that this exception does not impact the overall conclusion; that is, for the TF-IDF representation, the removal of stop words negatively influences the classification results. This means that, although stop words are, by definition, insignificant for determining the sentiment expressed in a sentence, given the fact that sentences, as opposed to documents, contain only brief opinions, the removal of stop words shortens the sentence even more, leading to a decreased classification performance.

The same conclusion holds for the LSI representation as well: all the averaged performance metrics are higher when not removing stop words, for all the classifiers used in the experiments. Thus, we can answer the first question: the removal of stop words does influence the classification results, in a negative manner.

Table 8. Results obtained for TF-IDF-based sentence-level classification with the RoProductReviews dataset. The highest value for each performance indicator is marked in bold.

Performance Indicator		Stopwords	SVM Mean	95% CI	LR Mean	95% CI	RF Mean	95% CI	NB Mean	95% CI
Accuracy	Avg	Without	0.774	0.012	0.778	0.012	0.751	0.017	0.663	0.015
		With	0.804	0.012	**0.805**	**0.012**	0.771	0.012	0.668	0.013
Precision	Positive	Without	**0.817**	**0.018**	0.806	0.016	0.776	0.025	0.643	0.017
		With	0.815	0.016	0.814	0.017	0.800	0.018	0.662	0.017
	Neutral	Without	0.300	0.287	0.000	0.000	0.265	0.172	0.190	0.082
		With	**0.400**	**0.307**	0.100	0.177	0.174	0.134	0.192	0.076
	Negative	Without	0.722	0.022	0.741	0.025	0.753	0.030	0.782	0.030
		With	0.787	0.021	**0.794**	**0.019**	0.763	0.021	0.745	0.023
Recall	Positive	Without	0.837	0.021	0.853	0.014	0.854	0.026	**0.938**	**0.010**
		With	0.899	0.014	0.907	0.013	0.868	0.016	0.905	0.013
	Neutral	Without	0.008	0.008	0.000	0.000	0.056	0.035	0.045	0.022
		With	0.012	0.009	0.004	0.006	0.039	0.021	**0.064**	**0.026**
	Negative	Without	**0.853**	**0.021**	0.842	0.020	0.759	0.040	0.421	0.026
		With	0.842	0.018	0.836	0.019	0.796	0.019	0.475	0.022
F1-Score	Positive	Without	0.827	0.014	0.828	0.014	0.812	0.014	0.763	0.013
		With	0.855	0.011	**0.858**	**0.012**	0.832	0.011	0.764	0.011
	Neutral	Without	0.017	0.016	0.000	0.000	0.080	0.045	0.070	0.033
		With	0.022	0.017	0.006	0.011	0.061	0.031	**0.093**	**0.036**
	Negative	Without	0.781	0.013	0.788	0.016	0.753	0.017	0.547	0.026
		With	0.813	0.015	**0.814**	**0.014**	0.778	0.013	0.579	0.019
Precision	Weighted Avg	Without	0.741	0.027	0.715	0.016	0.725	0.022	0.661	0.017
		With	0.772	0.026	**0.747**	**0.022**	0.734	0.019	0.657	0.015
Recall	Weighted Avg	Without	0.774	0.012	0.778	0.012	0.751	0.017	0.663	0.015
		With	0.804	0.012	**0.805**	**0.012**	0.771	0.012	0.668	0.013
F1-Score	Weighted Avg	Without	0.743	0.013	0.745	0.014	0.728	0.018	0.621	0.017
		With	0.770	0.014	**0.771**	**0.013**	0.748	0.012	0.637	0.016

Table 9. Results obtained for LSI-based sentence-level classification with the RoProductReviews dataset. The highest value for each performance indicator is marked in bold.

Performance Indicator		Stopwords	SVM Mean	95% CI	LR Mean	95% CI	RF Mean	95% CI	NB Mean	95% CI
Accuracy	Avg	Without	0.663	0.014	0.660	0.010	0.699	0.012	0.609	0.013
		With	0.724	0.013	0.713	0.012	**0.728**	**0.011**	0.669	0.012
Precision	Positive	Without	**0.781**	**0.018**	0.763	0.020	0.738	0.020	0.683	0.017
		With	0.745	0.018	0.725	0.013	0.749	0.013	0.698	0.014
	Neutral	Without	0.000	0.000	0.000	0.000	**0.229**	**0.116**	0.000	0.000
		With	0.000	0.000	0.000	0.000	0.271	0.171	0.017	0.052
	Negative	Without	0.574	0.019	0.577	0.016	0.662	0.019	0.537	0.020
		With	0.698	0.024	0.694	0.024	**0.708**	**0.022**	0.628	0.025
Recall	Positive	Without	0.639	0.017	0.641	0.019	0.781	0.017	0.632	0.018
		With	0.821	0.019	**0.833**	**0.017**	0.829	0.017	0.780	0.019
	Neutral	Without	0.000	0.000	0.000	0.000	**0.034**	**0.018**	0.000	0.000
		With	0.000	0.000	0.000	0.000	0.024	0.013	0.001	0.004
	Negative	Without	**0.837**	**0.021**	0.827	0.018	0.730	0.025	0.706	0.020
		With	0.749	0.024	0.701	0.020	0.743	0.020	0.659	0.020
F1-Score	Positive	Without	0.702	0.014	0.697	0.014	0.759	0.013	0.656	0.014
		With	0.781	0.012	0.775	0.010	**0.786**	**0.010**	0.736	0.010
	Neutral	Without	0.000	0.000	0.000	0.000	**0.057**	**0.029**	0.000	0.000
		With	0.000	0.000	0.000	0.000	0.045	0.025	0.002	0.006
	Negative	Without	0.681	0.018	0.680	0.014	0.694	0.014	0.610	0.017
		With	0.722	0.016	0.697	0.016	**0.724**	**0.014**	0.642	0.016
Precision	Weighted Avg	Without	0.636	0.016	0.629	0.013	0.667	0.016	0.570	0.014
		With	0.666	0.016	0.653	0.014	**0.695**	**0.018**	0.616	0.015
Recall	Weighted Avg	Without	0.663	0.014	0.660	0.010	0.699	0.012	0.609	0.013
		With	0.724	0.013	0.713	0.012	**0.728**	**0.011**	0.669	0.012
F1-Score	Weighted Avg	Without	0.637	0.015	0.633	0.011	0.675	0.013	0.584	0.013
		With	0.693	0.015	0.681	0.013	**0.701**	**0.013**	0.639	0.012

Once we have established that better results are obtained without removing the stop words, in order to answer the second question, we only compare the results obtained for TF-IDF and LSI representations when keeping the stop words, presented in the same tables (Tables 8 and 9, respectively). For all the averaged performance indicators, all algorithms yield higher values for the TF-IDF representation, with the exception of NB. Yet, the difference in accuracy and weighted recall is 0.1% between the two representations, while the difference in F1-score is 0.2%. Taking all of these into consideration, we can state that the TF-IDF representation is better suited for all the algorithms employed in the experiments. This conclusion can be motivated by the nature of the representations themselves since LSI attempts to reduce the dimensionality of the TF-IDF representation, and sentences can be viewed as very short documents, reducing the dimensionality leads to a loss of relevant information.

Finally, so as to choose the algorithm that is best suited for SLSA on the RoProductReviews dataset, we compare the performance indicators obtained with the TF-IDF representation for SVM, LR, RF, and NB. Figure 3 presents these values, gathered from Tables 8 and 9. The results for each category are not included in Figure 3, because we consider the averaged performance indicators to suffice for the intended comparison; however, the values for these metrics can be found in the respective tables. Therefore, considering these performance indicators, LR obtains the highest values for accuracy, weighted recall, and weighted F1-score, while SVM leads to the highest weighted precision value. Yet, since the difference in weighted precision between the two algorithms is 0.025, we can conclude that LR is the best-suited algorithm for the task of sentiment analysis at the sentence level, which coincides with the conclusion drawn for the document level. Therefore, we can state that sentiment analysis for Romanian can be performed at both the document and sentence levels using the LR algorithm.

If we are to look at the results obtained for each class, as presented in Table 8, one can notice that the results obtained for the neutral class are very low, which is explainable given the unbalanced dataset. In order to solve this problem, a higher number of neutral sentences, comparable to that of the positive and negative sentences, should be used for training the algorithms.

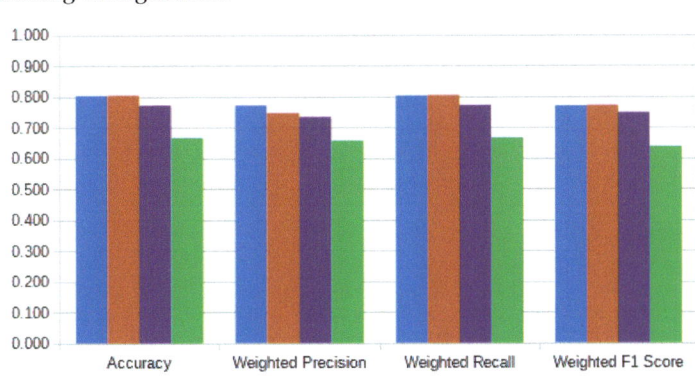

Figure 3. Sentence-level classification with the RoProductReviews dataset.

Concluding, from the results presented in Tables 8 and 9, in order to perform the task of SLSA on the RoProductReviews dataset, the LR algorithm should be applied on the TF-IDF representation of the sentences, without removing the stop words, leading to an accuracy score of 0.805, a weighted precision score of 0.747, a weighted recall score of 0.805, and a weighted F1-score of 0.771.

Given that CNN is the most effective model at the document level, embedding encoding and CNN are used in the deep learning technique at the sentence level on the RoProductReviews subset for multi-classification with three classes. The results are presented in Table 10, and are comparable to the other approaches presented previously for SLSA. The accuracy obtained is 0.790, while weighted precision is 0.780, weighted recall 0.790 and weighted F1-score 0.781. This means that, in comparison with the results obtained for LR, the deep learning approach leads to better precision and F1-score, while the classical ML algorithm obtains higher accuracy and recall values. Figure 4a presents this comparison, for an easier analysis. Since the differences are very small—0.015 in accuracy and 0.015 in weighted recall, in favor of LR, and 0.033 in weighted precision and 0.01 in weighted F1 in favor of CNN—a clear conclusion cannot be drawn: each of these two algorithms can be used to perform the task of SLSA.

Table 10. Multi-class classification using deep learning models at sentence level with three classes: negative, neutral, and positive. The highest value for each performance indicator is marked in bold.

Performance Indicators		CNN Mean	95% CI
Accuracy	Avg	**0.790**	0.011
Precision	Negative	0.795	0.025
	Neutral	0.360	0.078
	Positive	0.833	0.017
Recall	Negative	0.814	0.020
	Neutral	0.203	0.050
	Positive	**0.864**	0.021
F1-Score	Negative	0.803	0.010
	Neutral	0.246	0.045
	Positive	0.847	0.007
Precision	Weighted Avg	0.780	0.012
Recall	Weighted Avg	**0.790**	0.012
F1-Score	Weighted Avg	0.781	0.010

However, there are very big differences in the performance indicators per class. Given that the dataset is very unbalanced, this limits the deep learning model's learning (1092 instances for the positive class, 171 instances for the neutral class, 804 instances for the negative class). As such, the neutral class performs very poorly (the lowest value is 0.203 for recall), while the positive class performs the best (the highest value is 0.847 for the F1-score). In comparison to LR, as presented in Figure 4b, CNN performs better for the neutral class and obtains better precision for the positive and negative classes, while LR outperforms CNN in terms of recall and F1-score for both the positive and negative classes.

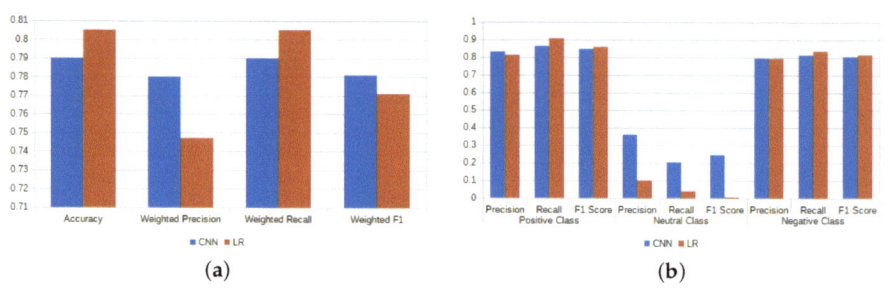

Figure 4. Comparison between CNN and LR for sentence-level classification with the RoProductReviews dataset: (**a**) overall and (**b**) with respect to class.

5.3. Aspect Level

5.3.1. Aspect Term Extraction

In general, in aspect-based sentiment analysis, *aspects* are specific to a product type. Users may be interested in the *battery life*, *photo/video quality*, and *performance* of a phone, but paying more attention to *memory* in case of an external hard drive and *coverage* for a wireless router. Naturally, there are common aspects that can be evaluated for multiple product types, which is owed to the overlap in the category taxonomy itself. For instance, *processing speed* can be evaluated on all electronics with a processing unit, as can *sound quality* on devices that support audio input and output. In this paper, we attempt to discover the most important aspects of a product category from our dataset using two clustering approaches.

Table 11 shows the results obtained for each of the two clustering algorithms employed, SOM and k-means, in terms of a mean over the random states and the 95% CI, for each of the product categories in the dataset. In terms of NPMI, in 8 out of 12 cases, the SOM algorithm provides better results, with k-means clusters achieving a higher score for *fitness bracelets*, *headphones*, and *monitor* product categories, though by small margins. For *smartwatches*, the generated clusters obtain the same score for both algorithms. If the clusters are evaluated using the LCH metric, for 7 out of 12 product categories, the SOM algorithm partitions the considered words better.

Overall, the low NPMI scores could be explained by the nature of the word groups. For some aspect categories, some aspect terms might be used interchangeably rather than co-occur in the same review. For instance, in terms of evaluating the *price* of a product, users most often limit themselves to either saying *A lot of money, but it's worth it* or *A good price for what it offers*, but not both in the same review, as the sentences have very similar meaning. Therefore, nouns *money* and *price* may occur less frequently together than in other types of text that discuss a finance topic. Alternatively, when evaluating the *functionalities* of a smartwatch, one could talk, in the same text span, about health monitoring using a number of different words: for instance, *somn/sleep* monitoring, *puls/heart rate* measuring, *tensiune/blood pressure*.

Table 11. Results for aspect term extraction and grouping in terms of NPMI and LCH. An average over the random states is provided along with the value for the 95% CI.

Product Category	SOM NPMI Mean	95% CI	LCH Mean	95% CI	K-Means NPMI Mean	95% CI	LCH Mean	95% CI
Fitness bracelets	−0.698	0.017	1.412	0.031	−0.697	0.028	1.390	0.023
Headphones	−0.627	0.025	1.484	0.036	−0.603	0.023	1.427	0.029
Keyboard	−0.660	0.024	1.421	0.022	−0.666	0.023	1.432	0.024
Laptop	−0.648	0.013	1.384	0.030	−0.685	0.017	1.385	0.025
Monitor	−0.596	0.025	1.364	0.016	−0.587	0.022	1.386	0.022
Mouse	−0.636	0.011	1.626	0.043	−0.654	0.019	1.526	0.026
Router	−0.616	0.027	1.609	0.027	−0.736	0.019	1.497	0.032
Smartphone	−0.700	0.016	1.406	0.034	−0.732	0.025	1.351	0.021
Smartwatch	−0.687	0.016	1.352	0.024	−0.687	0.012	1.395	0.024
Speakers	−0.632	0.019	1.487	0.016	−0.649	0.013	1.452	0.025
Tablet	−0.735	0.013	1.352	0.024	−0.753	0.017	1.347	0.031
Vacuum cleaner	−0.604	0.011	1.421	0.022	−0.642	0.016	1.448	0.019

The LCH score, on the other hand, might deal well with the first case, identifying *price* and *money* as similar concepts, but lacks the ability to contextually assess the relatedness of groups like the second example (e.g., *sleep, heart rate, blood pressure*).

In the following, we present more detailed results for a selected product category, *laptop*. Appendix A includes results for another product category, *monitors*, to showcase the ability of the approach to identify relevant aspect categories for different product types.

The noun groups $\mathcal{A}_{w_l}$ obtained in one example run for the category *laptop* are presented in Table 12, which shows the eight aspect clusters that were obtained. As it can be seen, these noun clusters are relatively easy to interpret. For the first cluster, $\mathcal{A}_{w_{l_1}}$, the label of *durability/reliability* was assigned, as the words within represent either words that refer to time (*perioadă/period, timp/time, an/year, lună/month*) or to the use of the product (*utilizare, folosire/usage*), with potential issues (*pană/breakdown, problemă/problem*). Temporal words are also used to form $\mathcal{A}_{w_{l_2}}$, but, in this case, it is more likely that the *battery life* of the laptop is discussed, since the referenced periods of time are shorter: *saptaman, saptamană/week, oră/hour*. This differentiation between temporal words used in *battery life* and *durability* aspect clusters indicates that using word2vec embeddings trained on the review corpus allows the clustering process to capture associations that go beyond classic semantic categories (e.g., grouping together words that refer to time). The ability of the learned representations to encode information from the specific usage patterns from the corpus they are trained on aids the formation of meaningful groups in terms of their ease of interpretability as aspect categories.

Table 12. Example clusters obtained using SOM for product type *laptop*.

	Terms	Assigned Label	NPMI	LCH
$\mathcal{A}_{w_{l_1}}$	perioadă, timp, pană, problemă, utilizare, inceput, an, lună, folosire *period, time, breakdown, problem, usage, start, year, month*	Durability	−0.481	1.805
$\mathcal{A}_{w_{l_2}}$	baterie, saptamană, saptaman, figură, oră *battery, week, issue, hour*	Battery life	−0.445	1.595
$\mathcal{A}_{w_{l_3}}$	așteptare, stea, ron, pret, ban, raport, leu *expectation, star, Romanian leu (RON), price, cent/money, ratio*	Price	−0.516	0.890
$\mathcal{A}_{w_{l_4}}$	mufă, wireless, pachet, adaptor, laptop, receiver, cutie, usb *socket, wireless, package, adapter, laptop, receiver, box, USB*	Connectivity	−0.543	1.708
$\mathcal{A}_{w_{l_5}}$	medie, design, slab, calitate, pro, ok, rest, aspect, dorit, material *average, design, poor, quality, pro, ok, otherwise, wanted, material*	Build quality/Design	−0.564	1.608
$\mathcal{A}_{w_{l_6}}$	foto, imagine, rezoluție, hd, display, ecran, caracteristică *photo, image, resolution, HD (High Definition), display, screen, characteristic*	Display	−0.635	1.385
$\mathcal{A}_{w_{l_7}}$	calculator, win, sită, desktop, stick, windows, ubunt *computer, win, site, desktop, stick, Windows, Ubuntu*	Operating system	−0.407	1.779
$\mathcal{A}_{w_{l_8}}$	modul, proces, driver, instalar, bios, drive, boot, parolă *module, process, driver, installation, BIOS, drive, boot, password*	Software components	−0.632	1.618

Cluster $\mathcal{A}_{w_{l_3}}$ can be interpreted as referring to *price* or the value for money, while $\mathcal{A}_{w_{l_4}}$ can be assigned a label of *connectivity* based on words such as *mufă/socket*, *adaptor/adapter*, *receiver*, *wireless*, *USB*. $\mathcal{A}_{w_{l_6}}$ is equally easy to interpret, as it contains nouns that almost exclusively refer to the *display* aspect category. As far as aspect clusters $\mathcal{A}_{w_{l_7}}$ and $\mathcal{A}_{w_{l_8}}$ are concerned, we highlight the distinction between the *operating system* and *software components* aspects, both of which can provide insights into the laptop's hardware, software and performance. However, the first terms (i.e., terms comprising $\mathcal{A}_{w_{l_7}}$) are relevant when discussing the laptop's compatibility with various software, operating systems, and its ability to access websites and web content effectively, while terms in $\mathcal{A}_{w_{l_8}}$ lean towards descriptions of internal components and the system configuration, often discussed in laptop reviews to evaluate its performance, ability to upgrade, and security features.

A somewhat less obvious cluster is $\mathcal{A}_{w_{l_5}}$. The terms included in this group are frequently used to either express an evaluation with regard to the *quality* of a product (terms *calitate/quality*, *pro*), or address some general aspects (e.g., "*În rest, n-au fost probleme*"/"*Otherwise, there were no issues*", "*În rest, e ok*"/"*Otherwise, it's fine*").

This, in turn, highlights one of the limitations of the proposed approach, namely the use of automatic PoS tagging, which may, at times, erroneously identify words as nouns, either because of homonymy (for instance, "bun" can be both an adjective, meaning *good*, or a noun, meaning *asset*) or the use of more informal constructions such as *super ok*, *super tare* (*super nice*), *super mulțumit* (*super content*), which the tagger may have difficulties in correctly processing.

5.3.2. Aspect Category Detection

In this subsection, we present results for the *aspect category detection* task, using the aspect clusters presented in Section 5.3.1 for the product type *laptop* to identify their presence in a review.

Table 13 provides a series of example reviews from the product category *laptop*, chosen to reflect the diversity of expression in the corpus, both in terms of the length of reviews, and in terms of the explicit and implicit discussion of aspects.

As it can be seen, our approach manages to identify both implicitly and explicitly referred aspects. This is owed to the use of word embeddings that capture subtle semantic similarities. For instance, if assessing the results obtained for reviews R_{l_6} or R_{l_7}, we observe that in R_{l_6}, only *operating systems* are referred to explicitly, while the updating issues point somewhat indirectly to the aspect *software components*. For R_{l_7}, it is interesting to see the distribution of the aspects, with *battery life*, *durability/reliability*, and *build quality/design* identified to cover, in large part, the target of the opinion expressed in the short review. While the use of a temporal quantifier (*3 zile/3 days*) makes the presence of the *durability/reliability* aspect expected, the presence of *battery life* is less so. A laptop not turning on may indeed involve an issue with the battery, which is knowledge the word2vec model likely learned by seeing the verb *a aprinde/turn on* in contexts which also involved discussions about the battery performance.

For an in-depth evaluation of the proposed approach's performance with respect to the length of reviews, we examine specific instances, namely reviews R_{l_2}, R_{l_3}, and R_{l_7}. The succinct information provided in R_{l_2} aligns with categories exhibiting the highest scores: *price* and *build quality/design*. The user's phrase "good for this money" effectively alludes to the laptop's value for money and overall quality. Longer reviews are addressed with equal proficiency, and increased references to discussed aspects may even contribute to a clearer distinction between aspect categories. For example, R_{l_3} is exclusively assigned to the *operating system* and *software components* categories. In contrast, R_{l_7}, which contains a profoundly implicit reference to the product's *durability* and *battery life*, is attributed to every aspect category to varying degrees. These observations lead us to the conclusion that the length of the considered text has a lesser role than the clarity with which aspects are referenced in the precise identification of aspect categories.

Lastly, while the results obtained provide encouraging results, there are cases in which the proposed method encounters difficulties, such as R_{l_9}. The *display* aspect is explicitly mentioned in the review, but it is unclear how *connectivity* and *durability/reliability* are discussed. Moreover, in a review such as R_{l_4}, it can be argued that *battery life* should have a higher score.

Table 13. Aspect category detection results with respect to a set of reviews from product category *laptop*.

	Review Text	Durability/ Reliability	Battery Life	Price	Connectivity	Build Quality/ Design	Display	Operating System	Software Components
R_{l_1}	Un laptop de buget se poate folosii pentru varsnici sau copii. Pentru banii ceruti este un produs foarte bun. A budget laptop can be used for seniors or children. For the money asked, it's a very good product.	0.004	0	0.792	0.001	0.203	0	0	0
R_{l_2}	Bun ptr bani astia Good for this money	0.015	0.007	0.497	0.003	0.470	0.006	0.002	0
R_{l_3}	Instalarea Windows-ului la laptopurile HP cu procesoare Intel de generatie 11 sau 12 necesita drivere speciale pentru fiecare model in parte, altfel masina nu vede hardul. Este un bag de fabricatie. Luati-le mai bine direct pe cele cu Windows-ul preinstalat. Installing Windows on HP laptops with 11th or 12th generation Intel processors requires special drivers for each model; otherwise, the system doesn't recognize the hard drive. It's a manufacturing glitch. It's better to get the ones with pre-installed Windows.	0	0	0	0	0	0.384	0	0.616
R_{l_4}	Nu încarcă bateria. Nu recomand decât dacă va doriți un laptop fix, gen PC It doesn't charge the battery. I only recommend it if you want a desktop-like laptop.	0.286	0.100	0.011	0.151	0.412	0.030	0.004	0
R_{l_5}	Fraților, nu vă sfătuiesc să vă zgârciți la câteva sute de lei pentru că acest produs este foarte slab! Îl am de o lună și deja s-a desfăcut toată rama din împrejurul display ului... Foarte slab... Brothers, I advise you not to skimp on a few hundred lei because this product is very weak! I've had it for a month, and the frame around the display has already come apart... Very poor...	0.090	0.001	0.210	0	0.695	0.003	0	0
R_{l_6}	Nemulțumit. Îl voi returna cât de curând. Se tot actualizează, ba se blochează. Are Windows-ul 10 instalat. Păcat de firma hp și de HDD de 1T. Unsatisfied. I will return it as soon as possible. It keeps updating, and it even freezes. It has Windows 10 installed. It's a shame for the HP brand and the 1TB HDD.	0.002	0.001	0.007	0.007	0.002	0.014	0.502	0.466
R_{l_7}	Dupa a 3 zi nu s-a mai aprins. After 3 days, it didn't turn on anymore	0.220	0.198	0.046	0.080	0.220	0.089	0.067	0.081
R_{l_8}	L. Am luat pentru gaming și deși are rtx 3050 ti in jocuri cu ray tracing nu depășește 25–30 cadre pe full hd, 2k/4k nu mai discutam.. I got it for gaming, and even though it has an RTX 3050 Ti, in games with ray tracing, it doesn't go beyond 25–30 frames per second at full HD. Let's not even discuss 2K/4K.	0.001	0	0.003	0	0.003	0.991	0	0.002
R_{l_9}	Laptopul este performant dar display-ul are probleme... The laptop is performant, but the display has issues...	0.438	0.026	0.019	0.119	0.039	0.243	0.070	0.046

6. Discussion

In this section, we present the results of a comparison between our approaches for document-level sentiment analysis and two existing approaches from the literature, as well as an overall analysis of the obtained results in order to provide insights into the research questions formulated in the Introduction.

6.1. Comparison to Related Work

In this study, we have also compared our approaches for document-level sentiment analysis with two existing approaches: one based on SentiWordnet and one based on searches using a search engine, proposed by Russu et al. in [28]. In addition, we have also evaluated our approaches on the movie reviews dataset Russu et al. have employed in their paper.

For a fair comparison, focused on the document representations, we have employed the same classifiers as in [28], namely RF, kNN, NB, and SVM, the same implementation for them (as offered by Weka) and the same evaluation methodology, that is, 10-fold cross-validation. We repeated 10-fold cross-validation ten times and report 95% confidence intervals for the performance measures.

The only two performance measures the authors report values for are weighted precision and weighted recall, so we have computed the same performance indicators for the LSI-based approach.

The experimental results are numerically presented in Table 14 and visually represented in Figure 5a,b. In Table 14, the best performances are highlighted.

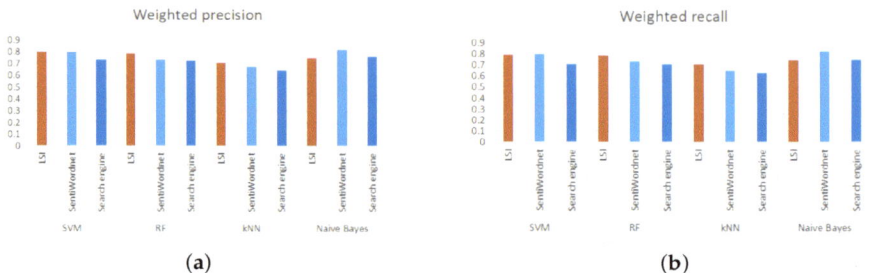

Figure 5. Comparison to related work: LSI-based versus SentiWordnet-based [28] and search-engine-based [28] document polarity binary classification with respect to two performance indicators: (**a**) weighted precision and (**b**) weighted recall.

It can be observed that, when using naïve Bayes as a classifier, the LSI-based approach is outperformed by the approaches proposed by Russu et al. [28], but when using support vector machines (SVM), the LSI-based approach outperforms the search-engine-based approach [28], while it is slightly outperformed by the SentiWordnet-based approach. However, when using both random forest and k-nearest neighbors as automatic classification algorithms, the LSI-based approach we propose outperforms both the SentiWordnet-based and the search-engine-based approaches proposed by Russu et al. [28].

When averaging the values for the performance indicators over the different classifiers employed, the LSI-based approach leads to an overall weighted precision of 0.757, compared to 0.755 for the SentiWordnet-based approach and 0.715 for the search-engine-based approach, and an overall weighted recall of 0.755, compared to 0.748 for the SentiWordnet-based approach and 0.694 for the search-engine-based approach. So, both performance indicators confirm that the performance of using LSI-based embeddings for representing review documents written in Romanian as a basis for automatic sentiment polarity classification leads to an overall slightly superior performance when compared to the SentiWordnet-based and search-engine-based approaches proposed by Russu et al. [28] for the considered movie reviews dataset.

As for the deep learning approach, dense embedding was integrated into the best-performing model up to this point, so CNN was used for classification, and the same evaluation methodology as in [28] was employed (namely, 10-fold cross-validation). The last line in Table 14 presents the results obtained for the two performance indicators utilized. While we notice the weighted precision 0.756 is comparable with the other approaches, the CNN model performs better than all search-engine-based approaches and kNN approaches, but it is outperformed by LSI-based representation used with SVM or RF. As for recall, this performance indicator is the weakest of all with a value of 0.534. In this case, the weaker performance of the deep learning approach in some cases could be explained by the small number of training instances in the dataset ($n = 1000$ instances), which limits the deep learning model's capacity to learn. For the previous experiments, there were 2067 instances for SLSA and 6434 instances for DLSA.

Table 14. Comparison to related work: LSI-based versus SentiWordnet-based [28] and search-engine-based [28] document polarity binary classification. The highest value for each performance indicator is marked in bold.

Classifier	Approach	Weighted Precision	Weighted Recall
SVM	LSI-based	0.794 ± 0.003	0.789 ± 0.002
	SentiWordnet-based [28]	**0.795**	**0.795**
	Search engine-based [28]	0.729	0.705
RF	LSI-based	**0.784 ± 0.005**	**0.783 ± 0.004**
	SentiWordnet-based [28]	0.735	0.732
	Search engine-based [28]	0.723	0.703
kNN	LSI-based	**0.704 ± 0.005**	**0.704 ± 0.005**
	SentiWordnet-based [28]	0.671	0.646
	Search engine-based [28]	0.645	0.625
NB	LSI-based	0.746 ± 0.005	0.743 ± 0.005
	SentiWordnet-based [28]	**0.818**	**0.818**
	Search engine-based [28]	0.763	0.744
CNN	Dense Embedding	0.756	0.534

6.2. Analysis

In this section, we provide an analysis of the results obtained in our study, considering the research questions we have started from.

RQ1: Is latent semantic indexing (LSI) in conjunction with conventional machine learning classifiers suitable for sentiment analysis of documents written in Romanian?

The results obtained in the sentiment analysis task at the document level for the Ro-ProductReviews dataset are presented in Section 5.1. The results provided in Tables 4 and 5 and the analysis of the performance of standard machine learning classifiers used in conjunction with an LSI representation indicate an affirmative answer to **RQ1**: using an LSI representation for documents written in Romanian as input for conventional machine learning classifiers leads to good results in our sentiment analysis task. The comparison with two existing approaches (presented in Section 6.1) also reinforces our conclusion.

RQ2: Can deep-learned embedding-based approaches improve the performance of document- and/or sentence-level sentiment analysis, as opposed to classical natural language processing (NLP) embedding-based non-deep-learning approaches?

In our study, we have experimented with deep learning approaches for sentiment analysis at both the document and sentence levels, in a binary and a multi-class setting. The obtained results at the document level are presented in Tables 6 and 7 and those obtained at sentence level are shown in Table 10. We have also compared them with the best results obtained using ML classifiers. The obtained results clearly show that deep learning approaches can improve performance compared to a classical ML classifier at the document level. For shorter texts, the improvement is less clear. Our experiments also point out the drawbacks of deep learning approaches, namely the higher cost in terms of resources such as running time and the need for a large dataset for training.

RQ3: What is the relevance of different textual representations in the task of sentence polarity classification, and what impact do additional preprocessing steps have in this task?

In our study, we have also examined different textual representations for sentence-level sentiment analysis to determine if the representation used affects the obtained results. In Tables 8 and 9, we have shown the results obtained by using conventional machine learning classifiers in conjunction with two representations (TF-IDF and LSI). From these results, we conclude that, while LSI is suitable for document-level analysis, its dimensionality reduction component is not improving the sentence polarity classification; on the contrary, thus, the TF-IDF method alone suffices for this granularity.

Regarding the impact of the preprocessing step, our results have shown that the additional step of stop words removal negatively influences the classification results. We consider that this may be due to the smaller dimension of the sentences, compared to the dimension of documents.

RQ4: In terms of aspect extraction, is it feasible for a clustering methodology relying on learned word embeddings to delineate groups of words capable of serving as aspect categories identified within a given corpus of documents?

We have experimented with clustering-based approaches for aspect term extraction and aspect category detection, the results obtained being presented in Section 5.3. The performance of these two approaches for aspect term extraction is presented in Tables 11 and 12, respectively, for a specific product category. From the results obtained, we can conclude that the proposed methodology produces coherent aspect clusters for given product types (namely, *laptop* and *monitor* in our experiments), resulting in interpretable and easy-to-label aspect categories. The approach used has the ability to identify aspect clusters (and, thus, aspect categories) with strong relevance to their respective product types.

RQ5: How can the aspect categories discussed within a document be identified, if an aspect category is given through a set of words?

For the aspect category detection task, we have used in our experiments a simple and completely unsupervised method based on word similarity in an embedding space, results for which are shown in Table 13. From the obtained results, we can conclude that a simple approach, like the one we have used, manages to correctly identify aspect categories in units of texts of varying lengths containing both implicit and explicit mentions of them.

In terms of the full aspect term extraction-aspect category detection pipeline, we have observed that the approach used demonstrates remarkable versatility, as it can be applied in order to analyze aspects of a single product type in depth, or it can be scaled up to handle more extensive categories of products. For instance, it can be effectively employed to explore and categorize aspects within the product type category of *peripherals*, making it a valuable tool for comprehensive product analysis. Moreover, the technique used for identifying aspects that are discussed in a review can be modified to address text units of varying lengths (e.g., sentences, sentence parts), which can then be assigned a sentiment label using the appropriate model.

While the approach holds promise, it is not without its limitations. The quality and effectiveness of the generated aspect clusters are directly influenced by the quality of the preprocessing pipeline. Elements such as part-of-speech tagging and lemmatization play a crucial role in the accuracy and relevance of the results. Additionally, the readability and complexity of the language used in the corpus can impact the quality of the clusters. Another limitation is the manual assignment of category labels, which can introduce subjectivity and potential inaccuracies in the analysis.

6.3. Potential Challenges and Limitations

Data accuracy and accessibility. A first challenge in implementing a sentiment analysis system may refer to the availability and quality of data gathered from online sources. The utility of such a sentiment analysis model is dependent on the representativeness of the training data, which should encompass a comprehensive set of diverse examples that cover the sentiments and language patterns that may be encountered in the target domain or application. Additionally, the dataset should be balanced, providing the model with sufficient information to capture the relevant patterns for each of the target classes. We have addressed these aspects in Section 4.1, specifically Sections 4.1.1 and 4.1.2, which describe our data collection process and its result.

Resistance to machine learning approaches. Another potential challenge in implementing an automated sentiment analysis system is the lack of transparency in the decision-making process of some models, as well as the hesitation to rely on machine predictions, especially for a task like sentiment analysis. Sentiment and emotion are complex concepts, and their interpretation and evaluation are at times difficult even for humans. In terms of the latter, we highlight the characteristics of the type of data we employ in our experiments. In product reviews, users evaluate a product, describing either their satisfaction or their dissatisfaction with the product (or, in some cases, both), thus purposefully expressing a valenced opinion. This often leads to a straightforward expression of sentiment, with rare use of ambiguous language or complex syntactic constructions, which may make it easier for models to learn the particularities of sentiment expression, and thus, lead to more confidence in the resulting predictions.

Generalization and adaptability. A limitation that follows from a focus on a specific type of data, such as reviews, is the SA system's decreased ability to handle other types of texts (e.g., tweets, news, etc). However, the aim of this study is an in-depth, multi-faceted analysis of the data considered, from which we hope to gain insights that may lead to building robust, general models in future work. As far as dependency on a domain, we have shown that, while we use a dataset of reviews about electronic devices as a case study, the proposed approach also provides good performances for other domains, such as movie reviews, as underlined in Section 6.1.

Ethical and Privacy Considerations. A crucial consideration in the analysis of user-generated content pertains to ethical and privacy concerns associated with potentially sensitive information. Notably, the RoProductReviews dataset utilized in all experiments within this study consists exclusively of publicly available data. Furthermore, no details regarding the identity of reviewers or any other personal information are included.

7. Conclusions and Further Work

In this study, an extensive examination of the performance of various machine learning approaches for sentiment analysis on Romanian-language texts was conducted, addressing multiple textual levels.

At the document level, the obtained results indicate that the LSI-based embedding is relevant for an automatic sentiment analysis of review documents written in Romanian, when feeding them into standard ML classifiers. Deep learning approaches, on the other hand, may provide a boost in performance when the available training dataset is sufficiently large, but at a higher cost with respect to resource utilization. Comparative studies using a range of dataset sizes would be necessary for future research in order to establish the precise contexts in which deep learning techniques outperform standard ML classifiers. Additionally, performing hyperparameter tuning would allow assessing the maximum potential of both conventional ML and deep learning classifiers.

At the sentence level, the results obtained for the task of sentiment analysis lead to the conclusion that, as opposed to the analysis at the document level, the dimensionality reduction step of the LSI algorithm hinders performance in the case of sentences, with the TF-IDF representation used in conjunction with standard ML classifiers resulting in higher performance. What is more, after examining the performance of a deep learning model for the sentiment analysis task at the sentence level, and taking into consideration the costs of deep learning methods, we conclude that standard ML algorithms are preferable for solving the task. As for future work, we intend to validate our conclusions on other datasets in Romanian and, additionally, to perform hyperparameter tuning so as to further improve the results.

In terms of the unsupervised extraction of aspect terms and categories, results show that the proposed technique based on word clustering manages to identify easily interpretable groups of words that can be viewed as aspect terms that form an aspect category. Additionally, a simple aspect category detection technique, based on word similarity in an embedding space, provides information regarding the aspect categories discussed in a review. Results for this task also reflect human interpretation to a high degree. To enhance the aspect term extraction-aspect category detection approach further, one avenue is the exploration of alternative word embeddings, such as BERT, which can potentially lead to a more precise and insightful analysis of product aspects. Finally, in future work, we aim to eliminate the manual aspect category label assignment step.

We also point out a future direction for research at all analysis levels: looking at language patterns used to express sentiment over time. This is because understanding the dynamics of sentiment expression would greatly improve the potential applicability of sentiment analysis systems, like the one this paper proposes, in real-world settings.

Author Contributions: Conceptualization, A.B., A.-D.C., D.-L.M. and C.M.-D.; Data curation, A.-D.C. and C.M.-D.; Formal analysis, A.B. and D.-L.M.; Investigation, A.B., A.-D.C., D.-L.M. and C.M.-D.; Methodology, D.-L.M. and V.P.; Resources, G.D.; Software, A.B., A.-D.C. and G.D.; Supervision, G.D.; Visualization, D.-L.M. and C.M.-D.; Writing—original draft, A.B., A.-D.C., D.-L.M., C.M.-D. and V.P.; Writing—review and editing, A.B., A.-D.C., C.M.-D. and V.P. All authors have read and agreed to the published version of the manuscript.

Funding: This work was supported by a grant of the European Regional Development Fund through the Competitiveness Operational Program 2014–2020, project "Produs software inovativ pentru analiza sentimentelor din textele în limba Româna—SENTITEXT", MySMIS code 156284.

Informed Consent Statement: Not applicable.

Data Availability Statement: The dataset collected and used in our experiments is not publicly available.

Conflicts of Interest: The study was conducted within the framework of a collaborative project involving Babeș-Bolyai University, Faculty of Mathematics and Computer Science, and T2 S.R.L., as outlined in the funding section. The research was carried out by a combined team from the Department of Computer Science of the Faculty of Mathematics and Computer Science and T2 S.R.L., sharing common objectives in exploring sentiment analysis models for the Romanian language. As a result, there is no conflict of interest in the collaboration, the investigation being performed without any commercial or financial affiliations outside of those declared in the article and that could thus be perceived as a possible conflict of interest.

Abbreviations

The following abbreviations are used in this manuscript:

CNN	Convolution Neural Network
DL	Deep Learning
DNN	Deep Neural Network
DT	Decision Trees
GAP	Global Average Pooling
GRU	Gated Recurrent Unit
kNN	k-Nearest Neighbors
LR	Logistic Regression
LSI	Latent Semantic Indexing
LSTM	Long Short-Term Memory
ML	Machine Learning
MLP	Multilayer Perceptron
NB	Naïve Bayes
RF	Random Forest
RNN	Recurrent Neural Network
SOM	Self-Organizing Maps
SVM	Support Vector Machines
TF-IDF	Term Frequency–Inverse Document Frequency
VP	Voted Perceptron

Appendix A

In this appendix, we include results for another product category, namely *monitors*, in order to showcase the adaptability of the proposed approach to aspect term extraction and aspect category detection with respect to identifying relevant aspect categories for different product types.

The word groups $\mathcal{A}_w$ obtained in one example run for the category *monitor* are presented in Table A1 in order of the cumulative frequency of the containing terms.

As it can be seen, the obtained noun clusters are, as it was the case for the *laptop* category, easily interpretable. $\mathcal{A}_{w_{m1}}, \mathcal{A}_{w_{m5}}, \mathcal{A}_{w_{m6}}$ describe various characteristics of the *display* of a monitor: image quality, display technology (IPS stands for in-plane switching technology, a type of display panel technology, while TN is short for twisted nematic, a type of LED panel display technology), and other display characteristics (HD stands for *high definition*). As it is a visual output device, having more than one aspect cluster that encompasses a larger, more general aspect category *display* is to be expected, especially as far as the technology used and the performance of the monitor in terms of color accuracy, brightness and contrast in different lighting conditions. *connectivity* is also a crucial aspect when buying a monitor, as a user will want to ensure that it has the necessary ports to connect to their device ($\mathcal{A}_{w_{m2}}$). The third aspect cluster is concerned with *price*, while the fourth is with the durability and reliability of the product.

Table A1. Example clusters obtained using SOM for product type *monitor*.

	Terms	Assigned Label	NPMI	LCH
$\mathcal{A}_{w_{m1}}$	culoare, intensitate, intuneric, scenecadră, expunere *color, intensity, darkness, scenes/frames, exposure*	Display (Image Quality)	−1.000	1.441
$\mathcal{A}_{w_{m2}}$	mufă, adaptor, cutie, cablu, usb *socket, adapter, box, cable, USB*	Connectivity	−1.000	2.009
$\mathcal{A}_{w_{m3}}$	asteptar, pret, produs, leu *expectation, price, product, Romanian leu (RON)*	Price	−0.384	1.000
$\mathcal{A}_{w_{m4}}$	săptămână, problemă, achiziție, an, saptaman, lună *week, problem, purchase, year, month*	Durability	−0.905	2.081
$\mathcal{A}_{w_{m5}}$	vizibilitate, pixel, ips, vizualizare, pixă, unghi, tn *visibility, pixel, IPS, visualization, angle, TN*	Display (Technology)	−0.382	1.493
$\mathcal{A}_{w_{m6}}$	imagine, monitor, hd, display, ecran *image, monitor, HD, display, screen*	Display (Characteristics)	0.258	1.279
$\mathcal{A}_{w_{m7}}$	medie, calitate, pro, ok, rest, bun, super *average, quality, pro, ok, otherwise, good, great*	Quality	−0.648	1.417

It is interesting to note the common aspect categories between the two types of products: *monitors* and *laptops*: durability ($\mathcal{A}_{w_{m4}}$), price ($\mathcal{A}_{w_{m3}}$), connectivity ($\mathcal{A}_{w_{m2}}$), and display ($\mathcal{A}_{w_{m6}}$). However, there are some differences in the aspect terms used for the categories for each product type. A stark contrast can be observed between the level of detail the *display* aspect category implied in the *monitor* reviews as opposed to the *laptop* reviews, which is an intuitive distinction, as for laptops, the display is only one of the components, while for a monitor, it can be argued that it is the most important one. Alternatively, the aspect of *durability/reliability* tends to be characterized by temporal words (i.e., *year, month, duration, time, beginning*) accompanied by synonyms of the word *usage* for both product types.

Table A2 provides a series of example reviews from the product category *monitors*, to exemplify the performance of the proposed aspect category detection technique on a different product category. In general, for this product type, we observe that short reviews such as R_{m_7}, which do not reference any particular aspects of the product, are dominated by the *quality/general* category. Other similar reviews with a marked presence of this aspect are: "Este destul de bun dar nu il recomand./It's decent, but I don't recommend it." (0.903), "Un monitor bun, claritate buna/A good monitor, good clarity." (0.988), "E chiar bun imi place/It's actually good, I like it" (0.936) or even simply "Bun/Good" (0.797). Alternatively, high *quality/general* scores are also obtained for long reviews in which no particular aspects are discussed. For example, a review consisting of approximately 50 words through which indications about a workaround for an issue (lack of component) was assigned a score of 0.999 for the *quality/general* aspect category.

However, in reviews such as R_{m_2} or R_{m_8}, the *quality/general* aspect category is present to a significant extent (for instance, *bun pentru birou/good for the office* in review R_{m_2} is a general evaluation), but so are other factors like connectivity (R_{m_2}—*conexiune VGA/VGA* connection, R_{m_8}—port HDMI, DisplayPort, USB), which are identified by the proposed method accordingly.

In addition, as it can be seen, aspects that are not explicitly referred (e.g., *display* in R_{m_4} or *durability/reliability* in R_{m_1} and R_{m_3} are also indicated by our approach, which supports the conclusion drawn regarding the wide applicability of the proposed aspect term extraction-aspect category detection pipeline.

Table A2. Aspect category detection results with respect to a set of reviews from product category *monitor*.

	Review Text	Display (Image Quality)	Connectivity	Price	Durability/ Reliability	Display (Technology)	Display Features	Quality/ General
R_{m_1}	*După o luna au apărut dungi pe ecran!!!* After a month, stripes appeared on the screen!	0.059	0.010	0.011	0.672	0.064	0.157	0.027
R_{m_2}	*Doar conexiune VGA și atât. Bun pentru birou.* Only VGA connection, and that's it. Good for the office	0.067	0.179	0.065	0.055	0.065	0.080	0.490
R_{m_3}	*Am monitorul de mai mult de 3 ani si sunt foarte multumit de el. Il folosesc doar pt gaming si se ridica asteptărilor. Cumpărați cu încredere* I've had the monitor for more than 3 years, and I am very satisfied with it. I use it exclusively for gaming, and it meets expectations. Buy with confidence.	0	0.001	0.105	0.817	0.002	0.006	0.068
R_{m_4}	*Are ghosting destul de urat.* Is ghosting quite ugly	0.176	0.057	0.082	0.060	0.178	0.183	0.264
R_{m_5}	*Pret calitate, DEZAMAGITOR!* Price quality, DISAPPOINTING!	0.005	0.003	0.147	0.037	0.020	0.017	0.771
R_{m_6}	*Nu am fost atent la detalii și am comandat unul cu port serial in loc de hdmi. Are doar o singura intrare si depinde de model…* I wasn't careful with the details, and I ordered one with a serial port instead of HDMI. It has only one input, and it depends on the model.	0.006	0.839	0.003	0.003	0.113	0.027	0.009
R_{m_7}	*Super ok! Se comporta bine!* Super ok! It performs well!	0	0	0.001	0.007	0	0	0.992
R_{m_8}	*Business as usual de la Dell. Un monitor excelent. ii dau totusi 4 stele pentru ca folosit cu doua deviceuri, dureaza foarte mult functia de autoscan, este mai rapid sa selectez manual input source cand am nevoie sa trec de la un PC la celalalt. E destul de incomod si faptul ca are doar un singur port HDMI si unul singur DisplayPort. USB-urile sunt excelente pentru cei fara docking station. Evident ca cei care au un singur device nu sunt catusi de putin incomodati de micile inconveniente sus mentionate.* Business as usual from Dell. An excellent monitor. However, I'm giving it four stars because when used with two devices, the autoscan function takes a long time. It's faster to manually select the input source when I need to switch from one PC to the other. It's quite inconvenient that it has only one HDMI port and one DisplayPort. The USB ports are excellent for those without a docking station. Clearly, those with only one device aren't bothered at all by the minor inconveniences mentioned above.	0.012	0.473	0	0	0.002	0	0.512

References

1. Liu, B. *Sentiment Analysis and Opinion Mining*; Springer Nature: Berlin/Heidelberg, Germany, 2022.
2. Vernikou, S.; Lyras, A.; Kanavos, A. Multiclass sentiment analysis on COVID-19-related tweets using deep learning models. *Neural Comput. Appl.* **2022**, *34*, 19615–19627. [CrossRef]
3. Hasib, K.M.; Habib, M.A.; Towhid, N.A.; Showrov, M.I.H. A Novel Deep Learning based Sentiment Analysis of Twitter Data for US Airline Service. In Proceedings of the 2021 International Conference on Information and Communication Technology for Sustainable Development (ICICT4SD), Dhaka, Bangladesh, 27–28 February 2021; pp. 450–455. [CrossRef]
4. Nagamanjula, R.; Pethalakshmi, A. Twitter sentiment analysis using Dempster shafer algorithm based feature selection and one against all multiclass SVM classifier. *Int. J. Adv. Res. Eng. Technol.* **2020**, *11*, 163–185. [CrossRef]
5. Mukta, M.S.H.; Islam, M.A.; Khan, F.A.; Hossain, A.; Razik, S.; Hossain, S.; Mahmud, J. A comprehensive guideline for Bengali sentiment annotation. *Trans. Asian Low-Resour. Lang. Inf. Process.* **2021**, *21*, 1–19. [CrossRef]
6. Elbagir, S.; Yang, J. Twitter sentiment analysis using natural language toolkit and VADER sentiment. In Proceedings of the International Multiconference of Engineers and Computer Scientists, Hong Kong, 13–15 March 2019; Volume 122, p. 16.
7. Su, J.; Chen, Q.; Wang, Y.; Zhang, L.; Pan, W.; Li, Z. Sentence-level Sentiment Analysis based on Supervised Gradual Machine Learning. *Sci. Rep.* **2023**, *13*, 14500. [CrossRef] [PubMed]
8. Liu, B. *Sentiment Analysis: Mining Opinions, Sentiments, and Emotions*; Cambridge University Press: Cambridge, UK, 2020.
9. Chebolu, S.U.S.; Dernoncourt, F.; Lipka, N.; Solorio, T. Survey of Aspect-based Sentiment Analysis Datasets. *arXiv* **2023**, arXiv:cs.CL/2204.05232.
10. Zhang, W.; Li, X.; Deng, Y.; Bing, L.; Lam, W. A survey on aspect-based sentiment analysis: Tasks, methods, and challenges. *IEEE Trans. Knowl. Data Eng.* **2023**, *35*, 11019–11038. [CrossRef]
11. He, R.; Lee, W.S.; Ng, H.T.; Dahlmeier, D. An Unsupervised Neural Attention Model for Aspect Extraction. In Proceedings of the 55th Annual Meeting of the Association for Computational Linguistics (Volume 1: Long Papers), Vancouver, BC, Canada, 30 July–4 August 2017; Association for Computational Linguistics: Vancouver, BC, Canada, 2017; pp. 388–397. [CrossRef]
12. Shi, T.; Li, L.; Wang, P.; Reddy, C.K. A simple and effective self-supervised contrastive learning framework for aspect detection. In Proceedings of the AAAI Conference on Artificial Intelligence, Vancouver, BC, Canada, 2–9 February 2021; Volume 35, pp. 13815–13824.
13. Chebolu, S.U.S.; Rosso, P.; Kar, S.; Solorio, T. Survey on aspect category detection. *ACM Comput. Surv.* **2022**, *55*, 1–37. [CrossRef]

14. Luo, L.; Ao, X.; Song, Y.; Li, J.; Yang, X.; He, Q.; Yu, D. Unsupervised Neural Aspect Extraction with Sememes. In Proceedings of the Twenty-Eighth International Joint Conference on Artificial Intelligence (IJCAI-19), Macao, China, 10–16 August 2019; pp. 5123–5129.
15. Tulkens, S.; van Cranenburgh, A. Embarrassingly Simple Unsupervised Aspect Extraction. In Proceedings of the 58th Annual Meeting of the Association for Computational Linguistics, Online, 5–10 July 2020; pp. 3182–3187. [CrossRef]
16. Dumitrescu, S.D.; Rebeja, P.; Lorincz, B.; Gaman, M.; Avram, A.; Ilie, M.; Pruteanu, A.; Stan, A.; Rosia, L.; Iacobescu, C.; et al. LiRo: Benchmark and leaderboard for Romanian language tasks. In Proceedings of the Neural Information Processing Systems Track on Datasets and Benchmarks, Online, 6–14 December 2021.
17. Tache, A.; Gaman, M.; Ionescu, R.T. Clustering Word Embeddings with Self-Organizing Maps. Application on LaRoSeDa—A Large Romanian Sentiment Data Set. In Proceedings of the 16th Conference of the European Chapter of the Association for Computational Linguistics: Main Volume, Association for Computational Linguistics, Online, 19–23 April 2021; pp. 949–956. [CrossRef]
18. Devlin, J.; Chang, M.; Lee, K.; Toutanova, K. BERT: Pre-training of Deep Bidirectional Transformers for Language Understanding. *arXiv* **2018**, arXiv:1810.04805.
19. Conneau, A.; Khandelwal, K.; Goyal, N.; Chaudhary, V.; Wenzek, G.; Guzmán, F.; Grave, E.; Ott, M.; Zettlemoyer, L.; Stoyanov, V. Unsupervised Cross-lingual Representation Learning at Scale. In Proceedings of the 58th Annual Meeting of the Association for Computational Linguistics, Online, 5–10 July 2020; pp. 8440–8451. [CrossRef]
20. Dumitrescu, S.D.; Avram, A.M.; Pyysalo, S. The birth of Romanian BERT. In Proceedings of the Findings of the Association for Computational Linguistics: EMNLP 2020, Online, 16–20 November 2020; pp. 4324–4328. [CrossRef]
21. Masala, M.; Ruseti, S.; Dascalu, M. RoBERT—A Romanian BERT Model. In Proceedings of the 28th International Conference on Computational Linguistics, Barcelona, Spain, 8–13 December 2020; pp. 6626–6637. [CrossRef]
22. Masala, M.; Iacob, R.C.A.; Uban, A.S.; Cidota, M.; Velicu, H.; Rebedea, T.; Popescu, M. jurBERT: A Romanian BERT Model for Legal Judgement Prediction. In Proceedings of the Natural Legal Language Processing Workshop 2021, Punta Cana, Dominican Republic, 10 November 2021; Association for Computational Linguistics: Punta Cana, Dominican Republic, 2021; pp. 86–94. [CrossRef]
23. Avram, A.; Catrina, D.; Cercel, D.; Dascalu, M.; Rebedea, T.; Pais, V.F.; Tufis, D. Distilling the Knowledge of Romanian BERTs Using Multiple Teachers. *arXiv* **2021**, arXiv:2112.12650.
24. Nicolae, D.; Yadav, R.; Tufis, D. A Lite Romanian BERT:ALR-BERT. *Computers* **2022**, *11*, 57. [CrossRef]
25. Joulin, A.; Grave, E.; Bojanowski, P.; Mikolov, T. Bag of Tricks for Efficient Text Classification. In Proceedings of the 15th Conference of the European Chapter of the Association for Computational Linguistics: Volume 2, Short Papers, Valencia, Spain, 3–7 April 2017; Association for Computational Linguistics: Valencia, Spain, 2017; pp. 427–431.
26. Burlăcioiu, C.; Boboc, C.; Mitre, B.; Dragne, I. Text Mining in Business. A Study of Romanian Client's Perception with Respect to Using Telecommunication and Energy Apps. *Econ. Comput. Econ. Cybern. Stud. Res.* **2023**, *57*, 221–234.
27. Jones, K.S. A statistical interpretation of term specificity and its application in retrieval. *J. Doc.* **2021**, *60*, 493–502. [CrossRef]
28. Russu, R.M.; Dinsoreanu, M.; Vlad, O.L.; Potolea, R. An opinion mining approach for Romanian language. In Proceedings of the 2014 IEEE 10th International Conference on Intelligent Computer Communication and Processing (ICCP), Cluj-Napoca, Romania, 4–6 September 2014; pp. 43–46. [CrossRef]
29. Esuli, A.; Sebastiani, F. SENTIWORDNET: A Publicly Available Lexical Resource for Opinion Mining. In Proceedings of the International Conference on Language Resources and Evaluation, European Language Resources Association (ELRA), Genoa, Italy, 22–28 May 2006.
30. Mikolov, T.; Sutskever, I.; Chen, K.; Corrado, G.S.; Dean, J. Distributed Representations of Words and Phrases and Their Compositionality. *Adv. Neural Inf. Process. Syst.* **2013**, *26*, 3111–3119.
31. Echim, S.V.; Smădu, R.A.; Avram, A.M.; Cercel, D.C.; Pop, F. Adversarial Capsule Networks for Romanian Satire Detection and Sentiment Analysis. In *Lecture Notes in Computer Science*; Springer Nature: Cham, Switzerland, 2023; Volume 13913, pp. 428–442. [CrossRef]
32. Neagu, D.C.; Rus, A.B.; Grec, M.; Boroianu, M.A.; Bogdan, N.; Gal, A. Towards Sentiment Analysis for Romanian Twitter Content. *Algorithms* **2022**, *15*, 357. [CrossRef]
33. Istrati, L.; Ciobotaru, A. Automatic Monitoring and Analysis of Brands Using Data Extracted from Twitter in Romanian. In *Intelligent Systems and Applications*; Springer International Publishing: Berlin/Heidelberg, Germany, 2022; pp. 55–75. [CrossRef]
34. Coita, I.F.; Cioban, S.; Mare, C. Is Trust a Valid Indicator of Tax Compliance Behaviour? A Study on Taxpayers' Public Perception Using Sentiment Analysis Tools. In *Digitalization and Big Data for Resilience and Economic Intelligence*; Springer International Publishing: Berlin/Heidelberg, Germany, 2022; pp. 99–108. [CrossRef]
35. Buzea, M.C.; Trăușan-Matu, Ș.; Rebedea, T. A three word-level approach used in machine learning for Romanian sentiment analysis. In Proceedings of the 2019 18th RoEduNet Conference: Networking in Education and Research (RoEduNet), Galați, Romania, 10–12 October 2019; pp. 1–6.
36. Roșca, C.M.; Ariciu, A.V. Unlocking Customer Sentiment Insights with Azure Sentiment Analysis: A Comprehensive Review and Analysis. *Rom. J. Pet. Gas Technol.* **2023**, *4*, 173–182. [CrossRef]
37. Hu, M.; Liu, B. Mining and summarizing customer reviews. In Proceedings of the Tenth ACM SIGKDD International Conference on Knowledge Discovery and Data Mining, Seattle, WA, USA, 22–25 August 2004; pp. 168–177. [CrossRef]
38. Popescu, A.M.; Etzioni, O. Extracting Product Features and Opinions from Reviews. In *Natural Language Processing and Text Mining*; Springer: London, UK, 2007; pp. 9–28. [CrossRef]

39. Wu, Y.; Zhang, Q.; Huang, X.J.; Wu, L. Phrase dependency parsing for opinion mining. In Proceedings of the 2009 Conference on Empirical Methods in Natural Language Processing: Volume 3, Singapore, 6–7 August 2009; pp. 1533–1541. [CrossRef]
40. Hai, Z.; Chang, K.; Kim, J.j. Implicit feature identification via co-occurrence association rule mining. In *Computational Linguistics and Intelligent Text Processing*; Springer: Berlin/Heidelberg, Germany, 2011; pp. 393–404. [CrossRef]
41. Schouten, K.; Van Der Weijde, O.; Frasincar, F.; Dekker, R. Supervised and Unsupervised Aspect Category Detection for Sentiment Analysis with Co-occurrence Data. *IEEE Trans. Cybern.* **2017**, *48*, 1263–1275. [CrossRef] [PubMed]
42. Titov, I.; McDonald, R. Modeling Online Reviews with Multi-Grain Topic Models. In Proceedings of the 17th International Conference on World Wide Web, Beijing, China, 21–25 April 2008; Association for Computing Machinery: New York, NY, USA, 2008; pp. 111–120. [CrossRef]
43. Brody, S.; Elhadad, N. An Unsupervised Aspect-Sentiment Model for Online Reviews. In Proceedings of the Human Language Technologies: The 2010 Annual Conference of the North American Chapter of the Association for Computational Linguistics, Los Angeles, CA, USA, 2–4 June 2010; Association for Computational Linguistics: Los Angeles, CA, USA, 2010; pp.804–812.
44. García-Pablos, A.; Cuadros, M.; Rigau, G. W2VLDA: Almost unsupervised system for Aspect Based Sentiment Analysis. *Expert Syst. Appl.* **2018**, *91*, 127–137. [CrossRef]
45. Ghadery, E.; Movahedi, S.; Faili, H.; Shakery, A. An Unsupervised Approach for Aspect Category Detection Using Soft Cosine Similarity Measure. *arXiv* **2018**, arXiv:1812.03361.
46. Sia, S.; Dalmia, A.; Mielke, S.J. Tired of Topic Models? Clusters of Pretrained Word Embeddings Make for Fast and Good Topics too! In Proceedings of the 2020 Conference on Empirical Methods in Natural Language Processing (EMNLP), Online, 16–20 November 2020; pp. 1728–1736. [CrossRef]
47. Viegas, F.; Canuto, S.; Gomes, C.; Luiz, W.; Rosa, T.; Ribas, S.; Rocha, L.; Gonçalves, M.A. CluWords: Exploiting Semantic Word Clustering Representation for Enhanced Topic Modeling. In Proceedings of the Twelfth ACM International Conference on Web Search and Data Mining, Melbourne, Australia, 11–15 February 2019; Association for Computing Machinery: New York, NY, USA, 2019; pp. 753–761. [CrossRef]
48. Comito, C.; Forestiero, A.; Pizzuti, C. Word Embedding Based Clustering to Detect Topics in Social Media. In Proceedings of the IEEE/WIC/ACM International Conference on Web Intelligence, Thessaloniki, Greece, 14–17 October 2019; Association for Computing Machinery: New York, NY, USA, 2019; pp. 192–199. [CrossRef]
49. Boroş, T.; Dumitrescu, S.D.; Burtica, R. NLP-Cube: End-to-End Raw Text Processing With Neural Networks. In Proceedings of the CoNLL 2018 Shared Task: Multilingual Parsing from Raw Text to Universal Dependencies, Brussels, Belgium, 31 October–1 November 2018; Association for Computational Linguistics: Brussels, Belgium, 2018; pp. 171–179. [CrossRef]
50. Lupea, M.; Briciu, A. Studying emotions in Romanian words using Formal Concept Analysis. *Comput. Speech Lang.* **2019**, *57*, 128–145. [CrossRef]
51. Deerwester, S.C.; Dumais, S.T.; Landauer, T.K.; Furnas, G.W.; Harshman, R.A. Indexing by Latent Semantic Analysis. *J. Am. Soc. Inf. Sci.* **1990**, *41*, 391–407. [CrossRef]
52. Řehůřek, R.; Sojka, P. Software Framework for Topic Modelling with Large Corpora. In Proceedings of the LREC 2010 Workshop on New Challenges for NLP Frameworks, Valletta, Malta, 22 May 2010; pp. 45–50. [CrossRef]
53. Nwankpa, C.; Ijomah, W.; Gachagan, A.; Marshall, S. Activation functions: Comparison of trends in practice and research for deep learning. *arXiv* **2018**, arXiv:1811.03378.
54. Nwankpa, C.E. Advances in optimisation algorithms and techniques for deep learning. *Adv. Sci. Technol. Eng. Syst. J.* **2020**, *5*, 563–577. [CrossRef]
55. Farhadloo, M.; Rolland, E. Multi-class sentiment analysis with clustering and score representation. In Proceedings of the 2013 IEEE 13th International Conference on Data Mining Workshops, Dallas, TX, USA, 7–10 December 2013; pp. 904–912.
56. Tache, A.M.; Gaman, M.; Ionescu, R.T. Clustering word embeddings with self-organizing maps. application on laroseda—A large romanian sentiment data set. *arXiv* **2021**, arXiv:2101.04197.
57. Bouma, G. Normalized (Pointwise) Mutual Information in Collocation Extraction. *Proc. Bienn. GSCL Conf.* **2009**, *30*, 31–40.
58. Lau, J.H.; Newman, D.; Baldwin, T. Machine Reading Tea Leaves: Automatically Evaluating Topic Coherence and Topic Model Quality. In Proceedings of the 14th Conference of the European Chapter of the Association for Computational Linguistics, Gothenburg, Sweden, 26–30 April 2014; Association for Computational Linguistics: Gothenburg, Sweden, 2014; pp. 530–539. [CrossRef]
59. Leacock, C. Combining local context and WordNet similarity for word sense identification. In *WordNet: A Lexical Reference System and Its Application*; The MIT Press: Cambridge, MA, USA, 1998; pp. 265–283.
60. Dumitrescu, S.D.; Avram, A.M.; Morogan, L.; Toma, S.A. RoWordNet—A Python API for the Romanian WordNet. In Proceedings of the 2018 10th International Conference on Electronics, Computers and Artificial Intelligence (ECAI), Iasi, Romania, 28–30 June 2018; pp. 1–6. [CrossRef]
61. Freund, Y.; Schapire, R.E. Large Margin Classification Using the Perceptron Algorithm. In Proceedings of the Eleventh Annual Conference on Computational Learning Theory, Madison, WI, USA, 24–26 July 1998; Association for Computing Machinery: New York, NY, USA, 1998; pp. 209–217. [CrossRef]

Disclaimer/Publisher's Note: The statements, opinions and data contained in all publications are solely those of the individual author(s) and contributor(s) and not of MDPI and/or the editor(s). MDPI and/or the editor(s) disclaim responsibility for any injury to people or property resulting from any ideas, methods, instructions or products referred to in the content.

Article

An Empirical Investigation on the Visual Imagery of Augmented Reality User Interfaces for Smart Electric Vehicles Based on Kansei Engineering and FAHP-GRA

Jin-Long Lin [1] and Meng-Cong Zheng [2,*]

[1] Doctoral Program in Design, College of Design, National Taipei University of Technology, 1, Sec. 3, Chung-hsiao E. Rd., Taipei 10608, Taiwan; t110859406@ntut.org.tw
[2] Department of Industrial Design, National Taipei University of Technology, 1, Sec. 3, Chung-hsiao E. Rd., Taipei 10608, Taiwan
* Correspondence: zmcdesign@gmail.com or zmcdesign@mail.ntut.edu.tw

Citation: Lin, J.-L.; Zheng, M.-C. An Empirical Investigation on the Visual Imagery of Augmented Reality User Interfaces for Smart Electric Vehicles Based on Kansei Engineering and FAHP-GRA. *Mathematics* **2024**, *12*, 2712. https://doi.org/10.3390/math12172712

Academic Editors: Grigoreta-Sofia Cojocar, Adriana-Mihaela Guran and Laura-Silvia Dioşan

Received: 28 June 2024
Revised: 27 August 2024
Accepted: 27 August 2024
Published: 30 August 2024

Copyright: © 2024 by the authors. Licensee MDPI, Basel, Switzerland. This article is an open access article distributed under the terms and conditions of the Creative Commons Attribution (CC BY) license (https://creativecommons.org/licenses/by/4.0/).

Abstract: Smart electric vehicles (SEVs) hold significant potential in alleviating the energy crisis and environmental pollution. The augmented reality (AR) dashboard, a key feature of SEVs, is attracting considerable attention due to its ability to enhance driving safety and user experience through real-time, intuitive driving information. This study innovatively integrates Kansei engineering, factor analysis, fuzzy systems theory, analytic hierarchy process, grey relational analysis, and factorial experimentation to evaluate AR dashboards' visual imagery and subjective preferences. The findings reveal that designs featuring blue planar and unconventional-shaped dials exhibit the best performance in terms of visual imagery. Subsequent factorial experiments confirmed these results, showing that drivers most favor blue-dominant designs. Furthermore, in unconventional-shaped dial designs, the visual effect of vertical 3D is more popular with drivers than horizontal 3D, while the opposite is true in round dials. This study provides a scientific evaluation method for assessing the emotional experience of AR dashboard interfaces. Additionally, these findings will help reduce the subjectivity in interface design and enhance the overall competitiveness of SEV vehicles.

Keywords: augmented reality dashboard; human-machine interface; multi-criteria decision-making; Kansei engineering; fuzzy analytic hierarchy process-grey relational analysis

MSC: 91C05; 90C70

1. Introduction

By 2030, the number of cars worldwide is expected to increase from 1.3 billion to 2 billion [1]. The huge increase in the number of cars will bring enormous environmental pressure to the region and the world, especially in terms of air pollution and the greenhouse effect [2,3]. Recently, smart electric vehicles (SEVs) have undoubtedly become a hot research topic for the Sustainable Development Goals [4,5], which have great potential to facilitate the energy crisis and environmental pollution and appeal to many consumers by emphasizing the user experience. The annual sales volume of new energy passenger vehicles in China in 2023 has reached 7.736 million units, of which SEVs accounted for 6.619 million units, with a penetration rate of 85.6% [6]. As a way to reduce carbon emissions and improve driver experience, SEVs have a bright future in China and worldwide. With the development of augmented reality (AR) and In-Vehicle Information Systems (IVISs), in-vehicle AR display technology has been widely applied and researched as an important functional system for SEVs.

AR is an advanced form of Human-Computer Interaction (HCI) that provides intuitive and rich interface information by embedding and overlaying virtual elements onto the real environment [7]. The applications of AR technology are extensive, spanning various domains such as gaming, education, entertainment, and manufacturing [8]. In the automotive sector, AR applications are primarily categorized into two types: one is in-vehicle display systems designed to provide information to drivers, and the other is auxiliary systems used during the automotive development process [7]. This study focuses on AR dashboard display systems intended for drivers. An AR dashboard combines augmented reality technology with dashboard displays, overlaying driving data, navigation, and assisted driving information onto live road video and presenting it to the driver through the dashboard display [9]. If AR is appropriately integrated with real-time road video, it can enhance drivers' situational awareness and thereby improve driving safety [10]. Some automakers have already adopted this technology in their production models. For example, China's SAIC Group launched the Rongwei MARVEL X in 2018, which pioneered the rendering of visual recognition results, fused positioning results, and map navigation information into AR images displayed in the in-vehicle dashboard. In addition, many scholars have conducted research on in-vehicle AR for the human-machine interface (HMI). Calvi and D'Amico [11] found that in-vehicle AR warnings significantly enhance the safety of left turns. Liu and Yin found through eye-tracking experiments that the reading performance on blue AR interfaces was the poorest, while green and adaptive colors demonstrated the most stable performance [12]. Zhong and Cheng [13] studied how environmental illuminance, interface color, and speed font design affect driver visual fatigue and visibility. Li and Wang [14] examined the impact of AR interface color combinations on the visual search performance and cognitive efficiency of drivers, considering gender and driving scenarios. However, most HMI research on in-vehicle AR has focused on driver safety [7,11,14–16], neglecting the experiential and emotional aspects of the driver. User experience is a pivotal determinant in enhancing user engagement and overall usage [17]. It encompasses both the behavior and emotions that users exhibit towards a particular object or system [18]. In addition, the user's emotional experience significantly affects purchase intention [19], usage intention, and user satisfaction [20]. Given its importance, this study aims to evaluate the emotional experience elicited by the user interface of an in-vehicle AR dashboard. Simultaneously, this study developed a method for evaluating the visual imagery and subjective preferences related to in-vehicle HMIs.

2. Theoretical Background
2.1. Kansei Engineering

Kansei engineering is a product design and development method based on human emotions and needs. Its core lies in the quantitative analysis of user emotions and feelings [21]. Kansei engineering focuses on capturing users' "Kansei" during the design process, which refers to their perceptions of aspects such as the color and shape of products or interfaces. This approach emphasizes addressing users' emotional needs, enabling designers to create products that better align with users' expectations and thus enhance user satisfaction. Kansei engineering typically involves matching adjectives (emotional words) with visual imagery and using inferential calculations to identify the most suitable design solutions [22]. This process includes four steps: selection of visual imagery and adjectives, semantic space expansion, properties space expansion, and relationship modeling [22]. Semantic space extension refers to the rational screening, categorizing, and evaluating perceptual adjectives [23]. Semantic space expansion can usually be performed through factor analysis, cluster analysis, principal component analysis, or other methods [24]. Properties space expansion refers to the systematic definition and description of specific properties of visual images. The purpose of this process is to create a detailed properties space that enables features of visual images to be associated with semantic space. Relational model construction refers to establishing a mathematical or statistical model to describe and quantify the relationship between the attributes of the visual image (properties space) and the user's emotional response (semantic space). Kansei engineering has been widely used in product development [24–27], user interface [28–30], and service design [31–34] and has achieved remarkable results. In the field of in-vehicle HMI, the dashboard's visual imagery is the driver's most frequently interacted element. For this reason, conducting a Kansei engineering study on the visual imagery of in-vehicle AR dashboards is necessary.

2.2. Multi-Criteria Decision Making (MCDM)

MCDM is a structured framework used to analyze decision problems with multiple complex objectives [35]. The core of MCDM lies in systematically analyzing and simplifying complex decision problems into manageable criteria and deriving the optimal decision through the trade-off of these criteria [36]. Handling uncertainty and subjectivity are common issues in the decision-making process, and MCDM methods provide decision makers with effective and robust decision support [37]. In practice, MCDM encompasses various methods, some of which include the analytic hierarchy process (AHP), grey relational analysis (GRA), the technique for order preference by similarity to the ideal solution (TOPSIS), and fuzzy TOPSIS [37]. These methods each offer unique advantages in addressing different types of decision problems and are suitable for various decision-making scenarios. The AHP, known for its structured approach and interpretability, is widely applied to various decision-making problems and remains one of the most commonly used MCDM methods to date [38]. Additionally, the AHP can be combined with triangular fuzzy numbers from fuzzy theory to make the decision-making process more realistic. However, when using the AHP or fuzzy AHP alone, the decision-maker judgment holds a dominant position within the hierarchy, which can lead to personal biases influencing the results [39]. GRA, on the other hand, is a flexible and adaptable MCDM method, but it is recommended to use weighted GRA, as it offers greater reliability and estimation accuracy compared to unweighted GRA [40]. TOPSIS is an MCDM method with relatively low computational complexity, making it suitable for handling large-scale decision problems. However, TOPSIS has certain limitations, such as the potential for rank reversal [41], and its use of Euclidean distance does not account for correlation, which may affect the results due to overlapping information [42]. Fuzzy TOPSIS, similar to the fuzzy AHP, incorporates triangular or trapezoidal fuzzy numbers to enhance decision-making accuracy.

In the field of Kansei engineering, evaluating visual imagery is a typical MCDM problem. For example, Jia and Tung [24] combined Kansei engineering with fuzzy theory to assess the visual imagery of wrist-worn wearable devices. Additionally, Lin and Zhai [26] applied TOPSIS within Kansei engineering to evaluate the visual imagery of automotive central touchscreens. In the realm of HMI, Li and Chen [28] conducted similar decision evaluations for visual imagery of waiting indicators. Wang and Yang [43] employed the GRA method to extract Kansei words related to wickerwork lamp products and conducted a study on Miryoku engineering. However, research combining MCDM with Kansei engineering in the automotive HMI domain remains relatively scarce. Although some scholars have used the AHP and GRA methods to evaluate the usability of automotive AR head-up displays (HUDs), they have not incorporated Kansei engineering methods [44]. In other research fields, fuzzy theory and TOPSIS have achieved certain successes in the study of visual imagery [24,26,28]. However, these methods are also limited by their respective theoretical foundations, and thus, they require a more comprehensive perspective. For instance, combining multiple MCDM methods can effectively address the limitations of individual methods, further enhancing the accuracy and reliability of decision analysis. Overall, MCDM methods have become important tools in modern decision analysis due to their scientific and systematic nature, with broad application prospects in complex systems or multi-criteria decision-making problems.

2.3. Fuzzy Analytic Hierarchy Process and Grey Relational Analysis (FAHP-GRA)

GRA is a significant method within MCDM. Its fundamental principle involves calculating grey relational degrees among variables to ascertain the degree of influence each factor has on the target variable, facilitating subsequent ranking and selection processes [45]. Compared to other decision-making methods, GRA exhibits clear advantages in handling uncertainty and fuzziness in MCDM processes [40]. In this study, the visual imagery investigation of the AR dashboard is evaluated based on the driver's perception, and human subjective judgment is subjective and fuzzy, so it is particularly suitable for using the GRA analysis method. In practical applications, GRA has been widely employed in decision-making problems across various fields, such as engineering, management, and design. Its outstanding flexibility and effectiveness have been well demonstrated [46–48].

In addition, when conducting MCDM, we need to consider the weight value of each factor to achieve a more accurate and reliable assessment [49]. Specifically, when using GRA for decision making, weighted GRA is the optimal choice [40]. The fuzzy analytic hierarchy process (FAHP) [50] is a weight calculation method that combines fuzzy theory [51] and the analytic hierarchy process [52]. Because of the characteristics of human thinking and cognitive patterns in the actual decision-making process, the quantitative numerical approach may not accurately reflect the cognitive preferences of the decision maker [53]. If cognitive preferences are expressed through fuzzy semantic variables, they can provide a more flexible way of judgment [54]. Therefore, combining the FAHP and GRA methods can solve the standardized weighting problem inherent in the GRA model and promote the accuracy and science of MCDM assessment [55]. Additionally, the characteristics and advantages of these methods in MCDM have already been discussed earlier, and the FAHP-GRA method will be applied in the Kansei engineering process to construct and analyze relational models, providing decision support and design guidance for the visual imagery of in-vehicle AR dashboards.

2.4. Research Objectives

Interface evaluation is a typical MCDM problem. Additionally, the influence of HMI on drivers' subjective preferences is complex and ambiguous. Therefore, this study employs a variety of rigorous analytical methods to conduct a comprehensive assessment of AR dashboard information design types. These methods include Kansei engineering, factor analysis, fuzzy theory, AHP, GRA, and factorial experiments. This study utilizes these objective research methods to review user perceptions and preferences regarding existing AR dashboard design types and conducts a design of experiments study on the main color, visual effects, and dial styling of AR dashboards. The objectives of this study are as follows:

1. To establish evaluation dimensions and indicator weights for the visual imagery of AR dashboards.
2. To rank the optimal design solutions for AR dashboards based on the visual imagery evaluation dimensions.
3. To investigate the effects of three independent variables—main color, visual effects, and dial styling—on drivers' preferences.
4. To discuss the cross-validation results between drivers' subjective evaluations and their visual imagery assessments of AR dashboards.

3. Methodological Procedures

The evaluation process for the AR dashboard HMI in this study is illustrated in Figure 1. Next, we will provide a detailed description of the three stages of Kansei engineering.

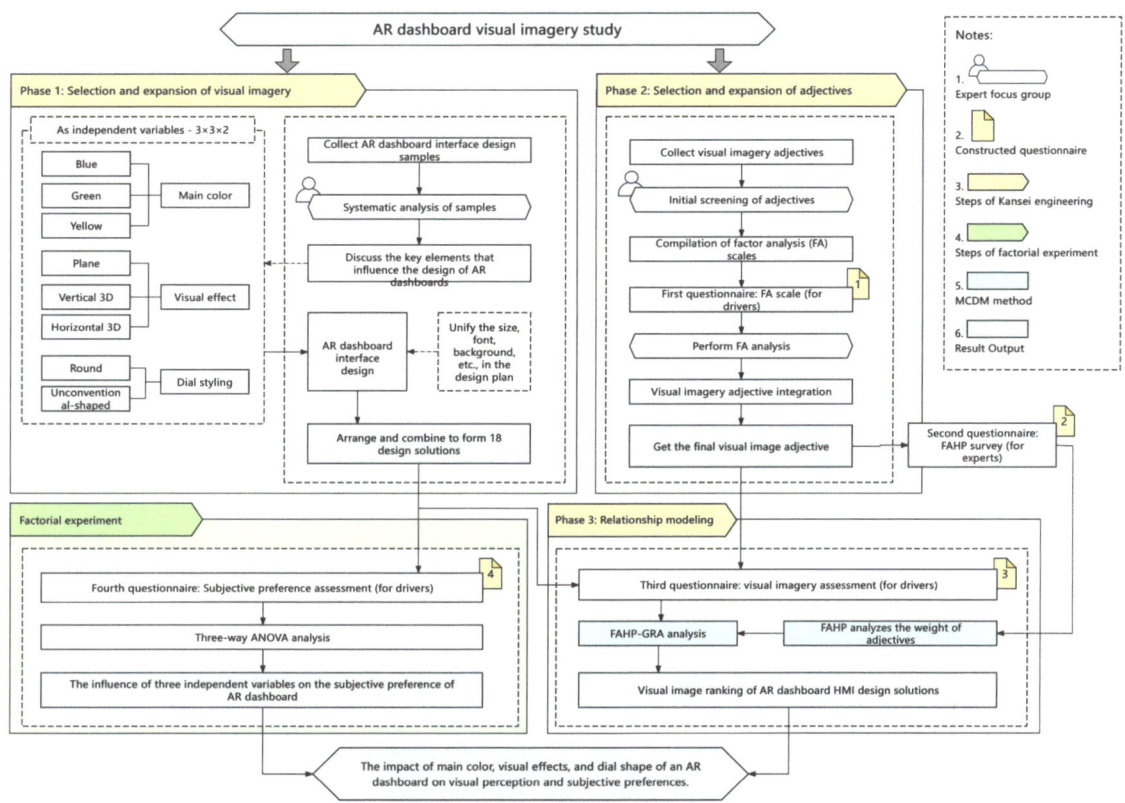

Figure 1. Assessment architecture diagram of this study.

3.1. Phase 1: Selection and Expansion of Visual Imagery

The researchers collected 335 samples of dashboard interface design pictures and invited 12 in-vehicle HMI design experts to systematically analyze and discuss these picture samples. Among them were three user interface design experts, three user experience experts, three human factors researchers, and three product managers. Based on the discussion results of the in-vehicle HMI design experts, the researchers carried out the factorial experiment planning and HMI design for the AR dashboard. After systematic analysis, the main color, visual effect, and dial styling of the AR dashboard will be used as the independent variables in the factorial experiment. Previous studies have also indicated that the color and shape of a product are major factors influencing users' emotional responses [56,57]. The visual effects and dial styling in this study are key aspects of the AR dashboard's shape, making them highly relevant for studying the visual imagery of automotive dashboards. The main color and visual effect are a within-subjects factor, while the styling of the dial is a between-subjects factor; the main color is divided into three levels: blue (H:200, S:100, B:100), green (H:120, S:100, B:100), and yellow (H:60, S:100, B:100); the visual effect is divided into three levels: plane, vertical 3D, and horizontal 3D; and the styling of the dial is divided into two levels: round and unconventionally shaped. In a usability study of speedometers, Francois and Crave [58] noted that combination dials outperformed both analog and digital dials in the tasks of reading information and detecting dynamic speed changes. A combination dial is a design that uses both numeric and indicator elements to convey speed information. Therefore, we redesigned the AR dashboard interface of the SEV based on the speedometer design guidelines proposed by

Francois and Crave [58]. The SEV-AR dashboard interface information in this experiment mainly consists of the speedometer and the power-to-weight ratio (PWR) dial. In designing the AR dashboard interface, we adhered to Nielsen's principles of consistency, aesthetics, and minimalism [59]. The specific design proposal is shown in Figure 2. Based on the different levels of the three independent variables, we developed 18 AR dashboard interface design proposals. For example, the first design in the first row (Proposal 1) of Figure 2 features a blue planar and round dial.

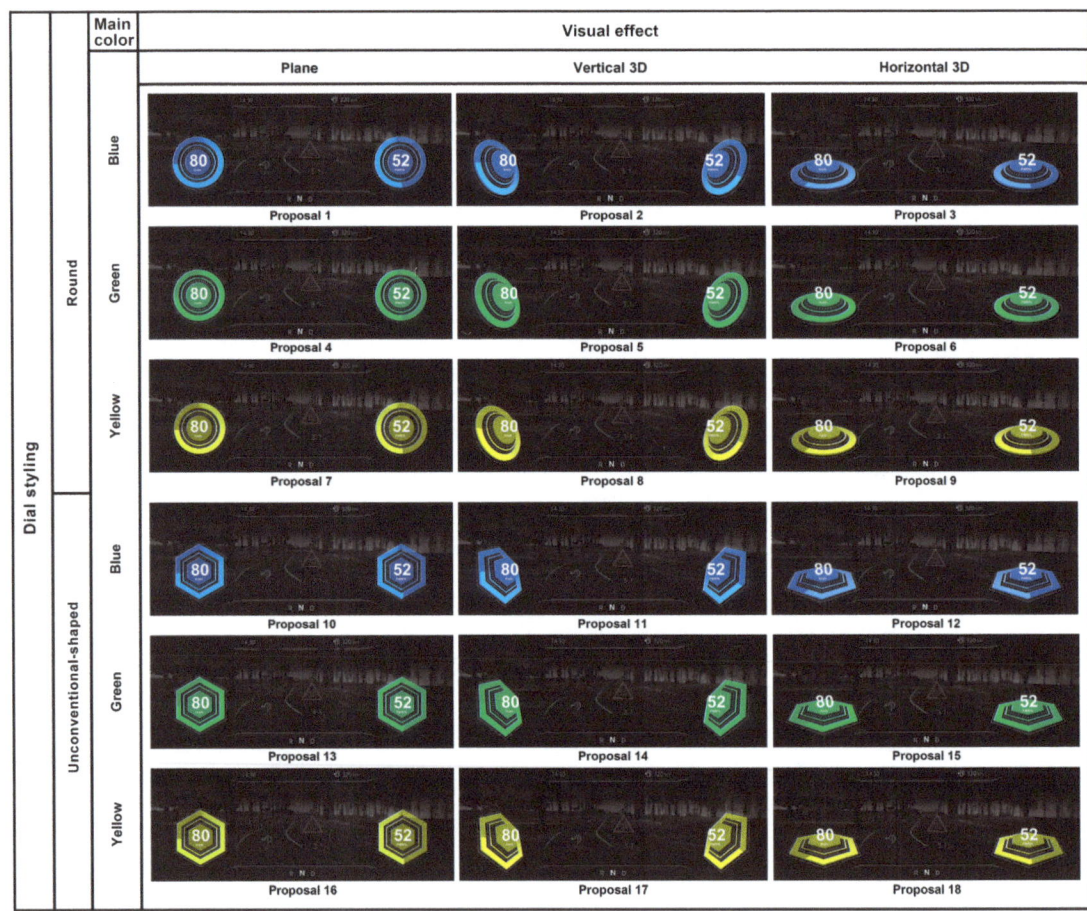

Figure 2. Design proposal for 18 AR dashboards.

The design proposals were formatted in a 12.3-inch (292.528mm × 109.698mm) format, and these designs were displayed on the liquid-crystal display. The evaluation task was carried out in a laboratory environment. We strictly followed the driver sight distance criterion proposed by Dreyfuss and Associates [60], where participants were asked to sit at a distance of 550 mm from the sight distance of the dashboard screen. While observing the design proposals, participants were able to swipe left and right to view each design proposal while completing the scale questionnaire. The scoring was on a 7-point Likert scale (1 for very low, 4 for average, 7 for very high). Figure 3 illustrates the process by which participants switched between different design schemes during the experiment.

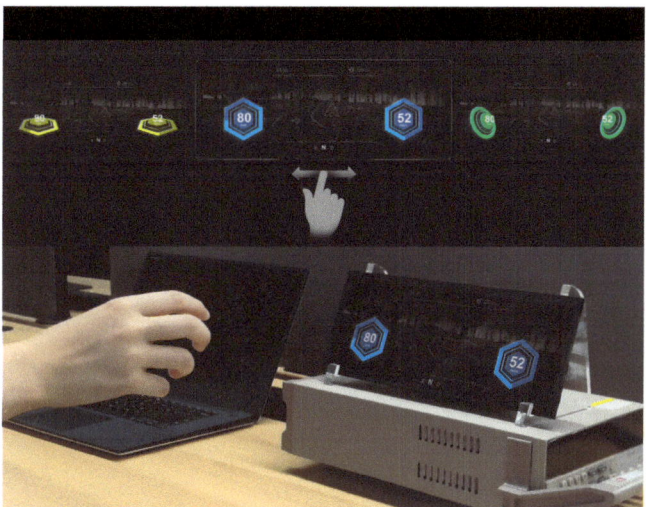

Figure 3. Schematic diagram of design proposal switching.

3.2. Phase 2: Selection and Expansion of Adjectives

Visual imagery adjectives can effectively respond to the user's mental feelings [28]. For instance, shapes and colors within visual imagery can have different impacts on users' psychological responses [56]. One of the key tasks for designers is to evoke specific emotional responses from users by manipulating visual imagery elements such as shapes and colors [57]. Therefore, controlling the visual imagery of AR dashboards is a critical method for designers to convey information to drivers and elicit emotional responses. At this stage, we first collected many adjectives related to the visual imagery of the dashboard from automotive portals, design resource websites, and the relevant research literature. For example, we extracted adjectives from user reviews of dashboard HMIs on automotive portals and design resource websites. Subsequently, after expert focus group discussions, adjectives unsuitable for describing the in-vehicle HMI were eliminated, leaving 130 adjectives for subsequent experiments. In the following study phase, we invited 12 designers and researchers related to the vehicle HMI to participate in the experiment. The participants were asked to select 40 to 50 adjectives from the aforementioned 130 that best describe the AR dashboard interface. Finally, the researchers selected the 40 most recognized adjectives based on the frequency of votes cast by the participants for the study of the factor analysis scale.

Factor analysis is a statistical method that uses a system of indicators to analyze or measure the extent to which multiple factors have an impression on an objective phenomenon [61]. Factor analysis is the most used analysis method in Kansei engineering, which can extract key perceptual factors from a large number of sensibility words, and these factors can be used to guide the subsequent design. Recently, many scholars have demonstrated that factor analysis is a scientific and reliable method for studying visual imagery [24,28,62]. Therefore, we used factor analysis in this phase to extract imagery adjectives for the AR dashboard interface. Specifically, participants were invited to experience the AR dashboard design sample from Phase 1 and then asked to evaluate 40 imagery adjectives using a 5-point Likert scale (1 for very inappropriate, 3 for average, 5 for very appropriate). The collected data will be factor analyzed to extract the adjectives that match the AR dashboard interface.

3.3. Phase 3a: Relationship Modeling—Fuzzy Analytic Hierarchy Process (FAHP) to Determine Visual Imagery Evaluation Dimension Weights

In this stage, FAHP weights are calculated for the adjectives (assessment dimensions) derived from the factor analysis, and the specific calculation steps are as follows.

Step 1: Perform a pairwise comparison of the assessment dimensions.

This study will invite user interface designers, user experience designers, and product managers to form an evaluation team to compare the importance of visual image dimensions in pairs. The measurement scale uses a semantic scale with a 1–9 level pairwise comparison [52], which is then converted into a triangular fuzzy number [50,63], as shown in Table 1 and Figure 4.

Table 1. Triangular fuzzy conversion scale.

Linguistic Scale	AHP Scale	Triangular Fuzzy Number Scale		
		Left Endpoint	Middle Value	Right Endpoint
Equal importance	1	1	1	3
Slight importance	3	1	3	5
Important	5	3	5	7
Strong importance	7	5	7	9
Extreme importance	9	7	9	9
Slight unimportance	1/3	1/5	1/3	1
Unimportant	1/5	1/7	1/5	1/3
Strong unimportance	1/7	1/9	1/7	1/5
Extreme unimportance	1/9	1/9	1/9	1/7

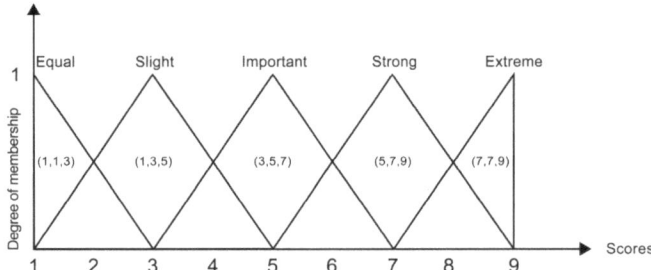

Figure 4. Linguistic variables describing weights of the FAHP.

Step 2: Create a pairwise comparison matrix.

The values of the pairwise comparison results of n image adjective dimensions are placed in the upper triangular part of the pairwise comparison matrix A, and the lower triangular part is the reciprocal of the relative position, that is, $a_{ji} = 1/a_{ij}$. Matrix A can be expressed as follows:

$$A = \begin{bmatrix} 1 & a_{12} & \cdots & a_{1n} \\ \frac{1}{a_{12}} & 1 & \cdots & a_{2n} \\ \vdots & \vdots & \ddots & \vdots \\ \frac{1}{a_{1n}} & \frac{1}{a_{2n}} & \cdots & 1 \end{bmatrix} \quad (1)$$

Step 3: Calculate the maximum eigenvalue and conduct consistency identification.

$$\overline{W_i} = \sqrt[n]{\prod_{i=1}^{n} A_{ij}} \quad (2)$$

$$W_i = \overline{W_i} / \sum_{i=1}^{n} W_i \quad (3)$$

Next, the maximum eigenvalue λ_{max} is found based on W_i and the comparison matrix A, as shown in Formula (4). Finally, find the random consistency ratio CR required in this step. When the CR value is not greater than 0.1, the importance matrix has satisfactory consistency. *CI* is the consistency index, and RI is the average random consistency index. The value range of the *RI* is visible in Table 2.

$$\lambda_{max} = \frac{1}{n} / \sum_{i=1}^{n} \frac{(AW)_i}{W_i} \quad (4)$$

$$CI = \frac{\lambda_{max} - n}{n - 1} \quad (5)$$

$$CR = CI/RI \quad (6)$$

Table 2. Value of random indexes (*RI*).

Matrix Size (*n*)	3	4	5	6	7
RI value	0.58	0.90	1.12	1.24	1.32

Step 4: Convert the original scores into triangular fuzzy numbers and establish a fuzzy pairwise comparison matrix.

After passing the consistency test, each internal value of the pairwise comparison matrix A is converted into a triangular fuzzy number $\tilde{M}_{ij}$, and a fuzzy pairwise comparison matrix M is established. That is, $\tilde{M}_{ij} = (L_{ij}, M_{ij}, R_{ij})$, the fuzzy number of the evaluation dimension *i* is relative to the evaluation dimension *j*, and the lower triangular part of the matrix M is $\tilde{M}_{ji} = 1/\tilde{M}_{ij}$. The matrix M can be expressed as follows:

$$M = [\tilde{M}_{ji}] = \begin{bmatrix} 1,1,1 & \tilde{M}_{12} = (L_{12}, M_{12}, R_{12}) & \cdots & \tilde{M}_{1j} = (L_{1j}, M_{1j}, R_{1j}) \\ \tilde{M}_{21} = 1/\tilde{M}_{12} & 1,1,1 & \cdots & \tilde{M}_{2j} = (L_{2j}, M_{2j}, R_{2j}) \\ \vdots & \vdots & \ddots & \vdots \\ \tilde{M}_{j1} = 1/\tilde{M}_{1j} & \tilde{M}_{j2} = 1/\tilde{M}_{2j} & \cdots & 1,1,1 \end{bmatrix} \quad (7)$$

Step 5: Calculate triangular fuzzy numbers and fuzzy weights.

Perform a geometric mean operation on the values in the fuzzy pairwise comparison matrix M to obtain the geometric mean triangular fuzzy number $\grave{M} = (\grave{L}_i, \grave{M}_i, \grave{R}_i)$ in each column of each evaluation dimension, and then add up the geometric mean triangular fuzzy numbers in each column. At the same time, to ensure that the left boundary value of the triangular fuzzyweight issmaller than the right boundary value, the summed triangular fuzzy number needs to be reciprocally converted. That is, $\grave{M} = (\grave{L}_r, \grave{M}_r, \grave{R}_r) = (1/\grave{R}_r, 1/\grave{M}_r, 1/\grave{L}_r,)$. Finally, the triangular blur weight $\tilde{W}_i = (1/\grave{R}_r L_i, 1/\grave{M}_r M_i, 1/\grave{L}_r R_i)$ is calculated. The weight calculation methods of the FAHP and AHP are similar and can be deduced concerning Formulas (2) and (3), which will not be described again.

Step 6: Defuzzification and normalization.

Defuzzification is performed on the obtained triangular fuzzy weight $\tilde{W}_i$, which is, converted into a real value DW_i. In addition, normalization needs to be performed again to make the sum of the importance of each evaluation dimension equal to 1. Finally, the fuzzy weight value $D\hat{W}_i$ of each element is obtained. Assuming the triangular fuzzy weight $\tilde{W}_i = (WL_i, WM_i, WR_i)$, the defuzzification and normalization formulas are as follows:

$$DW_i = \frac{(WR_i - WL_i) + (WM_i - WL_i)}{3} + WL_i \quad (8)$$

$$D\hat{W}_i = \frac{DW_i}{\sum_{i=1}^{n} DW_i} \tag{9}$$

3.4. Phase 3b: Relationship Modeling—Evaluating Visual Imagery Using FAHP-GRA

In this stage, a second user questionnaire was constructed based on the design proposals and adjectives derived from Phases 1 and 2, thereby measuring the driver's visual image evaluation of the AR instrument panel design proposal. The questionnaire adopts a 7-point Likert scale (1 for very low, 4 for medium, and 7 for very high). Subsequently, the questionnaire data were calculated by FAHP-GRA to obtain the scores of each AR dashboard design proposal. The calculation steps of FAHP-GRA are as follows.

Step 1: Construct reference and comparison sequences.

Based on the final scores of the 18 AR dashboards, the optimal value in each evaluation dimension is selected as the reference sequence C_0. At the same time, the scores of the 18 AR dashboards will be used as the comparison sequences $C_1, C_2, C_3, \ldots, C_{18}$.

Step 2: Perform non-dimensionalization.

Although all assessment dimensions use a 7-point Likert scale, differences in the resulting data range may lead to numerical instability or calculation accuracy issues. Therefore, the non-dimensionalization of reference and comparison sequences is required to improve the stability of data calculations.

$$X_i(k) = \frac{C_i(k)}{C_k} \tag{10}$$

Among them, $C_k = 1/(n+1)\sum_{i=0}^{n} C_i(k), k = 1, 2, \ldots, m$.

Step 3: Determine the optimal value range of the distinguishing coefficient ρ.

Before performing the gray correlation calculation, the distinguishing coefficient ρ value must be determined. The value range of ρ is (0, 1). Usually, ρ = 0.5 is taken. However, since the distinguishing coefficient will affect the arrangement of related sequences, we should not simply apply ρ = 0.5 or other values. Necessary calculations need to be performed to determine the ρ value [64]. Therefore, this step adopts the calculation formula for the value range of the distinguishing coefficient ρ proposed by Guo and Guo [65] as follows:

$$\rho_1 = \frac{\Delta_{0i}(k)}{\Delta_{max}} \cdot \frac{1}{e-1} \tag{11}$$

$$\rho_2 = (e-1) \cdot \rho_1 \tag{12}$$

For this gray relational system, the distinguishing coefficient value is optimal between [ρ1, ρ2].

Step 4: Calculate the grey relational degree of each sequence.

After determining the ρ value, the grey relational degree can be calculated [66]. The formula is as follows:

$$\xi^{(i)}(k) = \frac{\min_i\min_k \left|X^{(0)}(k) - X^{(i)}(k)\right| + \rho \max_i\max_k \left|X^{(0)}(k) - X^{(i)}(k)\right|}{\left|X^{(0)}(k) - X^{(i)}(k)\right| + \rho \max_i\max_k \left|X^{(0)}(k) - X^{(i)}(k)\right|} \tag{13}$$

Step 5: Calculate the weighting grey relational degree.

To compare different AR dashboard design proposals more scientifically and comprehensively, it is necessary to integrate the weight values and grey relational degree of each evaluation dimension [67]. Let the grey relational degree of each design proposal be γ^i, and its formula is as follows:

$$\gamma^{(i)} = \sum_{k=1}^{n} W_i \cdot \gamma^{(i)}(k) \tag{14}$$

When the γ^i value is larger, it indicates that the visual image of the AR dashboard design proposal is better.

4. Analysis and Results

4.1. Visual Imagery Adjective Extraction Results

After referring to the HMI design of AR dashboards, the expert team sifted and sorted out the 40 most common adjectives for evaluating AR dashboard interfaces from 130 imagery adjectives, which are all positive (see Table 3).

Table 3. Forty most common adjectives for visual imagery.

Visual Imagery Adjectives				
Detailed	Dynamic	Rich	Concise	Vivid
Responsive	Cool	Intelligent	Technological	Immersive
Innovative	Secure	Efficient	Futuristic	Aesthetic
Unique	Stunning	Abstract	Visual	Premium
Reliable	Smooth	Gorgeous	Personalized	Attractive
Harmonious	Natural	Interesting	Diverse	Practical
Orderly	Dreamlike	Clear	Sleek	Intuitive
Trustworthy	Grand	Rhythmic	Fresh	Agile

Next, we combined 40 adjectives with 18 AR dashboard HMI design proposals. Using purposive sampling, a total of 140 questionnaires were collected. All participants were required to have a driver's license and possess certain driving information recognition capabilities. In the end, 123 valid questionnaires were obtained, 60 from males and 63 from females, with and an average age of 28.61 (SD = 5.46). Subsequently, we conducted the first factor analysis on the questionnaire data and a second factor analysis on the 23 adjectives with factor loadings greater than 0.6 (see Table 4).

Table 4. The 23 adjectives with factor loadings higher than 0.6.

Adjectives	Initial	Extraction	Adjectives	Initial	Extraction
Premium	1.000	0.803	Efficient	1.000	0.722
Natural	1.000	0.762	Reliable	1.000	0.715
Unique	1.000	0.758	Intelligent	1.000	0.706
Aesthetic	1.000	0.758	Trustworthy	1.000	0.704
Attractive	1.000	0.751	Concise	1.000	0.701
Personalized	1.000	0.741	Diverse	1.000	0.699
Dreamlike	1.000	0.738	Stunning	1.000	0.679
Visual	1.000	0.736	Interesting	1.000	0.677
Smooth	1.000	0.735	Responsive	1.000	0.661
Gorgeous	1.000	0.734	Innovative	1.000	0.646
Technological	1.000	0.728	Rich	1.000	0.605
Clear	1.000	0.726			

Extraction method: principal component analysis.

As shown in Table 5, after the second factor analysis, KMO = 0.896, Bartlett = 1949.631, and $p < 0.001$ ($df = 253$), indicating a statistically significant difference. This result suggests that the correlation matrices in the original group have common factors and are suitable for factor analysis.

In addition, according to the principal component method and the eigenvalue principle, there are five factors with an eigenvalue greater than 1, and their total explained variance is 71.675% (see Table 6). Generally speaking, a value higher than 70% indicates a good level of explanation. Therefore, five groups of similar factors were extracted at this stage, as shown in Figure 5.

Table 5. The KMO and Bartlett test results.

Visual Imagery Adjectives		
Kaiser Meyer Olkin		0.896
Bartlett's Sphericity Test	Approximate Chi-Squared	1949.631
	df	253
	p	<0.001 ***

* Significantly different at α = 0.05 level (p < 0.05). ** Significantly different at α = 0.01 level (p < 0.01). *** Significantly different at α = 0.001 level (p < 0.001).

Table 6. Total variance explained.

Component	Initial Eigenvalues			Squares Loading Extraction			Transformed Squares Loading		
	Total	Variance (%)	Accumulative (%)	Total	Variance (%)	Accumulative (%)	Total	Variance (%)	Accumulative (%)
1	10.313	44.837	44.837	10.313	44.837	44.837	6.103	26.533	26.533
2	2.573	11.189	56.026	2.573	11.189	56.026	3.353	14.579	41.112
3	1.301	5.657	61.683	1.301	5.657	61.683	2.801	12.180	53.292
4	1.186	5.158	66.840	1.186	5.158	66.840	2.500	10.868	64.160
5	1.112	4.834	71.675	1.112	4.834	71.675	1.728	7.515	71.675

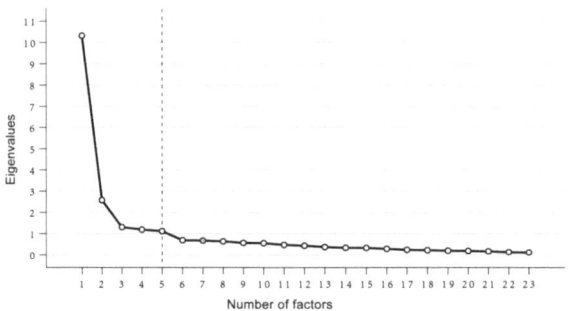

Figure 5. The scree plot of eigenvalues and the number of factors.

In Table 7, the difference between each adjective in the five components is obvious, and it does not overwhelm multiple components. Moreover, the loadings of the factors are all higher than the excellent standard of 0.6, indicating that these adjectives have very high structural validity for evaluating the design of the AR dashboard HMI.

Table 7. The transformed component matrices.

Adjectives	Component				
	Factor 1	Factor 2	Factor 3	Factor 4	Factor 5
Unique	0.841	0.157	0.132	0.022	0.093
Dreamlike	0.829	0.097	0.070	0.139	0.129
Gorgeous	0.781	0.198	−0.060	0.279	0.058
Innovative	0.767	0.161	0.136	0.032	0.110
Diverse	0.755	0.228	0.184	0.200	0.054
Stunning	0.751	0.200	0.028	0.195	0.190
Personalized	0.738	0.376	0.189	0.126	0.056
Interesting	0.704	0.356	0.046	0.057	0.222
Rich	0.612	0.309	0.195	0.312	0.012
Premium	0.260	0.755	0.054	0.320	0.248
Aesthetic	0.269	0.701	0.157	0.330	0.246
Attractive	0.312	0.698	0.236	0.322	0.084
Technological	0.403	0.692	0.262	−0.133	−0.018

Table 7. Cont.

Adjectives	Component				
	Factor 1	Factor 2	Factor 3	Factor 4	Factor 5
Intelligent	0.428	0.673	0.225	0.117	0.069
Visual	0.118	0.334	0.774	0.056	−0.090
Efficient	0.212	0.078	0.740	0.315	0.157
Clear	0.201	0.098	0.730	0.370	0.084
Concise	−0.053	0.155	0.716	0.029	0.400
Trustworthy	0.047	0.227	0.285	0.743	0.132
Responsive	0.329	0.205	0.078	0.709	−0.049
Reliable	0.254	0.085	0.310	0.672	0.310
Natural	0.264	0.101	0.103	0.021	0.819
Smooth	0.175	0.238	0.242	0.339	0.689

Extraction method: principal component analysis. Transformed method: Kaiser normalized maximum variance method.

After factor analysis, twenty-three adjectives in five groups were obtained in this stage. Since the adjectives in each group are related, we invited language and literature experts to rename each group. The results are shown in Table 8. These results created five basic visual image evaluation dimensions for the next stage of research.

Table 8. Renamed adjectives and their codes.

Factor	Adjective Groups	Factor Renaming	Code
1	Unique, Dreamlike, Gorgeous, Innovative, Diverse, Stunning, Personalized, Interesting, Rich	Novel and Splendid	N&S
2	Premium, Aesthetic, Attractive, Technological, Intelligent	Technological and Aesthetic	T&A
3	Visual, Efficient, Clear, Concise	Visible and Concise	V&C
4	Trustworthy, Responsive, Reliable	Agile and Reliable	A&R
5	Natural, Smooth	Smooth and Natural	S&N

4.2. Visual Imagery Weighting Results

At this stage, 12 experts were invited to rate important pairs of evaluation dimensions. Experts include in-vehicle HMI user interface (UI) designers, user experience (UE) designers, ergonomics researchers (ERs), and product managers (PMs). Next, we performed an AHP weight calculation (referring to Formulas (2) and (3)) and a consistency test (referring to Formulas (4), (5), and (6)) with the ratings of the 12 experts.

In Table 9, the CR values of all expert ratings are less than 0.1; that is, the weight matrix of each expert has satisfactory consistency. Therefore, the importance of weight calculation, defuzzification (refer to Formula (8)), and regularization (refer to Formula (9)) of the FAHP are performed again, and the results are shown in Table 10.

Table 9. AHP weights and consistency test results of experts.

Expert Code	N&S	T&A	V&C	A&R	S&N	CI	CR
UI 1	0.049	0.100	0.443	0.193	0.214	0.050	0.045
UI 2	0.050	0.050	0.367	0.379	0.155	0.070	0.063
UI 3	0.056	0.485	0.255	0.107	0.097	0.086	0.076
UE 1	0.043	0.071	0.057	0.335	0.494	0.076	0.068
UE 2	0.073	0.061	0.172	0.394	0.300	0.062	0.055
UE 3	0.055	0.173	0.239	0.318	0.216	0.039	0.035
ER 1	0.039	0.094	0.567	0.216	0.084	0.071	0.064

Table 9. Cont.

Expert Code	N&S	T&A	V&C	A&R	S&N	CI	CR
ER 2	0.046	0.078	0.228	0.206	0.441	0.072	0.064
ER 3	0.129	0.245	0.499	0.083	0.045	0.069	0.062
PM 1	0.037	0.171	0.439	0.182	0.171	0.026	0.024
PM 2	0.112	0.192	0.192	0.239	0.265	0.081	0.072
PM 3	0.046	0.079	0.166	0.355	0.355	0.060	0.053

Table 10. FAHP weights of experts.

Expert Code	N&S	T&A	V&C	A&R	S&N
UI 1	0.055	0.123	0.403	0.218	0.201
UI 2	0.056	0.048	0.389	0.341	0.166
UI 3	0.071	0.449	0.264	0.126	0.090
UX 1	0.052	0.078	0.050	0.343	0.477
UX 2	0.092	0.059	0.191	0.395	0.264
UX 3	0.062	0.217	0.252	0.302	0.168
ER 1	0.046	0.116	0.536	0.217	0.085
ER 2	0.050	0.084	0.257	0.198	0.411
ER 3	0.137	0.254	0.460	0.097	0.052
PM 1	0.036	0.213	0.408	0.191	0.153
PM 2	0.145	0.231	0.195	0.221	0.208
PM 3	0.050	0.085	0.187	0.366	0.312
Geometric mean	0.065	0.132	0.260	0.232	0.180
Normalized weight	0.074	0.152	0.299	0.268	0.207

The results show that the weight of novel and splendid (N&S) is 0.074, technological and aesthetic (T&A) is 0.152, visible and concise (V&C) is 0.299, agile and reliable (A&R) is 0.268, and smooth and natural (S&N) is 0.207.

4.3. FAHP-GRA Calculation Results

At this stage, 100 drivers (60 males and 40 females) were invited to evaluate the five dimensions of N&S, T&A, V&C, A&R, and S&N of 18 AR instrument panels. Their average age was 29.76 years (SD = 5.03). The evaluation score results are processed according to the average, and the AR dashboard design solution's performance value and comparison sequence are obtained (see Table 11).

Table 11 shows the reference sequence $C_0 = \begin{bmatrix} 5.220 & 5.260 & 5.380 & 4.820 & 4.980 \end{bmatrix}$ of the AR dashboard and the comparison sequence from Proposals 1 to 18. First, we performed non-dimensionalization processing on the reference and comparison sequences according to Formula (10). Next, we calculated the values of the distinguishing coefficients ρ1 and ρ2 according to Formulas (11) and (12). The results show that the distinguishing coefficient is optimal between 0.300 and 0.516. In this study, the ρ value takes the intermediate value of 0.4 for subsequent calculations. Finally, we calculated the gray relational degree of each proposal according to Formula (13). We substituted its gray relational degree and the FAHP results into Formula (14) to obtain the overall relational degree γ^i (see Table 12).

The closer the value of γ^i is to 1, the closer the proposal is to the ideal proposal (reference sequence). In Table 12, the blue planar and unconventional-shaped dial design (Proposal 10) has the closest value of γ^i to 1 (γ^{10} = 0.863). Therefore, this proposal is the best AR dashboard design.

Table 11. Performance scores of 18 proposals.

Proposal Codes	N&S	T&A	V&C	A&R	S&N
Proposal 1	4.380	4.500	5.380	4.800	4.980
Proposal 2	5.220	5.260	4.840	4.600	4.740
Proposal 3	4.740	4.580	4.700	4.580	4.480
Proposal 4	4.380	4.300	4.600	4.420	4.460
Proposal 5	4.460	4.420	4.340	4.280	4.420
Proposal 6	4.260	4.220	4.160	4.060	4.060
Proposal 7	3.900	3.880	4.040	3.840	3.840
Proposal 8	4.080	3.920	3.860	3.880	3.900
Proposal 9	3.860	3.840	3.960	3.940	3.920
Proposal 10	4.400	4.680	5.340	4.820	4.980
Proposal 11	4.820	4.820	4.440	4.220	4.260
Proposal 12	4.900	4.780	4.800	4.440	4.460
Proposal 13	4.300	4.280	4.760	4.480	4.560
Proposal 14	4.440	4.280	4.340	4.180	4.100
Proposal 15	4.840	4.640	4.620	4.400	4.280
Proposal 16	4.160	4.000	4.520	4.120	4.140
Proposal 17	4.220	4.060	3.920	3.740	3.580
Proposal 18	4.360	4.120	4.360	3.860	4.040

Table 12. Weighted relational degree of each proposal.

Proposal Codes	N&S	T&A	V&C	A&R	S&N	γ^i	Sequence
Proposal 1	0.031	0.066	0.299	0.259	0.207	0.862	2
Proposal 2	0.074	0.152	0.158	0.194	0.146	0.725	3
Proposal 3	0.041	0.071	0.141	0.189	0.111	0.553	5
Proposal 4	0.031	0.058	0.131	0.158	0.109	0.487	8
Proposal 5	0.033	0.063	0.110	0.138	0.105	0.449	10
Proposal 6	0.028	0.055	0.099	0.115	0.080	0.378	13
Proposal 7	0.023	0.046	0.093	0.099	0.070	0.331	17
Proposal 8	0.025	0.046	0.085	0.102	0.072	0.331	16
Proposal 9	0.023	0.045	0.090	0.106	0.073	0.336	15
Proposal 10	0.031	0.077	0.281	0.268	0.207	0.863	1
Proposal 11	0.044	0.087	0.117	0.131	0.092	0.472	9
Proposal 12	0.048	0.084	0.153	0.161	0.109	0.556	4
Proposal 13	0.029	0.057	0.148	0.168	0.120	0.523	6
Proposal 14	0.032	0.057	0.110	0.127	0.082	0.409	11
Proposal 15	0.045	0.074	0.133	0.155	0.094	0.501	7
Proposal 16	0.027	0.048	0.124	0.121	0.085	0.404	12
Proposal 17	0.028	0.050	0.088	0.093	0.061	0.319	18
Proposal 18	0.030	0.052	0.112	0.100	0.079	0.373	14

4.4. Factorial Experiment Results

This experiment utilizes a 3 (main color) × 3 (visual effect) × 2 (dial styling) mixed factorial design. During the experiment, drivers were asked to rate both the visual imagery of the AR dashboard proposal and their subjective preferences. We conducted a three-way ANOVA on the subjective preference outcome data. Additionally, LSD post hoc test analysis was performed on statistically significant variables. It is worth noting that during the ANOVA analysis of repeated measures data, it is necessary to first examine the sphericity of the data [68]. In this study, Mauchly's test of sphericity indicated a significant difference ($p < 0.05$), and we applied the Greenhouse Geisser correction to adjust the degrees of freedom [69,70]. The results are shown in Table 13.

Table 13. The mixed factorial ANOVA results of subjective preference (after correction).

Source	SS	df	MS	F	p	η^2	Post Hoc
Main color	100.287	1.704	58.847	30.710	<0.001 ***	0.239	Blue > Green > Yellow
Visual effect	0.507	1.819	0.279	0.154	0.838	0.002	
Dial styling	4.551	1.000	4.551	0.549	0.461	0.006	
Main color × visual effect	7.307	3.484	2.097	3.426	0.013 *	0.034	
Main color × dial styling	5.016	1.704	2.943	1.536	0.220	0.015	
Visual effect × dial styling	10.702	1.819	5.883	3.249	0.046 *	0.032	
Main color × visual effect × dial styling	1.711	3.484	0.491	0.802	0.509	0.008	

* Significantly different at α = 0.05 level ($p < 0.05$). ** Significantly different at α = 0.01 level ($p < 0.01$). *** Significantly different at α = 0.001 level ($p < 0.001$).

The main color has a significant main effect ($F_{1.704,98}$ = 30.710, $p < 0.001$; η^2 = 0.239). Further analysis using the LSD post hoc test showed significant differences in subjective preferences between blue (M = 4.587, SE = 0.096), green (M = 4.143, SE = 0.110), and yellow (M = 3.770, SE = 0.131). The subjective preference for blue is significantly higher than for green and yellow, while the subjective preference for green is also significantly higher than for yellow. However, the main effect of visual effects was not significant ($F_{1.819,98}$ = 0.154, p = 0.838 > 0.05; η^2 = 0.002). Similarly, dial styling has no significant main effect ($F_{1.000,98}$ = 0.549, p = 0.461 > 0.05; η^2 = 0.006).

The interaction between the main color and the visual effect was significant ($F_{3.484,98}$ = 3.426, p = 0.013 < 0.05; η^2 = 0.034). To test the differences between groups within a certain level of an independent variable [71], we conducted a simple effects analysis. A simple effects analysis on the main color reveals that only the visual effect of green is significantly different (see Figure 6). Specifically, when the main color is green, the visual effect of vertical 3D is significantly worse than that of flat and horizontal 3D.

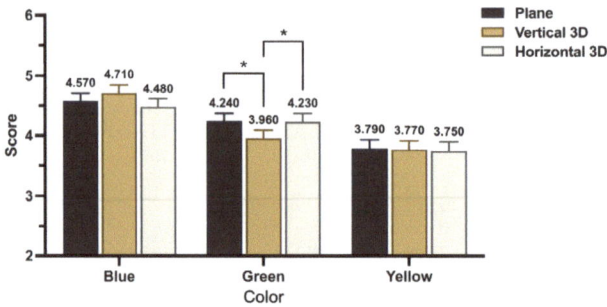

Figure 6. The results of the simple effects analysis of the main color within the interaction between the main color and visual effects. Error bars represent +1 SEM. (Notes: * $p \leq 0.05$, ** $p \leq 0.01$, *** $p \leq 0.001$).

Additionally, there is a significant interaction between visual effects and dial styling ($F_{1.819,98}$ = 3.249, p = 0.046 < 0.05; η^2 = 0.032). In the simple effects analysis of dial styling, significant differences were found in the visual effects of different dial styles. For round dials, the visual effect of vertical 3D is significantly better than horizontal 3D. For unconventional-shaped dials, the visual effect of horizontal 3D is significantly better than vertical 3D (see Figure 7).

Overall, the main color (η^2 = 0.239) has a greater impact on subjective preference than dial styling (η^2 = 0.006) and visual effects (η^2 = 0.002). In comparison, dial styling impacts subjective preference more than visual effects. According to the results of FAHP-GRA, the top five design solutions are all blue, with the highest-ranked design solution being a blue planar and unconventional-shaped dial design (Proposal 10).

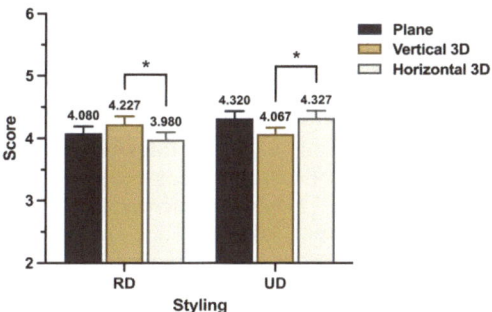

Figure 7. The results of the simple effects analysis of dial styling within the interaction between visual effects and dial styling. Error bars represent +1 SEM. (Notes: * $p \leq 0.05$, ** $p \leq 0.01$, *** $p \leq 0.001$).

5. Discussion

5.1. Discussion of the Results

This study discusses the effects of the main color, visual effect, and dial styling of AR dashboards on drivers' visual imagery evaluation and subjective preference. Previous studies have shown that in in-vehicle AR user interfaces, blue, green, and yellow colors exhibit superior robustness and response efficiency compared to other colors [72]. This study further concluded through visual imagery experiments that among the main colors, drivers prefer blue the most, followed by green, with yellow being the least preferred. However, recent studies have shown that AR heads-up displays (HUDs) with green as the main color have the shortest response time [12]. In addition, there are studies showing that red, yellow, green, and orange perform better than other colors in terms of visual search performance and cognitive efficiency [14]. These studies have inconsistent evaluation results regarding dominant colors, possibly due to experimental factors such as display technology [73], ambient illumination [13], and driving scenes [14]. For example, the photophysical properties of blue luminescent materials are worse than those of other colors [74], particularly in terms of luminous efficiency, maximum brightness, and the working life of blue quantum dots [75]. In any case, previous research mostly focused on the objective effectiveness of in-vehicle AR display technology and did not study the impact of in-vehicle AR interface displays on the driver's emotional experience. This research has identified a new direction for the automotive AR interface display field. From the dimensions of the driver's emotional experience, blue is the best choice. Although blue light display technology is more challenging to develop than other colors of light, we recommend that automobile manufacturers and related technicians prioritize advancing blue light display technology to meet the emotional needs of most drivers.

In addition, the interaction between visual effects and dial styling was significantly different. This is similar to the results of Chen and Lu [76], which showed no significant difference between round and unconventional-shaped (hexagonal) designs in balanced aesthetics experiments, but there is a significant difference between vertical and horizontal ellipse images. Our results indicate that there is a significant difference between the vertical 3D design of a circle and the horizontal 3D design of a round. The round vertical 3D design was more popular among drivers, and the visual imagery of this proposal was rated higher. Our study further revealed an interaction between round and unconventional-shapes in terms of visual effect, where the vertical 3D design of unconventional-shapes was significantly less preferred than the horizontal 3D design of unconventional-shapes. Drivers preferred the unconventional-shaped horizontal 3D design more, and the visual imagery of that proposal was rated higher. This finding complements Chen and Lu [76]'s theory on the interaction between styling and visual effect in visual aesthetics. Research on the emotional aspects of products suggests that emotional experiences will help increase product utilization and influence future purchase choices [77]. Therefore, in developing in-vehicle AR dashboard HMIs, automobile manufacturers should pay attention to the effects of the main color, visual effect, and dial styling on the driver's emotional experience.

5.2. Methodological Contributions

One of the important innovations of this study is the combination of various MCDM and Kansei engineering methods to evaluate the visual image of vehicle HMIs. The visual image evaluation of vehicle HMIs is influenced by factors such as participants' personal preferences, culture, and knowledge level and exhibits typical gray system characteristics and ambiguity [78]. Therefore, the decision-making method using FAHP-GRA is particularly suitable. Recently, Yunuo and Xia [44] confirmed in a study on vehicle-mounted AR-HUD that AHP-GRA is more reliable than entropy weights TOPSIS in determining weights. Although the study by Yunuo and Xia [44] described the implementation of AHP-GRA in HMIs in great detail, it did not use the methods of Kansei engineering and factor analysis to construct evaluation indicators, which may affect the objectivity of the program. In previous research, we made a preliminary attempt to apply AHP-GRA in the usability evaluation of application programming interfaces and determined the feasibility of this method in the HMI field through a triangulation model [79]. This study further combines fuzzy system theory with the AHP-GRA method and introduces the research method of Kansei engineering to conduct visual image research on vehicle-mounted AR instrument panels. Additionally, we conducted interactive verification of the subjective preference results and visual image assessment results through factorial experiments to ensure the reliability of the MCDM results.

5.3. Limitations and Future Directions

Despite the rigorous examination conducted in this study, several limitations should be considered. First, this research only explored the visual imagery of three variables within AR dashboards. Future studies could expand to include more variables, such as the size, layout, and brightness of elements in AR dashboards. Second, the participants in this study were primarily drivers from the Chinese region, so caution should be exercised when generalizing the findings to consumers in other countries or regions. Future research could involve a comparative analysis of drivers from different countries or regions. Finally, the results of this study have not yet been tested in real-world settings. Future research may need to conduct usability tests and incorporate eye-tracking data and driving performance into the evaluation.

6. Conclusions

This study is highly innovative, both from a methodological perspective and within the context of in-vehicle HMI research. Methodologically, this study integrates Kansei engineering, fuzzy system theory, AHP, and GRA, proposing a subjective evaluation method and process for assessing the visual imagery of in-vehicle HMIs. This approach helps reduce the uncertainty in HMI design and effectively addresses the ambiguity inherent in human factors. The FAHP results reveal that the dimensions affecting the visual imagery evaluation of AR dashboards include novelty and splendor, technological and aesthetic aspects, visibility and conciseness, agility and reliability, and smoothness and naturalness. Among these dimensions, "visibility and conciseness" received the highest weight, while "novelty and splendor" received the lowest. Further GRA analysis indicated that the design featuring blue planar and unconventional-shaped dials (Proposal 10) was the optimal choice based on visual imagery criteria. Conversely, the design with yellow vertical 3D and unconventional-shaped dials (Proposal 17) was the least favored, a finding that was corroborated by factorial experiments.

The factorial experiment results demonstrated that the main color of the AR dashboard had the most significant impact on drivers' subjective preferences. Blue was the most favored main color, followed by green, with yellow being the least favored. Avoiding vertical 3D visual effects in green AR dashboards is also recommended. The interaction between visual effects and dial styling in AR dashboards also requires special attention. In round dials, drivers preferred vertical 3D effects more than horizontal 3D effects. Conversely, horizontal 3D effects were more favored in unconventional-shaped dials than vertical 3D effects. These findings provide scientific and detailed guidance for future SEV-AR dashboard HMI designs, helping to enhance the in-vehicle user experience and, consequently, improving SEV vehicles' market competitiveness.

Author Contributions: Conceptualization, J.-L.L. and M.-C.Z.; Methodology, J.-L.L.; Validation, J.-L.L.; Investigation, J.-L.L.; Resources, M.-C.Z.; Data curation, M.-C.Z.; Writing—original draft, J.-L.L.; Writing—review & editing, J.-L.L. and M.-C.Z.; Visualization, J.-L.L.; Supervision, M.-C.Z.; Project administration, M.-C.Z. All authors have read and agreed to the published version of the manuscript.

Funding: This research received no external funding.

Data Availability Statement: Due to confidentiality agreements, supporting data can only be made available to bona fide researchers subject to a non-disclosure agreement. Details of the data and how to request access are available from Meng-Cong Zheng (zmcdesign@gmail.com) at the National Taipei University of Technology.

Acknowledgments: The authors would like to very thank the Desay SV Automotive Co., Ltd. CT_UXD Department (former name: IND) experts for their selfless support in the experimental process.

Conflicts of Interest: The authors declare no conflict of interest.

References

1. Martins, L.S.; Guimarães, L.F.; Junior, A.B.B.; Tenório, J.A.S.; Espinosa, D.C.R. Electric car battery: An overview on global demand, recycling and future approaches towards sustainability. *J. Environ. Manag.* **2021**, *295*, 113091. [CrossRef] [PubMed]
2. Aijaz, I.; Ahmad, A. Electric vehicles for environmental sustainability. In *Smart Technologies for Energy and Environmental Sustainability*; Springer: Cham, Switzerland, 2022; pp. 131–145.
3. Kumar, R.R.; Alok, K. Adoption of electric vehicle: A literature review and prospects for sustainability. *J. Clean. Prod.* **2020**, *253*, 119911. [CrossRef]
4. Haque, T.S.; Rahman, M.H.; Islam, M.R.; Razzak, M.A.; Badal, F.R.; Ahamed, M.H.; Moyeen, S.I.; Das, S.K.; Ali, M.F.; Tasneem, Z. A review on driving control issues for smart electric vehicles. *IEEE Access* **2021**, *9*, 135440–135472. [CrossRef]
5. Bhatti, G.; Mohan, H.; Singh, R.R. Towards the future of smart electric vehicles: Digital twin technology. *Renew. Sustain. Energy Rev.* **2021**, *141*, 110801. [CrossRef]
6. EqualOcean. China's SEV Annual Sales List Announced. 2024. Available online: https://www.iyiou.com/data/202401161059254 (accessed on 1 June 2024).
7. Boboc, R.G.; Gîrbacia, F.; Butilă, E.V. The application of augmented reality in the automotive industry: A systematic literature review. *Appl. Sci.* **2020**, *10*, 4259. [CrossRef]
8. Devagiri, J.S.; Paheding, S.; Niyaz, Q.; Yang, X.; Smith, S. Augmented Reality and Artificial Intelligence in industry: Trends, tools, and future challenges. *Expert Syst. Appl.* **2022**, *207*, 118002. [CrossRef]
9. Choi, K.-H.; Park, S.-Y.; Kim, S.-H.; Lee, K.-S.; Park, J.-H.; Cho, S.-I.; Park, J.-H. Methods to detect road features for video-based in-vehicle navigation systems. *J. Intell. Transp. Syst.* **2010**, *14*, 13–26. [CrossRef]
10. Akaho, K.; Nakagawa, T.; Yamaguchi, Y.; Kawai, Y.; Kato, H.; Nishida, S. Route guidance by a car navigation system based on augmented reality. *Electr. Eng. Jpn.* **2012**, *180*, 43–54. [CrossRef]
11. Calvi, A.; D'Amico, F.; Ferrante, C.; Ciampoli, L.B. Evaluation of augmented reality cues to improve the safety of left-turn maneuvers in a connected environment: A driving simulator study. *Accid. Anal. Prev.* **2020**, *148*, 105793. [CrossRef]
12. Liu, S.; Yin, G. Research on Color Adaptation of Automobile Head-up Display Interface. In Proceedings of the 2021 IEEE 8th International Conference on Industrial Engineering and Applications (ICIEA), Chengdu, China, 23–26 April 2021.
13. Zhong, X.; Cheng, Y.; Tian, L. Color Visibility Evaluation of In-Vehicle AR-HUD Under Different Illuminance. In Proceedings of the International Conference on Information Economy, Data Modeling and Cloud Computing, ICIDC 2022, Qingdao, China, 17–19 June 2022.
14. Li, Y.; Wang, Y.; Song, F.; Liu, Y. Assessing Gender Perception Differences in Color Combinations in Digital Visual Interfaces Using Eye tracking–The Case of HUD. *Int. J. Hum.–Comput. Interact.* **2023**, 1–17. [CrossRef]
15. Kim, H.; Gabbard, J.L. Assessing distraction potential of augmented reality head-up displays for vehicle drivers. *Hum. Factors* **2022**, *64*, 852–865. [CrossRef] [PubMed]
16. Abdi, L.; Meddeb, A. In-vehicle augmented reality system to provide driving safety information. *J. Vis.* **2018**, *21*, 163–184. [CrossRef]
17. Chatzopoulos, D.; Bermejo, C.; Huang, Z.; Hui, P. Mobile augmented reality survey: From where we are to where we go. *IEEE Access* **2017**, *5*, 6917–6950. [CrossRef]

18. Hassenzahl, M.; Tractinsky, N. User experience-a research agenda. *Behav. Inf. Technol.* **2006**, *25*, 91–97. [CrossRef]
19. Nasermoadeli, A.; Ling, K.C.; Maghnati, F. Evaluating the impacts of customer experience on purchase intention. *Int. J. Bus. Manag.* **2013**, *8*, 128. [CrossRef]
20. Deng, L.; Turner, D.E.; Gehling, R.; Prince, B. User experience, satisfaction, and continual usage intention of IT. *Eur. J. Inf. Syst.* **2010**, *19*, 60–75. [CrossRef]
21. Nagamachi, M. Kansei engineering: A new ergonomic consumer-oriented technology for product development. *Int. J. Ind. Ergon.* **1995**, *15*, 3–11. [CrossRef]
22. Nagamachi, M. Kansei engineering as a powerful consumer-oriented technology for product development. *Appl. Ergon.* **2002**, *33*, 289–294. [CrossRef]
23. Simon, T.; Eklund, J.; Jan, R.A.; Nagamachi, M. Concepts, methods and tools in Kansei engineering. *Theor. Issues Ergon. Sci.* **2004**, *5*, 214–231.
24. Jia, L.-M.; Tung, F.-W. A study on consumers' visual image evaluation of wrist wearables. *Entropy* **2021**, *23*, 1118. [CrossRef]
25. Chen, C.-H.; Lin, Z. The application of fuzzy theory in the evaluation of visual images of smartphone rear cameras. *Appl. Sci.* **2021**, *11*, 3555. [CrossRef]
26. Lin, Z.; Zhai, W.; Li, S.; Li, X. Evaluating the impact of the center control touch screen of new energy vehicles on user visual imagery and preferences. *Displays* **2023**, *78*, 102435. [CrossRef]
27. Wang, P.; Chu, J.; Yu, S.; Chen, C.; Hu, Y. A consumers' Kansei needs mining and purchase intention evaluation method based on fuzzy linguistic theory and multi-attribute decision making method. *Adv. Eng. Inform.* **2024**, *59*, 102267. [CrossRef]
28. Li, S.; Chen, C.-H.; Lin, Z. Evaluating the impact of wait indicators on user visual imagery and speed perception in mobile application interfaces. *Int. J. Ind. Ergon.* **2022**, *88*, 103280. [CrossRef]
29. Cao, X.; Watanabe, M.; Ono, K. How character-centric game icon design affects the perception of gameplay. *Appl. Sci.* **2021**, *11*, 9911. [CrossRef]
30. Guo, F.; Liu, W.L.; Cao, Y.; Liu, F.T.; Li, M.L. Optimization design of a webpage based on Kansei engineering. *Hum. Factors Ergon. Manuf. Serv. Ind.* **2016**, *26*, 110–126. [CrossRef]
31. Oey, E.; Ngudjiharto, B.; Cyntia, W.; Natashia, M.; Hansopaheluwakan, S. Driving process improvement from customer preference with Kansei engineering, SIPA and QFD methods-a case study in an instant concrete manufacturer. *Int. J. Product. Qual. Manag.* **2020**, *31*, 28–48. [CrossRef]
32. Chen, M.-C.; Hsu, C.-L.; Chang, K.-C.; Chou, M.-C. Applying Kansei engineering to design logistics services—A case of home delivery service. *Int. J. Ind. Ergon.* **2015**, *48*, 46–59. [CrossRef]
33. Restuputri, D.P.; Indriani, T.R.; Masudin, I. The effect of logistic service quality on customer satisfaction and loyalty using kansei engineering during the COVID-19 pandemic. *Cogent Bus. Manag.* **2021**, *8*, 1906492. [CrossRef]
34. Hartono, M. The modified Kansei Engineering-based application for sustainable service design. *Int. J. Ind. Ergon.* **2020**, *79*, 102985. [CrossRef]
35. Zeleny, M. *MCDM: Past Decade and Future Trends: A Source Book of Multiple Criteria Decision Making*; JAI Press: London, UK, 1984.
36. Keeney, R. *Decisions with Multiple Objectives: Preferences and Value Trade-Offs*; Cambridge University Press: Cambridge, UK, 1993.
37. Sahoo, S.K.; Goswami, S.S. A comprehensive review of multiple criteria decision-making (MCDM) Methods: Advancements, applications, and future directions. *Decis. Mak. Adv.* **2023**, *1*, 25–48. [CrossRef]
38. Munier, N.; Hontoria, E. *Uses and Limitations of the AHP Method*; Springer: Berlin/Heidelberg, Germany, 2021.
39. Munier, N.; Hontoria, E.; Munier, N.; Hontoria, E. Shortcomings of the AHP Method. In *Uses and Limitations of the AHP Method: A Non-Mathematical and Rational Analysis*; Springer: Cham, Switzerland, 2021; pp. 41–90.
40. Hsu, C.-J.; Huang, C.-Y. Comparison of weighted grey relational analysis for software effort estimation. *Softw. Qual. J.* **2011**, *19*, 165–200. [CrossRef]
41. Shin, Y.B.; Lee, S.; Chun, S.G.; Chung, D. A critical review of popular multi-criteria decision making methodologies. *Issues Inf. Syst.* **2013**, *14*, 358–365.
42. Çelikbilek, Y.; Tüysüz, F. An in-depth review of theory of the TOPSIS method: An experimental analysis. *J. Manag. Anal.* **2020**, *7*, 281–300. [CrossRef]
43. Wang, T.; Yang, L. Combining GRA with a fuzzy QFD model for the new product design and development of Wickerwork Lamps. *Sustainability* **2023**, *15*, 4208. [CrossRef]
44. Cheng, Y.; Zhong, X.; Ye, M.; Tian, L. Usability Evaluation of in-Vehicle AR-HUD Interface Applying AHP-GRA. *Hum.-Centric Intell. Syst.* **2022**, *2*, 124–137.
45. Deng, J. Introduction to grey system theory. *J. Grey Syst.* **1989**, *1*, 1–24.
46. Wang, P.; Meng, P.; Zhai, J.-Y.; Zhu, Z.-Q. A hybrid method using experiment design and grey relational analysis for multiple criteria decision making problems. *Knowl.-Based Syst.* **2013**, *53*, 100–107. [CrossRef]
47. Kuo, Y.; Yang, T.; Huang, G.-W. The use of grey relational analysis in solving multiple attribute decision-making problems. *Comput. Ind. Eng.* **2008**, *55*, 80–93. [CrossRef]
48. Wu, H.-H. A comparative study of using grey relational analysis in multiple attribute decision making problems. *Qual. Eng.* **2002**, *15*, 209–217. [CrossRef]
49. Singh, M.; Pant, M. A review of selected weighing methods in MCDM with a case study. *Int. J. Syst. Assur. Eng. Manag.* **2021**, *12*, 126–144. [CrossRef]

50. Van Laarhoven, P.J.; Pedrycz, W. A fuzzy extension of Saaty's priority theory. *Fuzzy Sets Syst.* **1983**, *11*, 229–241. [CrossRef]
51. Zadeh, L.A. Fuzzy sets. *Inf. Control* **1965**, *8*, 338–353. [CrossRef]
52. Saaty, T.L. The analytic hierarchy process (AHP). *J. Oper. Res. Soc.* **1980**, *41*, 1073–1076.
53. Liu, Y.; Eckert, C.M.; Earl, C. A review of fuzzy AHP methods for decision-making with subjective judgements. *Expert Syst. Appl.* **2020**, *161*, 113738. [CrossRef]
54. Herrera, F.; Herrera-Viedma, E.; Chiclana, F. Multiperson decision-making based on multiplicative preference relations. *Eur. J. Oper. Res.* **2001**, *129*, 372–385. [CrossRef]
55. Wang, T.-K.; Zhang, Q.; Chong, H.-Y.; Wang, X. Integrated supplier selection framework in a resilient construction supply chain: An approach via analytic hierarchy process (AHP) and grey relational analysis (GRA). *Sustainability* **2017**, *9*, 289. [CrossRef]
56. Crozier, R.; Crozier, W.R. *Manufactured Pleasures: Psychological Responses to Design*; Manchester University Press: Manchester, UK, 1994.
57. Hsiao, K.-A.; Chen, L.-L. Fundamental dimensions of affective responses to product shapes. *Int. J. Ind. Ergon.* **2006**, *36*, 553–564. [CrossRef]
58. Francois, M.; Crave, P.; Osiurak, F.; Fort, A.; Navarro, J. Digital, analogue, or redundant speedometers for truck driving: Impact on visual distraction, efficiency and usability. *Appl. Ergon.* **2017**, *65*, 12–22. [CrossRef]
59. Nielsen, J. Usability Heuristics for User Interface Design. Available online: https://www.nngroup.com/articles/ten-usability-heuristics/ (accessed on 25 May 2024).
60. Dreyfuss, H.; Associates, H.D.; Tilley, A.R. *The Measure of Man and Woman: Human Factors in Design*; Whitney Library of Design: New York, NY, USA, 1993.
61. Kline, P. *An Easy Guide to Factor Analysis*; Routledge: London, UK, 2014.
62. Wu, F.; Lu, P.; Lin, Y.-C. Research on the Influence of Wheelsets on the Visual Imagery of City Bicycles. *Sustainability* **2022**, *14*, 2762. [CrossRef]
63. Buckley, J.J. Fuzzy hierarchical analysis. *Fuzzy Sets Syst.* **1985**, *17*, 233–247. [CrossRef]
64. Azzeh, M.; Neagu, D.; Cowling, P.I. Fuzzy grey relational analysis for software effort estimation. *Empir. Softw. Eng.* **2010**, *15*, 60–90. [CrossRef]
65. Guo, y.; Guo, W. Method for Determining the Distinguishing Coefficient in Grey Relational Analysis. *Arid Environ. Monit.* **1994**, *8*, 132–135.
66. Deng, J.L. *A Course on Grey System Theory*; Huazhong University of Science and Technology Press: Wuhan, China, 1990.
67. Mu, R.; Zhang, J. Research of hierarchy synthetic evaluation based on grey relational analysis. *Syst. Eng. Theory Pract.* **2008**, *28*, 125–130.
68. Gamst, G.; Meyers, L.S.; Guarino, A. *Analysis of Variance Designs: A Conceptual and Computational Approach with SPSS and SAS*; Cambridge University Press: Cambridge, UK, 2008.
69. Blanca, M.J.; Arnau, J.; García-Castro, F.J.; Alarcón, R.; Bono, R. Repeated measures ANOVA and adjusted F-tests when sphericity is violated: Which procedure is best? *Front. Psychol.* **2023**, *14*, 1192453. [CrossRef]
70. Zahmat Doost, E.; Zhang, W. The Impact of Different Interruptions on Perceived Stress: Developing a Multimodal Measurement for Early Detection. *Int. J. Hum.–Comput. Interact.* **2024**, 1–21. [CrossRef]
71. Coulombe, D. Two-way ANOVA with and without repeated measurements, tests of simple main effects, and multiple comparisons for microcomputers. *Behav. Res. Methods Instrum. Comput.* **1984**, *16*, 397–398. [CrossRef]
72. Merenda, C.; Smith, M.; Gabbard, J.; Burnett, G.; Large, D. Effects of real-world backgrounds on user interface color naming and matching in automotive AR HUDs. In Proceedings of the 2016 IEEE VR 2016 Workshop on Perceptual and Cognitive Issues in AR (PERCAR), Greenville, SC, USA, 19 March 2016.
73. Firth, M. *Introduction to Automotive Augmented Reality Head-Up Displays Using TI DLP® Technology*; Technical document; Texas Instruments Incorporated: Dallas, TX, USA, 2019.
74. Shirasaki, Y.; Supran, G.J.; Bawendi, M.G.; Bulović, V. Emergence of colloidal quantum-dot light-emitting technologies. *Nat. Photonics* **2013**, *7*, 13–23. [CrossRef]
75. Kim, T.; Kim, K.-H.; Kim, S.; Choi, S.-M.; Jang, H.; Seo, H.-K.; Lee, H.; Chung, D.-Y.; Jang, E. Efficient and stable blue quantum dot light-emitting diode. *Nature* **2020**, *586*, 385–389. [CrossRef]
76. Chen, X.; Lu, Y.; Hao, G. Balanced Aesthetics: How Shape, Contrast, and Visual Force Affect Interface Layout. *Int. J. Hum.–Comput. Interact.* **2023**, 1–14. [CrossRef]
77. Jordan, P.W. Human factors for pleasure in product use. *Appl. Ergon.* **1998**, *29*, 25–33. [CrossRef] [PubMed]
78. Yan, H.-B.; Huynh, V.-N.; Murai, T.; Nakamori, Y. Kansei evaluation based on prioritized multi-attribute fuzzy target-oriented decision analysis. *Inf. Sci.* **2008**, *178*, 4080–4093. [CrossRef]
79. Lin, J.-L. Research on the Usability of Mobile Shopping Applications Based on Triangulation Model. National Cheng Kung University. 2021. Available online: https://nckur.lib.ncku.edu.tw/handle/987654321/204702 (accessed on 25 May 2024).

Disclaimer/Publisher's Note: The statements, opinions and data contained in all publications are solely those of the individual author(s) and contributor(s) and not of MDPI and/or the editor(s). MDPI and/or the editor(s) disclaim responsibility for any injury to people or property resulting from any ideas, methods, instructions or products referred to in the content.

Article

A Lightweight GCT-EEGNet for EEG-Based Individual Recognition Under Diverse Brain Conditions

Laila Alshehri and Muhammad Hussain *

Department of Computer Science, King Saud University, Riyadh 11421, Saudi Arabia; 441204115@student.ksu.edu.sa
* Correspondence: mhussain@ksu.edu.sa

Abstract: A robust biometric system is essential to mitigate various security threats. Electroencephalography (EEG) brain signals present a promising alternative to other biometric traits due to their sensitivity, non-duplicability, resistance to theft, and individual-specific dynamics. However, existing EEG-based biometric systems employ deep neural networks, such as convolutional neural networks (CNNs) and recurrent neural networks (RNNs), which face challenges such as high parameter complexity, limiting their practical application. Additionally, their ability to generalize across a large number of subjects remains unclear. Moreover, they have been validated on datasets collected in controlled environments, which do not accurately reflect real-world scenarios involving diverse brain conditions. To overcome these challenges, we propose a lightweight neural network model, GCT–EEGNet, which is based on the design ideas of a CNN model and incorporates an attention mechanism to pay attention to the appropriate frequency bands for extracting discriminative features relevant to the identity of a subject despite diverse brain conditions. First, a raw EEG signal is decomposed into frequency bands and then passed to GCT–EEGNet for feature extraction, which utilizes a gated channel transformation (GCT) layer to selectively emphasize informative features from the relevant frequency bands. The extracted features were used for subject recognition through a cosine similarity metric that measured the similarity between feature vectors of different EEG trials to identify individuals. The proposed method was evaluated on a large dataset comprising 263 subjects. The experimental results demonstrated that the method achieved a correct recognition rate (CRR) of 99.23% and an equal error rate (EER) of 0.0014, corroborating its robustness against different brain conditions. The proposed model maintains low parameter complexity while keeping the expressiveness of representations, even with unseen subjects.

Keywords: EEG brain signals; biometric recognition; convolutional neural network; deep learning

MSC: 68T07

1. Introduction

Identity recognition is crucial for verifying users and preventing imposters in various biometric applications. Traditional methods such as cards, keys, and passwords are widely used, but they are susceptible to loss or theft. Biometric traits such as fingerprints, iris appearance, voice, and gait offer promising alternatives, though each has its limitations [1,2]. For instance, biometrics involving the eyes, fingers, or faces cannot be easily replaced once compromised. To address these security concerns, EEG-based brain biometrics have emerged as a viable solution [3]. The EEG has been extensively used in medicine to assess brain health and in brain–computer interface systems, and is gaining acceptance as a biometric method due to its user-friendliness, the availability of portable headsets, and its non-invasive nature [4]. The EEG records electrical activity across the scalp using electrodes, offering advantages such as cost-effectiveness, temporal precision, resistance to theft, and the ability to verify live subjects. Each individual's EEG is unique, exhibiting

Citation: Alshehri, L.; Hussain, M. A Lightweight GCT-EEGNet for EEG-Based Individual Recognition Under Diverse Brain Conditions. *Mathematics* **2024**, *12*, 3286. https://doi.org/10.3390/math12203286

Academic Editors: Grigoreta-Sofia Cojocar, Adriana-Mihaela Guran and Laura-Silvia Dioşan

Received: 22 September 2024
Revised: 16 October 2024
Accepted: 16 October 2024
Published: 20 October 2024

Copyright: © 2024 by the authors. Licensee MDPI, Basel, Switzerland. This article is an open access article distributed under the terms and conditions of the Creative Commons Attribution (CC BY) license (https://creativecommons.org/licenses/by/4.0/).

minimal intra-subject and significant inter-subject variability [5]. The primary challenge lies in developing a reliable EEG-based recognition system that recognizes individuals despite their brain activity variability. Numerous EEG-based biometric methods have evolved from those based on hand-engineered features using conventional machine learning to more advanced modern techniques such as convolutional neural networks (CNNs) [6–10] and recurrent neural networks (RNNs) [11–14]. Traditional methods rely on hand-engineered features, and they often preprocess EEG recordings to remove unwanted artifacts such as power supply noise, eye blinking, or muscle activity [15]. After preprocessing, features are extracted using methods such as auto-regressive (AR) models [16,17] and power spectral density (PSD) [18–20]. They are often difficult to tune and time-consuming, and they usually require expert knowledge. The designs of methods based on white-box models, such as auto-regressive models, assume simple and linear relationships in the data, making them less effective in capturing intricate patterns in EEG signals [4,21]. Therefore, simpler models often miss essential details, whereas EEG signals vary between subjects and brain states, and intricate patterns play a key role in discriminating subjects' identities. In contrast, a deep learning model automatically learns intricate patterns from the data hierarchically, making it better suited to capture discriminative features relevant to the identity of subjects from their EEG signals. There are many research works based on deep learning for EEG-based recognition [6–14]. However, they are not generalizable because their designs are based on small datasets that were collected during specific tasks with fewer than 60 participants. This limits their applicability to real-world scenarios. Further research is needed to improve the generalizability and applicability of EEG-based biometric systems by developing task-independent feature extraction methods and ensuring low time and space complexity in the model design. This study proposes a solution to tackle these issues through a compact and efficient deep learning model that automatically captures discriminative information for individual identification, thereby enhancing the system's usability and applicability in real-world scenarios. The key contributions of this research include the following:

- A lightweight deep neural network model based on the design ideas of CNN models and an attention mechanism to selectively focus on salient frequency bands for extracting discriminative features relevant to the identity of a subject from an EEG trial under various brain conditions.
- A robust EEG-based system for identification and authentication that is agnostic to various brain conditions, i.e., resting states, emotions, alcoholism, etc., and one that uses a short EEG trial of one second to reveal or authenticate the identity of a subject.
- A thorough evaluation for validating the proposed EEG-based system using a large dataset of 263 subjects who underwent EEG trials that were captured in various brain states.

The remainder of this study is organized as follows: Section 2 presents an overview of the existing works and Section 3 describes the proposed method. Section 4 explains the evaluation method and Section 5 describes the detailed experiments with discussions. Finally, the findings are summed up and future research is discussed in Section 6.

2. Related Work

The use of EEG-based biometrics has been explored since the 1980s, leveraging distinct electrical activity patterns for individual identification [22]. Over the years, research efforts have increasingly focused on extracting discriminative information from EEG recordings. Maiorana [23] highlighted the effectiveness of deep learning techniques, particularly convolutional neural networks (CNNs) and recurrent neural networks (RNNs), in extracting unique features from various EEG representations and architectures. This section reviews the current literature on deep learning methods for EEG biometrics, covering both identification and verification approaches.

In the identification task, CNNs gained increasing attention due to their exceptional feature learning and classification abilities. Das et al. [11] applied a CNN–LSTM model to identify 109 subjects from PhysioNet dataset, achieving 99.9 for eyes-closed (EC) and 98% for eyes-open (EO) tasks in trials of 12 s. Similarly, Jijomon and Vinod [12] developed a CNN–LSTM model that was applied to a private dataset consisting of 20 subjects performing auditory tasks (AEPs), reaching a 99.5% CRR with trials of 2 s. Wilaiprasitporn et al. [14] also employed CNN–LSTM and CNN–GRU for 2D meshes on the DEAP dataset, which involved 32 subjects performing emotion-related tasks, achieving a CRR of over 99% with a 10 s trial length. Jin et al. [24] proposed the CTNN model, which was employed on a private dataset of 20 subjects performing different brain tasks, achieving a CRR of 99.9%.

Different CNN-based models have also been used for verification tasks, such as spatial–temporal convolutions [7], depth-wise separable convolutions [25], and Siamese networks [9]. Chen et al. [7] used a CNN with global spatial and local temporal kernels on multiple datasets with different brain tasks, achieving an EER of 2.94. Debie et al. [25] applied a depth-wise separable convolution technique to a CNN on two public datasets with fewer than 54 subjects, performing different kinds of tasks, achieving a false acceptance rate (FAR) and false rejection rate (FRR) of less than 2%. In [13], a CNN–LSTM model was applied to the PhysioNet dataset, achieving an EER of 0.41. Seha and Hatzinakos [10] used 3D tensors with a CNN encoder, and the features were classified using an SVM on a private dataset of 13 subjects performing AEPs, achieving EERs between 3 and 7.5%.

Some previous methods treated identification and verification tasks as classification problems, making them impractical in real-world applications. In contrast, other studies [26–28] treated these tasks as matching problems using CNNs and focusing on specific protocols such as eyes-open (EO) and eyes-closed (EC) tasks or time-locked brain protocols (e.g., event-related potentials, ERPs). Alsumari et al. [27] and Bidgoly et al. [26] used the PhysioNet dataset, achieving correct recognition rates (CRRs) of 99.05% and 98.04%, with error rates of 0.187 and 1.96, respectively. In [28], ERPs were extracted from two datasets with 40 and 41 subjects, achieving CRRs of 95.63% and 99.92% and equal error rates (EERs) of 1.37% and 0.14%, respectively.

Although EEG-based biometric systems have made great progress over the years, research in this area still faces significant challenges. First, some methods [7,11,14,19,24] stack layers to CNNs or apply an RNN on top of a CNN in an end-to-end model, leading to parameter explosion as the number of subjects increases. To lower the number of parameters, the recognition problem should be treated as a matching problem. Additionally, most research works rely on private datasets or datasets with fewer than 100 subjects, making them less generalizable. These systems often need repeated stimuli in controlled environments, requiring subjects' cooperation to create the same brain state each time, which is not always possible because brain states are dynamic and not constantly at rest. In addition, external factors such as fatigue, mood, and alcohol use are not considered in many studies such that most research focuses on datasets such as PhysioNet, DEAP, and private datasets, which are limited to specific tasks such as motor imagery (MI), visual evoked potentials (VEPs), and auditory evoked potentials (AEPs).

Further, although some studies such as [11,14] achieved high accuracies, they used long trial lengths of 10 and 12 s, respectively. Jijomon and Vinod [12] also achieved high identification with only two electrodes, but their study involved a small number of subjects, limiting its applicability to real-world scenarios. End-to-end models come with a high cost in terms of time and space, as they need to be retrained every time a new subject registers. With a large number of individuals, the number of parameters can grow rapidly. While some techniques, such as depth-wise separable convolutions [24], help reduce spatial complexity, the overall computational demands and the need to retrain models for new subjects further limit their scalability. All these problems make the models less efficient for real-time applications.

Despite advancements in EEG-based biometric systems, ensuring effective performance in the presence of varying mental and physical activities remains a challenge, as EEG signals are influenced by factors such as movement, artifacts, fatigue, and emotions. These issues necessitate the development of a model that focuses on learning intricate intrinsic and discriminative features from EEG trials across diverse brain states, including often neglected psychological factors such as fatigue. To address these issues, inspired by the design of EEGNet [29] and the limitations of the existing deep models for EEG-based recognition, we designed a model that incorporates depth-wise separable convolutions and attention mechanisms to focus on the most important EEG features, improving accuracy while reducing complexity.

3. The Proposed Method

We address the recognition problem using EEG brain signals as a biometric modality. First, we define and formulate the problem. The challenging part of the solution to this problem is the extraction of discriminative features from EEG signals. We present the details of a lightweight deep neural network model for feature extraction from EEG trials.

3.1. Problem Specification and Formulation

In biometric recognition, there are two primary tasks. Given an EEG trial (a query trial) of a subject, the aim is to reveal (identification problem) or authenticate (verification problem) the identity l of the subject. In the identification task, the system determines the identity of an unknown subject by matching the query EEG trial x against the trials of all subjects in the gallery set; this task is formulated as a one-to-many matching problem. Identification can be with a closed set, where the trials of the query subject are known to be in the gallery set, or an open set, where the query subject may not be in the gallery set; this trial design is more challenging. In the verification task, the system verifies the claimed identity of a subject by comparing the query EEG trial x with the EEG trials of the same subject in the gallery set; this task is formulated as a one-to-one matching problem.

We represent an EEG trial or epoch as a matrix of size $C \times T$, i.e., $x \in R^{C \times T}$, where C is the number of channels used to capture the brain's electrical activity over different locations on the scalp, and T is the number of timestamps recorded within a fixed time interval. Let $X = \{X_1, X_2, \ldots, X_N\}$ be the collection of EEG trials acquired from N subjects, such that $X_i = \{x_1^i, x_2^i, \ldots, x_n^i\}$ is the set of trials from the ith subject; for simplicity, we write this as $X_i = \{x_1, x_2, \ldots, x_{ni}\}$. In addition, let $L = \{1, 2, \ldots, N\}$ be the set of subject labels/IDs, and $l \in L$ be the ID or label of the lth subject. Let $V = \{V_1, V_2, \ldots, V_N\}$, where $V_i = \{v_1^i, v_2^i, \ldots, v_n^i\}$ is the set of feature vectors extracted from the EEG trials $x_1, x_2, \ldots, x_{ni}$ corresponding to the ith subject; for simplicity, we write this as $V_i = \{v_1, v_2, \ldots, v_{ni}\}$. The crucial part of the design of the recognition system is the extraction of discriminative features v_i from EEG trials x_i. Inspired by the outstanding performance of deep learning models in automatic feature learning in various applications and, specifically, EEG-based applications [6,7], we design a lightweight deep model f for feature extraction in such a way that $f(x; \theta) = v$, where x is the input EEG trial, v is the feature vector extracted by f, and θ represents the learnable parameters of f. The complexity of the model depends on the learnable parameters θ; f must be designed so that this complexity is low to avoid overfitting.

For the design of an identification or verification system, we divide the available data of each subject into query and gallery sets, V_i^q and V_i^g, respectively. Let v_q and v_g be the feature vectors extracted from a query and a gallery trial, respectively, i.e., $v_q \in V_i^q$ and $v_g \in V_i^g$. We compute the matching score $s_{q,g} \in [0 \ 1]$ of v_q and v_g using the metric $d(v_q, v_g)$ and let t be a predefined threshold. In case of an open-set identification problem, let $s_i^q = max\{0, s_{q,g} | s_{q,g} \geq t, v_g \in V_i^g\}$ be the maximum matching score of the query vector v_q from each of the gallery vectors $v_g \in V_i^g$ of the ith subject. The predicted label of the query trail x_q is l_q, where $l_q = \underset{1 \leq i \leq N}{max}\{s_i^q | i = 1, 2, \ldots, N\}$. If each s_i^q is zero, the subject does not exist. In case of verification, let $s_i^q = max\{0, s_{q,g} | s_{q,g} \geq t, v_g \in V_i^g\}$ be the maximum matching score of the query vector v_q from each of the gallery vectors $v_g \in V_i^g$ of the query subject. The attempt is genuine if $s_i^q \neq 0$; otherwise, it is an impostor.

We examine metrics such as Euclidean, Manhattan, and cosine similarity to compute the similarity between two trials.

3.2. Deep-Learning-Based Feature Extractor

This section presents the details of a lightweight and task-independent deep model, GCT–EEGNet. Its architecture is inspired by EEGNet's success and excellent generalizability in various BCI paradigms [29]. It is designed as a feature extractor f to extract discriminative features relevant to the identity of a subject from their EEG trial x. Figure 1 provides an overview of the model architecture, and Table 1 gives its complete specification. First, an EEG trial x is preprocessed using the mapping ψ_1, which normalizes the trial and then decomposes it into frequency sub-bands (rhythms) using the discrete wavelet transform (DWT). Then, mapping ψ_2 assigns weights to each rhythm according to its contribution to learning discriminative features; it is implemented as an attention block that helps to pay attention to the significant rhythms. It follows the mappings ψ_3 and ψ_4, which learn low-level spectral–spatio–temporal features using temporal convolution ($TConv$), depth-wise channel convolution ($DCConv$), and average pooling. Finally, the mapping ψ_5 learns high-level spectral–spatio–temporal features using separable temporal convolution ($STCov$) and global average pooling (GAP) blocks. The output of GAP is the feature vector (v) used for identification and verification. Mathematically, f is a composition of the following five mappings:

$$f(x;\theta) = \psi_5 \circ \psi_4 \circ \psi_3 \circ \psi_2 \circ \psi_1(x) \tag{1}$$

where $\theta = \{\theta_2, \theta_3, \theta_4, \theta_5\}$ and $\theta_2, \theta_3, \theta_4, \theta_5$ are learnable parameters of ψ_2, ψ_3, ψ_4, and ψ_5, respectively. The details of each mapping are given in the following paragraphs. The GCT–EEGNet is trained as an end-to-end classification model; for this purpose, an FC layer with the softmax function is added after GAP during the training time. After training, the classification layer is removed, and the model is used as a standalone feature extractor.

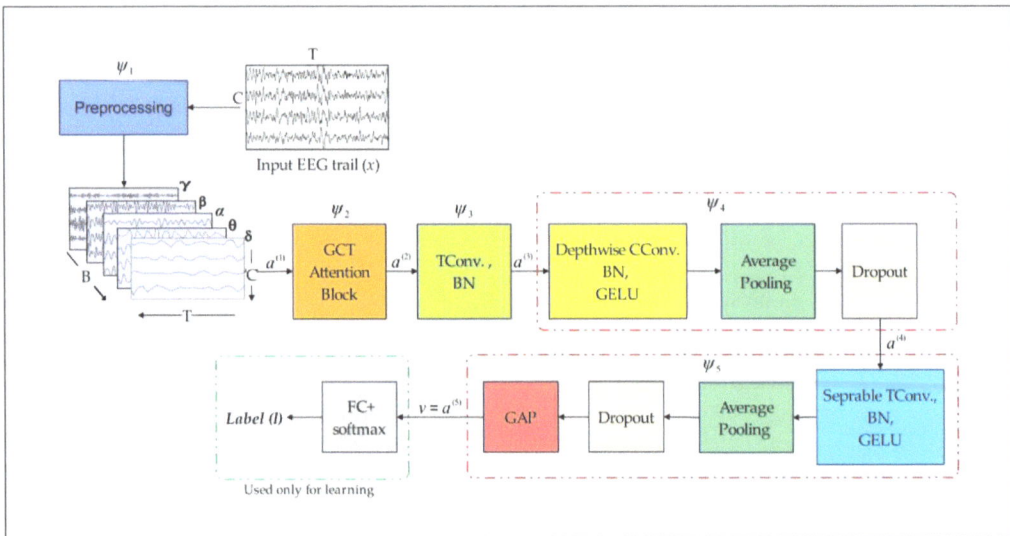

Figure 1. The architecture of the attention-based EEGNet model (GCT–EEGNet), where B is the number of frequency bands, T is the time points, C is the number of channels of the EEG signal, α, β, γ, θ, and δ are the alpha, beta, gamma, theta, and delta frequency bands, respectively. The $TConv$, $CConv$, BN, and GAP represent temporal and channel convolutions, batch normalization, and global average pooling layers, respectively, and v is the learned feature vector and l is the subject label.

Table 1. The specifications of the architecture of GCT–EEGNet, where C and D are hyperparameters, C is the number of channels, and D is a depth multiplier that specifies the number of spatial filters for each feature channel of the input feature map.

Transformation Mapping	Block Layers	#Kernel/Size	Output	Options	Learnable Parameters
	Input	-	32×128		0
ψ_1	Preprocessing	-	$5 \times 32 \times 128$		0
ψ_2	GCT	-	$5 \times 32 \times 128$		15
ψ_3	Conv2D	$64/1 \times 64$	$64 \times 32 \times 128$	Padding = same	20,480
	BatchNorm	-	$64 \times 32 \times 128$		512
ψ_4	Depthwise Conv2D	$D \times 64/C \times 1$	$64 \times 1 \times 128$	D = 1 C = 32	2048
	BatchNorm	-	$64 \times 1 \times 128$		512
	GELU	-	$64 \times 1 \times 128$		0
	Average Pooling2D	1×4	$64 \times 1 \times 32$		0
	Dropout	0.5	$64 \times 1 \times 32$		0
ψ_5	Separable Conv.	$128/1 \times 16$	$128 \times 1 \times 32$		9216
	BatchNorm	-	$128 \times 1 \times 32$		128
	GELU	-	$128 \times 1 \times 32$		0
	Average Pooling 2D	1×8	$128 \times 1 \times 4$		0
	Dropout	0.5	$128 \times 1 \times 4$		0
	GAP Layer	-	128		0
	FC + Softmax	-	236		30,444
	Total Parameters				62,764

3.2.1. Data Preprocessing

An EEG trial x is preprocessed with the mapping ψ_1, which is composed of the following two functions:

$$\psi_1(x) = \mathcal{F} \circ \aleph(x) \quad (2)$$

where the function $\aleph$ normalizes the input EEG trial x, and then the function $\mathcal{F}$ decomposes it into rhythms. The function $\aleph$ is defined using Z-score normalization [13] as follows:

$$x'_{c,t} = \frac{x_{c,t} - \mu_c}{\sigma_c}, \quad c = 1, 2, \ldots, C = 1, 2, \ldots, T \quad (3)$$

where c, t, μ_c, and σ_c refer to the channel identifier, the signal value at a specific time point, and the mean and standard deviation of the cth channel, respectively. Note that the function is applied on each channel individually to address differences in the feature unit and scale while improving the convergence speed. Instead of utilizing the entire frequency spectrum, which is rarely employed in biometrics, specific frequency bands or rhythms known to be more discriminative are used [30]. The study in [15] indicated that EEG bands below 50 Hz have higher energy for biometric identification. Consequently, the function $\mathcal{F}$ decomposes each EEG trial into frequency bands—delta (1–4 Hz), theta (4–8 Hz), alpha (8–16 Hz), beta (16–32 Hz), and gamma (32–50 Hz)—to assess their significance in the recognition process. Following a previous study [31], the function $\mathcal{F}$ is based on the DWT due to the nonstationary rapid fluctuations in EEG [32]. The DWT with the fourth-order Daubechies mother wavelet (db4) is used to decompose an EEG segment into the A5 (low-frequency) and D1–D5 (high-frequency) bands, where A5 is the delta (δ) band, while D2 to D5 are the theta (θ), alpha (α), beta (β), and low gamma (γ) bands, respectively. The choice of the DWT, specifically the db4 wavelet, is well suited for EEG analysis because its morphology is similar to that of EEG data [33,34]. Finally, the mapping ψ_1 transforms the input EEG trial $x \in R^{C \times T}$ into a tensor $a^{(1)} \epsilon R^{B \times C \times T}$ of B bands, C channels, and T time samples, as depicted in Figure 1.

3.2.2. GCT Attention Block

For subject recognition, not all brain rhythms and channels are equally important. Therefore, identifying the most significant ones without extensive experiments is crucial. To address this issue, we employ an attention mechanism using the GCT block with mapping ψ_2, which is a composition of the following mappings:

$$\psi_2\left(a^{(1)};\theta_2\right) = \mathcal{X}_4 \circ \mathcal{X}_3 \circ \mathcal{X}_2 \circ \mathcal{X}_1\left(a^{(1)};\eta\right) \tag{4}$$

where $\theta_2 = \{\eta, \lambda, \omega\}$ are learnable parameters of $\mathcal{X}_1$ and $\mathcal{X}_3$, respectively. The GCT [35] is a simple and effective attention module that simulates channel interactions without extra parameters. It helps prioritize and emphasize key rhythms and channels for the recognition task. It consists of the following three main components: global context embedding, channel normalization, and gating mechanism, as depicted in Figure 2.

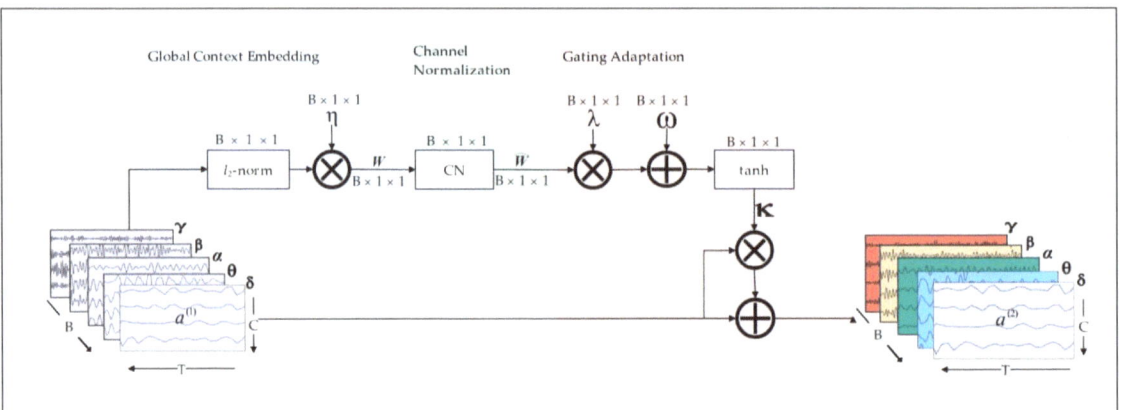

Figure 2. Gate channel transformation (GCT) module, where B is the number of frequency bands, T is the time points, C is the number of channels of the EEG signal, α, β, γ, θ, and δ are the alpha, beta, gamma, theta, and delta frequency bands, respectively. η denotes the trainable embedding weights, W represents the global context information, λ and ω represent the gating weights and biases, and κ is the output of tanh function. Different colors in the output $a^{(1)}$ indicate the varying significance assigned to each band.

Initially, global contextual information is captured by mapping $\mathcal{X}_1$ using the l_2-*norm* from the EEG trail $a^{(1)} \in R^{B \times C \times T}$ as follows:

$$\mathcal{X}_1\left(a^{(1)};\eta\right) = W = [w_1, w_2, \ldots, w_b]^t, \quad W \in R^{B \times 1 \times 1} \tag{5}$$

$$w_b = \eta_b \sqrt{\left[\sum_{i=1}^{C}\sum_{j=1}^{T}\left(a^{(1)}{}_b^{i,j}\right)^2\right] + \varepsilon}, \quad b = 1, 2, \ldots, B \tag{6}$$

where $W = [w_1, w_2, \ldots, w_b]^t$ represents the globally collected contextual information along each frequency band dimension $b \in B$, ε serves as a small constant to avoid the derivation problem at zero, η denotes the trainable embedding weights for controlling and emphasizing each frequency band's significance, and C and T refer to the number of channels and time points, respectively. Then, channel normalization (CN) is applied using mapping $\mathcal{X}_2$ by normalizing each component w_b of W, as shown in the following Equation (7):

$$\mathcal{X}_2(W) = \hat{W} = (\hat{w}_1, \hat{w}_2, \ldots, \hat{w}_b)^t, \quad \hat{W} \in R^{B \times 1 \times 1} \tag{7}$$

where

$$\hat{w}_b = \frac{\sqrt{B} \cdot w_b}{\sqrt{\left(\sum_{b=1}^{B} w_b^2\right) + \varepsilon}} \quad (8)$$

and the scaler $\sqrt{B}$ is used to adjust the scale of $\hat{W} = (\hat{w}_1, \hat{w}_2, \ldots, \hat{w}_b)$. This adjustment helps prevent $\hat{w}_b$ from becoming too small when the number of frequency bands is large. Channel normalization encourages channel interactions, whereas the l_2-*norm* operates across channels. It permits larger responses for some frequency band coefficients and suppresses others with smaller feedback. Finally, using the normalized vector $\hat{W}$ and the frequency bands $a^{(1)}$, gating adaptation takes place using mappings $\mathcal{X}_3$ and $\mathcal{X}_4$, as shown in the following:

$$\mathcal{X}_3(\hat{W}; \lambda, \omega) = \kappa = \tanh(\lambda \hat{W} + \omega), \ \kappa \in R^{B \times 1 \times 1}, \quad (9)$$

$$a^{(2)} = \mathcal{X}_4\left(a^{(1)}, \kappa\right) = a^{(1)} \oplus a^{(1)} \otimes \kappa \ ; \ a^{(2)} \in R^{B \times C \times T} \quad (10)$$

where λ and ω represent the gating weights and biases that control the activation of features, while $a^{(1)}$, $a^{(2)}$ denote input and output features for the gating mechanism module, respectively. The gating mechanism boosts competition and cooperation between frequency bands during the training process. To enhance feature extraction and classification performance, we employed convolutional layers to extract both temporal and spatial features.

3.2.3. Temporal Convolution Block

This block is designed to capture time-dependent features within an EEG trial, enabling the model to learn important temporal relationships that are crucial for distinguishing between different subjects. It operates along the time axis via a standard 2D convolutional layer φ_1, transforming the tensor $a^{(2)} \in R^{B \times C \times T}$ into the tensor $a^{(3)} \in R^{k_1 \times C \times T}$ through the mapping ψ_3 as defined below:

$$\psi_3\left(a^{(2)}; \theta_3\right) = BN \circ \varphi_1\left(a^{(2)}; \theta_3\right) \quad (11)$$

where k_1 is the number of kernels used for temporal convolution with a size of 1×64 to detect the temporal features for each frequency band. In our experiments, we set k_1 to 64. To enhance neural network performance and achieve faster training convergence, each convolutional layer is followed by a subsequent batch normalization (BN) layer [36].

3.2.4. Depth-Wise Channel Convolution Block

To reduce the model's computational complexity while extracting spatial features, a depth-wise channel convolution layer φ_2 is applied. Similar to the approaches used in Xception [37] and MobileNet [38], this layer applies a single filter per input channel, effectively isolating channel-specific features without the overhead of traditional convolution operations. Using φ_2, the mapping ψ_4 transforms $a^{(3)}$ into $a^{(4)} \in R^{k_2 \times 1 \times \frac{T}{4}}$ as follows:

$$\psi_4\left(a^{(3)}; \theta_4\right) = \mathcal{P}_a \circ g \circ BN \circ \varphi_2\left(a^{(3)}; \theta_4\right) \quad (12)$$

where k_2 is the number of kernels, each of size $C \times 1$, and C is the number of channels. These kernels are applied along the spatial (channel) axis, enabling the network to learn D spatial kernels, with each kernel being dedicated to a distinct feature map. The result is an output feature map of an extended dimension $D \times k_2$. This approach provides the following two key advantages: first, it serves as a spatial cross-channel feature learner, enhancing the global feature extraction, especially in multi-channel EEG data. Second, it reduces the number of learnable parameters, as this layer is not connected to all outputs from the preceding layer. Then, it is followed by *BN*. Unlike the original EEGNet activation function g, which utilizes exponential linear units (ELUs), we employ the Gaussian error linear unit (GELU) [39], which was motivated by its success in vision transformers (ViTs) [40]. It is applied in the second and third convolutional layers, combining the benefits of dropout [41] and randomly removing neurons during the training process. To further reduce dimensionality, an average pooling layer $\mathcal{P}_a$ with a window of size 1×4 is employed after the GELU layers. All convolution layers are applied with a stride of one.

3.2.5. Separable Temporal Convolution Block

Finally, the separable convolution layer φ_3 integrates depth-wise and pointwise convolutions to decompose the convolution process further, thereby enabling the model to process spatial and temporal features independently. This approach not only improves the model's ability to capture complex patterns in EEG data but also enhances its computational efficiency, leading to more robust and accurate classification output. Specifically, this layer employs a 1×16 kernel to aggregate individual feature maps. Then, a pointwise convolution with 128 kernels, each of size 1×1, is employed to combine these feature maps optimally. This setup effectively exploits temporal and spatial features for individual recognition. Employing φ_3, the transformation map ψ_5 that converts the tensor $a^{(4)} \epsilon\ R^{k_2 \times 1 \times \frac{T}{4}}$ into $a^{(5)} \epsilon\ R^{k_2 \times 1 \times \frac{T}{4 \times 8}}$ is defined as follows:

$$\psi_5\left(a^{(4)};\ \theta_5\right) = \mathcal{P}_g \circ \mathcal{P}_a \circ g \circ BN \circ \varphi_3\left(a^{(4)};\ \theta_5\right) \tag{13}$$

where BN, g, and $\mathcal{P}_a$ denote the batch normalization, GELU, and average pooling with a window of size 1×8, respectively. Instead of incorporating a fully connected layer, which would increase the model complexity, a GAP layer $\mathcal{P}_g$ is utilized, where $\mathcal{P}_g\left(a^{(5)}\right) = v$. This serves later as a feature extraction layer. This GAP layer reduces feature dimensionality and model parameters for efficient feature extraction. The resulting feature vector v is then fed into a softmax classifier with N units, corresponding to the total number of subjects that the model is trained on.

3.2.6. Training of GCT–EEGNet

The network was trained as an end-to-end model using a categorical cross-entropy loss for 100 epochs with a batch size of 500. The AdamW optimizer [42] with its default parameters was used for training. The training stopped if validation loss did not improve for three consecutive epochs, and an early stopping technique [43] was employed to prevent overfitting.

For model evaluation, a stratified 10-fold cross-validation was applied based on the subjects. In each fold, the subjects were divided into the following two groups: 90% were used for training, and the remaining 10% were used for testing. This format ensured that each fold used distinct subjects for testing [44]. After training, the model was utilized as a feature extractor, and the identification and authentication performances were assessed using 10% of the subjects reserved for testing. All results are reported as the average performance across folds.

4. Evaluation Protocol

This section first describes the datasets used to evaluate the proposed method. Then, it provides an overview of the performance metrics used for evaluation. For evaluation, 10-fold cross-validation was used, as described in Section 3.2.6.

4.1. Datasets

To validate the generalization of the proposed model across diverse brain activations, three publicly available EEG benchmark datasets were combined to create a larger dataset with a large number of subjects—263 in total—encompassing diverse human states. The EEG signals in each dataset were downsampled to 128 Hz, and the same channels were selected from all datasets.

The DEAP [45] was developed to analyze human affective states. It was recorded from 32 individuals using a BioSemi headset with 32 EEG channels placed on the skull based on a 10–20 system and a 512 Hz sampling rate. The subjects watched 40 one-minute music videos that corresponded to different emotional states, i.e., valence, arousal, dominance, and liking. For a fair comparison, we used the preprocessed version.

Physionet motor/imagination [46] is a well-known and widely used EEG dataset with 64 channels; 160 Hz EEG recordings were captured from 109 healthy subjects. The international 10–10 system for the placement of electrodes was utilized. Each participant's EEG was recorded over 14 tests. One baseline run lasted one minute in both "eyes-open" (EO) and "eyes-closed" (EC) conditions, and the last four minutes contained four motor/imagination (MI) activities.

The EEG UCI dataset was produced for alcoholism-related genetic studies and involves recordings from 122 patients, including 45 controls and 77 alcoholics, with each completing 120 one-second trials. It was collected using a 10–20 system with 64 electrodes at 256 Hz; subjects viewed black-and-white photos [47] for 300 ms, with a separation of 1.6 s. Subjects were asked to determine if the two photos were identical.

The combined dataset (CD) integrated data from all subjects across the *DEAP*, *UCI*, and *PhysioNet* datasets. Due to differences in EEG data collection equipment, 32 channels of each EEG trial were selected according to the 10–20 electrode placement system (see Figure 3). The EEG records were then segmented into non-overlapping one-second epochs (EEG trials), resulting in EEG trials of 32 × 128, where 32 was the number of channels, and 128 was the number of time samples. This dataset included EEG trials from a total of 263 subjects, with each having different brain activations. Subjects were numbered sequentially for training purposes, starting with those from DEAP, followed by PhysioNet and then UCI.

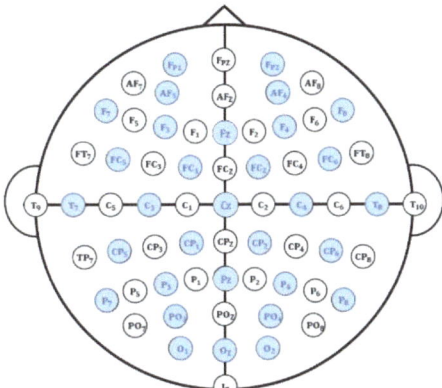

Figure 3. Channel positions of all 64 electrodes (channels) using a 10–20 system where the highlighted channels were used in experiments [24].

4.2. Performance Metrics

Commonly used metrics for identification and verification tasks were employed to evaluate the efficacy of GCT–EEGNet. The study considered the correct recognition rate (CRR) and cumulative match characteristic (CMC) curve for identification and the equal error rate (EER) and detection error trade-off (DET) curve for verification. A lower EER signifies a better performance in authentication scenarios.

5. Experimental Results and Discussion

This section presents the details of the experiments conducted to validate the performance of the method and discusses the results obtained. All experiments were performed on a computer with 128 GB of RAM and an NVIDIA Quadro RTX 6000 GPU. The model was implemented using Python v3.7, Pytorch Lightning v1.7, and torch v1.13.1.

5.1. Ablation Study

In this section, we discuss ablation experiments that were performed to assess the impact of each model component using 10-fold cross-validation. Initially, for each fold, we trained the model using all 32 channels and used 90% of the subjects for training; e.g., in the DEAP dataset, 28 subjects were used for training, and the remaining 10% were used for testing. We utilized the same hyperparameters in GCT–EEGNet that are common in EEGNet [29], the baseline network, which was trained for 100 epochs per fold. The impacts of various factors and hyperparameters on the performance of the model are shown in Table 2. The model configuration that gave the highest average validation accuracy over 10-fold cross-validation on the datasets was considered for further improvement.

5.1.1. Input Configuration and Optimizers

We compared the results obtained with the 3D input shape [5 × 32 × 128] with those obtained with the original 2D shape [32 × 128] while keeping all hyperparameters fixed in GCT–EEGNet as in the baseline EEGNet network. Besides the network's architectural design, the training method affects the model's performance [48]. The vision transformer [49,50] introduced a new collection of modules and new training methods (e.g., the AdamW optimizer). As shown in Table 2, the 3D input shape using the same optimizer achieved better performance for non-preprocessed datasets using the Adam optimizer, particularly the UCI dataset, with a difference of almost 13%. In addition, we observed that the AdamW optimizer yielded better outcomes for three datasets, with a slight decrease in validation accuracy of 0.05% for DEAP.

5.1.2. Number of Kernels and Activation Functions

Table 2 also shows the impact of altering the number of kernels from (8, 16) to (32, 64) and (64, 128) for the first and second convolution layers, respectively, in GCT–EEGNet while keeping the ELU activation function fixed. It is evident that using 64 and 128 kernels produced the best results. A larger number of kernels in the first layer resulted in better accuracy than a smaller number of kernels, with a slight improvement in the DEAP dataset, since it was preprocessed, and there was a significant improvement in the other two datasets in comparison with the small number of kernels (8, 16). In addition, the most often used activation functions were assessed, and the results indicated that the GELU activation function achieved the best results, with a modest improvement over ReLU and ELU; the SiLU activation function showed a slight improvement for some datasets, but its long training time is a major drawback.

Table 2. Ablation study of the performance of GCT–EEGNet; the performance is reported as the mean validation performance ± standard deviation using 10-fold cross-validation; *ELU* is the exponential linear unit, *Avg* is the average pooling layer, *ReLU* is the rectified linear unit, *GELU* is the Gaussian error linear units, *SiLU* is the sigmoid linear unit, *GAP* is global average pooling, *SE* is squeeze and excitation, *GCT* is gated channel transformation, and *RMSProp* is root mean squared propagation.

Experiment	Choices	Datasets			
		DEAP	**PhysioNet**	**EEG UCI**	**Combined**
	Raw 2D input without DWT decomposition (32 × 128)				
Optimizers, kernels 8, 16	Adam	99.87 ± 0.08	74.51 ± 2.75	49.10 ± 7.29	69.80 ± 3.02
	AdamW	99.92 ± 0.06	73.72 ± 2.14	50.50 ± 5.26	69.81 ± 3.05
	Raw 3D input with DWT decomposition (5 × 32 × 128)				
Optimizers, kernels 8, 16	Adam	99.88 ± 0.05	76.90 ± 1.63	62.57 ± 2.74	74.56 ± 1.35
	AdamW	**99.87 ± 0.11**	77.57 ± 0.87	64.22 ± 3.80	74.69 ± 1.41

Table 2. Cont.

Experiment	Choices	Datasets			
		DEAP	PhysioNet	EEG UCI	Combined
Number of kernels	32, 64	99.99 ± 0.02	99.13 ± 0.15	95.58 ± 0.64	98.69 ± 0.19
	64, 128	100 ± 0.01	99.75 ± 0.05	97.41 ± 0.94	99.54 ± 0.08
Activation functions	ReLU [51]	97.75 ± 0.77	99.67 ± 0.07	97.75 ± 0.77	99.39 ± 0.09
	SiLU [52]	97.84 ± 0.54	99.77 ± 0.07	97.84 ± 0.54	99.53 ± 0.04
	GeLU [39]	100 ± 0.01	99.79 ± 0.06	97.90 ± 0.52	99.50 ± 0.03
Pooling Layer	Max	100 ± 0.01	99.68 ± 0.08	97.50 ± 0.61	99.38 ± 0.09
GAP layer	GAP	100 ± 0.00	99.80 ± 0.06	98.51 ± 0.40	99.58 ± 0.08
Attention Layer	SE	100 ± 0.00	99.68 ± 0.06	98.73 ± 0.36	99.54 ± 0.10
	GCT	100 ± 0.00	99.84 ± 0.05	98.87 ± 0.33	99.66 ± 0.04
Dropout	0.5	-	-	-	99.66 ± 0.04
	0.25	-	-	-	99.63 ± 0.06
	Without dropout	-	-	-	99.24 ± 0.19

5.1.3. Pooling Layer

To reduce the feature map dimensionality, pooling layers were employed. We compared the following two most popular types of pooling in this experiment: average and maximum pooling. Because the average pooling layer was used from the beginning of the first test, all previous results included the average pooling layer. Table 2 shows that the average pooling achieved good accuracy compared with max pooling.

5.1.4. GAP and Attention Layer

Instead of simply flattening or adding an FC layer, we used a GAP layer. The GAP layer averaged spatial information to strengthen the input against spatial translations. The results in Table 2 show that the validation accuracy improved with a notable reduction in the learnable parameters. In addition, we evaluated two attention approaches to capture the channel importance. The GCT layer was shown to be better than the squeeze and excitation (SE) block, with a small difference.

5.1.5. The Effect of Employing GELU with Dropout

As the GELU activation function incorporated a dropout functionality, we needed to guarantee that this layer had a positive effect on the presence of GELU or that the validation accuracy would be reduced. As a result, we found that the dropout was beneficial for this application, as removing this layer would result in a modest decline in outcomes (see Table 2). Note that all previous experiments included dropout with a 50% rate. This experiment applied only to the combined dataset.

5.2. The Identification and Verification Results

The ablation study helped to find the best configuration of GCT–EEGNet. Using its best configuration, we extracted the feature vector of each EEG trial as the output of the GAP layer. Then, we matched pairs of EEG trials by determining the similarity between their feature vectors. We explored several similarity metrics for matching, including Euclidean, Manhattan, and cosine similarity. The choice of a similarity metric can significantly impact the results, and we aimed to identify the most effective one. Our findings revealed that the cosine similarity measure (red line) consistently outperformed the others in both the identification and verification scenarios (see Figures 4 and 5). Figure 4 shows the CMC curves for the identification scenario, illustrating the top ten ranks for the combined dataset. The best results were achieved using the cosine similarity measure with a CRR of 99.23%. For the verification scenario, we considered genuine pairs (within a class) and impostor (between classes) pairs, with 1080 and 28,080, respectively. The DET curves depicted in Figure 5 show that the cosine distance measure resulted in the lowest EER of 0.0014%. The EER represents the threshold at which the false acceptance rate (FAR) equals the false rejection rate (FRR). The results indicate that the cosine distance is the best similarity measure, and this outcome was also confirmed by the authors of [26] using the PhysioNet dataset.

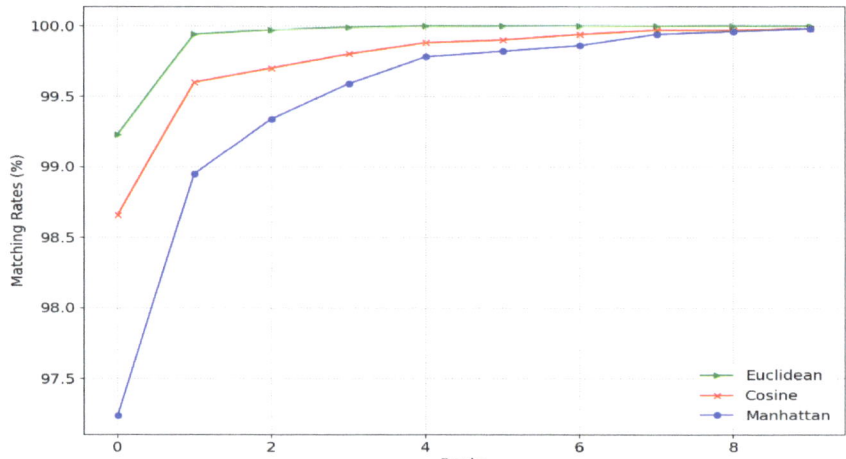

Figure 4. Performance in identification: CMC curves for the combined dataset.

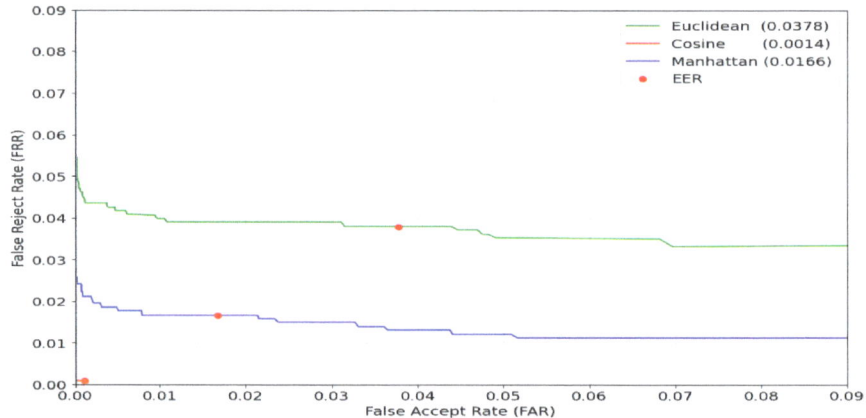

Figure 5. Performance in verification: DET curves for the combined dataset.

5.3. Robustness to Diverse Brain States

To replicate real-world scenarios and demonstrate the robustness of GCT–EEGNet across diverse brain states, we extracted epochs (EEG trials) from EEG signals, regardless of the onsets or offsets of cognitive tasks, and performed two experiments. This approach ensured the generalization of GCT–EEGNet across diverse cognitive states, as shown in Table 3. In the first experiment, the model was trained on cognitive states different from those employed during the testing stage. The results indicated that the model achieved a good CRR and EER on the DEAP dataset, where nearly equal samples were sampled from each cognitive state. Additionally, the results from the PhysioNet and UCI datasets highlighted the impact of the difference in training and testing sample sizes on the model performance. For example, in the PhysioNet dataset, the performance decreased by nearly 9% from 97.83% to 88.72% when the model trained on a small number of samples (13,195) for EO and EC conditions and tested on a much larger sample size of 161,647 for PHY and IMA. Conversely, when trained on the larger PHY and IMA sample, the model's performance improved, yielding a CRR of 97.83% and an EER of 0.0047. The performance was particularly good for the UCI dataset when trained on the alcoholic state, which was likely due to the larger sample size of 6989 for 77 subjects compared with the 4015 samples from 45 subjects in the non-alcoholic training phase. These findings emphasize the critical influence of the training data size on model performance.

Table 3. Test results of experiments with the CRR and EER (average ± standard deviation), where *HH* is high valence, high arousal; *HL* is high valence, low arousal; *LH* is low valence, high arousal; *LL* is low valence, low arousal; *EO* is eyes open; *EC* is eyes closed; *PHY* is motor physical activity; and *MI* or *IMA* is motor imagination activity.

	Experiment # 1			
Dataset	**Training States**	**Testing States**	**CRR**	**EER**
DEAP	LL, HH	LH, HL	99.99 ± 0.04	0.0215 ± 0.0183
	LL, HL	LH, HH	99.98 ± 0.05	0.0272 ± 0.0253
	LL, LH	HL, HH	99.96 ± 0.06	0.0283 ± 0.0106
	HH, HL	LL, LH	99.93 ± 0.09	0.1079 ± 0.0216
	HH, LH	LL, HL	99.98 ± 0.05	0.0860 ± 0.0597
	LH, HL	LL, HH	100.00 ± 0.00	0.0523 ± 0.0061
PhysioNet	EO, EC	PHY, IMA	88.72 ± 1.12	0.0514 ± 0.0105
	PHY, IMA	EO, EC	97.83 ± 1.66	0.0047 ± 0.0023
EEG UCI	Alcoholic	Non-Alcoholic	84.25 ± 0.83	0.0087 ± 0.0015
	Non-Alcoholic	Alcoholic	77.47 ± 0.56	0.0041 ± 0.0008
	Experiment # 2			
	Datasets		**CRR**	**EER**
	DEAP		100.00 ± 0.00	0.0004 ± 0.0008
	PhysioNet		98.90 ± 0.48	0.0043 ± 0.0014
	EEG UCI		99.25 ± 0.91	0.0009 ± 0.0016
	Combined		99.23 ± 0.50	0.0014 ± 0.0008

In addition, binding a system to a specific mental state during registration is often impractical in real-world biometric applications. To address this variation, the model was trained with diverse states, enabling it to adapt to subject variability. In the second experiment, data from various brain states were merged for both training and testing. This approach demonstrated that the proposed model achieved better identification results (more than 98% for all datasets) and verification results of less than 0.004. This indicated that the model generalized well over diverse cognitive states, even with new subjects that were never introduced during the training procedure. This adaptability to intra-person EEG variability makes the model a promising candidate for real-world biometric applications.

5.4. The Effects of Different Frequency Bands

This section examines how various frequency bands, including the delta, theta, alpha, beta, and gamma bands, impacted the brainprints derived from EEG-generated spontaneous brain activity. The GCT attention block within the model played a crucial role in determining the most contributive frequency bands for recognition. Attention weights were computed per frequency band generated in the testing samples and then averaged to account for subject variability, as the different subjects generated distinct attention patterns. Figure 6a shows that the beta (14–32 Hz) and gamma (32–50 Hz) bands dominated the combined dataset. These findings suggest that lower frequencies correspond to common brain activities, while higher frequencies are associated with individual distinctiveness. To reveal the significance of frequency bands, we applied the deepSHAP technique [53]. Figure 6b presents a global interpretation of the model's decisions, highlighting the prominence of the gamma band across all 32 channels, which aligns with the results observed in the GCT layer. This suggests that the attention layer of our model could provide valuable insights into identifying the frequency band with the greatest contribution.

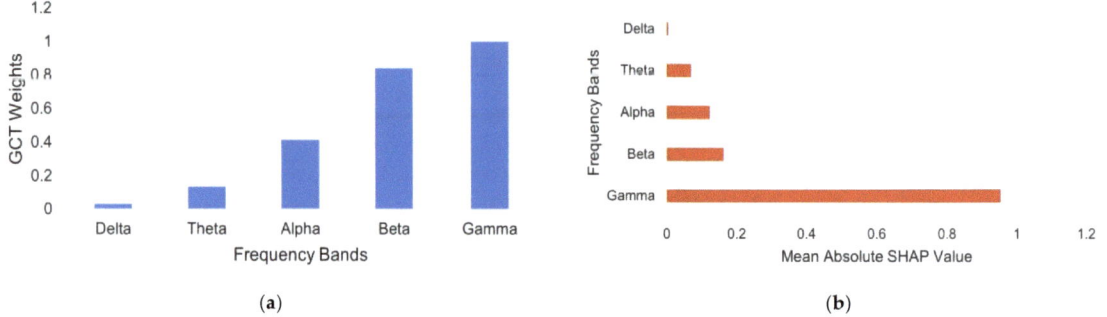

Figure 6. The effect of frequency bands on the combined dataset. (**a**) The GCT attention mechanism weights. (**b**) The respective mean SHAP values.

5.5. The Effect of Channel Reduction

In this experiment, we analyzed the effect of reducing the number of EEG channels on the model performance. To improve the system's user-friendliness, it was necessary to minimize the number of electrodes while maintaining satisfactory performance. Figure 7a–e displays five sets of EEG channels defined by Wilaiprasitporn et al. [14], with each covering the following distinct regions of the scalp: frontal (F), central and parietal (CP), temporal (T), occipital and parietal (OP), and frontal and parietal (FP). The results depicted in Figure 8a illustrate the performance of these channel subsets using all frequency bands on the combined dataset. The blue color represents the performance of five distinct channel sets, while the red color indicates the performance difference between these subsets and the full 32-channel configurations. The model performance was degraded as the number of electrodes decreased. Moreover, the channels from the CP region exhibited the best performance, exceeding 90%. Figure 8b shows the results when only the gamma band was used; though there was a slight decrease in the performance, the gamma band played key role in identification, as identified in the previous section.

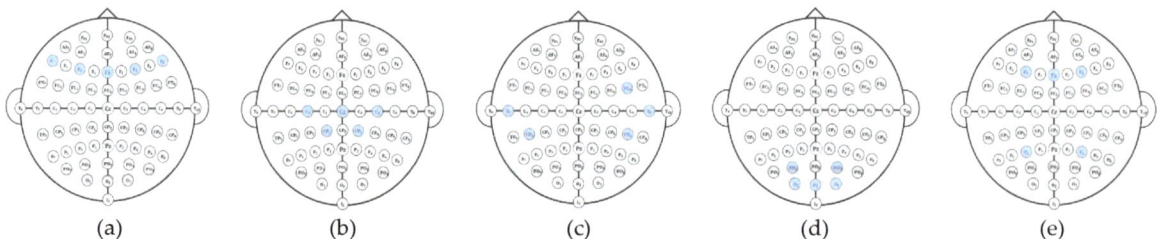

Figure 7. Five different channel configurations, each highlighting different regions of the scalp: (**a**) frontal (F), (**b**) central and parietal (CP), (**c**) temporal (T), (**d**) occipital and parietal (OP), (**e**) frontal and parietal (FP).

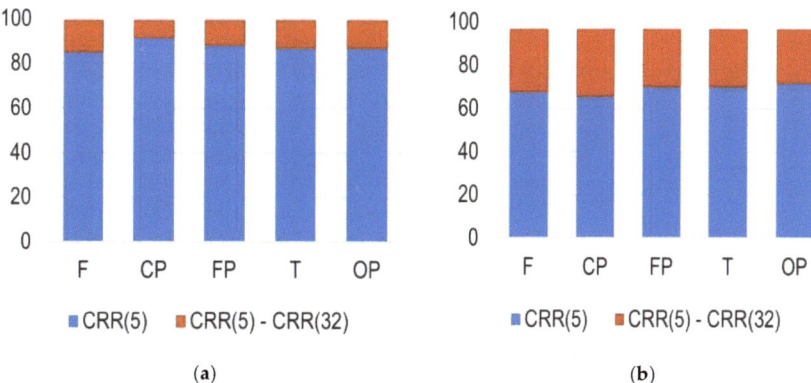

(a) (b)

Figure 8. Performance of the proposed method among five different sets of channels. (**a**) All frequency bands, (**b**) gamma band, where CRR (5) denotes the performance of the five distinct channel sets, while CRR (5)–CRR (32) indicate the performance differences among the five channel subsets and the 32 channels.

5.6. Comparison with the State of the Art

To demonstrate the effectiveness of the proposed method, we compared its performance with that of state-of-the-art EEG-based deep learning biometric techniques on public domain datasets, including DEAP, PhysioNet, UCI, and a combined dataset. It is to be noted that many state-of-the-art methods also used DEAP and PhysioNet for evaluation; the comparison of these datasets is given in Table 4.

Table 4. Comparison with state-of-the-art EEG-based biometric systems according to the number of subjects (# Sub.), trial length (TL), number of channels (# Chan.), network (NW), Euclidean distance (L2), and Manhattan distance (L1).

	Dataset	# Sub	Method	# Ch	TL (sec.)	CRR (%)	EER (%)	Parameters
Sun et al. [13]—2019	PhysioNet	109	CNN, LSTM	16	1	99.58	0.41	505,281,566
Wilaiprasitporn et al. [14]—2019	DEAP	32	CNN, LSTM CNN, GRU	5	10	>99	-	324,032 496,384
Jin et al. [24]—2020	MTED	20	CTNN	7	1	99	0.1	4600
Bidgoly et al. [26] 2022	PhysioNet	109	CNN, Cosine	3	1	98.04	1.96	NA
Alsumari et al. [27]—2023	PhysioNet	109	CNN, L1	2	5	99.05	0.187	74,071
Fallahi et al. [28]—2023	ERP CORE	40	Siamese NW, L2	30	0.10	95.63	1.37	NA
	Brain Invaders	41		32		99.92	0.14	
Proposed approach	DEAP	32	GCT–EEGNET, Cosine	32	1	100.00	0.0004	35,900
	PhysioNet	109				98.90	0.0043	45,000
	UCI	122				99.25	0.0009	62,100
	Combined	263				99.23	0.0014	62,800

Most of the state-of-the-art techniques were trained and evaluated on a single dataset involving a small number of tasks, limiting their performance evaluation to specific scenarios and often involving smaller groups of subjects. For instance, Sun et al. [13] evaluated their CNN–LSTM model on the PhysioNet dataset (109 subjects, 16 channels), achieving a high CRR of 99.58%. However, their model incorporated LSTM layers, increasing its complexity to over 505 million parameters, which raised the risk of overfitting, especially when trained on a dataset with only 109 subjects. The large number of parameters also makes the model computationally expensive and difficult to deploy in real-world systems, unlike the proposed method, which uses only 62,800 parameters while maintaining competitive performance. Similarly, Bidgoly et al. [26] utilized PhysioNet with three channels, achieving a CRR of 98.04% by stacking CNN layers. However, this method uses only three channels, thus it lacks the spatial information of EEG trials, leading to a relatively higher EER of 1.96%. In addition, Alsumari et al. [27] employed the PhysioNet dataset with only two channels, achieving a CRR of 99.05% but at the cost of higher error rates (EER of 0.187%). Their model's simplicity raises concerns about its robustness against diverse brain conditions. In contrast, the proposed model captures richer spatial–temporal information while maintaining low complexity and achieving a much lower EER of 0.0043% on the same dataset. Wilaiprasitporn et al. [14] employed the DEAP dataset (32 subjects, 5 EEG channels) with CNN–LSTM and CNN–GRU networks, yielding a CRR of more than 99%, but these models were tested on a relatively small number of subjects and brain conditions. This limitation of dataset size could affect the generalization of the model to larger populations. Similarly, the proposed model was applied to the DEAP dataset, gaining 100% with a small number of parameters of 35,900. Jin et al. [24] used the MTED dataset (20 subjects, 7 channels), which resulted in a CRR of 99% and an EER of 0.1%. Although these metrics are impressive, the small dataset size (20 subjects) raises concerns about the model's applicability to broader real-world conditions. In contrast, the proposed method demonstrated a much wider generalization by achieving an EER of 0.0014% on a dataset of 263 subjects in diverse brain states. Fallahi et al. [28] used the ERP CORE and Brain Invaders datasets with 40 and 41 subjects, respectively, achieving a CRR of 99.92%. However, their method relies on a Siamese network, which, while effective for specific tasks, introduces a relatively higher EER of 1.37%. Moreover, these datasets focus on specific cognitive tasks, limiting their applicability across broader EEG conditions. In contrast, the proposed method was designed to perform well across multiple brain states and cognitive conditions, as evidenced by its consistently low EER on the DEAP, PhysioNet, UCI, and combined datasets. The method was tested on a large combined dataset created from DEAP, PhysioNet, and UCI with a larger number of subjects, which helped to validate its broader generalization. Despite using a low-complexity architecture with fewer parameters, the method achieved competitive results. Specifically, it attained a CRR of 99.23% and an EER of 0.0014% across diverse brain states and short temporal intervals of one second. This indicated that the proposed model can handle the variability in real-world EEG-based biometric input more effectively than more complex models that are tuned for specific tasks or datasets. In conclusion, although the datasets vary in their characteristics, the proposed method offers a balanced solution with good accuracy, lower complexity, and greater flexibility across different EEG datasets. This highlights its practicality for real-world EEG-based biometric systems, particularly in scenarios that require adaptability across diverse brain conditions and subjects.

5.7. Visualization of the Features Learned by the Model from EEG Segments

To verify the effectiveness of the model, we employed the t-distributed stochastic neighbor embedding (t-SNE) [54] method to visualize the learned features in lower-dimensional 2D space from the GAP layer. This technique helped us evaluate whether the model had effectively learned features that distinguished individuals. Figure 9 shows the results for the combined dataset, with each color representing a different subject. The visualization shows the GAP layer's remarkable ability to classify the testing subjects into distinct groups. Although most subjects were well separated, there were a few outliers (i.e., S039, S034, and S099), which appeared to be incorrectly grouped with other subjects. Overall, this visualization indicated that our approach effectively extracted distinctive features from EEG data for each individual, achieving this with just two layers.

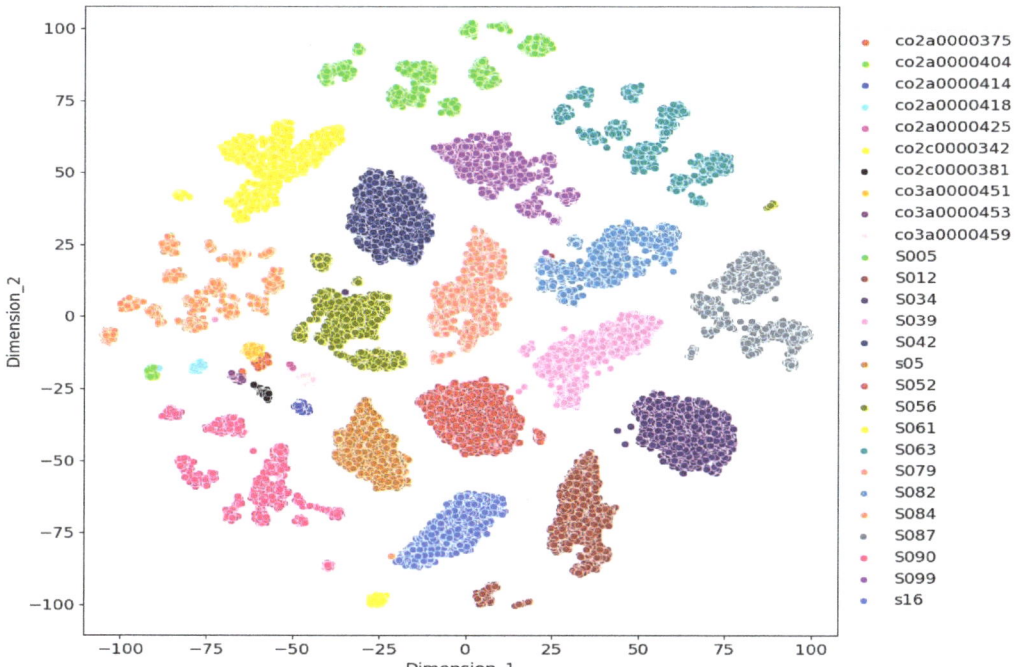

Figure 9. The t-SNE visualization for high-dimensional features of the GAP layer.

5.8. Discussion

This study presents an EEG-based biometric system based on GCT–EEGNET with a large number of individuals (263) and diverse mental states. While several models in [11–14] achieved high performance by integrating CNN and RNN layers to exploit both spatial and temporal features, their robustness and generalization to a large number of subjects are questionable due to increased complexity. To address this problem, our approach utilized depth-wise separable convolution layers within a CNN architecture. This design efficiently captured both spatial and temporal features while significantly reducing parameter complexity to just 62,764 parameters. This reduction enhanced the model's efficiency and generalization, even with a larger number of subjects. An ablation study on the model hyperparameter choices was discussed in Section 5.1.

Additionally, the method automatically selected optimal frequency bands through the analysis of the GCT layer attention scores, reducing the need for costly experiments (see Section 5.4). The results showed that the gamma and beta bands were the most significant frequency bands, which was consistent with the prior findings in [24,27,55,56]. This indicated that distinctive human features prevail in higher-frequency bands. Channel reduction simplified the system's equipment and applicability. We observed a decline in the model's performance when employing fewer channels compared with utilizing 32 channels. This decline may be attributed to the correlation between channels of an EEG segment. Figure 9 confirms the model's ability to discriminate against unseen subjects. Overall, the system has potential benefits for individuals with disabilities and security concerns.

The proposed EEG-based biometric system shows promising results for recognizing individuals with diverse brain states. However, several limitations need to be addressed for real-world adoption. Reducing the number of EEG channels decreases its performance, complicating practical use and requiring simpler setups. In addition, the limited availability of large, multi-session datasets spanning long time intervals consisting of a large number of subjects may affect the system's ability to generalize across different brain conditions. While the model performs well under diverse mental states, EEG signals exhibit high variability across sessions, even for the same individual. This variability could affect the system's long-term reliability in real-world applications, where EEG data may be collected over weeks or months. Addressing these issues will be key for real-world adoption, with future work focusing on improving robustness and acceptance by considering channel reduction, handling cross-session variability, and reducing computational requirements for broader applicability.

6. Conclusions

This study introduced an efficient, lightweight GCT–EEGNet model for EEG-based biometric recognition by leveraging attention mechanisms and advanced convolutional layers. Our model captures both temporal and spatial features from EEG signals, utilizing diverse cognitive states. The results demonstrated the model's effectiveness, achieving a high CRR of 99.23 and a low EER of 0.0014 with a short one-second temporal window while utilizing 32 electrodes on the combined dataset. The system required only a short one-second temporal window for identification and verification. The integrated GCT layer emphasized the significance of higher-frequency bands, particularly the beta and gamma bands, for individual distinction. A depth-wise separable convolution layer was employed to avoid excessive growth in the number of trainable parameters as the number of subjects increased. Furthermore, comparisons with state-of-the-art methods showed GCT–EEGNet's ability to balance high performance with minimal computational complexity, making it a strong candidate for scalable EEG-based biometric recognition. Future research could explore alternative attention mechanisms for automated channel selection and further investigate the system performance on multi-session datasets to enhance the system's real-world applicability and long-term usability.

Author Contributions: Conceptualization, L.A. and M.H.; Data curation, L.A.; Formal analysis, L.A. and M.H.; Funding acquisition, M.H.; Methodology, L.A. and M.H.; Project administration, M.H.; Resources, M.H.; Software, L.A.; Supervision, M.H.; Validation, L.A.; Visualization, L.A.; Writing—original draft, L.A.; Writing—review and editing, L.A. and M.H. All authors have read and agreed to the published version of the manuscript.

Funding: This research was supported under the Researchers Supporting Project, number (RSP2024R109), King Saud University, Riyadh, Saudi Arabia.

Data Availability Statement: Public-domain datasets were used for the experiments. The DEAP dataset is available at https://www.eecs.qmul.ac.uk/mmv/datasets/deap/download.html (accessed on 16 December 2023). The PhysioNet dataset is available at https://physionet.org/content/eegmmidb/1.0.0/ (accessed on 16 December 2023). The EEG UCI dataset is available at https://archive.ics.uci.edu/dataset/121/eeg+database (accessed on 16 December 2023).

Conflicts of Interest: The authors declare no competing interests.

References

1. Zhang, D.D. *Automated Biometrics: Technologies and Systems*; Springer: Berlin/Heidelberg, Germany, 2013; Volume 7.
2. Jain, A.K.; Ross, A.; Prabhakar, S. An Introduction to Biometric Recognition. *IEEE Trans. Circuits Syst. Video Technol.* **2004**, *14*, 4–20. [CrossRef]
3. Poulos, M.; Rangoussi, M.; Chrissikopoulos, V.; Evangelou, A. Parametric Person Identification from the EEG Using Computational Geometry. In Proceedings of the ICECS'99. 6th IEEE International Conference on Electronics, Circuits and Systems (Cat. No. 99EX357), Paphos, Cyprus, 5–8 September 1999; pp. 1005–1008.
4. Gui, Q.; Ruiz-Blondet, M.V.; Laszlo, S.; Jin, Z. A Survey on Brain Biometrics. *ACM Comput. Surv.* **2019**, *51*, 1–38. [CrossRef]
5. Van Dis, H.; Corner, M.; Dapper, R.; Hanewald, G.; Kok, H. Individual Differences in the Human Electroencephalogram during Quiet Wakefulness. *Electroencephalogr. Clin. Neurophysiol.* **1979**, *47*, 87–94. [CrossRef] [PubMed]
6. Zhang, X.; Yao, L.; Wang, X.; Zhang, W.; Zhang, S.; Liu, Y. Know Your Mind: Adaptive Cognitive Activity Recognition with Reinforced CNN. In Proceedings of the 2019 IEEE International Conference on Data Mining (ICDM), Beijing, China, 8–11 November 2019; pp. 896–905.
7. Chen, J.X.; Mao, Z.J.; Yao, W.X.; Huang, Y.F. EEG-Based Biometric Identification with Convolutional Neural Network. *Multimed. Tools Appl.* **2019**, *79*, 1–21. [CrossRef]

8. Xu, T.; Wang, H.; Lu, G.; Wan, F.; Deng, M.; Qi, P.; Bezerianos, A.; Guan, C.; Sun, Y. E-Key: An EEG-Based Biometric Authentication and Driving Fatigue Detection System. *IEEE Trans. Affect. Comput.* **2021**, *14*, 864–877. [CrossRef]
9. Maiorana, E. Learning Deep Features for Task-Independent EEG-Based Biometric Verification. *Pattern Recognit. Lett.* **2021**, *143*, 122–129. [CrossRef]
10. Seha, S.N.A.; Hatzinakos, D. Longitudinal Assessment of EEG Biometrics under Auditory Stimulation: A Deep Learning Approach. In Proceedings of the 2021 29th European Signal Processing Conference (EUSIPCO), Dublin, Ireland, 23–27 August 2021; pp. 1386–1390.
11. Das, B.B.; Kumar, P.; Kar, D.; Ram, S.K.; Babu, K.S.; Mohapatra, R.K. A Spatio-Temporal Model for EEG-Based Person Identification. *Multimed. Tools Appl.* **2019**, *78*, 28157–28177. [CrossRef]
12. Jijomon, C.M.; Vinod, A.P. Person-Identification Using Familiar-Name Auditory Evoked Potentials from Frontal EEG Electrodes. *Biomed. Signal Process. Control.* **2021**, *68*, 102739. [CrossRef]
13. Sun, Y.; Lo, F.P.-W.; Lo, B. EEG-Based User Identification System Using 1D-Convolutional Long Short-Term Memory Neural Networks. *Expert Syst. Appl.* **2019**, *125*, 259–267. [CrossRef]
14. Wilaiprasitporn, T.; Ditthapron, A.; Matcharparn, K.; Tongbuasirilai, T.; Banluesombatkul, N.; Chuangsuwanich, E. Affective EEG-Based Person Identification Using the Deep Learning Approach. *IEEE Trans. Cogn. Dev. Syst.* **2019**, *12*, 486–496. [CrossRef]
15. Yang, S.; Deravi, F. On the Usability of Electroencephalographic Signals for Biometric Recognition: A Survey. *IEEE Trans. Hum.-Mach. Syst.* **2017**, *47*, 958–969. [CrossRef]
16. Maiorana, E.; La Rocca, D.; Campisi, P. EEG-Based Biometric Recognition Using EigenBrains. In Proceedings of the 2015 IEEE International Conference on Multimedia & Expo Workshops (ICMEW), Turin, Italy, 29 June–5 July 2015; pp. 1–6.
17. Rodrigues, D.; Silva, G.F.; Papa, J.P.; Marana, A.N.; Yang, X.-S. EEG-Based Person Identification through Binary Flower Pollination Algorithm. *Expert Syst. Appl.* **2016**, *62*, 81–90. [CrossRef]
18. Thomas, K.P.; Vinod, A.P. EEG-Based Biometric Authentication Using Gamma Band Power during Rest State. *Circuits Syst. Signal Process.* **2018**, *37*, 277–289. [CrossRef]
19. Jijomon, C.M.; Vinod, A.P. EEG-Based Biometric Identification Using Frequently Occurring Maximum Power Spectral Features. In Proceedings of the 2018 IEEE Applied Signal Processing Conference (ASPCON), Kolkata, India, 7–9 December 2018; pp. 249–252.
20. Nakamura, T.; Goverdovsky, V.; Mandic, D.P. In-Ear EEG Biometrics for Feasible and Readily Collectable Real-World Person Authentication. *IEEE Trans. Inf. Forensics Secur.* **2017**, *13*, 648–661. [CrossRef]
21. Zhang, S.; Sun, L.; Mao, X.; Hu, C.; Liu, P. Review on EEG-Based Authentication Technology. *Comput. Intell. Neurosci.* **2021**, *2021*, 5229576. [CrossRef] [PubMed]
22. Stassen, H.H. Computerized Recognition of Persons by EEG Spectral Patterns. *Electroencephalogr. Clin. Neurophysiol.* **1980**, *49*, 190–194. [CrossRef]
23. Maiorana, E. Deep Learning for EEG-Based Biometric Recognition. *Neurocomputing* **2020**, *410*, 374–386. [CrossRef]
24. Jin, X.; Tang, J.; Kong, X.; Peng, Y.; Cao, J.; Zhao, Q.; Kong, W. CTNN: A Convolutional Tensor-Train Neural Network for Multi-Task Brainprint Recognition. *IEEE Trans. Neural Syst. Rehabil. Eng.* **2020**, *29*, 103–112. [CrossRef]
25. Debie, E.; Moustafa, N.; Vasilakos, A. Session Invariant EEG Signatures Using Elicitation Protocol Fusion and Convolutional Neural Network. *IEEE Trans. Dependable Secur. Comput.* **2021**, *9*, 2488–2500. [CrossRef]
26. Bidgoly, A.J.; Bidgoly, H.J.; Arezoumand, Z. Towards a Universal and Privacy Preserving EEG-Based Authentication System. *Sci. Rep.* **2022**, *12*, 1–12. [CrossRef]
27. Alsumari, W.; Hussain, M.; Alshehri, L.; Aboalsamh, H.A. EEG-Based Person Identification and Authentication Using Deep Convolutional Neural Network. *Axioms* **2023**, *12*, 74. [CrossRef]
28. Fallahi, M.; Strufe, T.; Arias-Cabarcos, P. BrainNet: Improving Brainwave-Based Biometric Recognition with Siamese Networks. In Proceedings of the 2023 IEEE International Conference on Pervasive Computing and Communications (PerCom), Atlanta, GA, USA, 13–17 March 2023; pp. 53–60.
29. Lawhern, V.J.; Solon, A.J.; Waytowich, N.R.; Gordon, S.M.; Hung, C.P.; Lance, B.J. EEGNet: A Compact Convolutional Neural Network for EEG-Based Brain–Computer Interfaces. *J. Neural Eng.* **2018**, *15*, 056013. [CrossRef] [PubMed]
30. Fraschini, M.; Hillebrand, A.; Demuru, M.; Didaci, L.; Marcialis, G.L. An EEG-Based Biometric System Using Eigenvector Centrality in Resting State Brain Networks. *IEEE Signal Process. Lett.* **2014**, *22*, 666–670. [CrossRef]
31. Kaur, B.; Singh, D.; Roy, P.P. A Novel Framework of EEG-Based User Identification by Analyzing Music-Listening Behavior. *Multimed. Tools Appl.* **2017**, *76*, 25581–25602. [CrossRef]
32. Kawabata, N. A Nonstationary Analysis of the Electroencephalogram. *IEEE Trans. Biomed. Eng.* **1973**, 444–452. [CrossRef]
33. Kumari, P.; Vaish, A. Brainwave Based User Identification System: A Pilot Study in Robotics Environment. *Robot. Auton. Syst.* **2015**, *65*, 15–23. [CrossRef]
34. Ting, W.; Guo-Zheng, Y.; Bang-Hua, Y.; Hong, S. EEG Feature Extraction Based on Wavelet Packet Decomposition for Brain Computer Interface. *Measurement* **2008**, *41*, 618–625. [CrossRef]
35. Yang, Z.; Zhu, L.; Wu, Y.; Yang, Y. Gated Channel Transformation for Visual Recognition. In Proceedings of the IEEE/CVF Conference on Computer Vision and Pattern Recognition, Seattle, WA, USA, 13 June 2020; pp. 11794–11803.
36. Ioffe, S.; Szegedy, C. Batch Normalization: Accelerating Deep Network Training by Reducing Internal Covariate Shift. *arXiv* **2015**, arXiv:1502.03167.

37. Chollet, F. Xception: Deep Learning with Depthwise Separable Convolutions. In Proceedings of the IEEE Conference on Computer Vision and Pattern Recognition, Honolulu, HI, USA, 21 July 2017; pp. 1251–1258.
38. Howard, A.G.; Zhu, M.; Chen, B.; Kalenichenko, D.; Wang, W.; Weyand, T.; Andreetto, M.; Adam, H. Mobilenets: Efficient Convolutional Neural Networks for Mobile Vision Applications. *arXiv* **2017**, arXiv:1704.04861. [CrossRef]
39. Hendrycks, D.; Gimpel, K. Gaussian Error Linear Units (Gelus). *arXiv* **2016**, arXiv:1606.08415. [CrossRef]
40. Dosovitskiy, A.; Beyer, L.; Kolesnikov, A.; Weissenborn, D.; Zhai, X.; Unterthiner, T.; Dehghani, M.; Minderer, M.; Heigold, G.; Gelly, S. An Image Is Worth 16x16 Words: Transformers for Image Recognition at Scale. *arXiv* **2020**, arXiv:2010.11929. [CrossRef]
41. Srivastava, N.; Hinton, G.; Krizhevsky, A.; Sutskever, I.; Salakhutdinov, R. Dropout: A Simple Way to Prevent Neural Networks from Overfitting. *J. Mach. Learn. Res.* **2014**, *15*, 1929–1958.
42. Loshchilov, I.; Hutter, F. Decoupled Weight Decay Regularization. *arXiv* **2017**, arXiv:1711.05101. [CrossRef]
43. Yao, Y.; Rosasco, L.; Caponnetto, A. On Early Stopping in Gradient Descent Learning. *Constr. Approx.* **2007**, *26*, 289–315. [CrossRef]
44. Lin, C.; Kumar, A. A CNN-Based Framework for Comparison of Contactless to Contact-Based Fingerprints. *IEEE Trans. Inf. Forensics Secur.* **2018**, *14*, 662–676. [CrossRef]
45. Koelstra, S.; Muhl, C.; Soleymani, M.; Lee, J.-S.; Yazdani, A.; Ebrahimi, T.; Pun, T.; Nijholt, A.; Patras, I. Deap: A Database for Emotion Analysis; Using Physiological Signals. *IEEE Trans. Affect. Comput.* **2011**, *3*, 18–31. [CrossRef]
46. Goldberger, A.L.; Amaral, L.A.; Glass, L.; Hausdorff, J.M.; Ivanov, P.C.; Mark, R.G.; Mietus, J.E.; Moody, G.B.; Peng, C.-K.; Stanley, H.E. PhysioBank, PhysioToolkit, and PhysioNet: Components of a New Research Resource for Complex Physiologic Signals. *Circulation* **2000**, *101*, e215–e220. [CrossRef]
47. Snodgrass, J.G.; Vanderwart, M. A Standardized Set of 260 Pictures: Norms for Name Agreement, Image Agreement, Familiarity, and Visual Complexity. *J. Exp. Psychol. Hum. Learn. Mem.* **1980**, *6*, 174. [CrossRef]
48. Liu, Z.; Mao, H.; Wu, C.-Y.; Feichtenhofer, C.; Darrell, T.; Xie, S. A Convnet for the 2020s. In Proceedings of the IEEE/CVF Conference on Computer Vision and Pattern Recognition, New Orleans, LA, USA, 18 June 2022; pp. 11976–11986.
49. Touvron, H.; Cord, M.; Douze, M.; Massa, F.; Sablayrolles, A.; Jégou, H. Training Data-Efficient Image Transformers & Distillation through Attention. In Proceedings of the International Conference on Machine Learning, Online, 18–24 July 2021; pp. 10347–10357.
50. Liu, Z.; Lin, Y.; Cao, Y.; Hu, H.; Wei, Y.; Zhang, Z.; Lin, S.; Guo, B. Swin Transformer: Hierarchical Vision Transformer Using Shifted Windows. In Proceedings of the IEEE/CVF International Conference on Computer Vision, Montreal, BC, Canada, 11 October 2021; pp. 10012–10022.
51. Agarap, A.F. Deep Learning Using Rectified Linear Units (Relu). *arXiv* **2018**, arXiv:1803.08375. [CrossRef]
52. Elfwing, S.; Uchibe, E.; Doya, K. Sigmoid-Weighted Linear Units for Neural Network Function Approximation in Reinforcement Learning. *Neural Netw.* **2018**, *107*, 3–11. [CrossRef]
53. Cui, J.; Yuan, L.; Wang, Z.; Li, R.; Jiang, T. Towards Best Practice of Interpreting Deep Learning Models for EEG-Based Brain Computer Interfaces. *arXiv* **2022**, arXiv:2202.06948. [CrossRef] [PubMed]
54. Van der Maaten, L.; Hinton, G. Visualizing Data Using T-SNE. *J. Mach. Learn. Res.* **2008**, *9*, 2579–2605.
55. Wang, M.; El-Fiqi, H.; Hu, J.; Abbass, H.A. Convolutional Neural Networks Using Dynamic Functional Connectivity for EEG-Based Person Identification in Diverse Human States. *IEEE Trans. Inf. Forensics Secur.* **2019**, *14*, 3259–3272. [CrossRef]
56. Fraschini, M.; Pani, S.M.; Didaci, L.; Marcialis, G.L. Robustness of Functional Connectivity Metrics for EEG-Based Personal Identification over Task-Induced Intra-Class and Inter-Class Variations. *Pattern Recognit. Lett.* **2019**, *125*, 49–54. [CrossRef]

Disclaimer/Publisher's Note: The statements, opinions and data contained in all publications are solely those of the individual author(s) and contributor(s) and not of MDPI and/or the editor(s). MDPI and/or the editor(s) disclaim responsibility for any injury to people or property resulting from any ideas, methods, instructions or products referred to in the content.

MDPI AG
Grosspeteranlage 5
4052 Basel
Switzerland
Tel.: +41 61 683 77 34

Mathematics Editorial Office
E-mail: mathematics@mdpi.com
www.mdpi.com/journal/mathematics

Disclaimer/Publisher's Note: The title and front matter of this reprint are at the discretion of the Guest Editors. The publisher is not responsible for their content or any associated concerns. The statements, opinions and data contained in all individual articles are solely those of the individual Editors and contributors and not of MDPI. MDPI disclaims responsibility for any injury to people or property resulting from any ideas, methods, instructions or products referred to in the content.

www.ingramcontent.com/pod-product-compliance
Lightning Source LLC
LaVergne TN
LVHW072340090526
838202LV00019B/2449